Lecture Notes in Computer Science 8409

Commenced Publication in 1973
Founding and Former Series Editors:
Gerhard Goos, Juris Hartmanis, and Jan van Leeuwen

Advanced Research in Computing and Software Science
Subline of Lectures Notes in Computer Science

Albert Cohen (Ed.)

Compiler Construction

23rd International Conference, CC 2014
Held as Part of the European Joint Conferences
on Theory and Practice of Software, ETAPS 2014
Grenoble, France, April 5-13, 2014
Proceedings

 Springer

Volume Editor

Albert Cohen
Inria
Paris, France
E-mail: albert.cohen@inria.fr

ISSN 0302-9743   e-ISSN 1611-3349
ISBN 978-3-642-54806-2   e-ISBN 978-3-642-54807-9
DOI 10.1007/978-3-642-54807-9
Springer Heidelberg New York Dordrecht London

Library of Congress Control Number: 2014933673

LNCS Sublibrary: SL 1 – Theoretical Computer Science and General Issues

Typesetting: Camera-ready by author, data conversion by Scientific Publishing Services, Chennai, India

Printed on acid-free paper

Springer is part of Springer Science+Business Media (www.springer.com)

Foreword

ETAPS 2014 was the 17th instance of the European Joint Conferences on Theory and Practice of Software. ETAPS is an annual federated conference that was established in 1998, and this year consisted of six constituting conferences (CC, ESOP, FASE, FoSSaCS, TACAS, and POST) including eight invited speakers and two tutorial speakers. Before and after the main conference, numerous satellite workshops took place and attracted many researchers from all over the globe.

ETAPS is a confederation of several conferences, each with its own Program Committee (PC) and its own Steering Committee (if any). The conferences cover various aspects of software systems, ranging from theoretical foundations to programming language developments, compiler advancements, analysis tools, formal approaches to software engineering, and security. Organizing these conferences in a coherent, highly synchronized conference program, enables the participation in an exciting event, having the possibility to meet many researchers working in different directions in the field, and to easily attend the talks of different conferences.

The six main conferences together received 606 submissions this year, 155 of which were accepted (including 12 tool demonstration papers), yielding an overall acceptance rate of 25.0%. I thank all authors for their interest in ETAPS, all reviewers for the peer reviewing process, the PC members for their involvement, and in particular the PC co-chairs for running this entire intensive process. Last but not least, my congratulations to all authors of the accepted papers!

ETAPS 2014 was greatly enriched by the invited talks of Geoffrey Smith (Florida International University, USA) and John Launchbury (Galois, USA), both unifying speakers, and the conference-specific invited speakers (CC) Benoît Dupont de Dinechin (Kalray, France), (ESOP) Maurice Herlihy (Brown University, USA), (FASE) Christel Baier (Technical University of Dresden, Germany), (FoSSaCS) Petr Jančar (Technical University of Ostrava, Czech Republic), (POST) David Mazières (Stanford University, USA), and finally (TACAS) Orna Kupferman (Hebrew University Jerusalem, Israel). Invited tutorials were provided by Bernd Finkbeiner (Saarland University, Germany) and Andy Gordon (Microsoft Research, Cambridge, UK). My sincere thanks to all these speakers for their great contributions.

For the first time in its history, ETAPS returned to a city where it had been organized before: Grenoble, France. ETAPS 2014 was organized by the Université Joseph Fourier in cooperation with the following associations and societies: ETAPS e.V., EATCS (European Association for Theoretical Computer Science), EAPLS (European Association for Programming Languages and Systems), and EASST (European Association of Software Science and Technology). It had

support from the following sponsors: CNRS, Inria, Grenoble INP, PERSYVAL-
Lab and Université Joseph Fourier, and Springer-Verlag.

The organization team comprised:

General Chair: Saddek Bensalem
Conferences Chair: Alain Girault and Yassine Lakhnech
Workshops Chair: Axel Legay
Publicity Chair: Yliès Falcone
Treasurer: Nicolas Halbwachs
Webmaster: Marius Bozga

The overall planning for ETAPS is the responsibility of the Steering Committee (SC). The ETAPS SC consists of an executive board (EB) and representatives of the individual ETAPS conferences, as well as representatives of EATCS,
EAPLS, and EASST. The Executive Board comprises Gilles Barthe (satellite
events, Madrid), Holger Hermanns (Saarbrücken), Joost-Pieter Katoen (chair,
Aachen and Twente), Gerald Lüttgen (treasurer, Bamberg), and Tarmo Uustalu
(publicity, Tallinn). Other current SC members are: Martín Abadi (Santa Cruz
and Mountain View), Erika Ábráham (Aachen), Roberto Amadio (Paris), Chris-
tel Baier (Dresden), Saddek Bensalem (Grenoble), Giuseppe Castagna (Paris),
Albert Cohen (Paris), Alexander Egyed (Linz), Riccardo Focardi (Venice), Björn
Franke (Edinburgh), Stefania Gnesi (Pisa), Klaus Havelund (Pasadena), Reiko
Heckel (Leicester), Paul Klint (Amsterdam), Jens Knoop (Vienna), Steve Kre-
mer (Nancy), Pasquale Malacaria (London), Tiziana Margaria (Potsdam), Fabio
Martinelli (Pisa), Andrew Myers (Boston), Anca Muscholl (Bordeaux), Catuscia
Palamidessi (Palaiseau), Andrew Pitts (Cambridge), Arend Rensink (Twente),
Don Sanella (Edinburgh), Vladimiro Sassone (Southampton), Ina Schäfer (Braun-
schweig), Zhong Shao (New Haven), Gabriele Taentzer (Marburg), Cesare Tinelli
(Iowa), Jan Vitek (West Lafayette), and Lenore Zuck (Chicago).

   I sincerely thank all ETAPS SC members for all their hard work in making the
17th ETAPS a success. Moreover, thanks to all speakers, attendants, organizers
of the satellite workshops, and Springer for their support. Finally, many thanks
to Saddek Bensalem and his local organization team for all their efforts enabling
ETAPS to return to the French Alps in Grenoble!

January 2014   Joost-Pieter Katoen

Preface

This volume contains the papers presented at CC 2014: the 23rd International Conference on Compiler Construction held on April 5–13, 2014 in Grenoble.

There were 47 complete submissions. Each submission was reviewed by at least 3 committee members. The review process and edition of the proceedings was conducted with EasyChair. The committee decided to accept 10 standard and 4 tool papers. The program also included 1 invited talk.

CC brings together a unique blend of scientists and engineers working on processing programs in a general sense. The conference is the most targeted forum for the discussion of progress in analyzing, transforming, or executing input that describes how a system operates, including traditional compiler construction as a special case. This year's topics of interest include, but are not limited to: compilation and interpretation techniques, including program representation and analysis, code generation, and code optimization; run-time techniques, including memory management and dynamic and just-in-time compilation; programming tools, from refactoring editors to checkers to compilers to virtual machines to debuggers; techniques for specific domains, such as secure, parallel, distributed, embedded or mobile environments; and design of novel language constructs and their implementation.

We take this opportunity to thank our invited speaker, to congratulate the authors, and to thank them for submitting their fine work to the Compiler Construction conference. Many thanks to the local organization team led by Saddek Bensalem, and to the steering committee of ETAPS for making CC 2014 possible.

January 2014   Albert Cohen

Organization

Program Committee

Nelson Amaral	University of Alberta, Canada
Sandrine Blazy	University of Rennes 1, France
Albert Cohen	INRIA, France
Dibyendu Das	AMD, India
Bjorn De Sutter	Ghent University, Belgium
Gabriel Dos Reis	Microsoft, USA
Evelyn Duesterwald	IBM, USA
Stephen Edwards	Columbia University, USA
Atsushi Igarashi	Kyoto University, Japan
Christoph Kessler	Linköping University, Sweden
Jens Knoop	TU Vienna, Austria
Jenq-Kuen Lee	National Tsinghua University, Taiwan
Claire Maiza	Grenoble INP, France
Fernando Pereira	Federal University of Minas Gerais, Brazil
Louis-Noël Pouchet	UCLA, USA
Helmut Seidl	TU Munich, Germany
Jan Vitek	Purdue University, USA
Jingling Xue	University of New South Wales, Australia
Qing Yi	University of Colorado at Colorado Springs, USA
Ayal Zaks	Intel, Israel

Additional Reviewers

Barany, Gergö	Laporte, Vincent
Barik, Raj	Mihaila, Bogdan
Berube, Paul	Moy, Matthieu
Bhattacharyya, Arnamoy	Paudel, Jeeva
Bodin, Martin	Puntigam, Franz
Carrier, Fabienne	Rastello, Fabrice
Casse, Hugues	Rohou, Erven
Cui, Huimin	Schulte, Christian
Ertl, M. Anton	Simon, Axel
Herter, Jörg	Thiessen, Rei
Herz, Alexander	Zhao, Peng
Ireland, Iain	Zhou, Hao
Kong, Martin	

Table of Contents

New Trends in Compilation

Using the SSA-Form in a Code Generator

Benoît Dupont de Dinechin

Kalray SA

Abstract. In high-end compilers such as Open64, GCC or LLVM, the Static Single Assignment (SSA) form is a structural part of the target-independent program representation that supports most of the code optimizations. However, aggressive compilation also requires that optimizations that are more effective with the SSA form be applied to the target-specific program representations operated by the code generator, that is, the set of compiler phases after and including instruction selection.

While using the SSA form in the code generator has definite advantages, the SSA form does not apply to all the code generator program representations, and is not suited for all optimizations. We discuss some of the issues of inserting the SSA form in a code generator, specifically: what are the challenges of maintaining the SSA form on a program representation based on machine instructions; how the SSA form may be used in the if-conversion optimizations; why the SSA form does not seem to benefit instruction scheduling; and what is the state-of-the-art in SSA form destruction on machine code.

Keywords: SSA Form, Code Generation, If-Conversion, Instruction Scheduling.

1 Introduction

In a compiler for imperative languages such as C, C++, or FORTRAN, the code generator covers the set of code transformations and optimizations that operate on a program representation close to the target machine ISA, and produce an assembly source or relocatable file with debugging information as result.

The main duties of code generation are: lowering the program intermediate representation to the target machine instructions and calling conventions; laying out data objects in sections and composing the stack frames; allocating variable live ranges to architectural registers; scheduling instructions to exploit micro-architecture; and producing assembly source or object code.

Historically, the 1986 edition of the "Compilers Principles, Techniques, and Tools" Dragon Book by Aho et al. lists the tasks of code generation as:

- Instruction selection and lowering of calling conventions.
- Control-flow (dominators, loops) and data-flow (variable liveness) analyses.
- Register allocation and stack frame building.
- Peephole optimizations.

A. Cohen (Ed.): CC 2014, LNCS 8409, pp. 1–17, 2014.

Ten years later, the 1997 textbook "Advanced Compiler Design & Implementation" by Muchnich extends code generation with the following tasks:

- Loop unrolling and basic block replication.
- Instruction scheduling and software pipelining.
- Branch optimizations and basic block alignment.

In current releases of high-end compilers such as Open64 or GCC, code generation techniques have significantly evolved, as they are mainly responsible for exploiting the performance-oriented features of architectures and micro-architectures. In these compilers, code generator optimizations include:

- If-conversion using SELECT, conditional move, or predicated, instructions.
- Use of specialized addressing modes such as auto-modified and modulo.
- Exploitation of hardware looping or static branch prediction hints.
- Matching fixed-point arithmetic and SIMD idioms to special instructions.
- Memory hierarchy optimizations, including pre-fetching and pre-loading.
- VLIW instruction bundling, that may interfere with instruction scheduling.

This sophistication of modern compiler code generation motivates the introduction of the SSA form on the program representation in order to simplify some of the analyses and optimizations. In particular, liveness analysis, unrolling-based loop optimizations, and exploitation of special instructions or addressing modes benefit significantly from the SSA form. On the other hand, the SSA form does not apply after register allocation, and there is still debate as to whether it should be used in the register allocator [3].

In this paper, we review some of the issues of inserting the SSA form in a code generator, based on experience with a family of code generators and linear assembly optimizers for the ST120 DSP core [21] [20,49,44], the Lx/ST200 VLIW family [23] [17,18,8,7,5], and the Kalray VLIW core [19]. Section 2 presents the challenges of maintaining the SSA form on a program representation based on machine instructions. Section 3 discusses two code generator optimizations that seem at odds with the SSA form, yet must occur before register allocation. One is if-conversion, whose modern formulations require an extension of the SSA form. The other is pre-pass instruction scheduling, which currently does not seem to benefit from the SSA form. Going in and out of SSA form in a code generator is required in such case, so Section 4 characterizes various SSA form destruction algorithms with regards to satisfying the constraints of machine code.

2   SSA Form Engineering Issues

2.1   Instructions, Operands, Operations, and Operators

An *instruction* is a member of the machine instruction set architecture (ISA). Instructions access values and modify the machine state through *operands*. We distinguish *explicit operands*, which are associated with a specific bit-field in the instruction encoding, from *implicit operands*, without any encoding bits.

Explicit operands correspond to allocatable architectural registers, immediate values, or instruction modifiers. Implicit operands correspond to single instance architectural registers and to registers implicitly used by some instructions, such as the status register, the procedure link register, or even the stack pointer.

An *operation* is an instance of an instruction that composes a program. It is seen by the compiler as an *operator* applied to a list of operands (explicit & implicit), along with operand naming constraints, and has a set of clobbered registers. The compiler view of operations also involves *indirect operands*, which are not apparent in the instruction behavior, but are required to connect the flow of values between operations. Implicit operands correspond to the registers used for passing arguments and returning results at function call sites, and may also be used for the registers encoded in register mask immediates.

2.2 Representation of Instruction Semantics

Unlike IR operators, there is no straightforward mapping between machine instructions and their operational semantics. For instance, a subtract with operands (a, b, c) may either compute $c \leftarrow a - b$ or $c \leftarrow b - a$ or any such expression with permuted operands. Yet basic SSA form code cleanups such as constant propagation and sign extension removal need to know what is actually computed by machine instructions. Machine instructions may also have multiple target operands, such as memory accesses with auto-modified addressing, or combined division-modulus instructions. There are two ways to address this issue.

- Add properties to the instruction operator and to its operands, a technique used by the Open64 compiler. Operator properties include *isAdd*, *isLoad*, etc. Typical operand properties include *isLeft*, *isRight*, *isBase*, *isOffset*, *isPredicated*, etc. Extended properties that involve the operator and some of its operands include *isAssociative*, *isCommutative*, etc.
- Associate a *semantic combinator*, that is, a tree of IR-like operators, to each target operand of a machine instruction. This more ambitious alternative was implemented in the SML/NJ [35] compiler and the LAO compiler [20].

An issue related to the representation of instruction semantics is how to factor it. Most information can be statically tabulated by the instruction operator, yet properties such as safety for control speculation, or being equivalent to a simple IR instruction, can be refined by the context where the instruction appears. For instance, range propagation may ensure that an addition cannot overflow, that a division by zero is impossible, or that a memory access is safe for control speculation. Alternate semantic combinators, or modifiers of the instruction operator semantic combinator, need to be associated with each machine instruction of the code generator internal representation.

Finally, code generation for some instruction set architectures require that pseudo-instructions with known semantics be available, besides variants of ϕ-functions and parallel COPY operations.

- Machine instructions that operate on register pairs, such as the long multiplies on the ARM, or more generally on register tuples, are common. In such cases there is a need for pseudo-instructions to compose wide operands in register tuples, and to extract independently register allocatable operands from wide operands.
- Embedded architectures such as the Tensilica Xtensa provide hardware loops, where an implicit conditional branch back to the loop header is taken whenever the program counter matches some address. The implied loop-back branch is also conveniently materialized by a pseudo-instruction.
- Register allocation for predicated architectures requires that the live-ranges of pseudo-registers or SSA variables with predicated definitions be contained by kill pseudo-instructions [26].

2.3   Operand Naming Constraints

Implicit operands and indirect operands are constrained to specific architectural registers either by the instruction set architecture (ISA constraints), or by the application binary interface (ABI constraints). An effective way to deal with such *dedicated register* naming constraints in the SSA form is by inserting parallel COPY operations that write to the constrained source operands, or read from the constrained target operands of instructions. The new SSA variables thus created are pre-colored with the required architectural register. With modern SSA form destruction [48,7], COPY operations are aggressively coalesced, and the remaining ones are sequentialized into machine operations.

Explicit instruction operands may be constrained to use the same resource (an unspecified architectural register) between a source and a target operand, as illustrated by most x86 instructions and by DSP-style auto-modified addressing modes. A related naming constraint is to require different resources between two source operands, as with the MUL instructions on the ARM. The *same resource* naming constraints are represented under the SSA form by inserting a COPY operation between the constrained source operand and a new variable, then using this new variable as the constrained source operand. In case of multiple constrained source operands, a parallel COPY operation is used. Again, these COPY operations are processed by the SSA form destruction.

A wider case of operand naming constraint is when a variable must be bound to a specific architectural register at all points in the program. This is the case with the stack pointer, as interrupt handling may reuse the run-time stack at any program point. One possibility is to inhibit the promotion of the stack pointer to a SSA variable. Stack pointer definitions including memory allocations through `alloca()`, activation frame creation/destruction, are then encapsulated as instances of a specific pseudo-instruction. Instructions that use the stack pointer must be treated as special cases for the SSA form analyses and optimizations.

2.4   Non-kill Target Operands

The SSA form requires that variable definitions be kills. This is not the case for target operands such as a status register that contains several independent bit-fields. Moreover, some instruction effects on bit-field may be *sticky*, that is, with an implied OR with the previous value. Typical sticky bits include exception flags of the IEEE 754 arithmetic, or the integer overflow flag on DSPs with fixed-point arithmetic. When mapping a status register to a SSA variable, any operation that partially reads or modifies the register bit-fields should appear as reading and writing the corresponding variable.

Predicated execution and conditional execution are other sources of definitions that do not kill their target register. The execution of predicated instructions is guarded by the evaluation of a single bit operand. The execution of conditional instructions is guarded by the evaluation of a condition on a multi-bit operand. We extend the ISA classification of [39] to distinguish four classes:

Partial Predicated Execution Support. SELECT instructions, first introduced by the Multiflow TRACE architecture [14], are provided. The Multiflow TRACE 500 architecture was to include predicated store and floating-point instructions [37].

Full Predicated Execution Support. Most instructions accept a Boolean predicate operand which nullifies the instruction effects if the predicate evaluates to false. EPIC-style architectures also provide predicate define instructions (PDIs) to efficiently evaluate predicates corresponding to nested conditions: Unconditional, Conditional, parallel-OR, parallel-AND [26].

Partial Conditional Execution Support. Conditional move (CMOV) instructions, first introduced by the Alpha AXP architecture [4], are provided. CMOV instructions are available in the ia32 ISA since the Pentium Pro.

Full Conditional Execution Support. Most instructions are conditionally executed depending on the evaluation of a condition of a source operand. On the ARM architecture, the implicit source operand is a bit-field in the status register and the condition is encoded on 4 bits. On the VelociTI™ TMS230C6x architecture [47], the source operand is a general register encoded on 3 bits and the condition is encoded on 1 bit.

2.5   Program Representation Invariants

Engineering a code generator requires decisions about what information is transient, or belongs to the invariants of the program representation. By invariant we mean a property which is ensured before and after each phase. Transient information is recomputed as needed by some phases from the program representation invariants. The applicability of the SSA form only spans the early phases of the code generation process: from instruction selection, down to register allocation. After register allocation, program variables are mapped to architectural registers or to memory locations, so the SSA form analyses and optimizations no longer apply. In addition, a program may be only partially converted to the SSA form. This motivates the engineering of the SSA form as extensions to a baseline code generator program representation.

Some extensions to the program representation required by the SSA form are better engineered as invariants, in particular for operands, operations, basic blocks, and control-flow graph. Operands which are SSA variables need to record the unique operation that defines them as a target operand, and possibly to maintain the list of where they appear as source operands. Operations such as ϕ-functions, σ-functions of the SSI form [6], and parallel copies may appear as regular operations constrained to specific places in the basic blocks. The incoming arcs of basic blocks need also be kept in the same order as the source operands of each of its ϕ-functions.

A program representation invariant that impacts SSA form engineering is the structure of loops. The modern way of identifying loops in a CFG is the construction of a loop nesting forest as defined by Ramalingam [43]. Non-reducible control-flow allows for different loop nesting forests for a given CFG, yet high-level information such as loop-carried memory dependences, or user-level loop annotations, are provided to the code generator. This information is attached to a loop structure, which thus becomes an invariant. The impact on the SSA form is that some loop nesting forests, such as the Havlak [29] loop structure, are better than others for key analyses such as SSA variable liveness [5].

Up-to-date live-in and live-out sets at basic block boundaries are also candidates for being program representation invariants. However, when using and updating liveness information under the SSA form, it appears convenient to distinguish the ϕ-function contributions from the results of dataflow fix-point computation. In particular, Sreedhar et al. [48] introduced the ϕ-function semantics that became later known as *multiplexing mode*, where a ϕ-function B_0 : $a_0 = \phi(B_1 : a_1, \ldots, B_n : a_n)$ makes a_0 live-in of basic block B_0, and $a_1, \ldots a_n$ live-out of basic blocks $B_1, \ldots B_n$. The classic basic block invariants LiveIn(B) and LiveOut(B) are then complemented with PhiDefs(B) and PhiUses(B) [5].

Finally, some compilers adopt the invariant that the SSA form be *conventional* across the code generation phases. This approach is motivated by the fact that classic optimizations such as SSA-PRE [32] require that 'the live ranges of different versions of the same original program variable do not overlap', implying the SSA form is conventional. Other compilers that use SSA numbers and omit the ϕ-functions from the program representation [34] are similarly constrained. Work by Sreedhar et al. [48] and by Boissinot et al. [7] clarified how to convert the transformed SSA form conventional wherever required, so there is no reason nowadays for this property to be an invariant.

3   Code Generation Phases and the SSA Form

3.1   Classic If-conversion

If-conversion refers to optimizations that convert a program region to straight-line code. It is primarily motivated by instruction scheduling on instruction-level parallel cores [39], as removing conditional branches enables to:

- eliminate branch resolution stalls in the instruction pipeline,
- reduce uses of the branch unit, which is often single-issue,
- increase the size of the instruction scheduling regions.

In case of inner loop bodies, if-conversion further enables vectorization [1] and software pipelining (modulo scheduling) [41]. Consequently, control-flow regions selected for if-conversion are acyclic, even though seminal techniques [1,41] consider more general control-flow.

The scope and effectiveness of if-conversion depends on the ISA support. In principle, any if-conversion technique targeted to full predicated or conditional execution support may be adapted to partial predicated or conditional execution support. For instance, non-predicated instructions with side-effects such as memory accesses can be used in combination with SELECT to provide a harmless effective address in case the operation must be nullified [39].

Besides predicated or conditional execution, architectural support for if-conversion is improved by supporting speculative execution. Speculative execution (control speculation) refers to executing an operation before knowing that its execution is required, such as when moving code above a branch [37] or promoting operation predicates [39]. Speculative execution assumes instructions have reversible side effects, so speculating potentially excepting instructions requires architectural support. On the Multiflow TRACE 300 architecture and later on the Lx VLIW architecture [23], non-trapping memory loads known as *dismissible* are provided. The IMPACT EPIC architecture speculative execution [2] is generalized from the *sentinel* model [38].

The classic contributions to if-conversion did not consider the SSA form.

Allen et al. [1] convert control dependences to data dependences, motivated by inner loop vectorization. They distinguish forward branches, exit branches, and backward branches, and compute Boolean guards accordingly. As this work predates the Program Dependence Graph [24], complexity of the resulting Boolean expressions is an issue. When comparing to later if-conversion techniques, only the conversion of forward branches is relevant.

Park & Schlansker [41] propose the RK algorithm based the control dependences. They assume a fully predicated architecture with only Conditional PDIs. The R function assigns a minimal set of Boolean predicates to basic blocks, and the K function express the way these predicates are computed. The algorithm is general enough to process cyclic and irreducible rooted flow graphs, but it practice it is applied to single entry acyclic regions.

Blickstein et al. [4] pioneer the use of CMOV instructions to replace conditional branches in the GEM compilers for the Alpha AXP architecture.

Lowney et al. [37] match the innermost if-then constructs in the Multiflow Trace Scheduling compiler in order to generate the SELECT and the predicated memory store operations.

Fang [22] assumes a fully predicated architecture with Conditional PDIs. The proposed algorithm is tailored to acyclic regions with single entry and multiple exits, and as such is able to compute R and K functions without relying on explicit control dependences. The main improvement of this algorithm over [41] is that it also speculates instructions up the dominance tree through predicate promotion, except for stores and PDIs. This work further proposes a pre-optimization pass to hoist or sink common sub-expressions before predication and speculation.

Leupers [36] focuses on if-conversion of nested if-then-else (ITE) statements on architectures with full conditional execution support. A dynamic programming technique appropriately selects either a conditional jump or a conditional instruction based implementation scheme for each ITE statement, and the objective is the reduction of worst-case execution time (WCET).

A few contributions to if-conversion did use the SSA form but only internally.

Jacome et al. [31] propose the Static Single Assignment - Predicated Switching (SSA-PS) transformation aimed at clustered VLIW architectures, with predicated move instructions that operate inside clusters (internal moves) or between clusters (external moves). The first idea of the SSA-PS transformation is to realize the conditional assignments corresponding to ϕ-functions via predicated switching operations, in particular predicated move operations. The second idea is that the predicated external moves leverage the penalties associated with inter-cluster data transfers. The SSA-PS transformation predicates non-move operations and is apparently restricted to innermost if-then-else statements.

Chuang et al. [13] introduce a predicated execution support aimed at removing non-kill register writes from the micro-architecture. They propose SELECT instructions called *phi-ops*, predicated memory accesses, Unconditional PDIs, and ORP instructions for OR-ing multiple predicates. A restriction of the RK algorithm to single-entry single-exit regions is proposed, adapted to the Unconditional PDIs and the ORP instructions. Their other contribution is the generation of phi-ops, whose insertion points are computed like the SSA form placement of the ϕ-functions. The ϕ-functions source operands are replaced by ϕ-lists, where each operand is associated with the predicate of its source basic block. The ϕ-lists are processed by topological order of the predicates to generate the phi-ops.

3.2   If-conversion under SSA Form

The ability to perform if-conversion on the SSA form of a program representation requires the handling of operations that do not kill the target operand because of predicated or conditional execution.

Stoutchinin & Ferrière [49] introduce ψ-functions in order to represent fully predicated code under the SSA form, which is then called the ψ-SSA form. The ψ-functions arguments are paired with predicates and are ordered in dominance order in the ψ-function argument list, a correctness condition re-discovered by Chuang et al. [13] for their phi-ops.

Stoutchinin & Gao [50] propose an if-conversion technique based on the predication of Fang [22] and the replacement of ϕ-functions by ψ-functions. They prove the conversion is correct provided the SSA form is conventional. The technique is implemented in Open64 for the ia64 architecture.

Bruel [10] targets VLIW architectures with SELECT and dismissible load instructions. The proposed framework reduces acyclic control-flow constructs from innermost to outermost, and the monitoring of the if-conversion benefits provides the stopping criterion. The core technique control speculates operations, reduces height of predicate computations, and performs tail duplication. It can also generate ψ-functions instead of SELECT operations.

Ferrière [25] extends the ψ-SSA form algorithms of [49] to architectures with partial predicated execution support, by formulating simple correctness conditions for the predicate promotion of operations that do not have side-effects. This work also details how to transform the ψ-SSA form to conventional ψ-SSA form by generating CMOV operations.

Thanks to these contributions, virtually all if-conversion techniques formulated without the SSA form can be adapted to the ψ-SSA form, with the added benefit that already predicated code may be part of the input. In practice, these contributions follow the generic steps of if-conversion proposed by Fang [22]:

- if-conversion region selection;
- code hoisting and sinking of common sub-expressions;
- assignment of predicates to the basic blocks;
- insertion of operations to compute the basic block predicates;
- predication or speculation of operations;
- and conditional branch removal.

The result of an if-converted region is a hyper-block, that is, a sequence of basic blocks with predicated or conditional operations, where control may only enter from the top, but may exit from one or more locations [40].

Although if-conversion based on the ψ-SSA form appears effective for the different classes of architectural support, the downstream phases of the code generator require at least some adaptations of the plain SSA form algorithms to handle the ψ-functions. The largest impact of handling ψ-function is apparent in the ψ-SSA form destruction [25], whose original description [49] was incomplete.

In order to avoid such complexities, the Kalray VLIW code generator adopts simpler solution than ψ-functions to represent the non-kill effects of conditional operations on target operands. This solution is based on the observation that under the SSA form, a CMOV operation is equivalent to a SELECT operation with a same resource naming constraint between one source and the target operand. Unlike other predicated or conditional instructions, a SELECT instruction kills its target register. Generalizing this observation provides a simple way to handle predicated or conditional operations in plain SSA form:

- For each target operand of the predicated or conditional instruction, add a corresponding source operand in the instruction signature.
- For each added source operand, add a same resource naming constraint with the corresponding target operand.

This simple transformation enables the SSA form analyses and optimizations to remain oblivious to predicated or conditional code. The drawback of this solution is that non-kill definitions of a given variable (before SSA variable renaming) remain in dominance order across program transformations, as opposed to ψ-SSA where predicate value analysis may enable this order to be relaxed.

3.3 Pre-pass Instruction Scheduling

Further down the code generator, the last major phase before register allocation is pre-pass instruction scheduling. Innermost loops with a single basic block, super-block or hyper-block body are candidates for software pipelining techniques such as modulo scheduling [45]. For innermost loops that are not software pipelined, and for other program regions, acyclic instruction scheduling techniques apply: basic block scheduling [27]; super-block scheduling [30]; hyper-block scheduling [40]; tree region scheduling [28]; or trace scheduling [37].

By definition, pre-pass instruction scheduling operates before register allocation. At this stage, instruction operands are mostly virtual registers, except for instructions with ISA or ABI constraints that bind them to specific architectural registers. Moreover, preparation to pre-pass instruction scheduling includes virtual register renaming, also known as register web construction, in order to reduce the number of anti dependences and output dependences in the instruction scheduling problem. Other reasons why it seems there is little to gain from scheduling instructions on a SSA form of the program representation include:

- Except in case of trace scheduling which pre-dates the use of SSA form in production compilers, the classic scheduling regions are single-entry and do not have control-flow merge. So there are no ϕ-functions in case of acyclic scheduling, and only ϕ-functions in the loop header in case of software pipelining. Keeping those ϕ-functions in the scheduling problem has no benefits and raises engineering issues, due to their parallel execution semantics and the constraint to keep them first in basic blocks.
- Instruction scheduling must account for all the instruction issue slots required to execute a code region. If the only ordering constraints between instructions, besides control dependences and memory dependences, are limited to true data dependences on operands, code motion will create interferences that must later be resolved by inserting COPY operations in the scheduled code region. (Except for interferences created by the overlapping of live ranges that results from modulo scheduling, as these are resolved by modulo renaming [33].) So scheduling instructions with SSA variables as operands is not effective unless extra dependences are added to the scheduling problem to prevent such code motion.

– Some machine instructions have partial effects on special resources such as the status register. Representing special resources as SSA variables even though they are accessed at the bit-field level requires coarsening the instruction effects to the whole resource, as discussed in Section 2.4. In turn this implies def-use variable ordering that prevents aggressive instruction scheduling. For instance, all sticky bit-field definitions can be reordered with regards to the next use, and an instruction scheduler is expected to do so. Scheduling OR-type predicate define operations [46] raises the same issues. An instruction scheduler is also expected to precisely track accesses to unrelated or partially overlapping bit-fields in a status register.

– Aggressive instruction scheduling relaxes some flow data dependences that are normally implied by SSA variable def-use ordering. A first example is *move renaming* [51], the dynamic switching of the definition of a source operand defined by a COPY operation when the consumer operations ends up being scheduled at the same cycle or earlier. Another example is *inductive relaxation* [16], where the dependence between additive induction variables and their use as base in base+offset addressing modes is relaxed to the extent permitted by the induction step and the range of the offset. These techniques apply to acyclic scheduling and to modulo scheduling.

To summarize, trying to keep the SSA form inside the pre-pass instruction scheduling appears more complex than operating on the program representation with classic compiler temporary variables. This representation is obtained after SSA form destruction and aggressive coalescing. If required by the register allocation, the SSA form should be re-constructed.

4   SSA Form Destruction Algorithms

The destruction of the SSA form in a code generator is required before the pre-pass instruction scheduling and software pipelining, as discussed earlier, and also before non-SSA register allocation. A weaker form is the conversion of transformed SSA form to conventional SSA form, which is required by classic SSA form optimizations such as SSA-PRE [32] and SSA form register allocators [42]. For all such cases, the main objective besides removing the SSA form extensions from the program representation is to ensure that the operand naming constraints are satisfied. Another objective is to avoid critical edge splitting, as this interferes with branch alignment [12], and is not possible on some control-flow edges of machine code such as hardware loop back edges.

The contributions to SSA form destruction techniques can be characterized as an evolution towards correctness, the ability to manage operand naming constraints, and the reduction of algorithmic time and memory requirements.

Cytron et al. [15] describe the process of *translating out of SSA* as 'naive replacement preceded by dead code elimination and followed by coloring'. They replace each ϕ-function $B_0 : a_0 = \phi(B_1 : a_1, \ldots, B_n : a_n)$ by n copies $a_0 = a_i$, one per basic block B_i, before applying Chaitin-style coalescing.

Briggs et al. [9] identify correctness issues in Cytron et al. [15] out of (transformed) SSA form translation and illustrate them by the *lost-copy problem* and the *swap problem*. These problems appear in relation with the critical edges, and because a sequence of ϕ-functions at the start of a basic block has parallel assignment semantics [7]. Two SSA form destruction algorithms are proposed, depending on the presence of critical edges in the control-flow graph. However the need for parallel COPY operations is not recognized.

Sreedhar et al. [48] define the ϕ-congruence classes as the sets of SSA variables that are transitively connected by a ϕ-function. When none of the ϕ-congruence classes have members that interfere, the SSA form is called *conventional* and its destruction is trivial: replace all the SSA variables of a ϕ-congruence class by a temporary variable, and remove the ϕ-functions. In general, the SSA form is *transformed* after program optimizations, that is, some ϕ-congruence classes contain interferences. In Method I, the SSA form is made conventional by inserting COPY operations that target the arguments of each ϕ-function in its predecessor basic blocks, *and also* by inserting COPY operations that source the target of each ϕ-function in its basic block. The latter is the key for not depending on critical edge splitting [7]. The code is then improved by running a new SSA variable coalescer that grows the ϕ-congruence classes with COPY-related variables, while keeping the SSA form conventional. In Method II and Method III, the ϕ-congruence classes are initialized as singletons, then merged while processing the ϕ-functions in some order. In Method II, two variables of the current ϕ-function that interfere directly or through their ϕ-congruence classes are isolated by inserting COPY operations for both. This ensures that the ϕ-congruence class which is grown from the classes of the variables related by the current ϕ-function is interference-free. In Method III, if possible only one COPY operation is inserted to remove the interference, and more involved choices about which variables to isolate from the ϕ-function congruence class are resolved by a maximum independent set heuristic. Both methods are correct except for a detail about the live-out sets to consider when testing for interferences [7].

Leung & George [35] are the first to address the problem of satisfying the same resource and the dedicated register operand naming constraints of the SSA form on machine code. They identify that Chaitin-style coalescing after SSA form destruction is not sufficient, and that adapting the SSA optimizations to enforce operand naming constraints is not practical. They operate in three steps: collect the renaming constraints; mark the renaming conflicts; and reconstruct code, which adapts the SSA destruction of Briggs et al. [9]. This work is also the first to make explicit use of parallel COPY operations.

Budimlić et al. [11] propose a lightweight SSA form destruction motivated by JIT compilation. It uses the (strict) SSA form property of dominance of variable definitions over uses to avoid the maintenance of an explicit interference graph. Unlike previous approaches to SSA form destruction that coalesce increasingly larger sets of non-interfering ϕ-related (and COPY-related) variables, they first construct SSA-webs with early pruning of obviously interfering variables, then de-coalesce the SSA webs into non-interfering classes. They propose the *dominance forest* explicit data-structure to speed-up these interference tests. This SSA form destruction technique does not handle the operand naming constraints, and also requires critical edge splitting.

Rastello et al. [44] revisit the problem of satisfying the *same resource* and *dedicated register* operand constraints of the SSA form on machine code, motivated by erroneous code produced by the technique of Leung & George [35]. Inspired by work of Sreedhar et al. [48], they include the ϕ-related variables as candidates in the coalescing that optimizes the operand naming constraints. This work avoids the patent of Sreedhar et al. (US patent 6182284).

Boissinot et al. [7] analyze the previous contributions to SSA form destruction to their root principles, and propose a generic approach to SSA form destruction that is proved correct, handles operand naming constraints, and can be optimized for speed. The foundation of the approach is to transform the program to conventional SSA form by isolating the ϕ-functions like in Method I of Sreedhar et al. [48]. However, the COPY operations inserted are parallel, so a parallel COPY sequentialization algorithm is provided. The task of improving the conventional SSA form is then seen as a classic aggressive variable coalescing problem, but thanks to the SSA form the interference relation between SSA variables is made precise and frugal to compute. Interference is obtained by combining the intersection of SSA live ranges, and the equality of values which is easily tracked under the SSA form across COPY operations. Moreover, the use of the dominance forest data-structure of Budimlić et al. [11] to speed-up interference tests between congruence classes is obviated by a linear traversal of these classes in pre-order of the dominance tree. Finally, the same resource operand constraints are managed by pre-coalescing, and the dedicated register operand constraints are represented by pre-coloring the congruence classes. Congruence classes with a different pre-coloring always interfere.

5 Summary and Conclusions

The target independent program representations of high-end compilers are nowadays based on the SSA form, as illustrated by the Open64 WHIRL, the GCC GIMPLE, or the LLVM IR. However support of the SSA form in the code generator program representations is more challenging. The main issues to address are the mapping of SSA variables to special architectural resources, the management of instruction set architecture (ISA) or application binary interface (ABI) operand naming constraints, and the representation of non-kill effects on the target operands of machine instructions. Moreover, adding the SSA form attributes and invariants to the program representations appears detrimental to the pre-pass instruction scheduling (including software pipelining).

The SSA form benefits most the phases of code generation that run before pre-pass instruction scheduling. In particular, we review the different approaches to if-conversion, a key enabling phase for the exploitation of instruction-level parallelism by instruction scheduling. Recent contributions to if-conversion leverage the SSA form but introduce ψ-functions in order to connect the partial definitions of predicated or conditional machine operations. This approach effectively extends the SSA form to the ψ-SSA form, which is more complicated to handle especially in the SSA form destruction phase.

We propose a simpler alternative for the representation of non-kill target operands without the ψ-functions, allowing the early phases of code generation to operate on the standard SSA form only. This proposal requires that the SSA form destruction phase be able to manage operand naming constraints. This motivated us to extend the technique of Sreedhar et al. (SAS'99), the only one at the time that was correct, and which did not require critical edge splitting. Eventually, this work evolved into the technique of Boissinot et al. (CGO'09).

References

1. Allen, J.R., Kennedy, K., Porterfield, C., Warren, J.: Conversion of control dependence to data dependence. In: Proc. of the 10th ACM SIGACT-SIGPLAN Symposium on Principles of Programming Languages, POPL 1983, pp. 177–189 (1983)
2. August, D.I., Connors, D.A., Mahlke, S.A., Sias, J.W., Crozier, K.M., Cheng, B.C., Eaton, P.R., Olaniran, Q.B., Hwu, W.M.W.: Integrated predicated and speculative execution in the impact epic architecture. In: Proc. of the 25th Annual International Symposium on Computer Architecture, ISCA 1998, pp. 227–237 (1998)
3. Barik, R., Zhao, J., Sarkar, V.: A decoupled non-ssa global register allocation using bipartite liveness graphs. ACM Trans. Archit. Code Optim. 10(4), 63:1–63:24 (2013)
4. Blickstein, D.S., Craig, P.W., Davidson, C.S., Faiman Jr., R.N., Glossop, K.D., Grove, R.B., Hobbs, S.O., Noyce, W.B.: The GEM optimizing compiler system. Digital Technical Journal 4(4), 121–136 (1992)
5. Boissinot, B., Brandner, F., Darte, A., de Dinechin, B.D., Rastello, F.: A non-iterative data-flow algorithm for computing liveness sets in strict ssa programs. In: Yang, H. (ed.) APLAS 2011. LNCS, vol. 7078, pp. 137–154. Springer, Heidelberg (2011)
6. Boissinot, B., Brisk, P., Darte, A., Rastello, F.: SSI properties revisited. ACM Trans. on Embedded Computing Systems (2012); special Issue on Software and Compilers for Embedded Systems
7. Boissinot, B., Darte, A., Rastello, F., de Dinechin, B.D., Guillon, C.: Revisiting Out-of-SSA Translation for Correctness, Code Quality and Efficiency. In: CGO 2009: Proc. of the 2009 International Symposium on Code Generation and Optimization, pp. 114–125 (2009)
8. Boissinot, B., Hack, S., Grund, D., de Dinechin, B.D., Rastello, F.: Fast Liveness Checking for SSA-Form Programs. In: CGO 2008: Proc. of the Sixth Annual IEEE/ACM International Symposium on Code Generation and Optimization, pp. 35–44 (2008)
9. Briggs, P., Cooper, K.D., Harvey, T.J., Simpson, L.T.: Practical Improvements to the Construction and Destruction of Static Single Assignment Form. Software – Practice and Experience 28, 859–881 (1998)

10. Bruel, C.: If-Conversion SSA Framework for partially predicated VLIW architectures. In: ODES 4, pp. 5–13 (March 2006)
11. Budimlic, Z., Cooper, K.D., Harvey, T.J., Kennedy, K., Oberg, T.S., Reeves, S.W.: Fast copy coalescing and live-range identification. In: Proc. of the ACM SIGPLAN 2002 Conference on Programming Language Design and Implementation, PLDI 2002, pp. 25–32. ACM, New York (2002)
12. Calder, B., Grunwald, D.: Reducing branch costs via branch alignment. In: Proc. of the Sixth International Conference on Architectural Support for Programming Languages and Operating Systems, ASPLOS VI, pp. 242–251. ACM, New York (1994)
13. Chuang, W., Calder, B., Ferrante, J.: Phi-predication for light-weight if-conversion. In: Proc. of the International Symposium on Code Generation and Optimization: Feedback-Directed and Runtime Optimization, CGO 2003, pp. 179–190 (2003)
14. Colwell, R.P., Nix, R.P., O'Donnell, J.J., Papworth, D.B., Rodman, P.K.: A vliw architecture for a trace scheduling compiler. In: Proc. of the Second International conference on Architectual Support for Programming Languages and Operating Systems, ASPLOS-II, pp. 180–192 (1987)
15. Cytron, R., Ferrante, J., Rosen, B.K., Wegman, M.N., Zadeck, F.K.: Efficiently Computing Static Single Assignment Form and the Control Dependence Graph. ACM Trans. on Programming Languages and Systems 13(4), 451–490 (1991)
16. de Dinechin, B.D.: A unified software pipeline construction scheme for modulo scheduled loops. In: Malyshkin, V.E. (ed.) PaCT 1997. LNCS, vol. 1277, pp. 189–200. Springer, Heidelberg (1997)
17. de Dinechin, B.D.: Time-Indexed Formulations and a Large Neighborhood Search for the Resource-Constrained Modulo Scheduling Problem. In: 3rd Multidisciplinary International Scheduling Conference: Theory and Applications, MISTA (2007)
18. Dupont de Dinechin, B.: Inter-Block Scoreboard Scheduling in a JIT Compiler for VLIW Processors. In: Luque, E., Margalef, T., Benítez, D. (eds.) Euro-Par 2008. LNCS, vol. 5168, pp. 370–381. Springer, Heidelberg (2008)
19. de Dinechin, B.D., Ayrignac, R., Beaucamps, P.E., Couvert, P., Ganne, B., de Massas, P.G., Jacquet, F., Jones, S., Chaisemartin, N.M., Riss, F., Strudel, T.: A clustered manycore processor architecture for embedded and accelerated applications. In: IEEE High Performance Extreme Computing Conference, HPEC 2013, pp. 1–6 (2013)
20. de Dinechin, B.D., de Ferrière, F., Guillon, C., Stoutchinin, A.: Code Generator Optimizations for the ST120 DSP-MCU Core. In: CASES 2000: Proc. of the 2000 International Conference on Compilers, Architecture, and Synthesis for Embedded Systems, pp. 93–102 (2000)
21. de Dinechin, B.D., Monat, C., Blouet, P., Bertin, C.: Dsp-mcu processor optimization for portable applications. Microelectron. Eng. 54(1-2), 123–132 (2000)
22. Fang, J.Z.: Compiler algorithms on if-conversion, speculative predicates assignment and predicated code optimizations. In: Sehr, D., Banerjee, U., Gelernter, D., Nicolau, A., Padua, D. (eds.) LCPC 1996. LNCS, vol. 1239, pp. 135–153. Springer, Heidelberg (1997)
23. Faraboschi, P., Brown, G., Fisher, J.A., Desoli, G., Homewood, F.: Lx: A Technology Platform for Customizable VLIW Embedded Processing. In: ISCA 2000: Proc. of the 27th Annual Int. Symposium on Computer Architecture, pp. 203–213 (2000)
24. Ferrante, J., Ottenstein, K.J., Warren, J.D.: The program dependence graph and its use in optimization. ACM Trans. Program. Lang. Syst. 9(3), 319–349 (1987)

25. de Ferrière, F.: Improvements to the Psi-SSA representation. In: Proc. of the 10th International Workshop on Software & Compilers for Embedded Systems, SCOPES 2007, pp. 111–121 (2007)

26. Gillies, D.M., Ju, D.C.R., Johnson, R., Schlansker, M.: Global predicate analysis and its application to register allocation. In: Proc. of the 29th Annual ACM/IEEE International Symposium on Microarchitecture, MICRO 29, pp. 114–125 (1996)

27. Goodman, J.R., Hsu, W.C.: Code scheduling and register allocation in large basic blocks. In: Proc. of the 2nd International Conference on Supercomputing, ICS 1988, pp. 442–452 (1988)

28. Havanki, W., Banerjia, S., Conte, T.: Treegion scheduling for wide issue processors. In: International Symposium on High-Performance Computer Architecture, 266 (1998)

29. Havlak, P.: Nesting of reducible and irreducible loops. ACM Trans. on Programming Languages and Systems 19(4) (1997)

30. Hwu, W.M.W., Mahlke, S.A., Chen, W.Y., Chang, P.P., Warter, N.J., Bringmann, R.A., Ouellette, R.G., Hank, R.E., Kiyohara, T., Haab, G.E., Holm, J.G., Lavery, D.M.: The superblock: An effective technique for vliw and superscalar compilation. J. Supercomput. 7(1-2), 229–248 (1993)

31. Jacome, M.F., de Veciana, G., Pillai, S.: Clustered vliw architectures with predicated switching. In: Proc. of the 38th Design Automation Conference, DAC, pp. 696–701 (2001)

32. Kennedy, R., Chan, S., Liu, S.M., Lo, R., Tu, P., Chow, F.: Partial redundancy elimination in ssa form. ACM Trans. Program. Lang. Syst. 21(3), 627–676 (1999)

33. Lam, M.: Software Pipelining: An Effective Scheduling Technique for VLIW Machines. In: PLDI 1988: Proc. of the ACM SIGPLAN 1988 Conference on Programming Language Design and Implementation, pp. 318–328 (1988)

34. Lapkowski, C., Hendren, L.J.: Extended ssa numbering: introducing ssa properties to languages with multi-level pointers. In: Proc. of the 1996 Conference of the Centre for Advanced Studies on Collaborative Research, CASCON 1996, pp. 23–34. IBM Press (1996)

35. Leung, A., George, L.: Static single assignment form for machine code. In: Proc. of the ACM SIGPLAN 1999 Conference on Programming Language Design and Implementation, PLDI 1999, pp. 204–214 (1999)

36. Leupers, R.: Exploiting conditional instructions in code generation for embedded vliw processors. In: Proc. of the Conference on Design, Automation and Test in Europe, DATE 1999 (1999)

37. Lowney, P.G., Freudenberger, S.M., Karzes, T.J., Lichtenstein, W.D., Nix, R.P., O'Donnell, J.S., Ruttenberg, J.: The multiflow trace scheduling compiler. J. Supercomput. 7(1-2), 51–142 (1993)

38. Mahlke, S.A., Chen, W.Y., Hwu, W.M.W., Rau, B.R., Schlansker, M.S.: Sentinel scheduling for vliw and superscalar processors. In: Proc. of the Fifth International Conference on Architectural Support for Programming Languages and Operating Systems, ASPLOS-V, pp. 238–247 (1992)

39. Mahlke, S.A., Hank, R.E., McCormick, J.E., August, D.I., Hwu, W.M.W.: A comparison of full and partial predicated execution support for ilp processors. In: Proc. of the 22nd Annual International Symposium on Computer Architecture, ISCA 1995, pp. 138–150 (1995),

40. Mahlke, S.A., Lin, D.C., Chen, W.Y., Hank, R.E., Bringmann, R.A.: Effective compiler support for predicated execution using the hyperblock. SIGMICRO Newsl. 23(1-2), 45–54 (1992)

41. Park, J.C., Schlansker, M.S.: On predicated execution. Tech. Rep. HPL-91-58, Hewlett Packard Laboratories, Palo Alto, California (1991)
42. Pereira, F.M.Q., Palsberg, J.: Register allocation by puzzle solving. In: Proc. of the ACM SIGPLAN 2008 Conference on Programming Language Design and Implementation, PLDI 2008, pp. 216–226. ACM (2008)
43. Ramalingam, G.: On loops, dominators, and dominance frontiers. ACM Trans. on Programming Languages and Systems 24(5) (2002)
44. Rastello, F., de Ferrière, F., Guillon, C.: Optimizing Translation Out of SSA Using Renaming Constraints. In: CGO 2004: Proc. of the International Symposium on Code Generation and Optimization, pp. 265–278 (2004)
45. Rau, B.R.: Iterative modulo scheduling. International Journal of Parallel Programming 24(1), 3–65 (1996)
46. Schlansker, M., Mahlke, S., Johnson, R.: Control cpr: A branch height reduction optimization for epic architectures. In: Proc. of the ACM SIGPLAN 1999 Conference on Programming Language Design and Implementation, PLDI 1999, pp. 155–168 (1999)
47. Seshan, N.: High velociti processing. IEEE Signal Processing Magazine, 86–101 (1998)
48. Sreedhar, V.C., Ju, R.D.C., Gillies, D.M., Santhanam, V.: Translating Out of Static Single Assignment Form. In: SAS 1999: Proc. of the 6th International Symposium on Static Analysis, pp. 194–210 (1999)
49. Stoutchinin, A., de Ferrière, F.: Efficient Static Single Assignment Form for Predication. In: Proc. of the 34th Annual ACM/IEEE International Symposium on Microarchitecture, MICRO 34, pp. 172–181 (2001)
50. Stoutchinin, A., Gao, G.: If-Conversion in SSA Form. In: Danelutto, M., Vanneschi, M., Laforenza, D. (eds.) Euro-Par 2004. LNCS, vol. 3149, pp. 336–345. Springer, Heidelberg (2004)
51. Young, C., Smith, M.D.: Better global scheduling using path profiles. In: Proc. of the 31st Annual ACM/IEEE International Symposium on Microarchitecture, MICRO 31, pp. 115–123 (1998)

Parameterized Construction of Program Representations for Sparse Dataflow Analyses

André Tavares[1], Benoit Boissinot[2], Fernando Pereira[1], and Fabrice Rastello[3]

[1] UFMG
[2] Ens Lyon
[3] Inria

Abstract. Data-flow analyses usually associate information with control flow regions. Informally, if these regions are too small, like a point between two consecutive statements, we call the analysis dense. On the other hand, if these regions include many such points, then we call it sparse. This paper presents a systematic method to build program representations that support sparse analyses. To pave the way to this framework we clarify the bibliography about well-known intermediate program representations. We show that our approach, up to parameter choice, subsumes many of these representations, such as the SSA, SSI and e-SSA forms. In particular, our algorithms are faster, simpler and more frugal than the previous techniques used to construct SSI - Static Single Information - form programs. We produce intermediate representations isomorphic to Choi *et al.*'s Sparse Evaluation Graphs (SEG) for the family of data-flow problems that can be partitioned per variables. However, contrary to SEGs, we can handle - sparsely - problems that are not in this family. We have tested our ideas in the LLVM compiler, comparing different program representations in terms of size and construction time.

1 Introduction

Many data-flow analyses bind information to pairs formed by a variable and a program point [4, 21, 24, 26, 30, 32, 36–39]. As an example, for each program point p, and each integer variable v live at p, Stephenson *et al.*'s [36] bit-width analysis finds the size, in bits, of v at p. Although well studied in the literature, this approach might produce redundant information. For instance, a given variable v may be mapped to the same bit-width along many consecutive program points. Therefore, a natural way to reduce redundancies is to make these analyses *sparser*, increasing the granularity of the program regions that they manipulate.

There exists different attempts to implement data-flow analyses sparsely. The Static Single Assignment (SSA) form [13], for instance, allows us to implement several analyses and optimizations, such as reaching definitions and constant propagation, sparsely. Since its conception, the SSA format has been generalized into many different program representations, such as the *Extended-SSA* form [4], the *Static Single Information* (SSI) form [1], and the *Static Single Use* (SSU) form [18, 23, 30]. Each of these representations extends the reach of the SSA form to sparser data-flow analyses; however, there is not a format that subsumes all

A. Cohen (Ed.): CC 2014, LNCS 8409, pp. 18–39, 2014.

the others. In other words, each of these three program representations fit specific types of data-flow problems. Another attempt to model data-flow analyses sparsely is due to Choi *et al.*'s *Sparse Evaluation Graph* (SEG) [9]. This datastructure supports several different analyses sparsely, as long as the abstract state of a variable does not interfere with the abstract state of other variables in the same program. This family of analyses is known as *Partitioned Variable Problems* in the literature [41].

In this paper, we propose a framework that includes all these previous approaches. Given a data-flow problem defined by (i) a set of control flow nodes, that produce information, and (ii) a direction in which information flows: forward, backward or both ways, we build a program representation that allows to solve the problem sparsely using def-use chains. The program representations that we generate ensure a key *single information property*: the data-flow facts associated with a variable are invariant along the entire live range of this variable.

We have implemented our framework in the LLVM compiler [22], and have used it to provide intermediate representations to well-known compiler optimizations: Wegman *et al.*'s [39] conditional constant propagation, and Bodik *et al.*'s [4] algorithm for array bounds check elimination. We compare these representations with the SSI form as defined by Singer. The intermediate program representations that we build increase the size of the original program by less than 5% - one order of magnitude less than Singer's SSI form. Furthermore, the time to build these program representations is less than 2% of the time taken by the standard suite of optimizations used in the LLVM compiler. Finally, our intermediate representations have already been used in the implementation of different static analyses, already publicly available [7, 15, 32, 34].

2   Static Single Information

Our objective is to generate program representations that bestow the *Static Single Information property* (Definition 6) onto a given data-flow problem. In order to introduce this notion, we will need a number of concepts, which we define in this chapter. We start with the concept of a *Data-Flow System*, which Definition 1 recalls from the literature. We consider a *program point* a point between two consecutive instructions. If p is a program point, then $preds(p)$ (resp. $succs(p)$) is the set of all the program points that are predecessors (resp. successors) of p. A *transfer function* determines how information flows among these program points. Information are elements of a *lattice*. We find a solution to a data-flow problem by continuously solving the set of transfer functions associated with each program region until a fix point is reached. Some program points are *meet nodes*, because they combine information coming from two or more regions. The result of combining different elements of a lattice is given by a *meet* operator, which we denote by $\wedge$.

Definition 1 (Data-Flow System). *A data-flow system E_{dense} is an equation system that associates, with each program point p, an element of a lattice $\mathcal{L}$, given by the equation $x^p = \bigwedge_{s \in preds(p)} F^{s,p}(x^s)$, where: x^p denotes the abstract state* *associated with program point p; preds(p) is the set of control flow predecessors of p; $F^{s,p}$ is the transfer function from program point s to program point p. The analysis can alternatively be written as a constraint system that binds to each program point p and each s $\in$ preds(p) the equation $x^p = x^p \wedge F^{s,p}(x^s)$ or, equivalently, the inequation $x^p \sqsubseteq F^{s,p}(x^s)$.*

The program representations that we generate lets us solve a class of data-flow problems that we call *Partitioned Lattice per Variable* (PLV), and that we introduce in Definition 2. Constant propagation is an example of a PLV problem. If we denote by $\mathcal{C}$ the lattice of constants, the overall lattice can be written as $\mathcal{L} = \mathcal{C}^n$, where n is the number of variables. In other words, this data-flow problem ranges on a product lattice that contains a term for each variable in the target program.

Definition 2 (Partitioned Lattice per Variable Problem (PLV)). *Let $\mathcal{V} = \{v_1, \ldots, v_n\}$ be the set of program variables. The Maximum Fixed Point problem on a data-flow system is a* Partitioned Lattice per Variable Problem *if, and only if, $\mathcal{L}$ can be decomposed into the product of $\mathcal{L}_{v_1} \times \cdots \times \mathcal{L}_{v_n}$ where each $\mathcal{L}_{v_i}$ is the lattice associated with program variable v_i. In other words x^s can be writen as $([v_1]^s, \ldots, [v_n]^s)$ where $[v]^s$ denotes the abstract state associated with variable v and program point s. $F^{s,p}$ can thus be decomposed into the product of $F_{v_1}^{s,p} \times \cdots \times F_{v_n}^{s,p}$ and the constraint system decomposed into the inequalities $[v_i]^p \sqsubseteq F_{v_i}^{s,p}([v_1]^s, \ldots, [v_n]^s)$.*

The transfer functions that we describe in Definition 3 have no influence on the solution of a data-flow system. The goal of a sparse data-flow analysis is to shortcut these functions. We accomplish this task by grouping contiguous program points bound to these functions into larger regions.

Definition 3 (Trivial/Constant/Undefined Transfer functions). *Let $\mathcal{L}_{v_1} \times \mathcal{L}_{v_2} \times \cdots \times \mathcal{L}_{v_n}$ be the decomposition per variable of lattice $\mathcal{L}$, where $\mathcal{L}_{v_i}$ is the lattice associated with variable v_i. Let F_{v_i} be a transfer function from $\mathcal{L}$ to $\mathcal{L}_{v_i}$.*

- *F_{v_i} is trivial if $\forall x = ([v_1], \ldots, [v_n]) \in \mathcal{L}, F_{v_i}(x) = [v_i]$*
- *F_{v_i} is constant with value $C \in \mathcal{L}_{v_i}$ if $\forall x \in \mathcal{L}, F_{v_i}(x) = C$*
- *F_{v_i} is undefined if F_{v_i} is constant with value $\top$, e.g., $F_{v_i}(x) = \top$, where $\top \wedge y = y \wedge \top = y$.*

A sparse data-flow analysis propagates information from the control flow node where this information is created directly to the control flow node where this information is needed. Therefore, the notion of *dependence*, which we state in Definition 4, plays a fundamental role in our framework. Intuitively, we say that a variable v depends on a variable v_j if the information associated with v might change in case the information associated with v_j does.

Definition 4 (Dependence). *We say that F_v depends on variable v_j if:*

$$\exists x = ([v_1], \ldots, [v_n]) \neq ([v_1]', \ldots, [v_n]') = x' \text{ in } \mathcal{L}$$
$$\text{such that } [\forall k \neq j, \ [v_k] = [v_k]' \wedge F_v(x) \neq F_v(x')]$$

In a *backward* data-flow analysis, the information that comes from the predecessors of a node n is combined to produce the information that reaches the successors of n. A *forward* analysis propagates information in the opposite direction. We call meet nodes those places where information coming from multiple sources are combined. Definition 5 states this concept more formally.

Definition 5 (Meet Nodes). *Consider a forward (resp. backward) monotone PLV problem, where (Y_v^p) is the maximum fixed point solution of variable v at program point p. We say that a program point p is a meet node for variable v if, and only if, p has $n \geq 2$ predecessors (resp. successors), $s_1, \ldots, s_n$, and there exists $s_i \neq s_j$, such that $Y_v^{s_i} \neq Y_v^{s_j}$.*

Our goal is to build program representations in which the information associated with a variable is invariant along the entire live range of this variable. A variable v is *alive* at a program point p if there is a path from p to an instruction that uses v, and v is not re-defined along the way. The live range of v, which we denote by *live(v)*, is the collection of program points where v is alive.

Definition 6 (Static Single Information property). *Consider a forward (resp. backward) monotone PLV problem E_{dense} stated as in Definition 1. A program representation fulfills the Static Single Information property if, and only if, it meets the following properties for each variable v:*

[**SPLIT-DEF**]: *for each two consecutive program points s and p such that $p \in$ live(v), and $F_v^{s,p}$ is non-trivial nor undefined, there should be an instruction between s and p that contains a definition (resp. last use) of v;*

[**SPLIT-MEET**]: *each meet node p with n predecessors $\{s_1, \ldots, s_n\}$ (resp. successors) should have a definition (resp. use) of v at p, and n uses (resp. definitions) of v, one at each s_i. We shall implement these defs/uses with ϕ/σ-functions, as we explain in Section 2.1.*

[**INFO**]: *each program point $p \not\subseteq$ live(v) should be bound to undefined transfer functions, e.g., $F_v^{s,p} = \lambda x. \top$ for each $s \subset preds(p)$ (resp. $s \in succs(p)$).*

[**LINK**]: *for each two consecutive program points s and p for which $F_v^{s,p}$ depends on some $[u]^s$, there should be an instruction between s and p that contains a (potentially pseudo) use (resp. def) of u.*

[**VERSION**]: *for each variable v, live(v) is a connected component of the CFG.*

2.1 Special Instructions Used to Split Live Ranges

We group control flow nodes in three kinds: interior nodes, forks and joins. At each place we use a different notation to denote live range splitting.

Interior nodes are control flow nodes that have a unique predecessor and a unique successor. At these control flow nodes we perform live range splitting via copies. If the control flow node already contains another instruction, then this copy *must* be done *in parallel* with the existing instruction. The notation,

$$inst \parallel v_1 = v_1' \parallel \ldots \parallel v_m = v_m'$$

denotes m copies $v_i = v_i'$ performed in parallel with instruction $inst$. This means that all the uses of $inst$ plus all v_i' are read simultaneously, then $inst$ is computed, then all definitions of $inst$ plus all v_i are written simultaneously.

In forward analyses, the information produced at different definitions of a variable may reach the same meet node. To avoid that these definitions reach the same use of v, we merge them at the earliest control flow node where they meet; hence, ensuring [SPLIT-MEET]. We do this merging via special instructions called ϕ-functions, which were introduced by Cytron et $al.$ to build SSA-form programs [13]. The assignment

$$v_1 = \phi(l^1 : v_1^1, \ldots, l^q : v_1^q) \parallel \ldots \parallel v_m = \phi(l^1 : v_m^1, \ldots, l^q : v_m^q)$$

contains m ϕ-functions to be performed in parallel. The ϕ symbol works as a multiplexer. It will assign to each v_i the value in v_i^j, where j is determined by l^j, the basic block last visited before reaching the ϕ-function. The above statement encapsulates m parallel copies: all the variables $v_1^j, \ldots, v_m^j$ are simultaneously copied into the variables $v_1, \ldots, v_m$. Note that our notion of control flow nodes differs from the usual notion of nodes of the CFG. A join node actually corresponds to the entry point of a CFG node: to this end we denote as $\text{In}(l)$ the point right before l. As an example in Figure 1(d), l_7 is considered to be an interior node, and the ϕ-function defining v_6 has been inserted at the join node $\text{In}(l_7)$.

In backward analyses the information that emerges from different uses of a variable may reach the same meet node. To ensure Property [SPLIT-MEET], the use that reaches the definition of a variable must be unique, in the same way that in a SSA-form program the definition that reaches a use is unique. We ensure this property via special instructions that Ananian has called σ-functions [1]. The σ-functions are the simetric of ϕ-functions, performing a parallel assignment depending on the execution path taken. The assignment

$$(l^1 : v_1^1, \ldots, l^q : v_1^q) = \sigma(v_1) \parallel \ldots \parallel (l^1 : v_m^1, \ldots, l^q : v_m^q) = \sigma(v_m)$$

represents m σ-functions that assign to each variable v_i^j the value in v_i if control flows into block l^j. These assignments happen in parallel, i.e., the m σ-functions encapsulate m parallel copies. Also, notice that variables live in different branch targets are given different names by the σ-function that ends that basic block. Similarly to join nodes, a fork node is the exit point of a CFG node: $\text{Out}(l)$ denotes the point right after CFG node l. As an example in Figure 1(d), l_2 is considered to be an interior node, and the σ-function using v_1 has been inserted at the fork node $\text{Out}(l_2)$.

2.2   Examples of PLV Problems

Many data-flow analyses can be classified as PLV problems. In this section we present some meaningful examples. Along each example we show the program representation that lets us solve it sparsely.

Class Inference: Some dynamically typed languages, such as Python, Java-Scrip, Ruby or Lua, represent objects as hash tables containing methods and

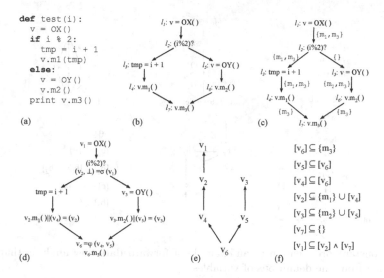

Fig. 1. Class inference as an example of backward data-flow analysis that takes information from the uses of variables

fields. In this world, it is possible to speedup execution by replacing these hash tables with actual object oriented virtual tables. A class inference engine tries to assign a virtual table to a variable v based on the ways that v is used. The Python program in Figure 1(a) illustrates this optimization. Our objective is to infer the correct suite of methods for each object bound to variable v. Figure 1(b) shows the control flow graph of the program, and Figure 1(c) shows the results of a dense implementation of this analysis. In a dense analysis, each program instruction is associated with a transfer function; however, some of these functions, such as that in label l_3, are trivial. We produce, for this example, the representation given in Figure 1(d). Because type inference is a backward analysis that extracts information from use sites, we split live ranges at these control flow nodes, and rely on σ-functions to merge them back. The use-def chains that we derive from the program representation, seen in Figure 1(e), lead naturally to a constraint system, which we show in Figure 1(f). A solution to this constraint system gives us a solution to our data-flow problem.

Constant Propagation: Figure 2 illustrates constant propagation, e.g., which variables in the program of Figure 2(a) can be replaced by constants? The CFG of this program is given in Figure 2(b). Constant propagation has a very simple lattice $\mathcal{L}$, which we show in Figure 2(c). Constant propagation is a PLV problem, as we have discussed before. In constant propagation, information is produced at the program points where variables are defined. Thus, in order to meet Definition 6, we must guarantee that each program point is reachable by a single definition of a variable. Figure 2(d) shows the intermediate representation that we create for the program in Figure 2(b). In this case, our intermediate representation is equivalent to the SSA form. The def-use chains implicit in our program

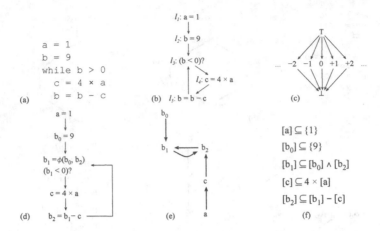

Fig. 2. Constant propagation as an example of forward data-flow analysis that takes information from the definitions of variables

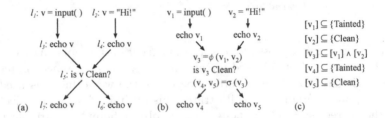

Fig. 3. Taint analysis is a forward data-flow analysis that takes information from the definitions of variables and conditional tests on these variables

representation lead to the constraint system shown in Figure 2(f). We can use the def-use chains seen in Figure 2(e) to guide a worklist-based constraint solver, as Nielson *et al.* [27, Ch.6] describe.

Taint Analysis: The objective of taint analysis [32, 33] is to find program vulnerabilities. In this case, a harmful attack is possible when input data reaches sensitive program sites without going through special functions called sanitizers. Figure 3 illustrates this type of analysis. We have used ϕ and σ-functions to split the live ranges of the variables in Figure 3(a) producing the program in Figure 3(b). Let us assume that *echo* is a sensitive function, because it is used to generate web pages. For instance, if the data passed to *echo* is a JavaScript program, then we could have an instance of cross-site scripting attack. Thus, the statement *echo* v_1 may be a source of vulnerabilities, as it outputs data that comes directly from the program input. On the other hand, we know that *echo* v_2 is always safe, for variable v_2 is initialized with a constant value. The

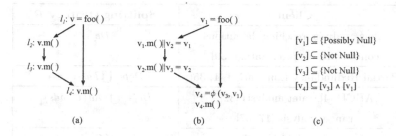

Fig. 4. Null pointer analysis as an example of forward data-flow analysis that takes information from the definitions and uses of variables

call *echo* v_5 is always safe, because variable v_5 has been sanitized; however, the call *echo* v_4 might be tainted, as variable v_4 results from a failed attempt to sanitize v. The def-use chains that we derive from the program representation lead naturally to a constraint system, which we show in Figure 3(c). The intermediate representation that we create in this case is equivalent to the *Extended Single Static Assignment* (e-SSA) form [4]. It also suits the ABCD algorithm for array bounds-checking climination [4], Su and Wagner's range analysis [37] and Gawlitza *et al.*'s range analysis [17].

Null Pointer Analysis: The objective of null pointer analysis is to determine which references may hold null values. Nanda and Sinha have used a variant of this analysis to find which method dereferences may throw exceptions, and which may not [26]. This analysis allows compilers to remove redundant null-exception tests and helps developers to find null pointer dereferences. Figure 4 illustrates this analysis. Because information is produced at use sites, we split live ranges after each variable is used, as we show in Figure 4(b). For instance, we know that the call $v_2.m()$ cannot result in a null pointer dereference exception, otherwise an exception would have been thrown during the invocation $v_1.m()$. On the other hand, in Figure 4(c) we notice that the state of v_4 is the meet of the state of v_3, definitely not-null, and the state of v_1, possibly null, and we must conservatively assume that v_4 may be null.

3   Building the Intermediate Program Representation

A *live range splitting strategy* $\mathcal{P}_v = I_\uparrow \cup I_\downarrow$ over a variable v consists of two sets of control flow nodes (see Section 2.1 for a definition of control flow nodes). We let $I_\downarrow$ denote a set of control flow nodes that produce information for a forward analysis. Similarly, we let $I_\uparrow$ denote a set of control flow nodes that are interesting for a backward analysis. The live-range of v must be split at least at every control flow node in $\mathcal{P}_v$. Going back to the examples from Section 2.2, we have the live range splitting strategies enumerated below. Further examples are given in Figure 5.

Client	Splitting strategy $\mathcal{P}$
Alias analysis, reaching definitions cond. constant propagation [39]	$Defs_\downarrow$
Partial Redundancy Elimination [1, 35]	$Defs_\downarrow \bigcup LastUses_\uparrow$
ABCD [4], taint analysis [32], range analysis [17, 37]	$Defs_\downarrow \bigcup \mathrm{Out}(Conds)_\downarrow$
Stephenson's bitwidth analysis [36]	$Defs_\downarrow \bigcup \mathrm{Out}(Conds)_\downarrow \bigcup Uses_\uparrow$
Mahlke's bitwidth analysis [24]	$Defs_\downarrow \bigcup Uses_\uparrow$
An's type inference [19], class inference [8]	$Uses_\uparrow$
Hochstadt's type inference [38]	$Uses_\uparrow \bigcup \mathrm{Out}(Conds)_\uparrow$
Null-pointer analysis [26]	$Defs_\downarrow \bigcup Uses_\downarrow$

Fig. 5. Live range splitting strategies for different data-flow analyses. We use *Defs* (*Uses*) to denote the set of instructions that define (use) the variable; *Conds* to denote the set of instructions that apply a conditional test on a variable; Out(*Conds*) the exits of the corresponding basic blocks; *LastUses* to denote the set of instructions where a variable is used, and after which it is no longer live.

- **Class inference** is a backward analysis that takes information from the uses of variables. Thus, for each variable, the live-range splitting strategy contains the set of control flow nodes where that variable is used. For instance, in Figure 1(b), we have that $\mathcal{P}_v = \{l_4, l_6, l_7\}_\uparrow$.
- **Constant propagation** is a forward analysis that takes information from definition sites. Thus, for each variable v, the live-range splitting strategy is characterized by the set of points where v is defined. For instance, in Figure 2(b), we have that $\mathcal{P}_b = \{l_2, l_5\}_\downarrow$.
- **Taint analysis** is a forward analysis that takes information from control flow nodes where variables are defined, and conditional tests that use these variables. For instance, in Figure 3(a), we have that $\mathcal{P}_v = \{l_1, l_2, \mathrm{Out}(l_5)\}_\downarrow$.
- Nanda *et al.*'s **null pointer analysis** [26] is a forward flow problem that takes information from definitions and uses. For instance, in Figure 4(a), we have that $\mathcal{P}_v = \{l_1, l_2, l_3, l_4\}_\downarrow$.

```
1 function SSIfy(var v, Splitting_Strategy Pv)
2     split(v, Pv)
3     rename(v)
4     clean(v)
```

Fig. 6. Split the live ranges of v to convert it to SSI form

The algorithm SSIfy in Figure 6 implements a live range splitting strategy in three steps: split, rename and clean, which we describe in the rest of this section.

Splitting Live Ranges through the Creation of New Definitions of Variables: To implement $\mathcal{P}_v$, we must split the live ranges of v at each control flow node listed by $\mathcal{P}_v$. However, these control flow nodes are not the only ones where splitting might be necessary. As we have pointed out in Section 2.1, we might have, for the same original variable, many different sources of information reaching a common meet point. For instance, in Figure 3(b), there exist two definitions of variable v: v_1 and v_2, that reach the use of v at l_5. Information that flows forward from l_3 and l_4 collide at l_5, the meet point of the if-then-else. Hence the live-range of v has to be split at the entry of l_5, e.g., at $In(l_5)$, leading to a new definition v_3. In general, the set of control flow nodes where information collide can be easily characterized by join sets [13]. The join set of a group of nodes P contains the CFG nodes that can be reached by two or more nodes of P through disjoint paths. Join sets can be over-approximated by the notion of iterated dominance frontier [40], a core concept in SSA construction algorithms, which, for the sake of completeness, we recall below:

- **Dominance**: a CFG node n dominates a node n' if every program path from the entry node of the CFG to n' goes across n. If $n \neq n'$, then we say that n *strictly* dominates n'.
- **Dominance Frontier** (DF): a node n' is in the dominance frontier of a node n if n dominates a predecessor of n', but does not strictly dominate n'.
- **Iterated dominance frontier** (DF^+): the iterated dominance frontier of a node n is the limit of the sequence:

$$DF_1 = DF(n)$$
$$DF_{i+1} = DF_i \cup \{DF(z) \mid z \in DF_i\}$$

Similarly, split sets created by the backward propagation of information can be over-approximated by the notion of *iterated post-dominance frontier* (pDF^+), which is the DF^+ [2] of the CFG where orientation of edges have been reverted. If $e = (u, v)$ is an edge in the control flow graph, then we define the dominance frontier of e, i.e., $DF(e)$, as the dominance frontier of a fictitious node n placed at the middle of e. In other words, $DF(e)$ is $DF(n)$, assuming that (u, n) and (n, v) would exist. Given this notion, we also define $DF^+(e)$, $pDF(e)$ and $pDF^+(e)$.

Figure 7 shows the algorithm that creates new definitions of variables. This algorithm has three phases. First, in lines 3-9 we create new definitions to split the live ranges of variables due to *backward* collisions of information. These new definitions are created at the iterated post-dominance frontier of control flow nodes that originate information. Notice that if the control flow node is a join (entry of a CFG node), information actually originate from each incoming edges (line 6). In lines 10-16 we perform the inverse operation: we create new definitions of variables due to the forward collision of information. Finally, in lines 17-23 we actually insert the new definitions of v. These new definitions might be created by σ functions (due exclusively to the splitting in lines 3-9); by ϕ-functions

```
1  function split(var v, Splitting_Strategy P_v = I↓ ∪ I↑)
2      "compute the set of split points"
3      S↑ = ∅
4      foreach i ∈ I↑:
5          if i.is_join:
6              foreach e ∈ incoming_edges(i):
7                  S↑ = S↑ ∪ Out(pDF⁺(e))
8          else:
9              S↑ = S↑ ∪ Out(pDF⁺(i))
10     S↓ = ∅
11     foreach i ∈ S↑ ∪ Defs(v) ∪ I↓:
12         if i.is_fork:
13             foreach e ∈ outgoing_edges(i)
14                 S↓ = S↓ ∪ In(DF⁺(e))
15         else:
16             S↓ = S↓ ∪ In(DF⁺(i))
17     S = P_v ∪ S↑ ∪ S↓
18     "Split live range of v by inserting φ, σ, and copies"
19     foreach i ∈ S:
20         if i does not already contain any definition of v:
21             if i.is_join: insert "v = φ(v, ..., v)" at i
22             elseif i.is_fork: insert "(v, ..., v) = σ(v)" at i
23             else: insert a copy "v = v" at i
```

Fig. 7. Live range splitting. We use $\text{In}(l)$ to denote a control flow node at the entry of l, and $\text{Out}(l)$ to denote a control flow node at the exit of l. We let $\text{In}(S) = \{l \in S \mid l \in S\}$. $\text{Out}(S)$ is defined in a similar way.

(due exclusively to the splitting in lines 10-16); or by parallel copies. Contrary to Singer's algorithm, originally designed to produce SSI form programs, we do not iterate between the insertion of ϕ and σ functions.

The Algorithm split preserves the SSA property, even for data-flow analyses that do not require it. As we see in line 11, the loop that splits meet nodes forwardly include, by default, all the definition sites of a variable. We chose to implement it in this way for practical reasons: the SSA property gives us access to a fast liveness check [5], which is useful in actual compiler implementations. This algorithm inserts ϕ and σ functions conservatively. Consequently, we may have these special instructions at control flow nodes that are not true meet nodes. In other words, we may have a ϕ-function $v = \phi(v_1, v_2)$, in which the abstract states of v_1 and v_2 are the same in a final solution of the data-flow problem.

Variable Renaming: The algorithm in Figure 8 builds def-use and use-def chains for a program after live range splitting. This algorithm is similar to the standard algorithm used to rename variables during the SSA construction [2, Algorithm 19.7]. To rename a variable v we traverse the program's dominance tree, from top to bottom, stacking each new definition of v that we find. The definition currently on the top of the stack is used to replace all the uses of v that

```
 1 function rename(var v)
 2     "Compute use-def & def-use chains"
 3     "We consider here that stack.peek() = undef if stack.isempty(),
 4       and that Def(undef) = entry"
 5     stack = ∅
 6     foreach CFG node n in dominance order:
 7         foreach m that is a predecessor of n:
 8             if exists dₘ of the form "lᵐ : v = ..." in a σ-function in Out(m):
 9                 stack.set_def(dₘ)
10             if exits uₘ of the form "··· = lᵐ : v" in a φ-function in In(n):
11                 stack.set_use(uₘ)
12         if exists a φ-function d in In(n) that defines v:
13             stack.set_def(d)
14         foreach instruction u in n that uses v:
15             stack.set_use(u)
16         if exists an instruction d in n that defines v:
17             stack.set_def(d)
18         foreach σ-function u in Out(n) that uses v:
19             stack.set_use(u)

21 function stack.set_use(instruction inst):
22     while Def(stack.peek()) does not dominate inst: stack.pop()
23     vᵢ = stack.peek()
24     replace the uses of v by vᵢ in inst
25     if vᵢ ≠ undef: set Uses(vᵢ) = Uses(vᵢ) ⋃ inst

27 function stack.set_def(instruction inst):
28     let vᵢ be a fresh version of v
29     replace the defs of v by vᵢ in inst
30     set Def(vᵢ) = inst
31     stack.push(vᵢ)
```

Fig. 8. Versioning

we find during the traversal. If the stack is empty, this means that the variable is not defined at that point. The renaming process replaces the uses of undefined variables by undef (line 3). We have two methods, $stack$.set_use and $stack$.set_def to build the chain relations between the variables. Notice that sometimes we must rename a single use inside a ϕ-function, as in lines 10-11 of the algorithm. For simplicity we consider this single use as a simple assignment when calling $stack$.set_use, as one can see in line 11. Similarly, if we must rename a single definition inside a σ-function, then we treat it as a simple assignment, like we do in lines 8-9 of the algorithm.

Dead and Undefined Code Elimination: The algorithm in Figure 9 eliminates ϕ-functions that define variables not actually used in the code, σ-functions that use variables not actually defined in the code, and parallel copies that ei-

```
1 function clean(var v)
2       let web = {v_i | v_i is a version of v}
3       let defined = ∅
4       let active = { inst | inst is actual instruction and web ∩ inst.defs ≠ ∅}
5       while exists inst in active s.t. web ∩ inst.defs \ defined ≠ ∅:
6             foreach v_i ∈ web ∩ inst.defs\defined:
7                   active = active ∪ Uses(v_i)
8                   defined = defined ∪ {v_i}
9       let used = ∅
10      let active = {inst |inst is actual instruction and web ∩ inst.uses ≠ ∅}
11      while exists inst ∈ active s.t. inst.uses\used ≠ ∅:
12            foreach v_i ∈ web ∩ inst.uses\used:
13                  active = active ∪ Def(v_i)
14                  used = used ∪ {v_i}
15      let live = defined ∩ used
16      foreach non actual inst ∈ Def(web):
17            foreach v_i operand of inst s.t. v_i ∉ live:
18                  replace v_i by undef
19            if inst.defs = {undef} or inst.uses = {undef}
20                  eliminate inst from the program
```

Fig. 9. Dead and undefined code elimination. Original instructions not inserted by split are called *actual* instruction. We let *inst*.defs denote the set of variables defined by *inst*, and *inst*.uses denote the set of variables used by *inst*.

ther define or use variables that do not reach any actual instruction. "Actual" instructions are those instructions that already existed in the program before we transformed it with split. In line 3 we let "*web*" be the set of versions of v, so as to restrict the cleaning process to variable v, as we see in lines 4-6 and lines 10-12. The set "*active*" is initialized to actual instructions in line 4. Then, during the loop in lines 5-8 we add to active ϕ-functions, σ-functions, and copies that can reach actual definitions through use-def chains. The corresponding version of v is then marked as *defined* (line 8). The next loop, in lines 11-14 performs a similar process to add to the active set the instructions that can reach actual uses through def-use chains. The corresponding version of v is then marked as *used* (line 14). Each non live variable (see line 15), i.e. either undefined or dead (non used) is replaced by undef in all ϕ, σ, or copy functions where it appears. This is done in lines 15-18. Finally useless ϕ, σ, or copy functions are removed in lines 19-20. As a historical curiosity, Cytron *et al.*'s procedure to build SSA form produced what is called *the minimal representation* [13]. Some of the ϕ-functions in the minimal representation define variables that are never used. Briggs *et al.* [6] remove these variables; hence, producing what compiler writers normally call *pruned SSA-form*. We close this section stating that the SSIfy algorithm preserves the semantics of the modified program [1]:

---

[1] The theorems in this paper are proved in the companion report, available on-line.

Theorem 1 (Semantics). SSIfy *maintains the following property: if a value n written into variable v at control flow node i' is read at a control flow node i in the original program, then the same value assigned to a version of variable v at control flow node i' is read at a control flow node i after transformation.*

The Propagation Engine: Def-use chains can be used to solve, sparsely, a PLV problem about any program that fulfills the SSI property. However, in order to be able to rely on these def-use chains, we need to derive a sparse constraint system from the original - dense - system. This sparse system is constructed according to Definition 7. Theorem 2 states that such a system exists for any program, and can be obtained directly from the Algorithm SSIfy. The algorithm in Figure 10 provides worklist based solvers for backward and forward sparse data-flow systems built as in Definition 7.

Definition 7 (SSI constrained system). *Let E_{dense} be a constraint system extracted from a program that meets the SSI properties. Hence, for each pair (variable v, program point p) we have equations $[v]^p = [v]^p \wedge F_v^{s,p}([v_1]^s, \ldots, [v_n]^s)$. We define a system of sparse equations E_{sparse}^{ssi} as follows:*

- *Let $\{a, \ldots, b\}$ be the variables used (resp. defined) at control flow node i, where variable v is defined (resp. used). Let s and p be the program points around i. The LINK property ensures that $F_v^{s,p}$ depends only on some $[a]^s \ldots [b]^s$. Thus, there exists a function G_v^i defined as the projection of $F_v^{s,p}$ on $\mathcal{L}_a \times \cdots \times \mathcal{L}_b$, such that $G_v^i([a]^s, \ldots, [b]^s) = F_v^{s,p}([v_1]^s, \ldots, [v_n]^s)$.*
- *The sparse constrained system associates with each variable v, and each definition (resp. use) point s of v, the corresponding constraint $[v] \sqsubseteq G_v^s([a], \ldots, [b])$ where $a, \ldots, b$ are used (resp. defined) at i.*

Theorem 2 (Correctness of SSIfy). *The execution of SSIfy$(v, \mathcal{P}_v)$, for every variable v in the target program, creates a new program representation such that:*

1. *there exists a system of equations E_{dense}^{ssi}, isomorphic to E_{dense} for which the new program representation fulfills the SSI property.*
2. *if E_{dense} is monotone then E_{dense}^{ssi} is also monotone.*

4   Our Approach vs Other Sparse Evaluation Frameworks

There have been previous efforts to provide theoretical and practical frameworks in which data-flow analyses could be performed sparsely. In order to clarify some details of our contribution, this section compares it with three previous approaches: Choi's Sparse Evaluation Graphs, Ananian's Static Single Information form and Oh's Sparse Abstract Interpretation Framework.

Sparse Evaluation Graphs: Choi's *Sparse Evaluation Graphs* [9] are one of the earliest data-structures designed to support sparse analyses. The nodes of

```
1  function forward_propagate(transfer_functions G)
2      worklist = ∅
3      foreach variable v: [v] = ⊤
4      foreach instruction i: worklist += i
5      while worklist ≠ ∅:
6          let i ∈ worklist
7          worklist -= i
8          foreach v ∈ i.defs:
9              [v]_new = [v] ∧ G_v^i([i.uses])
10             if [v] ≠ [v]_new:
11                 worklist += Uses(v)
12                 [v] = [v]_new
```

Fig. 10. Forward propagation engine under SSI. For backward propagation, we replace i.defs by i.uses / i.uses / Uses(v) by i.defs / Def(v).

this graph represent program regions where information produced by the dataflow analysis might change. Choi *et al.*'s ideas have been further expanded, for example, by Johnson *et al.*'s *Quick Propagation Graphs* [21], or Ramalingan's *Compact Evaluation Graphs* [31]. Nowadays we have efficient algorithms that build such data-structures [20, 29]. These graphs improve many data-flow analyses in terms of runtime and memory consumption. However, they are more limited than our approach, because they can only handle sparsely problems that Zadeck has classified as *Partitioned Variable*. In these problems, a program variable can be analyzed independently from the others. Reaching definitions and liveness analysis are examples of PVPs, as this kind of information can be computed for one program variable independently from the others. For these problems we can build intermediate program representations isomorphic to SEGs, as we state in Theorem 3. However, many data-flow problems, in particular the PLV analyses that we mentioned in Section 2.2, do not fit into this category. Nevertheless, we can handle them sparsely. The sparse evaluation graphs can still support PLV problems, but, in this case, a new SEG vertex would be created for every control flow node where new information is produced, and we would have a dense analysis.

Theorem 3 (Equivalence SSI/SEG). *Given a forward Sparse Evaluation Graph (SEG) that represents a variable v in a program representation Prog with CFG G, there exits a live range splitting strategy that once applied on v builds a program representation that is isomorphic to SEG.*

Static Single Information Form and Similar Program Representations: Scott Ananian has introduced in the late nineties the *Static Single Information* (SSI) form, a program representation that supports both forward and backward analyses [1]. This representation was later revisited by Jeremy Singer [35]. The σ-functions that we use in this paper is a notation borrowed from Ananian's work, and the algorithms that we discuss in Section 3 improve on Singer's ideas.

Contrary to Singer's algorithm we do not iterate between the insertion of phi and sigma functions. Consequently, as we will show in Section 5, we insert less phi and sigma functions. Nonetheless, as we show in Theorem 2, our method is enough to ensure the SSI properties for any combination of unidirectional problems. In addition to the SSI form, we can emulate several other different representations, by changing our parameterizations. Notice that for SSI we have $\{Defs_\downarrow \cup LastUses_\uparrow\}$. For Bodik's e-SSA [4] we have $Defs_\downarrow \bigcup Out(Conds)_\downarrow$. Finally, for SSU [18, 23, 30] we have $Uses_\uparrow$.

The SSI constrained system might have several inequations for the same left-hand-side, due to the way we insert phi and sigma functions. Definition 6, as opposed to the original SSI definition [1, 35], does not ensure the SSA or the SSU properties. These guarantees are not necessary to every sparse analysis. It is a common assumption in the compiler's literature that "data-flow analysis (...) can be made simpler when each variable has only one definition", as stated in Chapter 19 of Appel's textbook [2]. A naive interpretation of the above statement could lead one to conclude that data-flow analyses become simpler as soon as the program representation enforces a single source of information per live-range: SSA for forward propagation, SSU for backward, and the *original* SSI for bi-directional analyses. This premature conclusion is contradicted by the example of dead-code elimination, a backward data-flow analysis that the SSA form simplifies. Indeed, the SSA form fulfills our definition of the SSI property for dead-code elimination. Nevertheless, the corresponding constraint system may have several inequations, with the same left-hand-side, i.e., one for each use of a given variable v. Even though we may have several sources of information, we can still solve this backward analysis using the algorithm in Figure 10. To see this fact, we can replace G_v^i in Figure 10 by "*i is a useful instruction or one of its definitions is marked as useful*" and one obtains the classical algorithm for dead-code elimination.

Sparse Abstract Interpretation Framework: Recently, Oh *et al.* [28] have designed and tested a framework that sparsifies flow analyses modelled via abstract interpretation. They have used this framework to implement standard analyses on the interval [11] and on the octogon lattices [25], and have processed large code bodies. We believe that our approach leads to a sparser implementation. We base this assumption on the fact that Oh *et al.*'s approach relies on standard def-use chains to propagate information, whereas in our case, the merging nodes combine information before passing it ahead. As an example, lets consider the code if () then a=•; else a=•; endif if () then •=a; else •=a; endif under a forward analysis that generates information at definitions and requires it at uses. We let the symbol • denote unimportant values. In this scenario, Oh et al.'s framework creates four dependence links between the two control flow nodes where information is produced and the two control flow nodes where it is consumed. Our method, on the other hand, converts the program to SSA form; hence, creating two names for variable a. We avoid the

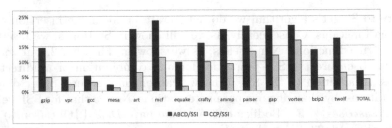

Fig. 11. Comparison of the time taken to produce the different representations. 100% is the time to use the SSI live range splitting strategy. The shorter the bar, the faster the live range splitting strategy. The SSI conversion took 1315.2s in total, the ABCD conversion took 85.2s, and the CCP conversion took 49.4s.

extra links because a ϕ-function merges the data that comes from these names before propagating it to the use sites.

5   Experimental Results

This section describes an empirical evaluation of the size and runtime efficiency of our algorithms. Our experiments were conducted on a dual core `Intel Pentium D` of 2.80GHz of clock, 1GB of memory, running `Linux Gentoo`, version 2.6.27. Our framework runs in LLVM 2.5 [22], and it passes all the tests that LLVM does. The LLVM test suite consists of over 1.3 million lines of C code. In this paper we show results for SPEC CPU 2000. To compare different live range splitting strategies we generate the program representations below. Figure 5 explains the sets *Defs, Uses* and *Conds*.

1. *SSI*: Ananian's Static Single Information form [1] is our baseline. We build the SSI program representation via Singer's iterative algorithm.
2. *ABCD*: ($\{Defs, Conds\}_{\downarrow}$). This live range splitting strategy generalizes the ABCD algorithm for array bounds checking elimination [4]. An example of this live range splitting strategy is given in Figure 3.
3. *CCP*: ($\{Defs, Conds_{eq}\}_{\downarrow}$). This splitting strategy, which supports Wegman *et al.*'s [39] conditional constant propagation, is a subset of the previous strategy. Differently of the ABCD client, this client requires that only variables used in equality tests, e.g., `==`, undergo live range splitting. That is, $Conds_{eq}(v)$ denotes the conditional tests that check if v equals a given value.

Runtime: The chart in Figure 11 compares the execution time of the three live range splitting strategies. We show only the time to perform live range splitting. The time to execute the optimization itself, removing array bound checks or performing constant propagation, is not shown. The bars are normalized to the running time of the SSI live range splitting strategy. On the average, the ABCD client runs in 6.8% and the CCP client runs in 4.1% of the time of SSI.

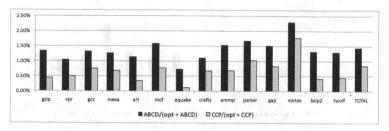

Fig. 12. Execution time of two different live range splitting strategies compared to the total time taken by machine independent LLVM optimizations (**opt** -O1). 100% is the time taken by **opt**. The shorter the bar, the faster the conversion.

These two forward analyses tend to run faster in benchmarks with sparse control flow graphs, which present fewer conditional branches, and therefore fewer opportunities to restrict the ranges of variables.

In order to put the time reported in Figure 11 in perspective, Figure 12 compares the running time of our live range splitting algorithms with the time to run the other standard optimizations in our baseline compiler[2]. In our setting, LLVM -O1 runs 67 passes, among analysis and optimizations, which include partial redundancy elimination, constant propagation, dead code elimination, global value numbering and invariant code motion. We believe that this list of passes is a meaningful representative of the optimizations that are likely to be found in an industrial strength compiler. The bars are normalized to the optimizer's time, which consists of the time taken by machine independent optimizations plus the time taken by one of the live range splitting clients, e.g, ABCD or CCP. The ABCD client takes 1.48% of the optimizer's time, and the CCP client takes 0.9%. To emphasize the speed of these passes, we notice that the bars do not include the time to do machine dependent optimizations such as register allocation.

Space: Figure 13 outlines how much each live range splitting strategy increases program size. We show results only to the ABCD and CCP clients, to keep the chart easy to read. The SSI conversion increases program size in 17.6% on average. This is an absolute value, i.e., we sum up every ϕ and σ function inserted, and divide it by the number of bytecode instructions in the original program. This compiler already uses the SSA-form by default, and we do not count as new instructions the ϕ-functions originally used in the program. The ABCD client increases program size by 2.75%, and the CCP client increases program size by 1.84%.

An interesting question that deserves attention is "What is the benefit of using a sparse data-flow analysis in practice?" We have not implemented dense versions of the ABCD or the CCP clients. However, previous works have shown that sparse analyses tend to outperform equivalent dense versions in terms of

---

[2] To check the list of LLVM's target independent optimizations try
```
llvm-as < /dev/null | opt -std-compile-opts -disable-output
-debug-pass=Arguments.
```

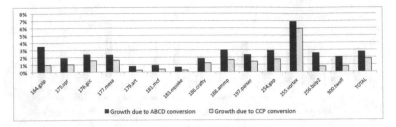

Fig. 13. Growth in program size due to the insertion of new ϕ and σ functions to perform live range splitting

time and space efficiency [9, 31]. In particular, the e-SSA format used by the ABCD and the CCP optimizations is the same program representation adopted by the tainted flow framework of Rimsa *et al.* [32, 33], which has been shown to be faster than a dense implementation of the analysis, even taking the time to perform live range splitting into consideration.

6   Conclusion

This paper has presented a systematic way to build program representations that suit sparse data-flow analyses. We build different program representations by splitting the live ranges of variables. The way in which we split live ranges depends on two factors: (i) which control flow nodes produce new information, e.g., uses, definitions, tests, etc; and (ii) how this information propagates along the variable live range: forwardly or backwardly. We have used an implementation of our framework in LLVM to convert programs to the Static Single Information form [1], and to provide intermediate representations to the ABCD array bounds-check elimination algorithm [4] and to Wegman *et al.*'s Conditional Constant Propagation algorithm [39]. Our framework has been used by Couto *et al.* [15] and by Rodrigues *et al.* [34] in different implementations of range analyses. We have also used our live range splitting algorithm, implemented in the phc PHP compiler [3], to provide the Extended Static Single Assignment form necessary to solve the tainted flow problem [32, 33].

Extending our Approach. For the sake of simplicity, in this paper we have restricted our discussion to: non relational analysis (PLV), intermediate-representation based appoach, and scalar variables without aliasing.

(1) *non relation analysis.* In this paper we have focused on PLV problems, i.e. solved by analyses that associate some information with each variable individually. For instance, we bind i to a range $0 \leq i < \text{MAX\_N}$, but we do not relate i and j, as in $0 \leq i < j$. A relational analysis that provides a all-to-all relation between all variables of the program is dense by nature, as any control flow node both produces and consumes information for the analysis. Nevertheless, our framework is compatible with the notion of *packing*. Each pack is a set of

variable groups selected to be related together. This approach is usually adopted in practical relational analyses, such as those used in Astrée [12, 25].

(2) *IR based approach.* Our framework constructs an intermediate representation (IR) that preserves the semantic of the program. Like the SSA form, this IR has to be updated, and prior to final code generation, destructed. Our own experience as compiler developers let us believe that manipulating an IR such as SSA has many engineering advantages over building, and afterward dropping, a separate sparse evaluation graph (SEG) for each analysis. Testimony of this observation is the fact that the SSA form is used in virtually every modern compiler. Although this opinion is admittedly arguable, we would like to point out that updating and destructing our SSI form is equivalent to the update and destruction of SSA form. More importantly, there is no fundamental limitation in using our technique to build a separate SEG without modifying the IR. This SEG will inherit the sparse properties as his corresponding SSI flavor, with the benefit of avoiding the quadratic complexity of direct def-use chains ($|\mathrm{Defs}(v)| \times |\mathrm{Uses}(v)|$ for a variable v) thanks to the use of ϕ and σ nodes. Note that this quadratic complexity becomes critical when dealing with code with aliasing or predication [28, pp.234].

(3) *analysis of scalar variables without aliasing or predication.* The most successful flavor of SSA form is the minimal and pruned representation restricted to scalar variables. The SSI form that we describe in this paper is akin to this flavor. Nevertheless, there exists several extensions to deal with code with predication (e.g. ψ-SSA form [14]) and aliasing (e.g. Hashed SSA [10] or Array SSA [16]). Such extensions can be applied without limitations to our SSI form allowing a wider range of analyses involving object aliasing and predication.

Acknowledgments. We thank the CC referees for very helpful comments on this paper, and we thank Laure Gonnord for enlightening discussions about the abstract interpretation framework. This project has been made possible by the cooperation FAPEMIG-INRIA, grant 11/2009.

References

1. Ananian, S.: The static single information form. Master's thesis. MIT (September 1999)
2. Appel, A.W., Palsberg, J.: Modern Compiler Implementation in Java, 2nd edn. Cambridge University Press (2002)
3. Biggar, P., de Vries, E., Gregg, D.: A practical solution for scripting language compilers. In: SAC, pp. 1916–1923. ACM (2009)
4. Bodik, R., Gupta, R., Sarkar, V.: ABCD: Eliminating array bounds checks on demand. In: PLDI, pp. 321–333. ACM (2000)
5. Boissinot, B., Hack, S., Grund, D., de Dinechin, B.D., Rastello, F.: Fast liveness checking for SSA-form programs. In: CGO, pp. 35–44. IEEE (2008)
6. Briggs, P., Cooper, K.D., Torczon, L.: Improvements to graph coloring register allocation. TOPLAS 16(3), 428–455 (1994)

7. Campos, V.H.S., Rodrigues, R.E., de Assis Costa, I.R., Pereira, F.M.Q.: Speed and precision in range analysis. In: de Carvalho Junior, F.H., Barbosa, L.S. (eds.) SBLP 2012. LNCS, vol. 7554, pp. 42–56. Springer, Heidelberg (2012)
8. Chambers, C., Ungar, D.: Customization: Optimizing compiler technology for self, a dynamically-typed object-oriented programming language. SIGPLAN Not. 24(7), 146–160 (1989)
9. Choi, J.-D., Cytron, R., Ferrante, J.: Automatic construction of sparse data flow evaluation graphs. In: POPL, pp. 55–66. ACM (1991)
10. Chow, F., Chan, S., Liu, S.-M., Lo, R., Streich, M.: Effective representation of aliases and indirect memory operations in SSA form. In: Gyimóthy, T. (ed.) CC 1996. LNCS, vol. 1060, pp. 253–267. Springer, Heidelberg (1996)
11. Cousot, P., Cousot, R.: Abstract interpretation: A unified lattice model for static analysis of programs by construction or approximation of fixpoints. In: POPL, pp. 238–252. ACM (1977)
12. Cousot, P., Cousot, R., Feret, J., Mauborgne, L., Miné, A., Rival, X.: Why does astrée scale up? Form. Methods Syst. Des. 35(3), 229–264 (2009)
13. Cytron, R., Ferrante, J., Rosen, B.K., Wegman, M.N., Zadeck, F.K.: Efficiently computing static single assignment form and the control dependence graph. TOPLAS 13(4), 451–490 (1991)
14. de Ferrière, F.: Improvements to the ψ-SSA representation. In: SCOPES, pp. 111–121. ACM (2007)
15. Teixeira, D.C., Pereira, F.M.Q.: The design and implementation of a non-iterative range analysis algorithm on a production compiler. In: SBLP, pp. 45–59. SBC (2011)
16. Fink, S.J., Knobe, K., Sarkar, V.: Unified analysis of array and object references in strongly typed languages. In: SAS 2000. LNCS, vol. 1824, pp. 155–174. Springer, Heidelberg (2000)
17. Gawlitza, T., Leroux, J., Reineke, J., Seidl, H., Sutre, G., Wilhelm, R.: Polynomial precise interval analysis revisited. Efficient Algorithms 1, 422–437 (2009)
18. George, L., Matthias, B.: Taming the IXP network processor. In: PLDI, pp. 26–37. ACM (2003)
19. An, J.H., Chaudhuri, A., Foster, J.S., Hicks, M.: Dynamic inference of static types for ruby. In: POPL, pp. 459–472. ACM (2011)
20. Johnson, R., Pearson, D., Pingali, K.: The program tree structure. In: PLDI, pp. 171–185. ACM (1994)
21. Johnson, R., Pingali, K.: Dependence-based program analysis. In: PLDI, pp. 78–89. ACM (1993)
22. Lattner, C., Adve, V.S.: LLVM: A compilation framework for lifelong program analysis & transformation. In: CGO, pp. 75–88. IEEE (2004)
23. Lo, R., Chow, F., Kennedy, R., Liu, S.-M., Tu, P.: Register promotion by sparse partial redundancy elimination of loads and stores. In: PLDI, pp. 26–37. ACM (1998)
24. Mahlke, S., Ravindran, R., Schlansker, M., Schreiber, R., Sherwood, T.: Bitwidth cognizant architecture synthesis of custom hardware accelerators. TCAD 20(11), 1355–1371 (2001)
25. Miné, A.: The octagon abstract domain. Higher Order Symbol. Comput. 19, 31–100 (2006)
26. Nanda, M.G., Sinha, S.: Accurate interprocedural null-dereference analysis for java. In: ICSE, pp. 133–143 (2009)
27. Nielson, F., Nielson, H.R., Hankin, C.: Principles of program analysis. Springer (2005)

28. Oh, H., Heo, K., Lee, W., Lee, W., Yi, K.: Design and implementation of sparse global analyses for c-like languages. In: PLDI, pp. 229–238. ACM (2012)
29. Pingali, K., Bilardi, G.: Optimal control dependence computation and the roman chariots problem. In: TOPLAS, pp. 462–491. ACM (1997)
30. Plevyak, J.B.: Optimization of Object-Oriented and Concurrent Programs. PhD thesis, University of Illinois at Urbana-Champaign (1996)
31. Ramalingam, G.: On sparse evaluation representations. Theoretical Computer Science 277(1-2), 119–147 (2002)
32. Rimsa, A., d'Amorim, M., Quintão Pereira, F.M.: Tainted flow analysis on e-SSA-form programs. In: Knoop, J. (ed.) CC 2011. LNCS, vol. 6601, pp. 124–143. Springer, Heidelberg (2011)
33. Rimsa, A.A., D'Amorim, M., Pereira, F.M.Q., Bigonha, R.: Efficient static checker for tainted variable attacks. Science of Computer Programming 80, 91–105 (2014)
34. Rodrigues, R.E., Campos, V.H.S., Pereira, F.M.Q.: A fast and low overhead technique to secure programs against integer overflows. In: CGO, pp. 1–11. ACM (2013)
35. Singer, J.: Static Program Analysis Based on Virtual Register Renaming. PhD thesis, University of Cambridge (2006)
36. Stephenson, M., Babb, J., Amarasinghe, S.: Bitwidth analysis with application to silicon compilation. In: PLDI, pp. 108–120. ACM (2000)
37. Su, Z., Wagner, D.: A class of polynomially solvable range constraints for interval analysis without widenings. Theoretical Computeter Science 345(1), 122–138 (2005)
38. Tobin-Hochstadt, S., Felleisen, M.: The design and implementation of typed scheme. In: POPL, pp. 395–406 (2008)
39. Wegman, M.N., Zadeck, F.K.: Constant propagation with conditional branches. TOPLAS 13(2) (1991)
40. Weiss, M.: The transitive closure of control dependence: The iterated join. TOPLAS 1(2), 178–190 (1992)
41. Zadeck, F.K.: Incremental Data Flow Analysis in a Structured Program Editor. PhD thesis, Rice University (1984)

Inter-iteration Scalar Replacement Using Array SSA Form

Rishi Surendran[1], Rajkishore Barik[2], Jisheng Zhao[1], and Vivek Sarkar[1]

[1] Rice University, Houston, TX
{rishi,jisheng.zhao,vsarkar}@rice.edu
[2] Intel Labs, Santa Clara, CA
rajkishore.barik@intel.com

Abstract. In this paper, we introduce novel simple and efficient analysis algorithms for scalar replacement and dead store elimination that are built on Array SSA form, a uniform representation for capturing control and data flow properties at the level of array or pointer accesses. We present extensions to the original Array SSA form representation to capture loop-carried data flow information for arrays and pointers. A core contribution of our algorithm is a subscript analysis that propagates array indices across loop iterations. Compared to past work, this algorithm can handle control flow within and across loop iterations and degrade gracefully in the presence of unanalyzable subscripts. We also introduce code transformations that can use the output of our analysis algorithms to perform the necessary scalar replacement transformations (including the insertion of loop prologues and epilogues for loop-carried reuse). Our experimental results show performance improvements of up to 2.29× relative to code generated by LLVM at -O3 level. These results promise to make our algorithms a desirable starting point for scalar replacement implementations in modern SSA-based compiler infrastructures such as LLVM.

Keywords: Static Single Assignment (SSA) form, Array SSA form, Scalar Replacement, Load Elimination, Store Elimination.

1 Introduction

Scalar replacement is a widely used compiler optimization that promotes memory accesses, such as a read of an array element or a load of a pointer location, to reads and writes of compiler-generated temporaries. Current and future trends in computer architecture provide an increased motivation for scalar replacement because compiler-generated temporaries can be allocated in faster and more energy-efficient storage structures such as registers, local memories and scratchpads. However, scalar replacement algorithms in past work [6,9,7,3,14,4,2,21,5] were built on non-SSA based program representations, and tend to be complex to understand and implement, expensive in compile-time resources, and limited in effectiveness in the absence of precise data dependences. Though the benefits of SSA-based analysis are well known and manifest in modern compiler

A. Cohen (Ed.): CC 2014, LNCS 8409, pp. 40–60, 2014.

infrastructures such as LLVM [13], it is challenging to use SSA form for scalar replacement analysis since SSA form typically focuses on scalar variables and scalar replacement focuses on array and pointer accesses.

In this paper, we introduce novel simple and efficient analysis algorithms for scalar replacement and dead store elimination that are built on Array SSA form [12], an extension to scalar SSA form that captures control and data flow properties at the level of array or pointer accesses. We present extensions to the original Array SSA form representation to capture loop-carried data flow information for arrays and pointers. A core contribution of our algorithm is a subscript analysis that propagates array indices across loop iterations. Compared to past work, this algorithm can handle control flow within and across loop iterations and degrades gracefully in the presence of unanalyzable subscript. We also introduce code transformations that can use the output of our analysis algorithms to perform the necessary scalar replacement transformations (including the insertion of loop prologs and epilogues for loop-carried reuse). These results promise to make our algorithms a desirable starting point for scalar replacement implementations in modern SSA-based compiler infrastructures.

The main contributions of this paper are:

- Extensions to Array SSA form to capture inter-iteration data flow information of arrays and pointers
- A framework for inter-iteration subscript analysis for both forward and backward data flow problems
- An algorithm for inter-iteration redundant load elimination analysis using our extended Array SSA form, with accompanying transformations for scalar replacement, loop prologs and loop epilogues.
- An algorithm for dead store elimination using our extended Array SSA form, with accompanying transformations.

The rest of the paper is organized as follows. Section 2 discusses background and motivation for this work. Section 3 contains an overview of scalar replacement algorithms. Section 4 introduces Array SSA form and extensions for inter-iteration data flow analysis. Section 5 presents available subscript analysis, an inter-iteration data flow analysis. Section 6 describes the code transformation algorithm for redundant load elimination, and Section 7 describes the analysis and transformations for dead store elimination. Section 8 briefly summarizes how our algorithm can be applied to objects and while loops. Section 9 contains details on the LLVM implementation and experimental results. Finally, Section 10 presents related work and Section 11 contains our conclusions.

2   Background

In this section we summarize selected past work on scalar replacement which falls into two categories. 1) inter-iteration scalar replacement using non-SSA representations and 2) intra-iteration scalar replacement using Array SSA form, to provide the background for our algorithms. A more extensive comparison with related work is presented later in Section 10.

(a) Original Loop	(b) After Scalar Replacement
1: **for** $i = 1$ to n **do** 2: $B[i] = 0.3333 * (A[i-1] + A[i] + A[i+1])$ 3: **end for**	1: $t_0 = A[0]$ 2: $t_1 = A[1]$ 3: **for** $i = 1$ to n **do** 4: $t_2 = A[i+1]$ 5: $B[i] = 0.3333 * (t_0 + t_1 + t_2)$ 6: $t_0 = t_1$ 7: $t_1 = t_2$ 8: **end for**

Fig. 1. Scalar replacement on a 1-D Jacobi stencil computation [1]

2.1 Inter-iteration Scalar Replacement

Figure 1(a) shows the innermost loop of a 1-D Jacobi stencil computation [1].
The number of memory accesses per iteration in the loop is four, which includes
three loads and a store. The read references involving array A present a reuse
opportunity in that the data read by $A[i + 1]$ is also read by $A[i]$ in the next
iteration of the loop. The same element is also read in the following iteration
by $A[i - 1]$. The reference $A[i + 1]$ is referred to as the *generator* [7] for the
redundant loads, $A[i]$ and $A[i - 1]$. The number of memory accesses inside the
loop could thus be reduced to one, if the data read by $A[i + 1]$ is stored in a
scalar temporary which could be allocated to faster memory. Assuming $n > 0$,
the loop after scalar replacement transformation is shown in 1(b). Non-SSA
algorithms for inter-iteration scalar replacement have been presented in past
work including [6,7,9]. Of these, the work by Carr and Kennedy [7] is described
below, since it is the most general among past algorithms for inter-iteration
scalar replacement.

2.2 Carr-Kennedy Algorithm

The different steps in the Carr-Kennedy algorithm [7] are 1) Dependence graph
construction, 2) Control flow analysis, 3) Availability analysis, 4) Reachability
analysis, 5) Potential generator selection, 6) Anticipability analysis, 7) Dependence graph marking, 8) Name partitioning, 9) Register pressure moderation, 10)
Reference replacement, 11) Statement insertion analysis, 12) Register copying,
13) Code motion, and 14) Initialization of temporary variables.

The algorithm is complex, requires perfect dependence information to be applicable and operates only on loop bodies without any backward conditional
flow. Further, the algorithm performs its profitability analysis on *name partitions*, where a name partition consists of references that share values. If a name
partition is selected for scalar replacement, all the memory references in that
name partition will get scalar replaced, otherwise none of the accesses in the
name partition are scalar replaced.

2.3 Array SSA Analysis

Array SSA is a program representation which captures precise element-level data-flow information for array variables. Every use and definition in the extended Array SSA form has a unique name. There are 3 different types of ϕ functions presented in [10].

1. A *control* ϕ (denoted simply as ϕ) corresponds to the ϕ function from scalar SSA. A ϕ function is added for a variable at a join point if multiple definitions of the variable reach that point.
2. A *definition* ϕ ($d\phi$) [12] is used to deal with *partially killing* definitions. A $d\phi$ function of the form $A_k = d\phi(A_i, A_j)$ is inserted immediately after each definition of the array variable, A_i, that does not completely kill the array value. A_j is the augmenting definition of A which reaches the point just prior to the definition of A_i. A $d\phi$ function merges the value of the element modified with the values that are available prior to the definition.
3. A *use* ϕ ($u\phi$) [10] function creates a new name whenever a statement reads an array element. The purpose of the $u\phi$ function is to link together uses of the same array in control-flow order. This is used to capture the read-after-read reuse (aka input dependence). A $u\phi$ function of the form $A_k = u\phi(A_i, A_j)$ is inserted immediately after the use of an array element, A_i. A_j is the augmenting definition of A which reaches the point just prior to the use of A_i.

[10] presented a unified approach for the analysis and optimization of object field and array element accesses in strongly typed languages using Array SSA form. But the approach had a major limitation in that it does not capture reuse across loop iterations. For instance, their approach cannot eliminate the redundant memory accesses in the loop in Figure 1. In Section 4, we introduce extensions to Array SSA form for inter-iteration analysis.

2.4 Definitely-Same and Definitely-Different Analyses

In order to reason about aliasing among array accesses, [10] describes two relations: $\mathcal{DS}$ represents the *Definitely-Same* binary relationship and $\mathcal{DD}$ represents the *Definitely-Different* binary relationship. $\mathcal{DS}(a, b) = true$ if and only if a and b are guaranteed to have the same value at all program points that are dominated by the definition of a and dominated by the definition of b. Similarly, $\mathcal{DD}(a, b) = true$ if and only if a and b are guaranteed to have different values at all program points that are dominated by the definition of a and dominated by the definition of b. The Definitely-same ($\mathcal{DS}$) and Definitely-different ($\mathcal{DD}$) relation between two array subscripts can be computed using different methods and is orthogonal to the analysis and transformation described in this paper.

3 Scalar Replacement Overview

In this section, we present an overview of the basic steps of our scalar replacement algorithms: redundant load elimination and dead store elimination. To simplify the description of the algorithms, we consider only a single loop. We also assume that the induction variable of the loop has been normalized to an increment of one. Extensions to multiple nested loops can be performed in hierarchical fashion, starting with the innermost loop and analyzing a single loop at a time. When analyzing an outer loop, the array references in the enclosed nested loops are summarized with subscript information [16].

The scalar replacement algorithms include three main steps:

1. *Extended Array SSA Construction*:
   In the first step, the extended Array SSA form of the original program is constructed. All array references are renamed and ϕ functions are introduced as described in Section 4. Note that the extended Array SSA form of the program is used only for the analysis (presented in step 2). The transformations (presented in step 3) are applied on the original program.

2. *Subscript analysis*:
   Scalar replacement of array references is based on two subscript analyses: (a) *available subscript analysis* identifies the set of redundant loads in the given loop, which is used for redundant load elimination (described in Section 6); (b) *dead subscript analysis* identifies the set of dead stores in the given loop, which is used in dead store elimination (described in Section 7). These analyses are performed on extended Array SSA form and have an associated tuning parameter: the maximum number of iterations for which the analysis needs to run.

3. *Transformation*:
   In this step, the original program is transformed using the information produced by the analyses described in step 2. For redundant load elimination, this involves replacing the read of array elements with read of scalar temporaries, generating copy statements for scalar temporaries and generating statements to initialize the temporaries. The transformation is presented in Section 6. Dead store elimination involves removing redundant stores and generating epilogue code as presented in Section 7.

4   Extended Array SSA Form

In order to model inter-iteration reuse, the lattice operations of the ϕ function in the loop header needs to be handled differently from the rest of the control ϕ functions. They need to capture what array elements are available from

```
1: for i = 1 to n do
2:     if A[B[i]] > 0 then
3:         A[i+1] = A[i-1] + B[i-1]
4:     end if
5:     A[i] = A[i] + B[i] + B[i+1]
6: end for
```

Fig. 2. Loop with redundant loads and stores

prior iterations. We introduce a *header* ϕ ($h\phi$) node in the loop header. We assume that every loop has one incoming edge from outside and thus, one of the arguments to the $h\phi$ denotes the SSA name from outside the loop. For each back edge from within the loop, there is a corresponding SSA operand added to the $h\phi$ function. Figure 2 shows a loop from [11, p. 387] extended with control flow. The three address code of the same program is given in 3(a) and the extended Array SSA form is given in 3(b). $A_1 = h\phi(A_0, A_{12})$ and $B_1 = h\phi(B_0, B_{10})$ are the two $h\phi$ nodes introduced in the loop header. A_0 and B_0 contain the definitions of array A which reaches the loop preheader.

While constructing Array SSA form, $d\phi$ and $u\phi$ functions are introduced first into the program. The control ϕ and $h\phi$ functions are added in the second phase. This will ensure that the new SSA names created due to the insertion of $u\phi$ and $d\phi$ nodes are handled correctly. We introduce at most one $d\phi$ function for each array definition and at most one $u\phi$ function for each array use. Past work have shown that the worst-case size of the extended Array SSA form is proportional to the size of the scalar SSA form that would be obtained if each array access is modeled as a definition [10]. Past empirical results have shown the size of scalar SSA form to be linearly proportional to the size of the input program [8].

(a) Three Address Code	(b) Array SSA form			
1: **for** $i = 1$ to n **do**	1:	$A_0 = \ldots$	17:	$A_7 = d\phi(A_6, A_5)$
2: $t1 = B[i]$	2:	$B_0 = \ldots$	18:	**end if**
3: $t2 = A[t1]$	3:	**for** $i = 1$ to n **do**	19:	$A_8 = \phi(A_3, A_7)$
4: **if** $t2 > 0$ **then**	4:	$A_1 = h\phi(A_0, A_{12})$	20:	$B_6 = \phi(B_3, B_5)$
5: $t3 = A[i-1]$	5:	$B_1 = h\phi(B_0, B_{10})$	21:	$t_6 = A_9[i]$
6: $t4 = D[i-1]$	6:	$t1 = D_2[i]$	22:	$A_{10} = u\phi(A_9, A_8)$
7: $t5 = t3 + t4$	7:	$B_3 = u\phi(B_2, B_1)$	23:	$t_7 = B_7[i]$
8: $A[i+1] = t5$	8:	$t2 = A_2[t1]$	24:	$B_8 = u\phi(B_7, B_6)$
9: **end if**	9:	$A_3 = u\phi(A_2, A_1)$	25:	$t_8 = B_9[i+1]$
10: $t6 = A[i]$	10:	**if** $t2 > 0$ **then**	26:	$B_{10} = u\phi(B_9, B_8)$
11: $t7 = B[i]$	11:	$t3 = A_4[i-1]$	27:	$t_9 = t_6 + t_7$
12: $t8 = B[i+1]$	12:	$A_5 = u\phi(A_4, A_3)$	28:	$t_{10} = t_9 + t_8$
13: $t9 = t6 + t7$	13:	$t4 = B_4[i-1]$	29:	$A_{11}[i] = t_{10}$
14: $t10 = t9 + t8$	14:	$B_5 = u\phi(B_4, B_3)$	30:	$A_{12} = d\phi(A_{11}, A_{10})$
15: $A[i] = t10$	15:	$t5 = t3 + t4$	31:	**end for**
16: **end for**	16:	$A_6[i+1] = t5$		

Fig. 3. Example Loop and extended Array SSA form

5   Available Subscript Analysis

In this section, we present the subscript analysis which is one of the key ingredients for inter-iteration redundant load elimination (Section 6) and dead store elimination transformation (Section 7). The subscript analysis takes as input the extended Array SSA form of the program and a parameter, τ, which represents the maximum number of iterations across which inter-iteration scalar replacement will be applied on. An upper bound on τ can be obtained by computing the maximum dependence distance for the given loop, when considering all dependences in the loop. However, since smaller values of τ may sometimes be better due to register pressure moderation reasons, our algorithm views τ as a tuning parameter. This paper focuses on the program analysis foundations of our scalar replacement approach — it can be combined with any optimization strategy for making a judicious choice for τ.

Our analysis computes the set of array elements that are available at all the ϕ, $u\phi$, $d\phi$ and $h\phi$ nodes. The lattice element for an array variable, A, is represented as $\mathcal{L}(A)$. The set denoted by $\mathcal{L}(A)$, represented as $\text{SET}(\mathcal{L}(A))$, is a subset of $\mathcal{U}_{ind}^A \times \mathbb{Z}_{\geq 0}$, where $\mathcal{U}_{ind}^A$ denotes the universal set of index values for A and $\mathbb{Z}_{\geq 0}$ denotes the set of all non-negative integers. The lattice elements are classified as:

1. $\mathcal{L}(A_j) = \top \Rightarrow \text{SET}(\mathcal{L}(A_j)) = \mathcal{U}_{ind}^A \times \mathbb{Z}_{\geq 0}$
   This case means that all the elements of A are available at A_j.
2. $\mathcal{L}(A_j) = \langle (i_1, d_1), (i_2, d_2)... \rangle \Rightarrow \text{SET}(\mathcal{L}(A_j)) = \{(i_1, d_1), (i_2, d_2), ...\}$
   This means that the array element $A[i_1]$ is available at A_j and is generated in the $k - d_1$th iteration, where k denotes the current iteration. Similarly $A[i_2]$ is available at A_j and is generated in the $k - d_2$th iteration and so on. d_1, d_2, ... is used to track the number of iterations that have passed since the corresponding array element was referenced.
3. $\mathcal{L}(A_j) = \bot \Rightarrow \text{SET}(\mathcal{L}(A_j)) = \{\}$
   This case means that, according to the current stage of analysis none of the elements in A are available at A_j.

The lattice element computations for the SSA nodes is defined in terms of SHIFT, JOIN, INSERT and UPDATE operations. The SHIFT operation is defined as follows, where $step_1$ denotes the coefficient of the induction variable in i_1, $step_2$ denotes the coefficient of the induction variable in i_2 and so on.

$$\text{SHIFT}(\{(i_1, d_1), (i_2, d_2), ...\}) = \{(i_1 - step_1, d_1 + 1), (i_2 - step_2, d_2 + 1), ...\}$$

The definitions of JOIN, INSERT and UPDATE operations are given below.

$$\text{JOIN}(\mathcal{L}(A_p), \mathcal{L}(A_q)) = \{(i_1, d) | (i_1, d_1) \in \mathcal{L}(A_p) \text{ and } \exists\, (i_1', d_1') \in \mathcal{L}(A_q) \text{ and }$$
$$\mathcal{DS}(i_1, i_1') = true \text{ and } d = max(d_1, d_1')\}$$

$$\text{INSERT}((i', d'), \mathcal{L}(A_p)) = \{(i_1, d_1) | (i_1, d_1) \in \mathcal{L}(A_p) \text{ and } \mathcal{DD}(i', i_1) = true\} \cup \{(i', d')\}$$

$$\text{UPDATE}((i', d'), \mathcal{L}(A_p)) = \{(i_1, d_1) | (i_1, d_1) \in \mathcal{L}(A_p) \text{ and } \mathcal{DS}(i', i_1) = false\} \cup \{(i', d')\}$$

Figures 4, 5, 6 and 7 describe the lattice element computations for the SSA nodes corresponding to $d\phi$, $u\phi$, ϕ, and $h\phi$ respectively. The lattice values are initialized as follows:

$$\mathcal{L}(A_i) = \begin{cases} \{(x, 0)\} & A_i \text{ is a definition of the form } A_i[x] \\ \{(x, 0)\} & A_i \text{ is a use of the form } A_i[x] \\ \top & A_i \text{ is defined outside the loop} \\ \bot & A_i \text{ is a SSA definition inside the loop} \end{cases}$$

Figure 8 illustrates available subscript analysis on the loop in Figure 3.

We now present a brief complexity analysis of the available subscript analysis. Let k be the total number of loads and stores of different array elements inside a loop. The number of $d\phi$ and $u\phi$ nodes inside the loop will be $O(k)$. Based on past empirical measurements for scalar SSA form [8], we can expect that the total number of ϕ nodes created will be $O(k)$. Our subscript analysis involves τ iterations in the SSA graph [8]. Therefore, in practice the complexity of the available subscript analysis is $O(\tau \times k)$, for a given loop.

$\mathcal{L}(A_r)$	$\mathcal{L}(A_p) = \top$	$\mathcal{L}(A_p) = \langle(i_1,d_1),\ldots\rangle$	$\mathcal{L}(A_p) = \bot$
$\mathcal{L}(A_q) = \top$	$\top$	$\top$	$\top$
$\mathcal{L}(A_q) = \langle(i',d')\rangle$	$\top$	$\text{INSERT}((i',d'),\langle(i_1,d_1),\ldots\rangle)$	$\langle(i',d')\rangle$
$\mathcal{L}(A_q) = \bot$	$\bot$	$\bot$	$\bot$

Fig. 4. Lattice computation for $\mathcal{L}(A_r) = \mathcal{L}_{d\phi}(\mathcal{L}(A_q), \mathcal{L}(A_p))$ where $A_r := d\phi(A_q, A_p)$ is a definition ϕ operation

$\mathcal{L}(A_r)$	$\mathcal{L}(A_p) = \top$	$\mathcal{L}(A_p) = \langle(i_1,d_1),\ldots\rangle$	$\mathcal{L}(A_p) = \bot$
$\mathcal{L}(A_q) = \top$	$\top$	$\top$	$\top$
$\mathcal{L}(A_q) = \langle(i',d')\rangle$	$\top$	$\text{UPDATE}((i',d'),\langle(i_1,d_1),\ldots\rangle)$	$\mathcal{L}(A_1)$
$\mathcal{L}(A_q) = \bot$	$\top$	$\mathcal{L}(A_p)$	$\bot$

Fig. 5. Lattice computation for $\mathcal{L}(A_r) = \mathcal{L}_{u\phi}(\mathcal{L}(A_q), \mathcal{L}(A_p))$ where $A_r := u\phi(A_q, A_p)$ is a use ϕ operation

$\mathcal{L}(A_r) = \mathcal{L}(A_q) \sqcap \mathcal{L}(A_p)$	$\mathcal{L}(A_p) = \top$	$\mathcal{L}(A_p) = \langle(i_1,d_1),\ldots\rangle$	$\mathcal{L}(A_p) = \bot$
$\mathcal{L}(A_q) = \top$	$\top$	$\mathcal{L}(A_p)$	$\bot$
$\mathcal{L}(A_q) = \langle(i_1',d_1'),\ldots\rangle$	$\mathcal{L}(A_q)$	$\text{JOIN}(\mathcal{L}(A_q), \mathcal{L}(A_p))$	$\bot$
$\mathcal{L}(A_q) = \bot$	$\bot$	$\bot$	$\bot$

Fig. 6. Lattice computation for $\mathcal{L}(A_r) = \mathcal{L}_{\phi}(\mathcal{L}(A_q), \mathcal{L}(A_p))$, where $A_r := \phi(A_q, A_p)$ is a control ϕ operation

$\mathcal{L}(A_r)$	$\mathcal{L}(A_p) = \top$	$\mathcal{L}(A_p) = \langle(i_1,d_1),\ldots\rangle$	$\mathcal{L}(A_p) = \bot$
$\mathcal{L}(A_q) = \top$	$\top$	$\mathcal{L}(A_p)$	$\bot$
$\mathcal{L}(A_q) = \langle(i_1',d_1'),\ldots\rangle$	$\text{SHIFT}(\mathcal{L}(A_q))$	$\text{JOIN}(\text{SHIFT}(\mathcal{L}(A_q)), \mathcal{L}(A_p))$	$\bot$
$\mathcal{L}(A_q) = \bot$	$\bot$	$\bot$	$\bot$

Fig. 7. Lattice computation for $\mathcal{L}(A_r) = \mathcal{L}_{h\phi}(\mathcal{L}(A_q), \mathcal{L}(A_p))$, where $A_r := h\phi(A_q, A_p)$ is a header ϕ operation

	Iteration 1	Iteration 2
$\mathcal{L}(A_1)$	$\bot$	$\{(i-1,1)\}$
$\mathcal{L}(B_1)$	$\bot$	$\{(i-1,1),(i,1)\}$
$\mathcal{L}(B_3)$	$\{(i,0)\}$	$\{(i-1,1),(i,0)\}$
$\mathcal{L}(A_3)$	$\{(t,0)\}$	$\{(i-1,1),(t,0)\}$
$\mathcal{L}(A_5)$	$\{(i-1,0),(t,0)\}$	$\{(i-1,0),(t,0)\}$
$\mathcal{L}(B_5)$	$\{(i-1,0),(i,0)\}$	$\{(i-1,0),(i,0)\}$
$\mathcal{L}(A_7)$	$\{(i-1,0),(i+1,0)\}$	$\{(i-1,0),(i+1,0)\}$
$\mathcal{L}(A_8)$	$\bot$	$\{(i-1,1)\}$
$\mathcal{L}(B_6)$	$\{(i,0)\}$	$\{(i-1,1),(i,0)\}$
$\mathcal{L}(A_{10})$	$\{(i,0)\}$	$\{(i-1,1),(i,0)\}$
$\mathcal{L}(B_8)$	$\{(i,0)\}$	$\{(i-1,1),(i,0)\}$
$\mathcal{L}(B_{10})$	$\{(i,0),(i+1,0)\}$	$\{(i-1,1),(i,0),(i+1,0)\}$
$\mathcal{L}(A_{12})$	$\{(i,0)\}$	$\{(i-1,1),(i,0)\}$

Fig. 8. Available Subscript Analysis Example

6   Load Elimination Transformation

In this section, we present the algorithm for redundant load elimination. There are two steps in the algorithm: *Register pressure moderation* described in Section 6.1, which determines a subset of the redundant loads for load elimination and *Code generation* described in Section 6.2, which eliminates the redundant loads from the loop.

The set of redundant loads in a loop is represented using *UseRepSet*, a set of ordered pairs of the form $(A_j[x], d)$, where the use $A_j[x]$ is redundant and d is the iteration distance from the generator to the use. $d = 0$ implies an intra-iteration reuse and $d \geq 1$ implies an inter-iteration reuse. *UseRepSet* is derived from the lattice sets computed by available subscript analysis.

$$UseRepSet = \{ (A_i[x], d) \mid \exists (y, d) \in \mathcal{L}(A_j),\ A_k = u\phi(A_i, A_j),\ \mathcal{DS}(x, y) = true\}$$

For the loop in Figure 3, $UseRepSet = \{(B_2[i], 1), (A_4[i-1], 1), (B_4[i-1], 1), (B_7[i], 0)\}$

6.1   Register Pressure Moderation

Eliminating all redundant loads in a loop may lead to generation of spill code which could counteract the savings from scalar replacement. To prevent this, we need to choose the most profitable loads which could be scalar replaced using the available machine registers. We define the most profitable loads as the ones which requires the least number of registers.

When estimating the total register requirements for scalar replacement, all redundant uses which are generated by the same reference need to be considered together. To do this *UseRepSet* is partitioned into $U_1, ...U_k$, such that generators of all uses in a partition are definitely-same. A partition represents a set of uses which do not dominate each other and are generated by the same use/def. A partition U_m is defined as follows, where $step$ is the coefficient of the induction variable in the subscript expression.

$U_m = \{(A_i[x_i], d_i) \mid \forall (A_j[x_j], d_j) \in U_m, \mathcal{DS}(x_i + d_i \times step, x_j + d_j \times step) = true\}$

If the array index expression is loop-invariant, the number of registers required for its scalar replacement is one. In other cases, the number of registers required for eliminating all the loads in the partition U_p is given by

$NumRegs(U_p) = \{d_i + 1 \mid (A_i[x_i], d_i) \in U_p \ \wedge \ \forall (A_j[x_j], d_j) \in U_p, \ d_i \ \geq \ d_j\}$

For the loop in Figure 3, the four elements in $UseRepSet$ will fall into four different partitions: $\{(B_2[i], 1)\}, \{(A_4[i-1], 1)\}, \{(B_4[i-1], 1)\}, \{(B_7[i], 0)\}$. The total number of registers required for the scalar replacement is 7.

The partitions are then sorted in increasing order of the number of registers required. To select the redundant loads for scalar replacement, we use a greedy algorithm in which at each step the algorithm chooses the first available partition. The algorithm terminates when the first available partition does not fit into the remaining machine registers.

6.2   Code Generation

The inputs to the code generation algorithm are the intermediate representation of the loop body, the Array SSA form of the loop, and the subset of $UseRepSet$ after register pressure moderation. The code transformation is performed on the original input program. The extended Array SSA form is used to search for the generator corresponding to a redundant use. The algorithm for the transformation is shown in Figure 9. A scalar temporary, A_t_x is created for every array access $A[i]$ that is scalar replaced where, $\mathcal{DS}(x, i) = true$. In the first stage of the algorithm all redundant loads are replaced with a reference to a scalar temporary as shown in lines 2-11 of Figure 9. For example the reads of array elements $B[i]$ in line 1, $A[i-1]$ in line 5, $B[i-1]$ in line 6 and $B[i]$ in line 11 of Figure 11(a) are replaced with reads of scalar temporaries as shown in Figure 11(b). The loop also computes the maximum iteration distance for all redundant uses to their generator. It also moves loop invariant array reads to loop preheader. The loop in lines 15-27 of Figure 9 generates copy statements between scalar temporaries and code to initialize scalar temporaries if it is a loop carried reuse. The code to initialize the scalar temporary is inserted in the loop preheader, the basic block that immediately dominates the loop header. Line 2-4 in Figure 11(b) is the code generated to initialize the scalar temporaries and lines 23-25 are the copy statements generated to carry values across iterations. The loop in lines 20-24 of Figure 9 guarantees that the scalar temporaries have the right values if the value is generated across multiple iterations. Lines 28-35 of Figure 9 identifies the generators and initializes the appropriate scalar temporaries. The generators are identified using the recursive search routine SEARCH, which takes two arguments: The first argument is a SSA function A_j and the second argument is an index i. The function returns the set of all uses/defs which generates $A[i]$. The

Input: Input loop, Array SSA form of the loop and *UseRepSet*
Output: Loop after eliminating redundant loads
1: $maxd \leftarrow 0$
2: **for all** $(A_i[x], d)$ in *UseRepSet* **do**
3:    Replace LHS $:= A_i[x]$ by LHS $:= A\_t_x$
4:    **if** $d > maxd$ and x is not a loop invariant **then**
5:       $maxd \leftarrow d$
6:    **end if**
7:    **if** x is loop invariant **then**
8:       Insert initialization of A_t_x in the loop preheader
9:       $UseRepSet \leftarrow UseRepSet - (A_i[x], d)$
10:   **end if**
11: **end for**
12: **for all** $(A_i[x], d)$ in *UseRepSet* **do**
13:    $n \leftarrow x$
14:    $dist \leftarrow d$
15:    **while** $dist \neq 0$ **do**
16:       **if** A_t_n is not initialized **then**
17:          Insert $A\_t_n := A\_t_{n+step}$ at the end of loop body
18:          Insert initialization of A_t_n in the loop preheader
19:       **end if**
20:       **for all** defs $A_j[k] :=$ RHS **do**
21:          **if** $\mathcal{DS}(n, k)$ **then**
22:             Replace the def by
                   $A\_t_n :=$ RHS; $A_j[k] := A\_t_n$
23:          **end if**
24:       **end for**
25:       $dist \leftarrow dist - 1$
26:       $n \leftarrow n + step$
27:    **end while**
28:    $genset \leftarrow$ SEARCH(A_h, n) where A_h is the $h\phi$
29:    **for all** uses $A_j \in genset$ **do**
30:       Replace the use by $A\_t_n := A_j[k]$; LHS $:= A\_t_n$
31:    **end for**
32:    **for all** defs $A_j \in genset$ **do**
33:       Replace the def by $A\_t_n :=$ RHS; $A_j[k] := A\_t_n$
34:    **end for**
35: **end for**
36: Introduce a $maxd$-trip count test for the scalar replaced loop

Fig. 9. Redundant Load Elimination Transformation Algorithm

```
 1: procedure SEARCH(A, i)
 2:     if A = hϕ(A₁, .., Aₖ) then
 3:         return ∪ⱼ₌₂,ₖ SEARCH(Aⱼ, i)
 4:     end if
 5:     if A = ϕ(A₁, .., Aₖ) then
 6:         return ∪ⱼ₌₁,ₖ SEARCH(Aⱼ, i)
 7:     end if
 8:     if A = dϕ(A₁, A₂) then
 9:         if ℒ(A₁) = {k} and 𝒟𝒮(i, k) then
10:             return {A₁}
11:         else
12:             return SEARCH(A₂, i)
13:         end if
14:     end if
15:     if A = uϕ(A₁, A₂) then
16:         if ℒ(A₁) = {k} and 𝒟𝒮(i, k) then
17:             return {A₁}
18:         else
19:             return SEARCH(A₂, i)
20:         end if
21:     end if
22: end procedure
```

Fig. 10. Subroutine to find the set of generators

(a) Original Loop	(b) After Redundant Load Elimination		
1: **for** $i = 1$ **to** n **do**			
2: $t1 = B[i]$	1: **if** $n > 2$ **then**	16: $t_7 = B\_t_{i-1}$	
3: $t2 = A[t1]$	2: $A\_t_{i-1} = A[0]$	17: $B\_t_{i+1} = B[i+1]$	
4: **if** $t2 > 0$ **then**	3: $B\_t_i = B[1]$	18: $t_8 = B\_t_{i+1}$	
5: $t3 = A[i-1]$	4: $B\_t_{i-1} = B[0]$	19: $t_9 = t_6 + t_7$	
6: $t4 = B[i-1]$	5: **for** $i = 1$ **to** n **do**	20: $t_{10} = t_9 + t_8$	
7: $t5 = t3 + t4$	6: $t1 = B\_t_i$	21: $A\_t_i = t_{10}$	
8: $A[i+1] = t5$	7: $t2 = A[t1]$	22: $A[i] = A\_t_i$	
9: **end if**	8: **if** $t2 > 0$ **then**	23: $A\_t_{i-1} = A\_t_i$	
10: $t6 = A[i]$	9: $t3 = A\_t_{i-1}$	24: $B\_t_{i-1} = B\_t_i$	
11: $t7 = B[i]$	10: $t4 = B\_t_{i-1}$	25: $B\_t_i = B\_t_{i+1}$	
12: $t8 = B[i+1]$	11: $t5 = t3 + t4$	26: **end for**	
13: $t9 = t6 + t7$	12: $A[i+1] = t5$	27: **else**	
14: $t_{10} = t9 + t8$	13: **end if**	28: original loop as shown in	
15: $A[i] = t_{10}$	14: $A\_t_i = A[i]$	Figure 11(a)	
16: **end for**	15: $t6 = A\_t_i$	29: **end if**	

Fig. 11. Redundant Load Elimination Example

SEARCH routine is given in Figure 10. The routine takes at most one backward traversal of the SSA graph to find the set of generators. Line 36 of the load elimination algorithm inserts a loop trip count test around the scalar replaced loop.

We now present a brief complexity analysis of the load elimination transformation described in Figure 9. Let k be the total number of loads and stores of array elements inside the loop and let l be the number of redundant loads. The algorithm makes l traversals of the SSA graph and examines the stores inside the loop a maximum of $l \times d$, where d is the maximum distance from the generator to the redundant use. Therefore the worst case complexity of the algorithm in Figure 9 for a given loop is $O((d+1) \times l \times k)$.

(a) Original Loop	(b) After Load Elimination
1: **for** $i = 1$ to n **do**	1: $A\_t\_init_i = A[1]$
2: $A[i+1] = e_1$	2: **for** $j = 1$ to n **do**
3: $A[i] = A[i] + e_2$	3: $A\_t_i = \phi(A\_t_{i+1}, A\_t\_init_i)$
4: **end for**	4: $A\_t_{i+1} = e_1$
	5: $A[i+1] = A\_t_{i+1}$
	6: $A\_t_i = A\_t_i + e_2$
	7: $A[i] = A\_t_i$
	8: **end for**
(c) Extended Array SSA	**(d) After Store Elimination**
1: $A_0 = ...$	1: $A\_t\_init_i = A[1]$
2: $A\_t\_init_i = A_1[1]$	2: **for** $j = 1$ to n **do**
3: $A_2 = u\phi(A_1, A_0)$	3: $A\_t_i = \phi(A\_t_{i+1}, A\_t\_init_i)$
4: **for** $j = 1$ to n **do**	4: $A\_t_{i+1} = e_1$
5: $A_3 = h\phi(A_2, A_7)$	5: $A\_t_i = A\_t_i + e_2$
6: $A\_t_i = \phi(A\_t_{i+1}, A\_t\_init_i)$	6: $A[i] = A\_t_i$
7: $A\_t_{i+1} = e_1$	7: **end for**
8: $A_4[i+1] = A\_t_{i+1}$	8: $A\_t_i = A\_t_{i+1}$
9: $A_5 = d\phi(A_4, A_3)$	9: $A[i+1] = e_1$
10: $A\_t_i = A\_t_i + e_2$	10: $A\_t_i = A\_t_i + e_2$
11: $A_6[i] = A\_t_i$	11: $A[i] = A\_t_i$
12: $A_7 = d\phi(A_6, A_5)$	
13: **end for**	

Fig. 12. Store Elimination Example

7   Dead Store Elimination

Elimination of loads can increase the number of dead stores inside the loop. For example, consider the loop in Figure 12(a). The store of $A[i+1]$ in line 2 is used by the load of $A[i]$ in line 3. Assuming $n > 0$, Figure 12(b) shows the same loop after scalar replacement and elimination of redundant loads. The store of $A[i+1]$

SSA function	Lattice Operation
$s_i : A_r = u\phi(A_q, A_p)$	$\mathcal{L}_u(A_p, s_i) = \mathcal{L}(A_r) - \{(v, d) \mid$ $\exists\, (w, 0) \in \mathcal{L}(A_p)\ s.t.\ \neg\mathcal{DD}(v, w)\}$
$s_i : A_r = d\phi(A_q, A_p)$	$\mathcal{L}_u(A_p, s_i) = \text{UPDATE}(\mathcal{L}(A_r), \mathcal{L}(A_q))$
$s_i : A_r = \phi(A_q, A_p)$	$\mathcal{L}_u(A_q, s_i) = \mathcal{L}(A_r)$ $\mathcal{L}_u(A_p, s_i) = \mathcal{L}(A_r)$
$s_i : A_r = h\phi(A_q, A_p)$	$\mathcal{L}_u(A_q, s_i) = \text{SHIFT}(\mathcal{L}(A_r))$ $\mathcal{L}_u(A_p, s_i) = \text{SHIFT}(\mathcal{L}(A_r))$

Fig. 13. Index Propagation for Dead Store Elimination

	Iteration 1	Iteration 2
$\mathcal{L}(A_7)$	$\perp$	{(i+1,1),(i+2,1)}
$\mathcal{L}(A_5)$	{(i,0)}	{(i,0),(i+1,1),(i+2,1)}
$\mathcal{L}(A_3)$	{(i,0),(i+1,0)}	{(i,0),(i+1,0),(i+2,1)}

Fig. 14. Dead Subscript Analysis

in line 5 for the first $n - 1$ iterations is now redundant since it gets overwritten by the store to $A[i]$ at line 7 in the next iteration with no uses in between.

Dead store elimination is run as a post pass to redundant load elimination and it uses a backward flow analysis of array subscripts similar to very busy expression analysis. The analysis computes set $\mathcal{L}(A_i)$ for every SSA function in the program. Similar to available subscript analysis presented in Section 5, the lattice for dead subscript analysis, $\mathcal{L}(A)$ is a subset of $\mathcal{U}_{ind}^A \times \mathbb{Z}_{\geq 0}$. Note that there could be multiple uses of the same SSA name. For instance, the SSA name A_3 is an argument of the $u\phi$ function in line 12 and the ϕ function in line 19 in the loop given in Figure 3(b). A backward data flow analysis will have to keep track of lattice values for each of these values. To achieve this, we associate a lattice element with each of the uses of the SSA variable represented as $\mathcal{L}_u(A_i, s_j)$, where s_j is a statement in the program which uses the SSA variable A_i.

During the backward flow analysis, index sets are propagated from left to right of ϕ functions. The lattice operations for the propagation of data flow information are shown in Figure 13. The computation of $\mathcal{L}(A_i)$ from all the augmented uses of A_i is given using the following equation.

$$\mathcal{L}(A_i) = \bigcap_{s_j \text{ is a } \phi \text{ use of } A_i} \mathcal{L}(A_i, s_j)$$

The lattice values are initialized as follows:

$$\mathcal{L}(A_i) = \begin{cases} \{(x, 0)\} & A_i \text{ is a definition of the form } A_i[x] \\ \{(x, 0)\} & A_i \text{ is a use of the form } A_i[x] \\ \top & A_i \text{ is defined outside the loop} \\ \perp & A_i \text{ is a SSA function defined inside the loop} \end{cases}$$

The SHIFT and UPDATE operations are defined as follows, where $step_1$ is the coefficient of the induction variable in i_1, $step_2$ is the coefficient of the induction variable in i_2 and so on.

$$\text{SHIFT}\langle (i_1, d_1), (i_2, d_2), \ldots \rangle = \langle (i_1 + step_1, d_1 + 1), (i_2 + step_2, d_2 + 1), \ldots \rangle$$

$$\text{UPDATE}((i', d'), \mathcal{L}(A_p)) = \{(i_1, d_1) | (i_1, d_1) \in \mathcal{L}(A_p) \text{ and } \mathcal{DS}(i', i_1) = false\} \cup \{(i', d')\}$$

The result of the analysis is used to compute the set of dead stores:

$$DeadStores = \{ (A_i[x], d) \mid \exists (y, d) \in \mathcal{L}(A_j) \text{ and } \mathcal{DS}(x, y) = true \text{ and } A_k = d\phi(A_i, A_j)\}$$

i.e., a store, $A_i[x]$ is redundant with respect to subsequent defs if $(y, d) \in \mathcal{L}(A_j)$ and $\mathcal{DS}(x, y) = true$, where $A_k = d\phi(A_i, A_j)$ is the $d\phi$ function corresponding to the use $A_i[x]$. d represents the number of iterations between the dead store and the killing store.

Figure 12(c) shows the extended Array SSA form of the program in Figure 12(b). Figure 14 illustrates dead subscript analysis on this loop. The set of dead stores for this loop is $DeadStores = \{(A_4[i + 1], 1)\}$.

Given the set $DeadStores = \{(S_1, d_1), \ldots (S_n, d_n)\}$, the algorithm for dead store elimination involves peeling the last k iterations of the loop, where $k = \max_{i=1..n} d_i$. The dead stores could be eliminated from the original loop, but they must be retained in the last k peeled iterations. The loop in Figure 12(b) after the elimination of dead stores is given in Figure 12(d).

Similar to available subscript analysis, the worst case complexity of dead subscript analysis for a given loop is $O(\tau \times k)$. The complexity of the transformation is $O(n)$, where n is the size of the loop body.

8   Extension to Objects and While Loops

In the previous sections, we introduced new scalar replacement analysis and transformations based on extended Array SSA form that can be used to optimize array accesses within and across loop iterations in counted loops. Past work has shown that scalar replacement can also be performed more generally on object fields in the presence of arbitrary control flow [10]. However, though the past work in [10] used Array SSA form, it could not perform scalar replacement across multiple iterations of a loop. In this section, we briefly illustrate how our approach can also perform inter-iteration scalar replacement in programs with while-loops containing accesses to object fields.

Figure 15(a) shows a simple example of a while loop in which the read of object field p.x can be replaced by a scalar temporary carrying the value from the previous iteration. This code assumes that $FIRST$ and $LAST$ refer to the first node and last node in a linked list, and the result of scalar replacement is shown in Figure 15(b). A value of $\tau = 1$ suffices to propagate *temp* from the previous iteration to the current iteration, provided a prologue is generated that is guarded by a zero-trip test as shown in Figure 15(b). It is worth noting that no shape analysis is necessary for the scalar replacement performed in Figure 15(b). If available, shape analysis [20] can be used as a pre-pass to further refine the DS and DD information for objects in while loops.

(a) Original Loop	(b) After Scalar Replacement
1: $p := FIRST$	1: $p := FIRST$
2: **while** $p \neq LAST$ **do**	2: **if** $p \neq LAST$ **then**
3: ... $= p.x$;	3: $temp = p.x$;
4: ...	4: **end if**
5: $p = p.next$;	5: **while** $p \neq LAST$ **do**
6: $p.x$ $= $ ...	6: ... $= temp$;
7: **end while**	7: ...
	8: $p = p.next$;
	9: $temp = $ ...
	10: $p.x$ $= temp$;
	11: **end while**

Fig. 15. Scalar replacement example for object accesses in a while loop

9   Experimental Results

In this section, we describe the implementation of our Array SSA based scalar replacement framework followed by an experimental evaluation of our scalar replacement and dead store analysis algorithms.

9.1   Implementation

We have implemented our algorithms in LLVM compiler release 3.2. A high-level view of the implementation is presented in Figure 16. To perform subscript analysis, we employed scalar evolution [17] as a pre-pass that computes closed form expressions for all scalar integer variables in a given program. This is followed by extended Array SSA construction, available subscript analysis, and redundant load elimination. Since there are $u\phi$s associated with the loads that were eliminated, an Array SSA repair pass is required after load elimination to cleanup the $u\phi$s and fix the arguments of control ϕs. The dead subscript analysis and dead store elimination follows the Array SSA repair pass. Finally, the program is translated out of Array SSA form.

9.2   Evaluation

Stencil computations offer opportunities for inter-iteration scalar replacement. We evaluated our scalar replacement transformation on 7 stencil applications: Jacobi 1-D 3-point, Jacobi 2-D 5-point, Jacobi 3-D 7-point, Jacobi 3-D 13-point,

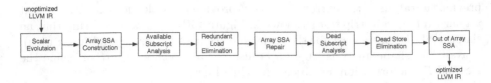

Fig. 16. High Level View of LLVM Implementation

Jacobi 3-D 19-point, Jacobi 3-D 27-point and Rician Denoising. For Jacobi 2-D 5-point example, we employed unroll-and-jam as a pre-pass transformation with an unroll factor of 4 to increase scalar replacement opportunities. No unrolling was performed on the remaining 3-D kernels, since they already contain sufficient opportunities for scalar replacement. We used $\tau = 5$, which is sufficient to capture all the load elimination opportunities in the applications.

The experimental results were obtained on a 32-core 3.55 GHz IBM Power7 system with 256 GB main memory and running SUSE Linux. The focus of our measurements was on obtaining dynamic counts of load operations[1] and the runtime improvement due to scalar replacement algorithms. When we report timing information, we report the best wall-clock time from five runs. We used the PAPI [15] interface to find the dynamic counts of load instructions executed for each of the programs. We compiled the programs with two different set of options described below.

- O3 : LLVM -O3 with basic alias analysis.
- O3SR : LLVM -O3 with basic alias analysis and scalar replacement

Table 1. Comparison of Load Instructions Executed and Runtimes

Benchmark	O3 Loads	O3SR Loads	O3 Time (secs)	O3SR Time (secs)
Jacobi 1-D 3-Point	5.58E+8	4.59E+8	.25	.25
Jacobi 2-D 5-Point	4.35E+8	4.15E+8	.43	.32
Jacobi 3-D 7-Point	1.41E+9	1.29E+9	1.66	.74
Jacobi 3-D 13-Point	1.89E+9	1.77E+9	2.73	1.32
Jacobi 3-D 19-Point	2.39E+9	1.78E+9	3.95	1.72
Jacobi 3-D 27-Point	2.88E+9	1.79E+9	5.45	3.16
Rician Denoising	2.71E+9	2.46E+9	4.17	3.53

Table 1 shows the dynamic counts of load instructions executed and the execution time for the programs without scalar replacement and with scalar replacement. All the programs show a reduction in the number of loads when scalar

---

[1] We only counted the load operations because these benchmarks do not offer opportunities for store elimination.

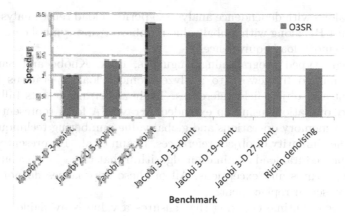

Fig. 17. Speedup : O3SR with respect to O3

replacement is enabled. Figure 17 shows the speedup for each of the benchmarks due to scalar replacement. All the programs, except Jacobi 1-D 3-Point displayed speedup due to scalar replacement. The speedup due to scalar replacement ranges from 1.18× to 2.29× for different benchmarks.

10   Related Work

Region Array SSA [19] is an extension of Array SSA form with explicit aggregated array region information for array accesses. Each array definition is summarized using a region representing the elements that it modifies across all surrounding loop nests. This region information then forms an integral part of normal ϕ operands. A region is represented using an uniform set of references (USR) representation. Additionally, the region is augmented with predicates to handle control flow. This representation is shown to be effective for constant propagation and array privatization, but the aggregated region representation is more complex than the subscript analysis presented in Section 5 and does not have enough maximum distance information to help guide scalar replacement to meet a certain register pressure. More importantly, since the region Array SSA representation explicitly does not capture use information, it would be hard to perform scalar replacement across iterations for array loads without any intervening array store.

A large body of past work has focused on scalar replacement [11,6,7,3,14] in the context of optimizing array references in scientific programs for better register reuse. These algorithms are primarily based on complex data dependence analysis and for loops with restricted or no control flow (e.g., [7] only handles loops with forward conditional control flow). Conditional control flow is often ignored when testing for data dependencies in parallelizing compilers. Moreover, [7] won't be able to promote values if dependence distances are not consistent. More recent algorithms such as [3,14] use analyses based on partial redundancy elimination along with dependence analysis to perform load reuse analysis. Bodik et al. [4] used PRE along with global value-numbering and symbolic information to capture memory load equivalences.

For strongly typed programming languages, Fink, Knobe and Sarkar [10] presented a unified framework to analyze memory load operations for both array-element and object-field references. Their algorithm detects fully redundant memory operations using an extended Array SSA form representation for array-element memory operations and global value numbering technique to disambiguate the similarity of object references. Praun et al. [18] presented a PRE based inter-procedural load elimination algorithm that takes into account Java's concurrency features and exceptions. All of these approaches do not perform inter-iteration scalar replacement.

[5] employed runtime checking that ensures a value is available for strided memory accesses using arrays and pointers. Their approach is applicable across loop iterations, and also motivated the specialized hardware features such as rotating registers, valid bits, and predicated registers in modern processors.

[21] extend the original scalar replacement algorithm of [7] to outer loops and show better precision. Extensions for multiple induction variables for scalar replacement are proposed in [2].

[9] presents a data flow analysis framework for array references which propagates iteration distance (aka dependence distance) across loop iterations. That is, instances of subscripted references are propagated throughout the loop from points where they are generated until points are encountered that kill the instances. This information is then applied to optimizations such as redundant load elimination. Compared to their work, our available subscript analysis operates on SSA form representation and propagates indices instead of just distances.

11   Conclusions

In this paper, we introduced novel simple and efficient analysis algorithms for scalar replacement and dead store elimination that are built on Array SSA form, an extension to scalar SSA form that captures control and data flow properties at the level of array or pointer accesses. A core contribution of our algorithm is a subscript analysis that propagates array indices across loop iterations. Compared to past work, this algorithm can handle control flow within and across loop iterations and degrades gracefully in the presence of unanalyzable subscripts. We also introduced code transformations that can use the output of our analysis algorithms to perform the necessary scalar replacement transformations (including the insertion of loop prologues and epilogues for loop-carried reuse). Our experimental results show performance improvements of up to $2.29\times$ relative to code generated by LLVM at -O3 level. These results promise to make our analysis algorithms a desirable starting point for scalar replacement implementations in modern SSA-based compiler infrastructures such as LLVM, compared to the more complex algorithms in past work based on non-SSA program representations.

References

1. Polybench: Polyhedral benchmark suite.
   http://www.cse.ohio-state.edu/~pouchet/software/polybench/
2. Baradaran, N., Diniz, P.C., Park, J.: Extending the applicability of scalar replacement to multiple induction variables. In: Eigenmann, R., Li, Z., Midkiff, S.P. (eds.) LCPC 2004. LNCS, vol. 3602, pp. 455–469. Springer, Heidelberg (2005)
3. Bodik, R., Gupta, R.: Array Data-Flow Analysis for Load-Store Optimizations in Superscalar Architectures. In: Huang, C.-H., Sadayappan, P., Banerjee, U., Gelernter, D., Nicolau, A., Padua, D.A. (eds.) LCPC 1995. LNCS, vol. 1033, pp. 1–15. Springer, Heidelberg (1996)
4. Bodík, R., Gupta, R., Soffa, M.L.: Load-reuse analysis: Design and evaluation. SIGPLAN Not. 34(5), 64–76 (1999)
5. Budiu, M., Goldstein, S.C.: Inter-iteration scalar replacement in the presence of conditional control flow. In: 3rd Workshop on Optimizations for DSO and Embedded Systems, San Jose, CA (March 2005)
6. Callahan, D., Carr, S., Kennedy, K.: Improving Register Allocation for Subscripted Variables. In: Proceedings of the ACM SIGPLAN 1990 Conference on Programming Language Design and Implementation, White Plains, New York, pp. 53–65 (June 1990)
7. Carr, S., Kennedy, K.: Scalar Replacement in the Presence of Conditional Control Flow. Software—Practice and Experience (1), 51–77 (1994)
8. Cytron, R., Ferrante, J., Rosen, B.K., Wegman, M.N., Zadeck, F.K.: Efficiently computing static single assignment form and the control dependence graph. ACM Trans. Program. Lang. Syst. 13(4), 451–490 (1991)
9. Duesterwald, E., Gupta, R., Soffa, M.L.: A practical data flow framework for array reference analysis and its use in optimizations. In: Proceedings of the ACM SIGPLAN 1993 Conference on Programming Language Design and Implementation, PLDI 1993, pp. 68–77. ACM, New York (1993)
10. Fink, S.J., Knobe, K., Sarkar, V.: Unified analysis of array and object references in strongly typed languages. In: Proceedings of the 7th International Symposium on Static Analysis, SAS 2000, pp. 155–174. Springer, London (2000)
11. Kennedy, K., Allen, J.R.: Optimizing compilers for modern architectures: A dependence-based approach. Morgan Kaufmann Publishers Inc., San Francisco (2002)
12. Knobe, K., Sarkar, V.: Array SSA form and its use in Parallelization. In: 25th Annual ACM SIGACT-SIGPLAN Symposium on the Principles of Programming Languages (January 1998)
13. Lattner, C., Adve, V.: LLVM: A Compilation Framework for Lifelong Program Analysis & Transformation. In: Proceedings of the 2004 International Symposium on Code Generation and Optimization (CGO 2004), Palo Alto, California (March 2004)
14. Lo, R., Chow, F., Kennedy, R., Liu, S.-M., Tu, P.: Register promotion by sparse partial redundancy elimination of loads and stores. SIGPLAN Not. 33(5), 26–37 (1998)
15. Mucci, P.J., Browne, S., Deane, C., Ho, G.: Papi: A portable interface to hardware performance counters. In: Proceedings of the Department of Defense HPCMP Users Group Conference, pp. 7–10 (1999)
16. Paek, Y., Hoeflinger, J., Padua, D.: Efficient and precise array access analysis. ACM Trans. Program. Lang. Syst. 24(1), 65–109 (2002)

17. Pop, S., Cohen, A., Silber, G.-A.: Induction variable analysis with delayed abstractions. In: Conte, T., Navarro, N., Hwu, W.-m.W., Valero, M., Ungerer, T. (eds.) HiPEAC 2005. LNCS, vol. 3793, pp. 218–232. Springer, Heidelberg (2005)
18. Von Praun, C., Schneider, F., Gross, T.R.: Load Elimination in the Presence of Side Effects, Concurrency and Precise Exceptions. In: Rauchwerger, L. (ed.) LCPC 2003. LNCS, vol. 2958, pp. 390–405. Springer, Heidelberg (2004)
19. Rus, S., He, G., Alias, C., Rauchwerger, L.: Region array ssa. In: Proceedings of the 15th International Conference on Parallel Architectures and Compilation Techniques, PACT 2006, pp. 43–52. ACM, New York (2006)
20. Sagiv, M., Reps, T., Wilhelm, R.: Parametric shape analysis via 3-valued logic. ACM Trans. Program. Lang. Syst. 24(3), 217–298 (2002)
21. So, B., Hall, M.: Increasing the applicability of scalar replacement. In: Duesterwald, E. (ed.) CC 2004. LNCS, vol. 2985, pp. 185–201. Springer, Heidelberg (2004)

Recovery of Class Hierarchies and Composition Relationships from Machine Code*

Venkatesh Srinivasan[1] and Thomas Reps[1,2]

[1] University of Wisconsin, Madison, WI, USA
[2] GrammaTech, Inc., Ithaca, NY, USA

Abstract. We present a reverse-engineering tool, called Lego, which recovers class hierarchies and composition relationships from stripped binaries. Lego takes a stripped binary as input, and uses information obtained from dynamic analysis to (i) group the functions in the binary into classes, and (ii) identify inheritance and composition relationships between the inferred classes. The software artifacts recovered by Lego can be subsequently used to understand the object-oriented design of software systems that lack documentation and source code, e.g., to enable interoperability. Our experiments show that the class hierarchies recovered by Lego have a high degree of agreement—measured in terms of precision and recall—with the hierarchy defined in the source code.

1 Introduction

Reverse engineering of software binaries is an activity that has gotten an increasing amount of attention from the academic community in the last decade (e.g., see the references in [2, §1]). However, most of this work has had the goal of recovering information to make up for missing symbol-table/debugging information [1,18,24,16,6,10], to create other basic intermediate representations (IRs) similar to the standard IRs that a compiler would produce [2,3,22], or to recover higher-level protocol abstractions or file formats [5,17,9].

In this paper, we address a problem that is complementary to prior work on reverse engineering of machine code,[1] namely, the problem of *recovery of class structure* at the machine-code level. In particular, we present a technique

---

* Supported, in part, by NSF under grants CCF- {0810053, 0904371}; by ONR under grants N00014- {09-1-0510, 11-C-0447}; by ARL under grant W911NF-09-1-0413; by AFRL under grants FA9550-09-1-0279 and FA8650-10-C-7088; and by DARPA under cooperative agreement HR0011-12-2-0012. Any opinions, findings, and conclusions or recommendations expressed in this publication are those of the authors, and do not necessarily reflect the views of the sponsoring agencies. T. Reps has an ownership interest in GrammaTech, Inc., which has licensed elements of the technology reported in this publication.

[1] We use the term "machine code" to refer generically to low-level code, and do not distinguish between actual machine-code bits/bytes and assembly code to which it is disassembled.

to group a program's procedures into classes, and to identify inheritance and composition relationships between classes.

Class hierarchies and composition relationships recovered from machine code can be used to understand the object-oriented design of legacy software binaries while porting them to newer platforms. They can also be used while designing new software that is aimed to be interoperable with existing software binaries. For instance, in the United States, the Digital Millennium Copyright Act (DMCA) prohibits users from circumventing access-control technologies [8]. However, the DMCA specifically grants a small number of exceptions, including one for reverse engineering for the purpose of interoperability (§1201(f)). Others [6] have used similar artifacts as fingerprints of code polymorphic viruses for malware detection.

We present a tool, called Lego, which takes a stripped executable as input and uses dynamic analysis to recover the class structure of the program, including inheritance and composition relationships. Lego is based on two common features of object-oriented languages. The first is the *this-pointer idiom*: at the machine-code level, the object pointer is passed as an explicit first argument to a class's methods. Lego exploits this idiom to group calls to instance methods (methods that have the *this*-pointer as an explicit first argument), including dynamically dispatched ones, that have a common receiver object. The second idiom is the presence of a *unique finalizer method* in most class declarations, which is called at the end of an object's lifetime to do cleanup. Lego exploits this idiom, along with the aforementioned method-call groupings, to group methods into classes, and to recover inheritance and composition relationships between recovered classes.

We tested Lego on ten open-source applications. Using the class structure declared in the source code as ground truth, the classes recovered by Lego had an average precision of 88% and an average recall of 86.7%.

The contributions of our work include the following:

- We show that even if an executable is stripped of symbol-table and debugging information, and, even if run-time-type information (RTTI) is not present in the executable, it is still possible to reconstruct a class hierarchy, including inheritance and composition relationships, with fairly high accuracy. Our technique is based on common semantic features of object-oriented languages, and is not tied to a specific language, compiler, or executable format. It can be used on any binary generated from a language that uses the *this*-pointer and the unique-finalizer features, and a compiler that faithfully implements those features.
- Our methods have been implemented in a tool, called Lego, that uses dynamic analysis to recover a class hierarchy. (Because Lego uses dynamic analysis, it can recover classes only for the parts of the program that are exercised during execution.)
- We present a scoring scheme that takes the structure of class hierarchies into account while scoring a recovered hierarchy with respect to a ground-truth hierarchy.

```
class Vehicle {              class Car : public Vehicle {     void foo(bool flag) {
  public:                      public:                           if (flag) {
    Vehicle();                   Car();                            Car c;
    ~Vehicle();                  Car(int n);                       c.print_car();
    void print_vehicle();        ~Car();                         } else {
};                               void print_car();                 Car c(10);
                               private:                            c.print_car();
class GPS {                      GPS g;                          }
  public:                    };                                }
    GPS();
    ~GPS();                  class Bus : public Vehicle {      int main() {
};                             public:                           Vehicle v;
                                 Bus();                          Bus b;
                                 ~Bus();                         v.print_vehicle();
                                 void print_bus();               foo(true);
                               private:                          foo(false);
                                 void helper();                  b.print_bus();
                             };                                  return 0;
                                                               }
```

Fig. 1. C++ program fragment, with inheritance and composition

– Lego is immune to certain compiler idiosyncrasies and optimization side-
  effects, such as reusing stack space for different objects in a given procedure
  activation-record.

2   Overview

Lego recovers class structure from binaries in two steps:

1. Lego executes the program binary, monitoring the execution to gather data
   about the various objects allocated during execution, the lifetime of those
   objects, and the methods invoked on those objects. Once the program terminates, Lego emits a set of object-traces (defined below) that summarizes
   the gathered data.
2. Lego uses the object-traces as evidence, and infers a class hierarchy and
   composition relationships that agree with the evidence.

This section presents an example to illustrate the approach.

In our study, all of the binaries analyzed by Lego come from source-code
programs written in C++. Fig. 1 shows a C++ program fragment, consisting of
four class definitions along with definitions of the methods main and foo. Classes
Vehicle, Car, and Bus constitute an inheritance hierarchy with Vehicle being
the base class, and Car and Bus being derived classes. There is a composition
relationship between Car and GPS. (Car has a member of class GPS.) Assume
that, in the class definition, helper() is called by ~Bus(). Also assume that
the complete version of the program shown in Fig. 1 is compiled and stripped
to create a stripped binary.

Lego takes a stripped binary and a test input or inputs, and does dynamic
binary instrumentation. When the execution of the binary under the test input
terminates, Lego emits a set of object-traces, one object-trace for every unique
object identified by Lego during the program execution. An *object-trace* of an
object O is a sequence of method calls and returns that have O as the receiver
object. Additionally, the set of methods directly called by each method in the

```
v_1:
 Vehicle() C
 Vehicle() R
 print_vehicle() C    c_1:              c_2:              b_1:
 print_vehicle() R     Car() C           Car(int) C        Bus() C
 ~Vehicle() C          Vehicle() C       Vehicle() C       Vehicle() C
 ~Vehicle() R          Vehicle() R       Vehicle() R       Vehicle() R
                       Car() R           Car(int) R        Bus() R
g_1:                    Vehicle()          Vehicle()          Vehicle()
 GPS() C                GPS()              GPS()            print_bus() C
 GPS() R              print_car() C      print_car() C      print_bus() R
 ~GPS() C             print_car() R      print_car() R      ~Bus() C
 ~GPS() R              ~Car() C           ~Car() C          helper() C
                       ~Vehicle() C       ~Vehicle() C      helper() R
g_2:                    ~Vehicle() R       ~Vehicle() R      ~Vehicle() C
 GPS() C                ~Car() R           ~Car() R          ~Vehicle() R
 GPS() R                ~GPS()             ~GPS()            ~Bus() R
 ~GPS() C              ~Vehicle()         ~Vehicle()         helper()
 ~GPS() R                                                    ~Vehicle()
```

Fig. 2. Object-traces for the example program. The records in the return-only suffixes are underlined.

sequence is also available in the object-trace. Concretely, an object-trace for an object O is a sequence of object-trace records. Each object-trace record has the following form,

$$\langle method, C \mid R, calledMethods \rangle,$$

where *method* denotes a method that was called with O as the receiver. Because we are dealing with binaries, methods are represented by their effective addresses, and so *method* is an effective address. C denotes a call event for *method*; R denotes a return event. *calledMethods* denotes the set of effective addresses of methods directly called by *method*. Each method in *calledMethods* can have any receiver object (not necessarily O). Object-traces are the key structure used for recovering class hierarchies and composition relationships.

In the rest of this section, when we use the term "method" in the context of object-traces or recovered classes, we are referring to the effective address of the method. However, to make our examples easier to understand, we will use method names rather than method effective addresses.

Fig. 2 shows the set of object-traces obtained from executing our example binary with Lego. In the figure, the objects encountered by Lego are denoted by appending instance numbers to the source-code object names: c_1 and c_2 correspond to different objects in two different activations of method foo, and g_1 and g_2 correspond to the instances of the GPS class in those objects.

We now describe how Lego obtains the class hierarchy and composition relationships from the set of object-traces. Lego computes a *fingerprint* for each object-trace. The fingerprint is a string obtained by concatenating the methods that constitute a return-only suffix of the object-trace. For our example, the fingerprint for the object-trace of v_1 is ~Vehicle(), and for the object-trace of c_1, it is ~Vehicle() ~Car(). The object-trace records that are underlined in Fig. 2 contribute to fingerprints. A fingerprint represents the methods that were involved in the cleanup of an object. A fingerprint's length indicates the

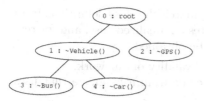

Fig. 3. Trie constructed by Lego using the object-trace fingerprints for the example program

Table 1. Methods in the set of recovered classes

Trie node	Methods in the recovered class
1	Vehicle(), print_vehicle(), ~Vehicle()
2	GPS(), ~GPS()
3	Bus(), print_bus(), ~Bus(), helper()
4	Car(), Car(int), print_car(), ~Car()

possible number of levels in the inheritance hierarchy from the object's class to the root. The methods in a fingerprint represent the potential finalizers in the class and its ancestor classes.

Next, Lego constructs a trie by inserting the fingerprints into an empty trie and creating a new trie node for each new method encountered. For the fingerprints of the object-traces in Fig. 2, the constructed trie is shown in Fig. 3. Each node's key is a finalizer method. Event order (i.e., left-to-right reading order in Fig. 2) corresponds to following a path down from the root of the trie (cf. Fig. 3).

Lego links each object-trace ot to the trie node N that "accepts" ot's fingerprint. In particular, N's key is the last method in ot's fingerprint. In our example, the object-trace of v_1 is linked to node 1 of Fig. 3, the object-traces of g_1 and g_2 to node 2, the object-trace of b_1 to node 3, and the object-traces of c_1 and c_2 to node 4.

Using the linked object-traces, Lego computes, for each trie node, the *methods set* and the *called-methods set*. For a trie node N and a set of object-traces OT_N linked to N, N's methods set is the set of methods that appear in some object-trace record in OT_N; N's called-methods set is the set union of the *calledMethods* field of the last object-trace record in each object-trace in OT_N. For instance, node 4's methods set is {Car(), Car(int), Vehicle(), print_car(), ~Car(), ~Vehicle()}, and its called-methods set is {~GPS(), ~Vehicle()}. If methods present in the methods set of ancestor nodes are also present in the methods set of descendants, Lego removes the common methods from the descendants. The resulting trie nodes and their methods sets constitute the recovered classes, and the resulting trie constitutes the recovered class hierarchy. The methods of each recovered class are shown in Table 1.

To determine composition relationships between recovered classes, for all pairs of trie nodes m and n, where neither is an ancestor of the other, Lego checks if n's key is present in the called-methods set of m. If so, the recovered class corresponding to m has a member whose class is the one corresponding to n, and thus there exists a composition relationship between m and n. For instance, in our example, the objects c_1 and c_2 (associated with node 4) both call ~GPS(), which is the key of node 2; consequently, Lego reports a composition relationship between nodes 4 and 2.

In this example, the recovered classes exactly match the class definitions from the source code. However, this example illustrates an idealized case, and for real applications an exact correspondence may not be obtained.

Threats to validity. There are five threats to the validity of our work.

1. The binaries given as input to Lego must come from a language that uses the *this*-pointer idiom.

2. Lego assumes that every class has a unique finalizer method that is called at the end of an object's lifetime. If a class has no finalizer or multiple finalizers, the information recovered by Lego might not be accurate. Lego also assumes that a parent-class finalizer is called only at the end of a child-class finalizer.

   In C++, the class destructor acts as the finalizer. Even if the programmer has not declared a destructor, in most cases, the compiler will generate one. A C++ base-class's destructor is called at the very end of a derived-class's destructor. The C++ compiler will sometimes create up to three versions of the class destructor in the binary [14]. Information that certain methods are alternative versions of a given destructor can be passed to Lego. However, our experiments show that there is little change in the results when such information is not provided to Lego (Fig. 9).

3. If the binary has stand-alone methods that do not belong to any class, but have an object pointer as the first argument, Lego might include those stand-alone methods in the set of methods of some recovered class. Although the recovered classes will not match the source-code class structure, it is arguable that they reflect the "actual" class structure used by the program.

   In addition, stand-alone methods that have a non-object pointer as the first argument may end up in stand-alone classes that are not part of any hierarchy.

4. Lego relies on the ability to observe a program's calls and returns. Ordinarily, these actions are implemented using specific instructions—e.g., `call` and `ret` in the Intel x86 instruction set. Code that is obfuscated—either because it is malicious, or to protect intellectual property—may deliberately perform calls and returns in non-standard ways.

5. Inlining of method calls also causes methods to be unobservable. In particular, if a method has been uniformly inlined by the compiler, it will never be observed by Lego.

For real software systems, these issues are typically not completely avoidable. Our experiments are based on C++, which uses the *this*-pointer idiom, and issues 4 and 5 were deemed out of scope. The experiments show that, even if issues 2 and 3 are present in an executable, Lego recovers classes and a class hierarchy that is reasonably accurate.

3   Algorithm

Lego needs to accomplish two tasks: (i) compute object-traces, and (ii) identify class hierarchies and composition relationships. In this section, we describe the algorithms used during these two phases of Lego.

Algorithm 1. Algorithm to compute full object-traces

Input: Currently executing instruction I
1. **if** InstrFW.isCall(I) **then**
2.   m ← InstrFW.eaOfCalledMethod(I)
3.   ShadowStack.top().calledMethods.insert(m)
4.   ID ← InstrFW.firstArgValue(I)
5.   expectedRetAddr ← InstrFW.eaOfNextInstruction(I)
6.   ShadowStack.push(⟨ID, expectedRetAddr, ∅⟩)
7.   OTM[ID].append(m, C, ∅)
8. **else if** InstrFW.isReturn(I) **then**
9.   **if not** IgnoreReturn(I) **then**
10.   m ← InstrFW.eaOfReturningMethod(I)
11.   ⟨ID, expectedRetAddr, calledMethods⟩ ← ShadowStack.top()
12.   ShadowStack.pop()
13.   OTM[ID].append(m, R, calledMethods)
14.   **end if**
15. **else**
16.   // Do Nothing
17. **end if**

3.1 Phase 1: Computing Object-Traces

The input to Phase 1 is a stripped binary; the output is a set of object-traces. The goal of Phase 1 is to compute and emit an object-trace for every unique object allocated during the program execution. This ideal is difficult to achieve because Lego works with a stripped binary and a runtime environment that is devoid of object types. We start by presenting a naïve algorithm; we then present a few refinements to obtain the algorithm that is actually used in Lego. In the algorithms that follow, a data structure called the Object-Trace Map (OTM) is used to record object-traces. The OTM has the type: OTM:*ID* → *ObjectTrace*, where *ID* is a unique identifier for a runtime object that Lego has identified.

3.1.1 Base Algorithm

A naïve first cut is to assume that every method in the binary belongs to some class, and to treat the first argument of every method as a valid *this* pointer (address of an allocated object). When Lego encounters a `call` instruction, it obtains the first argument's value, treats it as an *ID*, and creates an object-trace call-record for the called method. It then appends the record to *ID*'s object-trace in the OTM. (It creates a new object-trace if one does not already exist.) The highlighted lines of Alg. 1 show this strawman algorithm.

The algorithms of Phase 1 work in the context of a dynamic binary-instrumentation framework. They use the framework to answer queries (represented as calls to methods of an `InstrFW` object) about static properties of the binary ("Is this instruction a `call`?") and the dynamic execution state. ("What is the value of the first argument to the current call?") In this version of the algorithm, an *ID* is a machine integer. An *ID* for which there is an entry in the

---

Algorithm 2. Algorithm IgnoreReturn

Input: Instruction I
Output: **true** or **false**
 1. actualRetAddress ← InstrFW.`targetRetAddr`(I)
 2. ⟨firstArgValue, expectedRetAddr, calledMethods⟩ ← ShadowStack.top()
 3. **if** actualRetAddr ≠ expectedRetAddr **then**
 4.   **if** ShadowStack.`matchingCallFound`(actualRetAddr) **then**
 5.   ShadowStack.`popUnmatchedFrames`(actualRetAddr)
 6.   **else**
 7.   **return true**
 8.   **end if**
 9. **end if**
10. **return false**

OTM corresponds to the value of the first argument of some method called at runtime.

To enable the strawman algorithm to append an object-trace return-record for a method m, Lego must remember the value of m's first argument to use as *ID* when it encounters m's **return** instruction. To accomplish this, Lego uses a shadow stack. Each shadow-stack frame corresponds to a method m; a stack frame is a record with a single field, *firstArgValue*, which holds the value of m's first argument. At a call to m, Lego pushes the value of m's first argument on the shadow stack. At a return from m, Lego obtains the value at the top of the shadow stack, treats it as the *ID*, creates an object-trace return-record for m, and appends it to *ID*'s object-trace in the OTM. It then pops the shadow stack.

Due to optimizations, or obfuscations that use calls or returns as obfuscated jumps [21], some binaries may have calls with unmatched returns, and returns with unmatched calls. Unmatched calls and returns would make Lego's shadow stack inconsistent with the runtime stack, leading to incorrect object-traces. To address this issue, Lego does call-return matching. The actions taken are those of line 9 of Alg. 1, and Alg. 2.

To record the methods called by a method in an object-trace record, we add another field, *calledMethods*, to each shadow-stack frame. For a frame corresponding to method m, *calledMethods* is the set of methods that are directly called by m (dynamically). The basic algorithm that computes full object-traces along with call-return matching is shown in Alg. 1 (both the highlighted and non-highlighted lines). Note that the *calledMethods* set is empty for call-records.

3.1.2   Blacklisting Methods

Alg. 1 records the necessary details that we want in object-traces. However, because Alg. 1 assumes that all methods receive a valid *this* pointer as the first argument, stand-alone methods and static methods, such as the following would end up in object-traces:

```
void foo();
static void Car::setInventionYear(int a);
```

The algorithm actually used in Lego tries to prevent methods that do not receive a valid *this* pointer as their first argument from appearing in object-traces. Because inferring pointer types at runtime is not easy, when the instrumentation framework provides the first argument's value v for a method m, Lego checks whether v could be interpreted as a pointer to some allocated portion of the global data, heap, or stack. If so, Lego heuristically treats v as a pointer (i.e., it uses v as an object *ID*); if not, Lego *blacklists* m. Once m is blacklisted, it is not added to future object-traces; moreover, if m is present in already computed object-traces, it is removed from them.

The metadata maintained by Lego is only an estimate. For example, Lego keeps track of the stack bounds by querying the instrumentation framework for the value of the stack pointer at calls and returns. If the estimates are wrong, it is possible for a method that receives a valid *this* pointer to be blacklisted. If the estimates are correct, methods that receive a valid *this* pointer are unlikely to ever be blacklisted. In contrast, methods that do not receive a valid *this* pointer are likely to be blacklisted at some point, and thereby prevented from appearing in any object-trace. One final point is worth mentioning: methods that expect a valid pointer as their first argument, but not necessarily a valid *this* pointer, will not be blacklisted (threat 3 to the validity of our approach).

3.1.3   Object-Address Reuse

§3.1.2 presented a version of the algorithm to compute object-traces that, on a best-effort basis, filters out methods that do not receive a valid *this* pointer as the first argument. However, there are several possible ways for the methods of two unrelated classes to appear in the same object-trace. Consider the example shown in Fig. 4. Assuming standard compilation and runtime environments, a and b will be allocated at the same address on the stack (but in two different activation-record instances). As a consequence, printA() and printB() will end up in the same object-trace. Methods of unrelated classes can also end up in the same object-trace when the same heap address is reused for the allocation of different objects of different classes.

Lego detects reuse of the same object address by versioning addresses. When Lego treats the value v of a method's first argument as a valid *this* pointer, Lego associates a version number with v. If v is deallocated (i.e., if it is freed in the heap, or if the method in whose activation record v was allocated returns), Lego increments the version number for v. An *ID* now has the form $\langle Addr, n \rangle$, where *Addr* is the object address and n is the version number.

3.1.4   Spurious Traces

Even with address versioning, it is possible for methods of two unrelated classes to end up in the same object-trace. This grouping of unrelated methods in the same object-trace is caused by the idiosyncrasies of the compiler in reusing stack space for objects in the same activation record (as opposed to reusing stack space

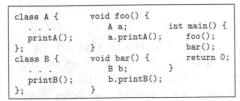

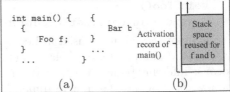

Fig. 4. Example program to illustrate reuse of stack space for objects in different activation records

Fig. 5. (a) Example to illustrate reuse of stack space for objects in the same activation record; (b) a stack snapshot

in different activation records, which §3.1.3 dealt with). We call such traces *spurious traces*. Consider the example program and its stack snapshot shown in Fig. 5. Because f and b are two stack-allocated objects in disjoint scopes, the compiler could use the same stack space for f and b (at different moments during execution). Note that object-address versioning does not solve this issue because an object going out of scope within the same activation record cannot be detected by a visible event (such as a method return or a heap-object deallocation).

To handle this issue, once the object-traces have been created by Alg. 1, Lego computes a set of potential initializers and finalizers by examining each object-trace *ot*. It adds the method of *ot*'s first entry to the set of potential initializers, and the method of *ot*'s last entry to the set of potential finalizers. It then scans each object-trace, and splits a trace at any point at which one of the potential finalizers is immediately followed by one of the potential initializers. This scheme breaks up spurious traces into correct object-traces. Note that if a class does not have an initializer or a finalizer, many methods of that class might end up in the set of potential initializers and the set of potential finalizers. As a consequence, non-spurious object-traces of objects of that class might be split. We examine the effects of splitting and not splitting spurious traces in our experiments (§4.4).

3.2 Phase 2: Computing Class Hierarchies

If the application does not use inheritance, the object-trace of an object will contain only the methods of the object's class. However, if the application uses inheritance, the object-trace of an object will contain methods of the object's class, plus those of the class's ancestors. In this section, we describe how Lego teases apart methods of different classes in a hierarchy. The input to this phase is a set of object-traces from Phase 1. The output is the recovered hierarchy.

3.2.1 Identifying Candidate Classes

A common semantics in object-oriented languages is that a derived class's finalizer cleans up the derived part of an object, and calls the base class's finalizer just before returning (to clean up the base part of the object). This behavior is visible in the object-traces that Lego gathers. Consider the example program and object-trace snippet of a D object shown in Fig. 6. The snippet covers all of the records between and including the last return record and its matching

class A {	class B:	class C:	class D:	~D() C	<u>~A() R</u>
	public A {	public B {	public C {	~C() C	<u>~B() R</u>
~A();	~B();	~C();	~D();	~B() C	<u>~C() R</u>
};	};	};	};	~A() C	<u>~D() R</u>

| (a) | (b) |

Fig. 6. (a) Example program, and (b) object-trace snippet to illustrate an object-trace fingerprint (underlined returns)

Algorithm 3. Algorithm to populate candidate classes

Input: OTM, Trie T
Output: Trie T with candidate classes populated with methods
1. **for** each object-trace ot in OTM **do**
2.   lastRec ← ot.getLastRecord()
3.   m ← lastRec.method
4.   c ← T.getCandidateClassWithFinalizer(m)
5.   c.calledMethods ← lastRec.calledMethods
6.   **for** each object-trace record r in ot **do**
7.   m′ ← r.method
8.   c.methods.insert(m′)
9.   **end for**
10. **end for**

---

call record. (The values of *calledMethods* fields of the object-trace records are omitted.)

We construct a string by concatenating the *method* fields that appear in the return-only suffix of an object-trace. We call such a string the *fingerprint* of the object-trace. We can learn two useful things from the fingerprint.

1. Because the fingerprint contains the methods involved in the cleanup of the object and its inherited parts, a fingerprint's length indicates the number of levels in the inheritance hierarchy from the object's class to the root.
2. The methods in the fingerprint correspond to potential finalizers in the class and its ancestor classes.

Lego computes a fingerprint for every computed object-trace, and creates a trie from the fingerprints (see §2). Every node in the trie corresponds to a *candidate class*, with the node's key constituting the candidate class's finalizer.

3.2.2   Populating Candidate Classes

Every computed object-trace *ot* is linked to the trie node (candidate class) that accepts *ot*'s fingerprint. Every candidate class has a *methods* set and a *called-methods* set. The methods set represents the set of methods in the object-traces linked to the candidate class, and is used in the computation of the final set of methods in each recovered class (see §3.2.3). The called-methods set represents the methods called by the finalizer of the candidate class, and is used to find composition relationships between recovered classes. The algorithm to populate the sets is given as Alg. 3.

Algorithm 4. Algorithm to find composition relationships

Input: Trie T
Output: Set of candidate class pairs $\langle A, B \rangle$ such that A has a member whose class is
     B
1. compositionPairs $= \emptyset$
2. **for** each pair of non-ancestors $\langle c, c' \rangle$ in T **do**
3.   **if** c'.finalizer $\in c$.calledMethods **then**
4.   compositionPairs $\leftarrow$ compositionPairs $\cup \langle c, c' \rangle$
5.   **end if**
6. **end for**

3.2.3 Trie Reorganizations

Some methods may appear both in the methods set of a candidate class C and candidate classes that are descendants of C. To remove this redundancy, Lego processes the candidate classes in the trie from the leaves to the root, and eliminates the redundant methods from the methods sets of candidate classes of descendants.

If two candidate classes C_1 and C_2, neither of which is an ancestor of the other, have a common method m in their methods sets, m is removed from the methods sets of C_1 and C_2, and put in the methods set of their lowest common ancestor. This reorganization handles cases where a class C was never instantiated during the program's execution, but its descendants C_1 and C_2 were, and the descendants had methods inherited from C in their object-traces.

After these two transformations, if a candidate class has no methods in its methods set, its trie node is removed from the trie. The resulting candidate classes and their corresponding methods sets constitute the final set of classes recovered by Lego. The final trie represents the recovered class hierarchy.

3.2.4 Composition Relationships

A composition relationship is said to exist between two classes A and B if A has a member whose class is B. The instance of the member is destroyed when the enclosing object is destroyed. However, unlike inheritance, A and B do not have an ancestor-descendant relationship. The algorithm for determining composition relationships is shown in Alg. 4.

Certain relationships between classes exist only at the source level. At the binary level, they become indistinguishable from other relationships. Lego cannot distinguish between certain composition relationships and inheritance. Consider the example shown in Fig. 7. Because the member g is the first member of a Car object, it might result in the Car object having the same object address as g. Methods of g end up in the object-trace of the Car object, and Lego would recover a hierarchy in which GPS becomes the base class of Car.

Because Lego operates at the binary level, Lego sees multiple inheritance as a combination of single inheritance and composition. Consider the example shown in Fig. 8(a). For the object layout shown in Fig. 8(b), Lego would recover

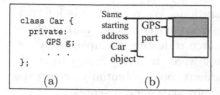

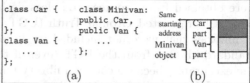

Fig. 7. (a) Example class-definition snippet; (b) a possible object layout to illustrate a composition relationship

Fig. 8. (a) Example class-definition snippet; (b) a possible object layout to illustrate multiple inheritance

a class hierarchy in which `Car` is the base class, `Minivan` is derived from `Car`, and `Minivan` has a member whose class is `Van`.

4 Experiments

This section describes Lego's implementation, the scoring scheme used to score the conformance of Lego's output with ground-truth, and the experiments performed.

4.1 Implementation

Lego uses Pin [20] for dynamic binary instrumentation, and Phase 1 of Lego is written as a "Pintool". Pin can instrument binaries at the instruction, basic-block, routine, and image level. (Lego mainly uses instruction instrumentation for the algorithms of Phase 1; it uses image instrumentation for instrumenting routines for dynamic memory allocation and deallocation.) Pin executes the binary for each given test input, while performing Lego's Phase 1 instrumentation and analysis actions. Object-traces are computed and stored in memory, and emitted at the end of the execution of the program. A post-processing step of Phase 1 reads the object-traces, removes spurious traces, and emits the final set of object-traces. Phase 2 reads the final object-traces and emits four output files:

1. The set of recovered classes: each class is a set of methods; each class is uniquely identified by an *ID*.
2. The recovered class hierarchy: a trie with every node (except the root) having a class's *ID* as its key.
3. The recovered finalizers: a set of methods in which each method is identified as the finalizer of some class recovered by Lego.
4. The recovered composition relationships: a set of class *ID* pairs. Each pair ⟨*A*, *B*⟩ indicates that class *A* has a member whose class is *B*.

4.2 Ground Truth

We used C++ applications to test Lego. To score the outputs created by Lego, we collected ground-truth information for our test suite. For each application, the methods in each class and the set of destructors were obtained from the unstripped, demangled binary. The class hierarchy and composition relationships

were obtained from source-code class declarations. We refer to this information as Unrestricted Ground Truth (UGT). We removed classes and methods
of libraries that were not included in the source code (for example, the C++
standard library) from the UGT (even if they were statically linked to create
the executable) because common library functions could potentially occupy the
bulk of UGT for all our test applications, thereby skewing our scores.

We cannot use UGT to score Lego's outputs because it contains *all* the methods and classes in the program, whereas Lego's outputs contain only the subset
of classes and methods that was *exercised* during Phase 1. We give the UGT
files to Lego as an additional input—used only to prepare material for scoring
purposes—and Lego emits "exercised" versions of the ground-truth files at the
end of Phase 1. We refer to these files as Partially-Restricted Ground Truth
(PRGT). Only methods that were exercised, and only classes that had at least
one of their methods exercised, appear in the PRGT files. (For example, the destructors file now has only the set of exercised destructors, and the composition-
relationships file contains only pairs ⟨A, B⟩ for which methods of A and methods
of B were exercised.)

Lego tries to group only methods that receive a *this* pointer, and it expects
every class in the binary to have a unique finalizer that should be called whenever an instance of the class is deallocated. However, PRGT does not comply
with Lego's goals and restrictions. Some classes in PRGT might contain static
methods, and some might not have a finalizer. (Even if they did, the finalizer
might not have been exercised during Phase 1.) To see how Lego performs in the
ideal case where the ground-truth complies with Lego's goals and restrictions, we
create another set of ground-truth files called Restricted Ground Truth (RGT).
RGT is a subset of PRGT: RGT is PRGT with all static methods removed,
and all classes removed that lack a destructor, or whose destructors were not
exercised during Phase 1. When Lego's results are scored against RGT, we are
artificially suppressing threats 2 and 3 to the validity of our study. Note that
the set of exercised destructors is the same for PRGT and RGT.

Scoring against RGT corresponds to the ideal case, whereas scoring against
PRGT corresponds to the more realistic case that would be encountered in
practice. We report Lego's results for both PRGT and RGT in §4.4.

4.3   Scoring

This section describes the algorithms used to score Lego's outputs against
ground-truth files. In this section, when we say "ground-truth" we mean RGT
or PRGT.

4.3.1   Scoring Finalizers

This output is the easiest to score because the ground-truth and Lego's output
are both sets of methods. We merely compute the precision and recall of the
recovered set of destructors against ground-truth.

4.3.2   Scoring the Class Hierarchy

It is not straightforward to score recovered classes because we are dealing with sets of sets of methods, which are related by inheritance relationships. We do not want to match ground-truth classes against recovered classes because a perfect matching may not always be possible. (For example, due to spurious traces, Lego may coalesce methods of two ground-truth classes into one recovered class.) Thus, as our general approach to scoring, we see if any of the recovered classes match a ground-truth class, both in terms of the set of methods, as well as its position in the hierarchy.

A naïve way to score would be as follows: Compare the set of methods in each ground-truth class against the set of methods in each recovered class to determine the maximum precision and maximum recall obtainable for each ground-truth class. Note that different recovered classes can contribute to maximum precision and maximum recall, respectively, for the ground-truth class. However, this simple approach treats classes as flat sets, and does not account for inheritance relationships between classes. As a consequence, the penalty for a recovered class having an extra method from an *unrelated* class will be the same as having an extra method from an *ancestor* class.

The scoring scheme used below addresses the inheritance issue. For every class in the ground-truth hierarchy and in the recovered hierarchy (except the dummy root nodes), we compute the *extended-methods set*. The extended-methods set of a class is the set union of its methods and the methods of all of its ancestors. For every ground-truth class, we compare the extended-methods set against every recovered class's extended-methods set to determine a maximum precision and maximum recall for the ground-truth class. This scoring scheme incorporates inheritance into scoring, by scoring with respect to paths of the inheritance hierarchy, rather than with respect to nodes. For every unique path in the inheritance hierarchy, it measures how close are the paths in the recovered hierarchy.

Scoring could also be done in the converse sense—comparing the extended-methods set of each recovered class with the extended-methods sets of all ground-truth classes—to determine a maximum precision and maximum recall for each recovered class. However, recovered classes may contain classes and methods not present in ground-truth (for example, library methods). For this reason, we do not score in this converse sense.

We can also view our scoring problem as one of computing an appropriate similarity measure. For this task we make use of the Jaccard Index. The Jaccard Index for a pair of sets A and B is defined as

$$J(A, B) = \frac{|A \cap B|}{|A \cup B|}$$

For every ground-truth class, we compare the extended-methods set against every recovered class's extended-methods set to determine the recovered class with the maximum Jaccard Index for the ground-truth class. In contrast, when computing maximum precision and maximum recall for a ground-truth class, the respective maxima might be associated with the extended-methods set of two independent recovered classes.

To obtain the precision, recall, and Jaccard Index for the entire ground-truth hierarchy, we compute the weighted average of, respectively, the maximum precision, maximum recall, and maximum Jaccard Index computed for each ground-truth class, using the number of methods in each ground-truth class as its weight. We compute a weighted average because we want classes with a larger number of methods to contribute more to the overall score than classes with a smaller number of methods.

4.3.3   Scoring Composition Relationships

For each ground-truth composition pair and each recovered composition pair, we compute the *composed-methods* set. The composed-methods set of a pair of classes is the set union of the methods of the two classes. We compare the composed-methods set of each ground-truth composition pair against the composed-methods sets of recovered composition pairs to determine the maximum precision, maximum recall, and maximum Jaccard Index. (We compute the Jaccard Index for scoring composition pairs as well because two different recovered composition pairs might contribute to maximum precision and maximum recall, respectively, for one ground-truth composition pair.) Finally, we compute the weighted-average precision, recall, and Jaccard Index for all ground-truth composition pairs, using the size of the composed-methods set of each pair as its weight.

4.4   Results

We tested Lego on ten open-source C++ applications obtained from SourceForge [25], the GNU software repository [13] and FreeCode [12]. The characteristics of the applications are listed in Table 2. The applications were compiled using the GNU C++ compiler. The test suite that came with the applications was used to create test inputs for the binary for Phase 1. The experiments were run on a system with a dual-core, 2.66GHz Intel Core i7 processor; however, all the applications in our test suite and all the analysis routines in Lego are single-threaded. The system has 4 GB of memory, and runs Ubuntu 10.04.

Our experiments had three independent variables:
1. Partially-restricted ground-truth (PRGT) vs. restricted ground-truth (RGT): See §4.2.
2. Destructor versions provided (Destr) vs. destructor versions not provided (NoDestr): Recall that some compilers produce up to three versions of a single declared destructor. In one set of experiments, for each destructor D we supplied all compiler-generated versions of D as additional inputs to Phase 1. This information was used to compute object-traces as if each class had a unique destructor in the binary. In another set of experiments, we did not coalesce the different destructor versions, and generated object-traces based on multiple destructors per class.
3. Split spurious traces (SST) vs. do not split spurious traces (NoSST): We described the additional pass to remove spurious traces from the object-traces emitted at the end of Phase 1 in §3.1.4. In one set of experiments

Table 2. Characteristics of our test suite. The applications are sorted by increasing method coverage.

Software	KLOC	No. of classes in program	No. of methods in program	No. of classes with multiple de-structor versions	No. of classes in PRGT	No. of methods in PRGT (Method coverage)	No. of methods in PRGT belonging to classes with un-exercised destructors	No. of classes in RGT	No. of methods in RGT
TinyXML - XML Parser	5	16	302	13	16	236 (78.14%)	19	13	203
Astyle - source-code beautifier	10.5	19	350	14	12	195 (55.71%)	3	10	192
gperf - perfect hash function generator	5.5	25	207	16	20	109 (52.65%)	37	13	72
cppcheck - C/C++ static code analyzer	121	77	1354	46	62	657 (48.52%)	31	54	567
re2c - scanner generator	7.5	36	257	29	32	119 (46.30%)	54	16	57
lshw - hardware lister	18.5	13	161	4	6	61 (37.88%)	2	4	59
smartctl - SMART disk analyzer	50.5	34	192	30	18	36 (18.75%)	16	8	19
pdftohtml - pdf to html converter	52.5	131	1693	126	57	314 (18.54%)	37	50	267
lzip - LZMA compressor	3.2	12	74	0	6	11 (14.86%)	7	2	4
p7zip - file archiver	122	372	2461	216	105	365 (14.83%)	38	74	327

(SST), we executed this pass and used the resulting object-traces for Phase 2. In another set of experiments (NoSST), we did not execute this pass.

The first set of experiments measured the conformance of the *recovered class hierarchy with the ground-truth hierarchy*. Fig. 9 shows the weighted-average precision, recall, and Jaccard Index obtained for different combinations of independent variables. The applications in the figure are sorted by increasing method coverage.

The aggregate precision, aggregate recall, and aggregate Jaccard Index reported for the entire test suite is the weighted average of the reported numbers, with the number of methods in the corresponding ground-truth as the weight. (The number of methods in PRGT is used as the weight in computing PRGT aggregates, and the number of methods in RGT is used as the weight in computing RGT aggregates.) One observation is that there is only a slight variation in precision, recall, and Jaccard Index in the Destr vs. NoDestr case. This tells us that the destructor versions are not essential inputs to recover accurate class hierarchies. Also, we can see that there is very little difference between precision, recall, and Jaccard Index numbers for the RGT vs. PRGT case. This tells us that even if we do not know if the binary came from clean object-oriented source-code, Lego's output can generally be trusted.

Another observation is that for some applications like TinyXML, cppcheck, etc., comparing against PRGT causes an increase in precision numbers compared to RGT (which seems counter-intuitive). This increase in precision is because of the fact that the recovered classes corresponding to the extra classes present in PRGT (and absent in RGT) get fragmented, with each fragment containing very

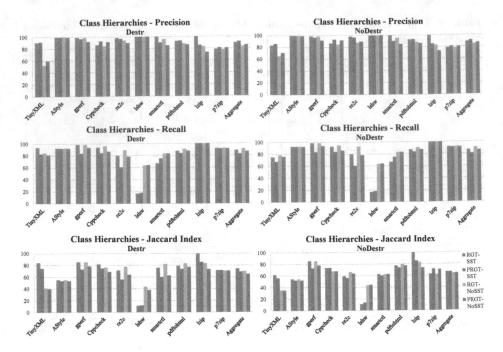

Fig. 9. Weighted-average precision, recall, and Jaccard Index for recovered class hierarchies

few methods of the class and they are not mixed with other recovered classes' methods. Because we compute weighted-average precision, this fragmentation causes an increase over the RGT weighted-average precision. However, if the methods of the extra classes get mixed with other recovered classes' methods, we see the intuitive decrease in weighted-average precision for PRGT (cf. lzip).

With SST, the precision increases or stays the same compared with NoSST. The increase is more pronounced if the source-code heavily uses code blocks within the same method—for example, TinyXML—à la Fig. 9. The recall for the SST case is better only if destructor versions were provided and if the source-code heavily uses code blocks (TinyXML). If, say, by inspecting and testing the binary, we suspect that code blocks are used, we could ask Lego to run the split-spurious-traces pass before recovering classes.

The second set of experiments measured the conformance of *recovered composition relationships with ground-truth composition relationships*. Lego detects a composition relationship by looking for finalizers called from the enclosing class's finalizer. It makes the most sense to use only RGT as the ground truth while scoring recovered composition relationships because all classes in the composition pairs of RGT have their destructors exercised during Phase 1. (All classes in PRGT may not satisfy this property.) Fig. 10 shows the results. Note that applications that do not have any composition relationships between classes in RGT are not shown in the figure. One of the applications (TinyXML) had a

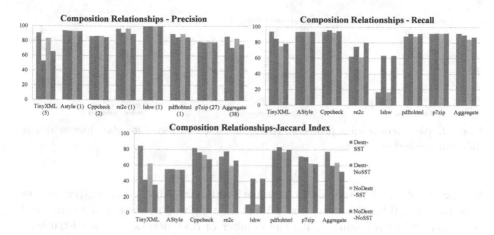

Fig. 10. Weighted-average precision, recall, and Jaccard Index for recovered composition relationships

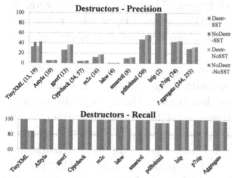

Fig. 11. Precision and recall for recovered destructors

Table 3. Time measurements (seconds). SD indicates slowdown.

Software	pin NULL	pinINSTR (SD)	I/O	Phase 2
tinyxml	3.62	30.54 (8.43x)	7.24	0.49
astyle	6.61	25.04 (3.78x)	2.74	0.88
gperf	2.05	6.51 (3.17x)	0.66	0.085
cppcheck	17.41	60.08 (3.45x)	5.14	1.04
re2c	3.31	7.44 (2.24x)	0.05	0.02
lshw	4.55	20.63 (4.53x)	0.46	0.33
smartctl	5.35	80.58 (15.06x)	1.78	0.15
pdftohtml	4.26	60.60 (14.22x)	15.22	6.40
p7zip	6.88	54.66 (7.94x)	9.73	0.04
lzip	1.47	3.70 (2.51x)	0.02	0.03

composition pair in RGT, in which the enclosing class's first member was a class. Because Lego sees this composition relationship as single inheritance (as described in §3.2.4), we removed this pair from the set of composition relationships (and added it as single inheritance in the RGT class hierarchy). The number of composition relationships between classes for each application is listed below its label in the precision graph. The aggregate precision, aggregate recall, and aggregate Jaccard Index for the entire test suite is the weighted average of the computed precision, recall, and Jaccard Index values with the sum of the sizes of all the composed-methods sets (§4.3.3) of an application as its weight.

The third set of experiments measured the conformance of *recovered destructors with ground-truth destructors*. Fig. 11 shows the results. Recall that RGT and PRGT have the same set of destructors (§4.2), so we report the results only for the RGT case. The number of destructors in each application is below its label in the precision graph. (Applications with different numbers of destructors

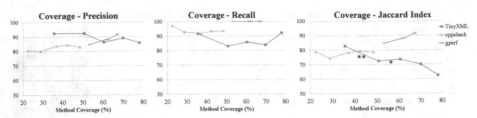

Fig. 12. Weighted-average precision, recall, and Jaccard Index for class hierarchies at different method coverages

for the Destr and NoDestr cases have both numbers listed.) The aggregate precision and recall for the entire test suite is the weighted average of the computed precision and recall values, with the number of destructors in ground-truth as the weight for each application. Lego identifies all of the destructors in most cases. In TinyXML, NoSST fails to expose a few destructors that are trapped in the middle of spurious object-traces. In pdftohtml, a few destructors get blacklisted by Lego and never end up in object-traces. Although Lego succeeds in identifying most of the destructors (high recall), the overall precision is low because destructors of classes in libraries—which are not present in the ground truth—are also reported by Lego.

Table 3 shows the timing measurements for our test suite. pinNULL represents the execution time of the application on pin, with Lego's analysis routines commented out. pinINSTR represents the execution time of the application on pin, with Lego's analysis routines performing dynamic analysis. The instrumentation and analysis overhead can be seen in the slowdown reported for each application. I/O represents the time taken to do file I/O in Phase 1 (reading ground-truth and destructor versions, writing object-traces, and exercised ground truth). pinIN-STR + I/O represents the total running time of Phase 1 of Lego. Phase 2 reports the wall-clock time for Phase 2.

The fourth set of experiments aimed to study the *impact of code coverage* on the scoring metrics. For three applications (tinyxml, gperf, and cppcheck) we aggregated the object-traces from 5 test runs: just run 1; 1 and 2; 1 through 3; 1 through 4; and 1 through 5, resulting in five different amounts of method coverage for each application, and fed those object traces to Phase 2 of Lego. The combination of independent variables used in this set of experiments was Destr-RGT-NoSST. The results are shown in Fig. 12. We did not observe any global trends for precision, recall, or Jaccard Index with respect to increasing coverage. We observed that any of the following might happen when there is additional method coverage in Phase 1:

1. The additional coverage covers methods of a new class, thereby boosting the overall score for the test suite (see plots for gperf).
2. The additional coverage covers inherited methods of a class that is a sibling of a class already explored by Lego. This results in common inherited methods being hoisted to the parent class (see §3.2.3), thereby boosting similarity (see the line segment marked "*" in the Jaccard Index plot for TinyXML).

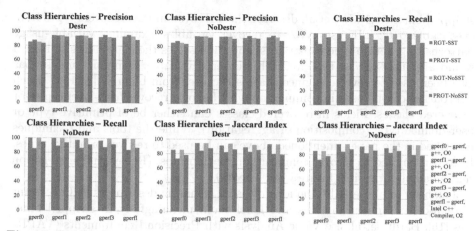

Fig. 13. Weighted-average precision, recall, and Jaccard Index for recovered class hierarchies measured for binaries generated from different compilers and at different optimization levels

3. The additional coverage causes Lego to encounter an object of a class A, but not objects of A's ancestors or siblings. This results in methods of A's ancestors ending up in the class recovered for A, thereby lowering the the similarity (see the line segment marked "**" in the Jaccard Index plot for TinyXML).

We also varied the compiler and optimization levels that were used to generate the binaries used in our experiments, and tested Lego on the newly generated binaries. Fig. 13 summarizes the results. We chose gperf as a representative application and compiled it using the Intel C++ compiler. We also compiled it using the GNU C++ compiler with different optimization levels. (We used the optimization flags -O0, -O1, -O2, and -O3.) The PRGT of the binaries generated using the -O1, -O2, and -O3 flags had 82 fewer methods than that of the binary generated using the -O0 flag. Methods being optimized away led to recovered classes that had fewer inherited base-class methods (which causes the slight increase in precision that one sees by comparing the gperf0 case to the other cases in Fig. 13).

To test Lego on binaries generated from a different object-oriented language, we collected applications written in the D programming language [7]. Lego did poorly in this experiment because D is garbage-collected, and thus many classes in the collected applications lacked a destructor. This failed experiment illustrates threat 2 to the validity of our approach, listed in §2.

5   Related Work

Reverse-Engineering Low-Level Software Artifacts from Binaries.
Many prior works have explored the recovery of lower-level artifacts from binaries. Balakrishnan and Reps use a conjunction of Value Set Analysis (VSA) and Aggregate Structure Identification (ASI) to recover variable-like entities from

stripped binaries [1]. Lee et al. describe the TIE system that recovers types from executables [16]. TIE uses VSA to recover variables, examines variable-usage patterns to generate type constraints, and then solves the constraints to infer a sound and most-precise type for each recovered variable. Dynamic analysis has also been used to reverse engineer data structures from binaries [24,18,6]. Such approaches can be used in conjunction with Lego to recover high-level types for recovered classes. Fields in recovered classes can either be of primitive type or user-defined type (composition or aggregation). While the tools and techniques described in the papers mentioned above can be used to recover primitive types, Lego can be used to recover composition relationships. (Recovering aggregation relationships is possible future work – see §6.)

Jacobson et al. describe the idea of using semantic descriptors to fingerprint system-call wrapper functions and label them meaningfully in stripped binaries [15]. Bardin et al. use Value Analysis with Precision Requirements (VAPR) for recovering a Control Flow Graph (CFG) from an unstructured program [3]. Schwartz et. al. describe the semantics-preserving structural-analysis algorithm used in Phoenix, their x86-to-C decompiler [22], to recover control structures. Fokin et al. describe techniques for decompilation of binaries generated from C++ [11]. During decompilation, they use run-time-type information (RTTI) and virtual function tables in conjunction with several analyses to recover polymorphic parts (virtual methods) of class hierarchies. The artifacts recovered by Lego complement those recovered by the aforementioned tools and techniques.

Recovering Protocol/File Formats from Executables. Prior works have also explored recovering higher-level abstractions from binaries. Cho et al. use concolic execution in conjunction with the L* learning algorithm to construct and refine the protocol state machine from executables that implement protocols [5]. Lim et al. describe recovering output file formats from x86 binaries using Hierarchical Finite State Machines (HFSMs) along with information from VSA and ASI [17]. Driscoll et al. use Finite Automata (FA) and Visibly Pushdown Automata (VPA) to infer I/O format of programs and check conformance of producer and consumer programs [9].

Modularizing Legacy Code. Formal Concept Analysis (FCA) has been extensively used for software-reengineering tasks [26,19,23]. Siff and Reps used FCA to modularize C code [23]. They used types and def/use information as attributes in a context relation to create a concept lattice, which was partitioned to obtain a set of concepts. Each concept was a maximal group of C functions that acted as a module. Bojic and Velasevic describe using dynamic analysis in conjunction with FCA to recover a high-level design for legacy object-oriented systems [4]. The high-level goals of Lego and these works are the same—namely, to recover a modular structure. However, Lego works at the binary level, where types are either absent or difficult to precisely obtain.

6   Conclusion and Future Work

In this paper, we described Lego, a tool that uses dynamic analysis to recover class hierarchies and composition relationships from stripped object-oriented binaries. We presented the algorithms used in Lego, and evaluated it on ten open-source C++ software applications by comparing the class hierarchies recovered by Lego with ground truth obtained from source code. Our experiments show that the class hierarchies recovered by Lego have a high degree of agreement—measured in terms of precision and recall—with the hierarchy defined in the source code. On average, the precision is 88% and the recall is 86.7%.

One possible direction for future work would be to use concolic execution to generate more inputs to achieve better coverage. For the Lego context, a concolic-execution engine should aim to maximize method coverage, not merely path coverage. A second direction would be to see how run-time-type information and virtual-function-table information could be used to improve the class hierarchy produced by Lego. When such information is available, it allows a portion of the source-code class hierarchy to be recovered exactly. (The hierarchy is incomplete because it contains only the program's virtual functions.) A third direction would be to use Lego's object-traces and recovered classes to infer temporal invariants on method-call order.

Another direction for future work is to use the information maintained by Lego about objects allocated during program execution to find aggregation relationships between inferred classes.

References

1. Balakrishnan, G., Reps, T.: DIVINE: DIscovering Variables IN Executables. In: VMCAI 2007. LNCS, vol. 4349, pp. 1–28. Springer, Heidelberg (2007)
2. Balakrishnan, G., Reps, T.: WYSINWYX: What You See Is Not What You eXecute. TOPLAS 32(6) (2010)
3. Bardin, S., Herrmann, P., Védrine, F.: Refinement-based CFG reconstruction from unstructured programs. In: Jhala, R., Schmidt, D. (eds.) VMCAI 2011. LNCS, vol. 6538, pp. 54–69. Springer, Heidelberg (2011)
4. Bojic, D., Velasevic, D.: A Use-case driven method of architecture recovery for program understanding and reuse reengineering. In: CSMR (2000)
5. Cho, C.Y., Babić, D., Poosankam, P., Chen, K.Z., Wu, E.X., Song, D.: MACE: Model inference assisted concolic exploration for protocol and vulnerability discovery. In: USENIX Sec. Symp. (2011)
6. Cozzie, A., Stratton, F., Xue, H., King, S.T.: Digging for data structures. In: OSDI (2008)
7. D Programming Language, http://dlang.org
8. DMCA §1201. Circumvention of Copyright Protection Systems, www.copyright.gov/title17/92chap12.html#1201
9. Driscoll, E., Burton, A., Reps, T.: Checking compatibility of a producer and a consumer. In: FSE (2011)
10. ElWazeer, K., Anand, K., Kotha, A., Smithson, M., Barua, R.: Scalable variable and data type detection in a binary rewriter. In: PLDI (2013)
11. Fokin, A., Derevenetc, E., Chernov, A., Troshina, K.: SmartDec: Approaching C++ decompilation. In: WCRE (2011)
12. Freecode, www.freecode.com
13. GNU Software Repository, www.gnu.org/software/software.html

14. Itanium C++ ABI, refspecs.linux-foundation.org/cxxabi-1.83.html
15. Jacobson, E.R., Rosenblum, N., Miller, B.P.: Labeling library functions in stripped binaries. In: PASTE (2011)
16. Lee, J., Avgerinos, T., Brumley, D.: TIE: Principled reverse engineering of types in binary programs. In: NDSS (2011)
17. Lim, J., Reps, T., Liblit, B.: Extracting output formats from executables. In: WCRE (2006)
18. Lin, Z., Zhang, X., Xu, D.: Automatic reverse engineering of data structures from binary execution. In: NDSS (2010)
19. Lindig, C., Snelting, G.: Assessing modular structure of legacy code based on mathematical concept analysis. In: ICSE (1997)
20. Luk, C.-K., Cohn, R., Muth, R., Patil, H., Klauser, A., Lowney, G., Wallace, S., Reddi, V.J., Hazelwood, K.: Pin: Building customized program analysis tools with dynamic instrumentation. In: PLDI (2005)
21. Roundy, K.A., Miller, B.P.: Binary-code obfuscations in prevalent packer tools. ACM Computing Surveys 46(1) (2013)
22. Schwartz, E.J., Lee, J., Woo, M., Brumley, D.: Native x86 decompilation using semantics-preserving structural analysis and iterative control-flow structuring. In: USENIX Sec. Symp. (2013)
23. Siff, M., Reps, T.: Identifying modules via concept analysis. TSE 25(6) (1999)
24. Slowinska, A., Stancescu, T., Bos, H.: Howard: A Dynamic excavator for reverse engineering data structures. In: NDSS (2011)
25. SourceForge, http://sourceforge.net
26. Tonella, P.: Concept analysis for module restructuring. TSE 27(4) (2001)

Liveness-Based Garbage Collection

Rahul Asati[1], Amitabha Sanyal[1], Amey Karkare[2], and Alan Mycroft[3]

[1] IIT Bombay, Mumbai 400076, India
{rahulasati,as}@cse.iitb.ac.in,
[2] IIT Kanpur, Kanpur 208016, India
karkare@cse.iitk.ac.in,
[3] Computer Laboratory, University of Cambridge, CB3 0FD, UK
alan.mycroft@cl.cam.ac.uk

Abstract. Current garbage collectors leave much heap-allocated data uncollected because they preserve data *reachable* from a root set. However, only *live* data—a subset of reachable data—need be preserved.

Using a first-order functional language we formulate a context-sensitive liveness analysis for structured data and prove it correct. We then use a 0-CFA-like conservative approximation to annotate each allocation and function-call program point with a finite-state automaton—which the garbage collector inspects to curtail reachability during marking. As a result, fewer objects are marked (albeit with a more expensive marker) and then preserved (e.g. by a copy phase).

Experiments confirm the expected performance benefits—increase in garbage reclaimed and a consequent decrease in the number of collections, a decrease in the memory size required to run programs, and reduced overall garbage collection time for a majority of programs.

1 Introduction

Most modern programming languages support dynamic allocation of heap data. Static analysis of heap data is much harder than analysis of static and stack data. Garbage collectors, for example, conservatively approximate the liveness of heap objects by their reachability from a set of memory locations called the *root set*. Consequently, many objects that are reachable but not live remain uncollected, causing a larger-than-necessary memory demand. This is confirmed by empirical studies on Haskell [1], Scheme [2] and Java [3] programs.

Here we consider a first-order pure functional language and propose a liveness analysis which annotates various program points with a description of variables and fields whose object references may be dereferenced in the future. The garbage collector then only marks objects pointed to by live references and leaves other, merely reachable, objects to be reclaimed. (Although not strictly necessary, a collector would normally *nullify* dead variables and fields rather than leaving dangling references.) Since there are fewer live objects than reachable objects, more memory is reclaimed. Additionally, since the collector traverses a smaller portion of the heap, the time spent for each collection is also smaller. The work is presented in the context of a stop-the-world non-incremental garbage collector

A. Cohen (Ed.): CC 2014, LNCS 8409, pp. 85–106, 2014.

(mark-and-sweep, compacting or copying) for which we also show a monotonicity result: that our technique can never cause more garbage collections to occur in spite of changing the rather unpredictable execution points at which collections occur. We anticipate that our technique is applicable to more modern collectors (generational, concurrent, parallel), but leave such extensions to future work.

We first define a *fully context-sensitive* (in the sense that its results are unaffected by function inlining) liveness analysis and prove it correct. However, fully context-sensitive methods often do not scale, and this analysis would also require us to determine, at run-time, the internal liveness of a function body at each call. Hence, similarly to the 0-CFA approach, we determine a context-independent *summary* of liveness for each function which safely approximates the context-dependence of all possible calls [4,5,6]. (Note that an intraprocedural context-insensitive method which assumes no information about function callers would be too imprecise for our needs.) In essence our approach sets up interprocedural data-flow equations for the liveness summaries of functions and shows how these can be solved symbolically as context-free grammars (CFGs). We can then determine a CFG for each program point; these are then safely approximated with finite-state automata which are encoded as tables for each program point. For garbage collection purposes only automata corresponding to *GC points* need to be stored. GC points are program points associated with a call to a user function or to **cons**—see Section 4.

We previously proposed an intraprocedural method for heap liveness analysis for a Java-like language [7] which statically inserted statements nullifying dead references to improve garbage collection; by contrast nullification here occurs dynamically (which can work better with aliasing) when the garbage collector acts on liveness annotations to avoid traversing dead references. A workshop paper [8] outlined the basic 0-CFA-style-summary interprocedural approach to functional-program liveness analysis. The current paper adds the context-sensitive analysis and better formalisation along with experimental results.

Motivating Example. Figure 1(a) shows an example program. The label π of an expression e denotes a program point. During execution of the program, it represents the instant of time just before the evaluation of e. We view the heap as a graph. Nodes in the heap, also called (**cons**) *cells* contain **car** and **cdr** *fields* containing values. Edges in the graph are *references* and emanate from *variables* or fields. Variable and field values may also be atomic values (**nil**, integers etc.) While it is convenient to box these in diagrams, our presented analysis treats them as non-heap values.

Figure 1(b) shows the heap at π. The edges shown by thick continuous arrows are those which are made live by the program. In addition, assuming that the value of any reachable part of the program result may be explored or printed, the edges marked by thick dashed arrows are also live. A cell is marked and preserved during garbage collection, only if it is reachable from the root set through a path of live edges. All other cells can be reclaimed. We model the liveness properties of the heap as automata and pass these automata to the garbage collector. Thus

```
(define (append l1 l2)
  (if (null? l1) l2
    (cons (car l1)
          (append (cdr l1) l2))))

(let z ←(cons (cons 4 (cons 5 nil))
              (cons 6 nil)) in
 (let y ← (cons 3 nil) in
  (let w ← (append y z) in
   π:(car (cdr w)))))
```

(a) Example program.

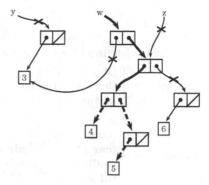

(b) Memory graph at π. Thick edges denote live links. Traversal stops during garbage collection at edges marked ✕ .

Fig. 1. Example Program and its Memory Graph

if a garbage collection happens at π with the heap shown in Figure 1(b), only the cells w and (**cdr** w), along with (**car** (**cdr** w)) and all cells reachable from it, will be marked and preserved.

Organisation of the Paper. Section 2 gives the syntax and semantics of the language used to illustrate our analysis along with basic concepts and notations. Liveness analysis is described in Section 3 followed by a sketch of a correctness proof relative to a non-standard semantics. Section 4 shows how to encode liveness as finite-state automata. Section 5 reports experimental results and Section 6 proves that a liveness-based collector can never do more garbage collections than a reachability-based collector.

2   The Target Language—Syntax and Semantics

We let x, y, z range over variables, f over user-functions and p over primitive functions (**cons**, + etc.). The syntax of our language is shown in Figure 2; it has eager semantics and restricts programs to be in Administrative Normal Form (ANF) [9] where all actual parameters to functions are variables. This restriction does not affect expressibility (and indeed we feel free to ignore it in examples when inessential), but simplifies the analysis formulation. Additionally, as in the three-address instruction form familiar from compiler texts, it forces each temporary to be named and function calls to be serialised (necessary to get an unambiguous definition of liveness). We further require that each variable in a program is distinct, so that no scope shadowing occurs—this simplifies proofs of soundness. In this formulation expressions: either perform a test (**if**), make a computation step (**let**) or return (**return**). The **return** keyword is logically redundant, but we find it clarifies the semantics and analysis.

$$
\begin{aligned}
p \in Prog &::= d_1 \ldots d_n \; e_{\mathbf{main}} & &- \; program \\
d \in Fdef &::= (\mathbf{define} \; (f \; x_1 \; \ldots \; x_n) \; e) & &- \; function \; definition
\end{aligned}
$$

$$
e \in Expr ::= \begin{cases}
(\mathbf{if} \; x \; e_1 \; e_2) & - \; conditional \\
(\mathbf{let} \; x \leftarrow s \; \mathbf{in} \; e) & - \; let \; binding \\
(\mathbf{return} \; x) & - \; return \; from \; function
\end{cases}
$$

$$
s \in Stmt ::= \begin{cases}
k & - \; constant \; (numeric \; or \; \mathbf{nil}) \\
(\mathbf{cons} \; x_1 \; x_2) & - \; constructor \\
(\mathbf{car} \; x) \qquad (\mathbf{cdr} \; x) & - \; selectors \\
(\mathbf{null?} \; x) \qquad (+ \; x_1 \; x_2) & - \; tester \; and \; generic \; arithmetic \\
(\mathbf{id} \; x) & - \; identity \; function \; (for \; inlining) \\
(f \; x_1 \; \ldots \; x_n) & - \; function \; application
\end{cases}
$$

Fig. 2. The syntax of our language

The body of the program is the expression denoted by $e_{\mathbf{main}}$; for analysis purposes it is convenient to regard $e_{\mathbf{main}}$ as part of a function definition (**define** (main) $e_{\mathbf{main}}$) as in C. We write $\pi : e$ to associate the label π (not part of the language syntax) with the program point just before expression e.

In spite of the ANF restrictions it is still possible to inline non-recursive functions (a fact we use to prove the safety of liveness analysis). A user-function call (**let** $x \leftarrow (f \, y_1 \; \ldots \; y_n)$ **in** e) to a function defined (after renaming its formals and locals to be disjoint from existing variables) by (**define** $(f \; z_1 \; \ldots \; z_n) \; e_f$) is replaced by a sequence of **let**s of the form $z_i \leftarrow (\mathbf{id} \; y_i)$ followed by the body e_f but with its (**return** w) expressions replaced by (**let** $x \leftarrow (\mathbf{id} \; w)$ **in** e). (We prefer to use **id** as a form of no-op function rather than introducing the form (**let** $x \leftarrow w$ **in** e) where the $Stmt$ part of **let** is a simple variable.)

Semantics. We now give an operational semantics for our language. Later, a refinement of the operational semantics, which we call minefield semantics, will serve to prove liveness analysis correct. We give a small-step semantics because, unlike big-step semantics, correctness for non-terminating programs does not need special treatment. We start with the domains used by the semantics:

$$
\begin{aligned}
v : Val &= \mathbb{N} + \{\mathbf{nil}\} + Loc & &- \text{Values} \\
\rho : Env &= Var \rightarrow Val & &- \text{Environment} \\
H : Heap &= Loc \rightarrow (Val \times Val) & &- \text{Heap}
\end{aligned}
$$

Here Loc is a countable set of locations which hold **cons** cells. A value is either a number, the empty list **nil**, or a location ℓ. Our liveness analysis does not track numeric values, and thus is neutral as to whether these are boxed or represented as immediates. An environment is a finite mapping from variables to values, and a heap a finite mapping from locations to pairs of values. Finally, S is a stack (using • for push and [] for empty stack) of frames of unfinished function calls.

$$\frac{}{\rho, H, k \rightsquigarrow H, k} \text{ (ORD-CONST)} \qquad \frac{\ell \notin \text{dom}(H) \text{ is a fresh location}}{\rho, H, (\textbf{cons } x \ y) \rightsquigarrow H[\ell \mapsto (\rho(x), \rho(y))], \ell} \text{ (ORD-CONS)}$$

$$\frac{H(\rho(x)) = (v_1, v_2)}{\rho, H, (\textbf{car } x) \rightsquigarrow H, v_1} \text{ (ORD-CAR)} \qquad \frac{H(\rho(x)) = (v_1, v_2)}{\rho, H, (\textbf{cdr } x) \rightsquigarrow H, v_2} \text{ (ORD-CDR)}$$

$$\frac{}{\rho, H, (\textbf{id } x) \rightsquigarrow H, \rho(x)} \text{ (ORD-ID)} \qquad \frac{\rho(x) \in \mathbb{N} \qquad \rho(y) \in \mathbb{N}}{\rho, H, (+ \ x \ y) \rightsquigarrow H, \rho(x) + \rho(y)} \text{ (ORD-PRIM)}$$

$$\frac{\rho(x) \neq \textbf{nil}}{\rho, H, (\textbf{null? } x) \rightsquigarrow H, 0} \qquad \frac{\rho(x) = \textbf{nil}}{\rho, H, (\textbf{null? } x) \rightsquigarrow H, 1} \text{ (ORD-NULL)}$$

$$\frac{\rho(x) \in \mathbb{N} \setminus \{0\}}{\rho, S, H, (\textbf{if } x \ e_1 \ e_2) \longrightarrow \rho, S, H, e_1} \qquad \frac{\rho(x) = 0}{\rho, S, H, (\textbf{if } x \ e_1 \ e_2) \longrightarrow \rho, S, H, e_2} \text{ (ORD-IF)}$$

$$\frac{\rho, H, s \rightsquigarrow H', v \qquad s \text{ is not } (f \ y_1 \dots y_n)}{\rho, S, H, (\textbf{let } x \leftarrow s \textbf{ in } e) \longrightarrow \rho[x \mapsto v], S, H', e} \text{ (ORD-LET-NONFN)}$$

$$\frac{s \text{ is } (f \ y_1 \dots y_n) \qquad f \text{ defined as } (\textbf{define } (f \ z_1 \ \dots \ z_n) \ e_f)}{\rho, S, H, (\textbf{let } x \leftarrow s \textbf{ in } e) \longrightarrow [\vec{z} \mapsto \rho(\vec{y})], (\rho, x, e) \bullet S, \ H, e_f} \text{ (ORD-LET-FNCALL)}$$

$$\frac{}{\rho, (\rho', x', e') \bullet S, H, (\textbf{return } x) \longrightarrow \rho'[x' \mapsto \rho(x)], S, H, e'} \text{ (ORD-RETURN)}$$

Fig. 3. The small-step operational semantics

A frame is a triple (e, x, ρ) representing the call site $(\textbf{let } x \leftarrow (f \ y_1 \dots y_n) \textbf{ in } e)$ being evaluated in environment ρ. Frames can also be viewed as continuations, in this view the (ORD-RETURN) rule in the small-step operational semantics (Figure 3) invokes them.

The semantics of statements s are given by the judgement form $\rho, H, s \rightsquigarrow H', v$ and those for expressions e by the form $\rho, S, H, e \rightarrow \rho', S', H', e'$. The start state is $(\{\}, [], \{\}, e_{\textbf{main}})$ and the program terminates successfully with result value $\rho(x)$ on reaching the halt state $(\rho, [], H, (\textbf{return } x))$

Notation: we write $\rho[x \mapsto v]$ for the environment which is as ρ but has value v at x. We also write $[\vec{x} \mapsto \vec{v}]$ which respectively has values $v_1, \dots, v_n$ at $x_1, \dots, x_n$ and write $[\vec{x} \mapsto \rho(\vec{y})]$ when $v_1, \dots, v_n$ are $\rho(y_1), \dots, \rho(y_n)$.

Stuck states. Note that certain forms of e do not reduce with $\rightarrow$ (perhaps because $\rightsquigarrow$ could not reduce a contained s). Some of these we eliminate syntactically, e.g. ensuring all variables and functions are defined and are called with the correct number of parameters. Others include $(\textbf{cdr nil}), (\textbf{car } 3), (+ \textbf{ nil } 4)$ and $(\textbf{if nil } e_1 \ e_2)$. All but the first can be eliminated with a static type system but, treating our program as dynamically typed, we regard all these as stuck states.

3   Liveness

In classical liveness analysis a variable is either 'live' (its value may be used in future computation) or 'dead' (definitely not used). Semantically, a variable is dead at a given program point if arbitrary changes to its value have no effect on the computation. Later we will use $\bot$ to represent a value which 'explodes' when it is used in a computation; dead variables can safely have their value replaced with $\bot$. For heap-allocated data we need a richer model of liveness in that both variables and fields of **cons** cells may be dead or live. Using $\mathbf{0}, \mathbf{1}$ to represent access using **car**, **cdr** respectively, liveness of the structure reachable from a variable is a set of *access paths* which we represent as a subset of $\{\mathbf{0}, \mathbf{1}\}^*$, and use conventional grammar notation. Thus the liveness of x being $\{\mathbf{10}, \mathbf{110}\}$ means that future computation can only refer to the second and third members of x considered as a list. Semantically, access paths are prefix-closed, as accessing a field requires accessing all the paths from the variable to the field, and hence the above liveness is properly written $\{\epsilon, \mathbf{1}, \mathbf{10}, \mathbf{11}, \mathbf{110}\}$. The classical notions of a scalar variable being live or dead correspond to $\{\epsilon\}$ and $\{\}$.

The overall liveness (also written *liveness environment* for emphasis) at a program point is conceptually a mapping from variables to subsets of $\{\mathbf{0}, \mathbf{1}\}^*$, but we often abuse notation, for example writing $\{x.\mathbf{01}, x.\mathbf{1}, y.\epsilon\}$ instead of the map $[x \mapsto \{\epsilon, \mathbf{0}, \mathbf{01}, \mathbf{1}\}, y \mapsto \{\epsilon\}, z \mapsto \{\}]$. Analogously to classical liveness, the liveness at program point π in $\pi : e$ is the liveness just before executing e.

A complementary notion to liveness is *demand*. The demand for expression e is again an access path—that subset of $\{\mathbf{0}, \mathbf{1}\}^*$ which the context of e may explore of e's result. So, for example given a demand σ and the expression $\pi : (\mathbf{return}\ x)$, the liveness at π is exactly $x.\sigma$. The classical analogy of this is in *strong liveness*, where an assignment node $n : x := y + z$ causes y and z to be live on entry to n if (and only if) x is live at exit of n—the liveness of x at exit from n becomes the demand on $y + z$. Note that, for an operation like division which may raise an exception, the assignment $n : x := y/z$ makes y and z live regardless of the liveness of x.

We use σ to range over demands, α to range over access paths and L to range over liveness environments. The notation $\sigma_1\sigma_2$ denotes the set $\{\alpha_1\alpha_2 \mid \alpha_1 \in \sigma_1, \alpha_2 \in \sigma_2\}$. Often we shall abuse notation to juxtapose an edge label and a set of access paths: $\mathbf{0}\sigma$ is a shorthand for $\{\mathbf{0}\}\sigma$. Finally, we use LF to range over *demand transformers*; given user function f, LF_f transforms demands on a call to f into demands on its formal parameters: if f is defined by $(\mathbf{define}\ (f\ x_1\ \dots\ x_n)\ e_f)$ and called with demand σ, then $\mathsf{LF}_f^i(\sigma)$ is the liveness of x_i at e_f.

Note that liveness refers to variables and fields, and not to **cons** cells (i.e. to edges in the memory graph, not to locations themselves). Hence liveness of $\{x.\epsilon, x.\mathbf{0}\}$ means that future computation may refer to the value ℓ of variable x, and also to the **car** field of location ℓ. In the absence of other pointers to heap location ℓ, we are certain that the **cdr** field of ℓ will not be referenced and may hence be corrupted arbitrarily. Note therefore, that while ℓ cannot be garbage collected, any location ℓ' stored in the **cdr** field of ℓ would be garbage (again provided there are no other aliases to ℓ or ℓ').

3.1   Liveness Analysis

First recall the classical formulation of liveness (as sets of simple variables) on three-address instructions, $live_{in}(I) = live_{out}(I) \setminus def(I) \cup ref(I)$, and then note that *strong liveness* needs, when I is the instruction $z := x + y$, that $ref(I)$ be refined to $\{x, y\}$ if $z \in live_{out}(I)$ and $\{\}$ otherwise.

Our liveness analysis formulated in Figure 4 is analogous. Firstly, the function *ref*, when given a statement s, returns the liveness *generated* by s. Because we generalise *strong* liveness, *ref* needs a second parameter, specifying the demand σ on the result of s, to determine which access paths of its free variables are made live. The cases for (**id** x) and (+ x y) exemplify this. A demand of σ on (**car** x) is transformed to the demand 0σ on x. In addition, **car** always dereferences its argument (even if its result is never used). This generates the liveness $\{x.\epsilon\} \cup x.0\sigma$ (note σ may be $\{\}$). In the opposite sense, the demand of 0σ on (**cons** x y) is transformed to the demand σ on x. Note that **cons** does not, by itself, dereference its arguments. Thirdly, for the case of a user-function call, a third parameter LF to *ref* expresses how the demand σ on the result is transformed into demands on its parameters. Constants generate no liveness.

The function $\mathcal{L}$ now gives the (total) liveness of an expression e. The cases **return** and **if** are straightforward, but note the liveness $x.\epsilon$ generated by the latter. The case (**let** $z \leftarrow s$ **in** e') resembles a three-address instruction: the liveness of e is given by taking the liveness, L, of e', killing any liveness of z and adding any liveness generated by s. The main subtlety is how the liveness of z in L is converted to a demand $L(z)$ to be placed on s via $ref(s, L(z), LF)$.

Finally, the judgement form $Prog \vdash^l LF$ is used to determine LF. Analogously to classical liveness being computed as a solution of dataflow equations, we require, via inference rule (LIVE-DEFINE), LF to satisfy the fixed-point property that: when we assume LF to be the demand transformer for the program then the calculated liveness of each function body $\mathcal{L}(e_f, \sigma, LF)$ agrees with the assumed LF_f. As usual, there are often multiple solutions to LF; all are safe (see Section 3.2) but we prefer the least one as giving the least liveness subject to safety—and hence greatest amount of garbage collected.

We make three observations: firstly the rule (LIVE-DEFINE) has a least solution as $\mathcal{L}(\cdot)$ is monotonic in σ; secondly that (LIVE-DEFINE) resembles the rule for type inference of mutually recursive function definitions, and thirdly the asymmetry of demand and liveness (compared to post- and pre-liveness classically) is due to the functional formulation here.

Section 4 shows how the demand transformer LF for a program (representing a fully context-sensitive analysis) can be safely approximated, for each function, by a *procedure summary* (unifying the contexts in the style of 0-CFA). The summary consists of a pair of a single demand and, for this demand, the corresponding tuple of demands the function makes on its arguments.

3.2   Minefield Semantics and Correctness

This section gives a modified semantics which checks liveness annotations at run time, and 'explodes' when these are found to be inconsistent with execution

$$ref(\kappa, \sigma, \mathsf{LF}) = \{\,\}, \text{ for } \kappa \text{ a constant, including } \mathbf{nil}$$
$$ref((\mathbf{cons}\ x\ y), \sigma, \mathsf{LF}) = \{x.\alpha \mid 0\alpha \in \sigma\} \cup \{y.\alpha \mid 1\alpha \in \sigma\}$$
$$ref((\mathbf{car}\ x), \sigma, \mathsf{LF}) = \{x.\epsilon\} \cup \{x.0\alpha \mid \alpha \in \sigma\}$$
$$ref((\mathbf{cdr}\ x), \sigma, \mathsf{LF}) = \{x.\epsilon\} \cup \{x.1\alpha \mid \alpha \in \sigma\}$$
$$ref((\mathbf{id}\ x), \sigma, \mathsf{LF}) = \{x.\sigma\}$$
$$ref((+\ x\ y), \sigma, \mathsf{LF}) = \{x.\epsilon, y.\epsilon\}$$
$$ref((\mathbf{null?}\ x), \sigma, \mathsf{LF}) = \{x.\epsilon\}$$
$$ref((f\ y_1\ \cdots\ y_n), \sigma, \mathsf{LF}) = \bigcup_{i=1}^{n} y_i.\mathsf{LF}_f^i(\sigma)$$

$$\mathcal{L}((\mathbf{return}\ x), \sigma, \mathsf{LF}) = x.\sigma$$
$$\mathcal{L}((\mathbf{if}\ x\ e_1\ e_2), \sigma, \mathsf{LF}) = \mathcal{L}(e_1, \sigma, \mathsf{LF}) \cup \mathcal{L}(e_2, \sigma, \mathsf{LF}) \cup \{x.\epsilon\}$$
$$\mathcal{L}((\mathbf{let}\ x \leftarrow s\ \mathbf{in}\ e), \sigma, \mathsf{LF}) = \mathsf{L} \setminus x.\{0,1\}^* \cup ref(s, \mathsf{L}(x), \mathsf{LF}), \text{ where } \mathsf{L} = \mathcal{L}(e, \sigma, \mathsf{LF})$$

$$\frac{\mathcal{L}(e_f, \sigma, \mathsf{LF}) = \bigcup_{i=1}^{n} z_i.\mathsf{LF}_f^i(\sigma) \text{ for each } f \text{ and } \sigma}{d_1 \ldots d_k \vdash^l \mathsf{LF}} \text{ (LIVE-DEFINE)}$$
where $(\mathbf{define}\ (f\ z_1\ \ldots\ z_n)\ e_f)$ is a member of $d_1 \ldots d_k$

Fig. 4. Liveness equations and judgement rule

behaviour, but otherwise behaves as the standard semantics. We show that such explosions never occur and hence run-time checks can be elided. We first assume an arbitrary demand transformer LF (below we assume $Prog \vdash^l \mathsf{LF}$). We then enrich the abstract machine state $\rho, \mathsf{S}, \mathsf{H}, e$ to $\rho, \mathsf{S}, \mathsf{H}, e, \sigma, \Sigma$. Here σ is the demand to the currently active function, thus the liveness L at e is $\mathcal{L}(e, \sigma, \mathsf{LF})$,[1] and Σ is a stack of demands—one for each function frame pushed in S.

Second, we augment Val with a value $\bot$. To model strong liveness $\bot$ may be copied freely, including into a **cons** cell, but explodes when used computationally (in a primitive operation other than a copy). Additionally we define $GC(\mathsf{L}, \Sigma)$: $(\rho, \mathsf{H}, \mathsf{S}) \mapsto (\rho', \mathsf{H}', \mathsf{S}')$ which determines $live\text{-}reachability$[2] using ρ and the ρ's in S as the root set and following links in H $only\ as\ far\ as\ allowed\ by\ \mathsf{L}\ and$ Σ. Hence $GC(\mathsf{L}, \Sigma)$ replaces live-unreachable values—in ρ, in H and the ρ's in S—with $\bot$. For example, if $x.\epsilon \notin \mathsf{L}$ then $\rho'(x) = \bot$. Only $GC(\cdots)$ introduces $\bot$.

Third, we update the semantics in four ways: (i) we arrange that all ($\rightarrow$) transitions on expressions e first use $GC(\cdots)$ to update the state and then continue as before; and (ii) whenever the value $\bot$ is used computationally in a reduction ($\rightsquigarrow$), we enter a distinguished stuck state BANG. For example, supposing $\rho(x) = \bot$ then $\rho, \mathsf{H}, s \rightsquigarrow$ BANG if s is (**car** x), (**cdr** x) or $(+\ x\ y)$, but not if s is (**id** x), (**cons** $x\ y$) or $(f\ x\ y)$. Finally (iii) we make a similar change to the ($\rightarrow$) reduction for (ORD-IF) and (iv) augment the (ORD-LET) rule for primitives to propagate BANG from ($\rightsquigarrow$) to ($\rightarrow$).

---

[1] This a simple liveness propagation using $\mathcal{L}(\cdots)$ and $ref(\cdots)$ as LF is assumed given.
[2] Reachability curtailed by liveness information.

The resulting minefield semantics behaves identically (identical heap, identical steps, including possible non-termination) to the standard semantics, except for the sole possibility of the minefield semantics going BANG while the standard semantics continues (either to a halt state, to a stuck state, or reduces forever).

We now prove a result that relates liveness analysis to the semantics.

Proposition 1. *Given program P with $P \vdash^l LF$, then in the minefield semantics $P \to$ BANG can never occur (cf. 'well-typed programs do not go wrong').*

Proof outline: Space does not permit a full proof, but we give the two main steps. We proceed by contradiction and assume there is a program P for which $P \vdash^l LF$ can enter state BANG. The first step is to construct a program P' with identical behaviour, but with no user-function definitions, using inlining. This is possible because a program which goes BANG does so after a finite number of reductions, and hence even recursive functions have only had a finite number of invocations. We hence repeatedly inline-expand user-function calls in P until we obtain a program P' which behaves identically[3] to P in the standard semantics, but executes no user-function calls. Any remaining, non-executed, calls can be replaced with a new primitive with the same demand-to-liveness transfer function—thus making P' a simple expression e'. Not only do the program points in reducing e' correspond one-one to states during evaluation of P, but also the liveness associated with a point in e' is identical to the liveness at the corresponding state $(\rho, S, H, e, \sigma, \Sigma)$ of P (concatenating the liveness $\mathcal{L}(e, \sigma, LF)$ at e with the liveness, obtained from Σ, of the call sites in S and after renaming the variables correspondingly to the inlining which produced e'). This assertion relies on the analysis being fully context-sensitive, and noting that while the change of scope caused by inlining changes variable visibility between P and e' it does not change the liveness—as local-to-a-function **let**-variables whose scope has been prolonged due to inlining are dead in the prolonged scope.

The second step of the proof is to show that e' cannot go BANG. We proceed by induction. Correctness of the **if** and final **return** forms are immediate; the (**let** $z \leftarrow s$ **in** e) form requires showing the inference rules ensure that any value referenced via z in e was already live-reachable (via another variable and path) in any enclosing expression (so that $GC(\cdots)$ could not re-write it to $\bot$).

4   Computing Liveness and Its Encoding as a Table

Section 3 gave a context-sensitive liveness analysis and proved it correct with reference to a *minefield* semantics. For practical use we need to solve the liveness equations *finitely and symbolically*. As expressed mathematically, and given a fixed program, three things are potentially unbounded: (i) the number of call strings (and hence arguments σ to LF); (ii) the length of access paths $\alpha \in \sigma$ and (iii) the number of such access paths.

We commonly first solve (i) by reducing the number of distinct calling contexts (e.g. to a single unified context in 0-CFA style). However, it turns out

---

[3] Modulo replacement of (ORD-CALL) and (ORD-RETURN) steps with (ORD-ID) steps.

that we can solve the equations for LF symbolically without this reduction, so here we defer this to Section 4.2. (It also allows easier extension to dynamically determined liveness—future work.) We address (*ii*) and (*iii*) by re-interpreting the liveness definitions in Figure 4 symbolically as a grammar rather than a mutually recursive set of equations on sets of access paths.

This requires two ideas. Firstly we have to control the use of functions—they tend to be infinitary and do not occur naturally in CFGs; in particular our L maps names to access paths, and LF maps access paths to a tuple of access paths. The former is achieved by using a separate meta-variable (later non-terminal) L_i^x for each variable x and each program point π_i (L_i^x represents $L(x)$ at π_i). Section 4.1 shows how the latter LF_f^i is also expressible finitely (it is a linear form).

Secondly, there are also two technical issues in re-interpreting Figure 4 as a grammar. One is the use of the set-difference operator $\setminus$ in "$\cdots \setminus x.\{0,1\}^*$" reflecting the classical *gen/kill* dataflow formulation. However after separating, as above, liveness environments into per-variable liveness L_i^x the '$\setminus$' operator reduces to the harmless grammar rule $L_i^x = \{\}$ (assuming i labels the (**let** $x \cdots$) expression). The other is that *ref* for **cons** decomposes strings and thus gives a general grammar not a CFG. Below we show how symbols $\bar{0}$, $\bar{1}$ can give an equivalent CFG.

Finally, Section 4.3 uses a construction due to Mohri and Nederhof [10] to over-approximate context-free grammars with regular grammars; these are more appropriate for run-time use. Hence the overall 'big picture' view is that each GC point is annotated with a table encoding the DFA for that program point. When garbage collection occurs, each saved return address on the run-time stack identifies the call-site GC point. The DFA annotating each such GC point is then used by the garbage collector to curtail (to access paths accepted by the DFA) its local-variable reachability-based marking.

GC Points. Given a call site (an expression π_1: (**let** $x \leftarrow (f \ y_1 \ \dots \ y_n)$ **in** π_2: e)) its associated GC point is π_2, as it is liveness at π_2 that should be encoded in the DFA associated with the call.[4] In the case of a call to **cons** as in π_1: (**let** $x \leftarrow (\textbf{cons} \ y_1 \ y_2)$ **in** π_2: e), the situation is slightly more complex. We may either treat **cons** as doing a full procedure call (and mark its formal parameters separately during garbage collection, which again leads to its GC point being π_2), or we may regard **cons** as being inlined, in which case it is vital that liveness of y_1 and y_2 are represented in the DFA (which is achieved by using π_1 rather than π_2 as the GC point). We adopt the latter approach.

Modifying the cons Rule. The *ref* rule for **cons**, shown in Figure 4, requires us to remove the leading **0** and **1** from access paths in σ. Mathematically this is

---

[4] A subtlety is that at machine code level the assignment to x does not take place until after the call, and so for garbage-collection purposes the DFA need not represent liveness of x.

```
(define (append l1 l2)
    π₁: (let test ← (null? l1) in
       π₂: (if test π₃:(return l2)
          π₄: (let tl ← (cdr l1) in
             π₅: (let rec ← (append tl l2) in
                π₆: (let hd ← (car l1) in
                   π₇: (let ans ← (cons hd rec) in (return ans))))))))

  π_main: ...
       π₈: (let y ← (append a b) in
          π₉: (let w ← (append y z) in
             π₁₀: (let c ← (cdr w) in
                π₁₁: (let d ← (car c) in (return d)))))))
```

Fig. 5. An example program. GC points are π_6, π_7, π_9 and π_{10}.

fine but causes problems when solving the liveness equations *symbolically* since such decomposition cannot be expressed as a context-free grammar. To handle this, we introduce two new symbols $\bar{0}$ and $\bar{1}$ with the properties:

$$\bar{0}\sigma \triangleq \{\alpha \mid 0\alpha \in \sigma\} \qquad \text{and} \qquad \bar{1}\sigma \triangleq \{\alpha \mid 1\alpha \in \sigma\}$$

We can now rewrite the **cons** rule as:

$$ref((\textbf{cons } x \ y), \sigma, \textsf{LF}) = x.\bar{0}\sigma \cup y.\bar{1}\sigma$$

We call the liveness equations with this modification $\mathcal{L}'$. The definitions of $\bar{0}$ and $\bar{1}$ induce the following relation $\hookrightarrow$ over sets of access paths:

$$\sigma_1\bar{0}\sigma_2 \hookrightarrow \sigma_1\sigma_2', \text{ where } \sigma_2' = \{\alpha \mid 0\alpha \in \sigma_2\}, \quad \text{and}$$
$$\sigma_1\bar{1}\sigma_2 \hookrightarrow \sigma_1\sigma_2', \text{ where } \sigma_2' = \{\alpha \mid 1\alpha \in \sigma_2\}$$

The reflexive transitive closure of $\hookrightarrow$ will be denoted as $\overset{*}{\hookrightarrow}$. The following proposition relates $\mathcal{L}$ and $\mathcal{L}'$:

Proposition 2. *Assume that a liveness computation based on $\mathcal{L}$ gives the liveness of the variable x at a program point π_i as σ (symbolically, $\mathsf{L}_i^x = \sigma$). Further, suppose $\mathsf{L}_i^x = \sigma'$ when $\mathcal{L}'$ is used for liveness computation instead of $\mathcal{L}$. Then $\sigma' \overset{*}{\hookrightarrow} \sigma$.*

To see why the proposition is true, consider an analysis based on $\mathcal{L}'$ in which σ appears in the context $ref((\textbf{cons } x \ y), \sigma, \textsf{LF})$. Let $\alpha \in \sigma$. The symbol $\bar{0}$ (respectively $\bar{1}$) merely marks a place in α where the original **cons** rule would have erased an immediately following **0** (respectively **1**), or, in absence of such a symbol, would have dropped α itself. Since the application of any rule in $\mathcal{L}'$ merely adds symbols at the beginning of α, the markers and other symbols in

α are propagated to other dependent parts of program in their same relative positions. Consequently, the erasure carried out at the end of the analysis with $\overset{*}{\hookrightarrow}$ gives the same result as obtained through $\mathcal{L}$.

4.1   Generating Equations for the Demand Transformer LF

We shall consider the program in Figure 5 as a running example. Unlike the program in Figure 1, this program is in ANF.

To generate the equations defining LF_f, we follow the rule DEFINE-LIVE. We start with a *symbolic demand* σ and determine $\mathsf{L} = \mathcal{L}(e_f, \sigma, \mathsf{LF})$, treating LF as an uninterpreted function symbol. We then generate equations of the form $\mathsf{LF}_f^i(\sigma) = \mathsf{L}(x_i)$ where x_i is the ith formal parameter of f and $\mathsf{L}(x_i)$ is the liveness of x_i. For our example program which has a single function **append**, this generates the following equations:

$$\mathsf{LF}^1_{\mathbf{append}}(\sigma) = \{\epsilon\} \cup \mathbf{0\bar{0}}\sigma \cup \mathbf{1}\mathsf{LF}^1_{\mathbf{append}}(\bar{\mathbf{1}}\sigma)$$
$$\mathsf{LF}^2_{\mathbf{append}}(\sigma) = \sigma \cup \mathsf{LF}^2_{\mathbf{append}}(\bar{\mathbf{1}}\sigma)$$

In general, the equations for LF are recursive since L may, in turn, be expressed in terms of LF. We assume that LF_f is expressible in the closed form as:[5]

$$\mathsf{LF}_f^i(\sigma) = \mathsf{I}_f^i \cup \mathsf{D}_f^i\sigma \tag{1}$$

where I_f^i and D_f^i are sets of strings over the alphabet $\{\mathbf{0}, \mathbf{1}, \bar{\mathbf{0}}, \bar{\mathbf{1}}\}$. The reason why LF has this form is as follows. Recall that $\mathsf{LF}_f^i(\sigma)$ gives the access paths starting from i that have to be dereferenced to produce the sub-structure σ of the result of f. I_f^i represents the access paths that would be dereferenced, but do not contribute to the result. This happens, for instance, when the argument is used only within the condition of an **if**. D_f^i, in contrast, represents the paths that are dereferenced to actually produce the result.

To solve for LF_f, we substitute the guessed form into its equations. $\mathsf{LF}_{\mathbf{append}}$ gives:

$$\mathsf{I}^1_{\mathbf{append}} \cup \mathsf{D}^1_{\mathbf{append}}\sigma = \{\epsilon\} \cup \mathbf{0\bar{0}}\sigma \cup \mathbf{1}(\mathsf{I}^1_{\mathbf{append}} \cup \mathsf{D}^1_{\mathbf{append}}\bar{\mathbf{1}}\sigma)$$
$$\mathsf{I}^2_{\mathbf{append}} \cup \mathsf{D}^2_{\mathbf{append}}\sigma = \sigma \cup \mathsf{I}^2_{\mathbf{append}} \cup \mathsf{D}^2_{\mathbf{append}}\bar{\mathbf{1}}\sigma$$

Equating the terms containing σ on the two sides of each equation, and doing the same for the terms without σ, we get equations for I_f^i and D_f^i that are independent of σ.

$$\mathsf{I}^1_{\mathbf{append}} = \{\epsilon\} \cup \mathbf{1}\mathsf{I}^1_{\mathbf{append}} \qquad\qquad \mathsf{I}^2_{\mathbf{append}} = \mathsf{I}^2_{\mathbf{append}}$$
$$\mathsf{D}^1_{\mathbf{append}} = \{\mathbf{0\bar{0}}\} \cup \mathbf{1}\mathsf{D}^1_{\mathbf{append}}\bar{\mathbf{1}} \qquad\qquad \mathsf{D}^2_{\mathbf{append}} = \{\epsilon\} \cup \mathsf{D}^2_{\mathbf{append}}\bar{\mathbf{1}}$$

---

[5] This is similar to solving the differential equation $ay'' + by' + c = 0$, where we guess that the solution has the form $y = e^{rx}$. Substituting the solution in the equation yields a quadratic equation in r, and each solution of r gives rise to a solution of the differential equation (in our setup we can effectively pick the least solution rather than needing linear combinations).

Note that these equations can be viewed as CFGs, with all but D_{append}^1 being regular, and that any solution of I_f^i and D_f^i yields a solution of LF_f.

4.2   Generating Liveness Equations L for Function Bodies

We now calculate a 0-CFA-style summary liveness for each GC point of a program. There are two parts to this. First, for each function f, we determine a *summary demand* σ_f over-approximating any demand σ passed to f. Such demands are caused by calls to f occurring at call sites. We introduce the notation $\delta_f(\pi, g)$ for the contribution to σ_f caused a call site π occurring in function g. So, suppose function g contains a call site π to f, say $\pi:(\textbf{let } x \leftarrow (f \, y_1 \, \dots \, y_n) \textbf{ in } e)$. Under the assumption that the demand on g is σ_g, the liveness at e is $L = \mathcal{L}(e, \sigma_g, LF)$, and the **let** case of Figure 4 tells us this call site contributes $L(x)$ to the demand σ_f placed on f; hence $\delta_f(\pi, g)$ is simply $L(x)$.

Now, supposing the k call sites to function f are π^1 (in function g^1) $\dots \pi^k$ (in function g^k), then the over-approximation requirement on σ_f is achieved by taking $\sigma_f = \delta_f(\pi^1, g^1) \cup \dots \cup \delta_f(\pi^k, g^k)$.

The expression e_{main} is a special case; we assume it may be called externally with demand $\sigma_{main} = \{0,1\}^*$ (denoted σ_{all}). This is because any part of its value may be used by the environment—for printing the result, for instance.

For the running example, **append** has calls from **main** at π_9 and a recursive call at π_5. So $\sigma_{append} = \delta_{append}(\pi_9, \textbf{main}) \cup \delta_{append}(\pi_5, \textbf{append})$. Calculating the $\delta_{append}(\pi, g)$ for the two call sites, and substituting gives:

$$\sigma_{append} = (\{\epsilon, 1\} \cup 10\sigma_{all}) \ \cup \ \bar{1}\sigma_{append}$$

Second, for each function f (possibly **main**) we need the liveness at each contained GC point π. Given σ_f calculated above, this is simply $\mathcal{L}(\pi, \sigma_f, LF)$. For the running example, containing GC points π_6, π_7 in **append** and π_9, π_{10} in e_{main}, this gives (recall Equation (1) above states $LF_f^i(\sigma) = I_f^i \cup D_f^i.\sigma$):

$$L_6^{11} = \{\epsilon\} \cup 0\bar{0}\sigma_{append} \qquad\qquad L_6^{rec} = \bar{1}\sigma_{append}$$
$$L_7^{hd} = \bar{0}\sigma_{append} \qquad\qquad\qquad L_7^{rec} = \bar{1}\sigma_{append}$$

$$L_9^y = LF_{append}^1(\{\epsilon,1\} \cup 10\sigma_{all}) \qquad L_9^z = LF_{append}^2(\{\epsilon,1\} \cup 10\sigma_{all})$$
$$L_{10}^w = \{\epsilon, 1\} \cup 10\sigma_{all}$$

In summary, the equations generated during liveness analysis are:

1. For each function f, equations defining I_f^i and D_f^i for use by LF_f.
2. For each function f, an equation defining the summary demand σ_f on e_f.
3. For each function f (including **main** for e_{main}) an equation defining liveness at each GC point of e_f.

4.3   Solving Liveness Equations—The Grammar Interpretation

The liveness equations above (of the form $X = \dots$) can now be re-interpreted as a context-free grammar (CFG) on the alphabet $\{0, 1, \bar{0}, \bar{1}\}$. We use $\langle X \rangle$ to denote

the corresponding non-terminal which then appears in a production $\langle X \rangle \to \ldots$.
We can think of the resulting productions as being associated with several grammars, one for each non-terminal $\langle L_i^x \rangle$ regarded as a start symbol. As an example, the grammar for $\langle L_9^y \rangle$ comprises the following productions:

$$\langle L_9^y \rangle \to \langle I_{\mathsf{append}}^1 \rangle \mid \langle D_{\mathsf{append}}^1 \rangle (\epsilon \mid 1 \mid 10 \langle \sigma_{all} \rangle)$$
$$\langle I_{\mathsf{append}}^1 \rangle \to \epsilon \mid 1 \langle I_{\mathsf{append}}^1 \rangle$$
$$\langle D_{\mathsf{append}}^1 \rangle \to 0\bar{0} \mid 1 \langle D_{\mathsf{append}}^1 \rangle \bar{1}$$
$$\langle \sigma_{all} \rangle \to \epsilon \mid 0 \langle \sigma_{all} \rangle \mid 1 \langle \sigma_{all} \rangle$$

Other equations can be converted similarly. The language generated by $\langle L_i^x \rangle$, denoted $\mathscr{L}(\langle L_i^x \rangle)$, is the desired solution of L_i^x. However, recall from our earlier discussion that the decision problem that we are interested in during garbage collection is:

Let $x.\alpha$ be a *forward access path*—consisting only of edges 0 and 1 (but not $\bar{0}$ or $\bar{1}$). Let $\mathscr{L}(\langle L_i^x \rangle) \overset{*}{\hookrightarrow} \sigma$, where σ consists of forward paths only. Then does $\alpha \in \sigma$?

We could convert the rules defining $\hookrightarrow$ into productions and add them to the grammar. However, this results in an *unrestricted grammar* [11], and the membership problem for such grammars is undecidable. We circumvent the problem by over-approximating the CFG generated by the analysis to *strongly regular* CFGs which have easy translations to non-deterministic finite state automata (NFA). The NFAs are then simplified on the basis of the $\hookrightarrow$ rules to enable checking of membership of forward access paths. The resulting NFAs are finally converted to DFAs for use during garbage collection.

Approximating CFGs Using NFAs. We use the algorithm by Mohri and Nederhof [10] to approximate a CFG to a *strongly regular* grammar. The transformation has the property that if L is a non-terminal in the grammar G and G' is the grammar after the Mohri-Nederhof transformation, then $\mathscr{L}_G(L) \subseteq \mathscr{L}_{G'}(L)$. This is required for the approximation to be safe with respect to liveness.

We exemplify the Mohri-Nederhof transformation on the $\langle L_9^y \rangle$ grammar above. We pick the only production that is affected by the transformation—the production for D_{append}^1. The production for I_{append}^1, while recursive, is already in strongly regular form and is therefore unaffected by the transformation.

$$\langle D_{\mathsf{append}}^1 \rangle \to 0\bar{0} \langle D_{\mathsf{append}}^1 \rangle' \mid 1 \langle D_{\mathsf{append}}^1 \rangle$$
$$\langle D_{\mathsf{append}}^1 \rangle' \to \bar{1} \langle D_{\mathsf{append}}^1 \rangle' \mid \epsilon$$

The languages generated for $\langle D_{\mathsf{append}}^1 \rangle$ in the original grammar and the new grammar are $1^i 0\bar{0} \bar{1}^i$ and $1^* 0\bar{0} \bar{1}^*$, showing a loss of precision.

Input: NFA $\overline{N}$ with underlying alphabet $\{0, 1, \bar{0}, \bar{1}\}$
Output: NFA N with underlying alphabet $\{0, 1\}$ such that $\mathscr{L}(\overline{N}) \overset{*}{\hookrightarrow} \mathscr{L}(N)$.
Steps:

   $i \leftarrow 0$
   $N_0 \leftarrow$ Equivalent NFA of $\overline{N}$ without ϵ-moves [11]
   repeat
      $N'_{i+1} \leftarrow N_i$
      for all states q in N_i such that q has an incoming edge from q' with label $\bar{0}$
      and outgoing edge to q'' with label **0 do**
         add an edge in N'_{i+1} from q' to q'' with label ϵ. {bypass $\bar{0}0$ using ϵ}
      end for
      for all states q in N_i such that q has an incoming edge from q' with label $\bar{1}$
      and outgoing edge to q'' with label **1 do**
         add an edge in N'_{i+1} from q' to q'' with label ϵ. {bypass $\bar{1}1$ using ϵ}
      end for
      $N_{i+1} \leftarrow$ Equivalent NFA of N'_{i+1} without ϵ-moves
      $i \leftarrow i + 1$
   until $(N_i = N_{i-1})$
   $N \leftarrow N_i$

Fig. 6. Algorithm for transforming an NFA to accept forward paths only

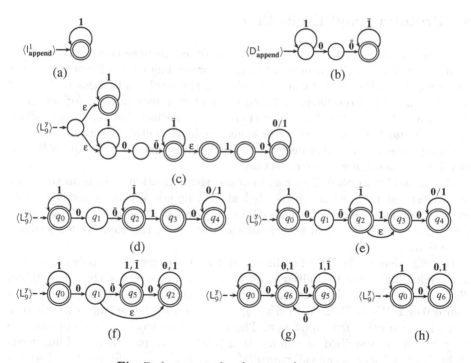

Fig. 7. Automata for the example program

Transforming NFAs to Accept Forward Paths: The strongly regular CFGs obtained after the Mohri-Nederhof transformation are first converted into NFAs. The algorithm described in Figure 6 converts an NFA $\overline{N}$ to a NFA N such that $\mathscr{L}(\overline{N}) \overset{*}{\hookrightarrow} \mathscr{L}(N)$, where N accepts forward paths only. Thus N can be used to check membership of forward paths.

The algorithm repeatedly introduces ϵ edges to bypass a pair of consecutive edges labelled $\overline{0}0$ or $\overline{1}1$. The process is continued until a fixed point is reached. When the fixed point is reached, the resulting NFA contains all possible reductions corresponding to all the paths in the original NFA. The proofs of the termination and correctness of the algorithm are given in our earlier paper [8].

We illustrate the algorithm in Figure 6 by constructing the automaton for $\langle L_9^y \rangle$. Figure 7 (c) shows the automaton for $\langle L_9^y \rangle$ constructed by composing the automata for $\langle I_{\mathbf{append}}^1 \rangle$, $\langle D_{\mathbf{append}}^1 \rangle$ and $(\epsilon \mid 1 \mid 10\sigma_{all})$. After ϵ removal we get (d). We add an ϵ edge from q_2 to q_3 bypassing the $\overline{1}1$ pair from q_2 to q_2 and then to q_3. This is shown in (e). The ϵ edge is removed in (f) and a second ϵ is added to the automaton bypassing the $\overline{0}0$ pair from q_1 to q_2. Removing this ϵ edge gives the automaton shown in (g). Restricting this automaton to forward edges only, we get the final automaton shown in (h). This automaton recognises $1^* \mid 1^*0\sigma_{all}$, showing that the entire list y, including its elements, is live at π_9. Also note that the language accepted by the final automaton satisfies the prefix-closed property.

5   Prototype and Evaluation

To demonstrate the effectiveness of liveness-based garbage collection, we have built a prototype consisting of an interpreter for our language, a liveness analyser and a copying collector that can optionally use the results of liveness analysis for marking instead of reachability. When the collector uses liveness for marking, we call it a *liveness-based collector* (LGC), else we use the term *reachability-based collector* (RGC). The collector is neither incremental nor generational. As a consequence, any cell that becomes unreachable or dead is assuredly collected in the next round of garbage collection.

When LGC is invoked (by a call to **cons**) the activation records on the stack all correspond to functions suspended at GC points, and by construction at each GC point we have a DFA specifying liveness of each local variable in the activation record. As usual such local variables form the root set for garbage collection.

Let dfa_π^x denote the DFA for the variable and program point pair (x, π). We write $\mathsf{initial}(\mathsf{dfa}_\pi^x)$ for the initial state of dfa_π^x. Considering a DFA as a table, $\mathsf{dfa}_\pi^x(q, sym)$ returns the next state for the state q and the symbol sym, where sym is 0 or 1. We shall also write $\mathsf{dfa}_\pi^x(q, sym)?$ for a predicate indicating whether there is a transition from q on sym. The LGC action to chase the root variable x at π can be described as follows: If $\mathscr{L}(\mathsf{dfa}_\pi^x)$ is empty, then nothing needs to be done. Otherwise we call $\mathsf{copy}(\mathsf{dfa}_\pi^x, \mathsf{initial}(\mathsf{dfa}_\pi^x), x)$ in Figure 8 and assign the returned pointer to x. The function $\mathsf{move\_to\_tospace}(x)$ copies the value of x in the other semi-space and returns the new address. It hides details such as

```
function copy(dfa, q, x)
    let y ← move_to_tospace(x)
    if x.tag ≠ cons then skip
    else if dfa(q, 0)? then y.car = copy(dfa, dfa(q, 0), x.car)
         if dfa(q, 1)? then y.cdr = copy(dfa, dfa(q, 1), x.cdr)
    return y
```

Fig. 8. Function for copying a root set variable

returning the forwarding pointer if the value of x is already copied, and creating the forwarding pointer otherwise.

The graphs in Figure 9[6] show the number of cells in the heap over time for RGC and LGC—here time is measured in terms of the number of **cons** cells allocated. In addition, they also show the number of reachable cells and the number of cells that are actually live (this is statically approximated by our liveness analysis). Since the programs have different memory requirements, we have tuned the size of heap for each program to ensure a reasonable number of collections. An invocation of RGC decreases the number of cells in heap until it touches the curve of reachable cells. An invocation of LGC decreases the number of heap cells to no lower than the curve of live cells.

To construct the reachable and live curves, we record for every cell its creation time (`Create_time`), its last use time (`Use_time`), and the earliest time when the cell becomes unreachable and can be garbage collected (`Collection_time`). For accurate recording of `Collection_time`, we force frequent invocations of a reachability-based collector in a separate run. A cell is live at time T if `Create_time` $\leq T \leq$ `Use_time`. If `Create_time` $\leq T \leq$ `Collection_time`, it is reachable.

The benchmark programs are drawn from the `no-fib` suite and other sources and have been manually converted to ANF. All graphs except `fibheap` show strictly fewer garbage collector invocations for LGC; `fibheap` is an exception in that the number of reachable cells first grows steadily until it almost fills the heap. This triggers garbage collections in both LGC and RGC. The number of reachable cells then drops steeply to a low level and remains low resulting in no further garbage collections. The graphs also show the precision of our liveness analysis. For all programs except `nperm` and `lambda`, LGC manages to collect a good portion of the cells that are not live.

5.1   Results

The increased effectiveness of LGC over RGC is also shown in the tables in Figure 10. The first table provides statistics regarding the analysis itself. The number of states and the analysis times are within tolerable limits. Precision of analysis refers to the percentage of dead cells that is collected by LGC, averaged

---

[6] For better clarity, visit `http://www.cse.iitk.ac.in/users/karkare/fhra` for coloured versions of the graphs.

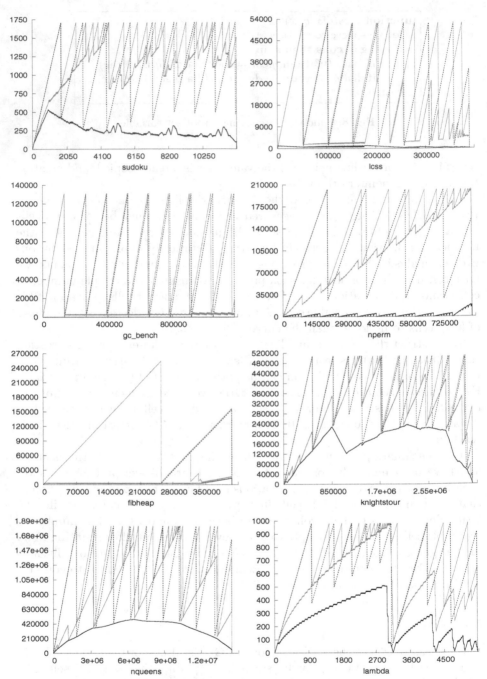

Fig. 9. Memory usage of programs. The dotted-grey and the dashed-black curves indicate the number of **cons** cells in the active semi-space for RGC and LGC respectively. The solid-grey curve represents the number of reachable cells and the solid-black curve represents the number of cells that are actually live (of which liveness analysis does a static approximation). x-axis is the time measured in number of **cons** cells allocated. y-axis is the number of **cons** cells.

Program	sudoku	lcss	gc_bench	nperm	fibheap	knightstour	treejoin	nqueens	lambda
Time (msec)	120.95	2.19	0.32	1.16	2.4	3.05	2.61	0.71	20.51
DFA size	4251	726	258	526	675	922	737	241	732
Precision(%)	87.5	98.8	99.9	87.1	100	94.3	99.6	98.8	83.8

(a)

Program	# Collected cells per GC		# Touched cells per GC		#GCs		MinHeap (#cells)		Avg. Drag (#cells)		GC time (sec)	
	RGC	LGC	RGC	LGC	RGC	LGC	RGC	LGC	RGC	LGC	RGC	LGC
sudoku	490	1306	1568	774	22	9	1704	589	858	146	.028	.122
lcss	46522	51101	6216	1363	8	7	52301	1701	5147	588	.045	.144
gc_bench	129179	131067	1894	4	9	9	131071	6	16970	4	.086	.075
nperm	47586	174478	201585	60882	14	4	202597	37507	171878	76618	1.406	.9
fibheap	249502	251525	5555	2997	1	1	254520	13558	78720	0	.006	.014
knightstour	2593	314564	907502	319299	1161	10	508225	307092	206729	82112	464.902	14.124
treejoin	288666	519943	297570	5547	2	1	525488	7150	212653	1954	.356	.217
nqueens	283822	1423226	2133001	584143	46	9	1819579	501093	521826	39465	70.314	24.811
lambda	205	556	2072	90345	23	8	966	721	303	95	.093	2.49

(b)

Fig. 10. Experimental results comparing RGC and LGC. Table (a) gives data related to liveness analysis, and (b) gives garbage collection data.

over all invocations. The second table shows garbage collection statistics for RGC and LGC. LGC collects larger garbage per invocation, drags cells for lesser time and requires a smaller heap size (*MinHeap*) for program to run in comparison with RGC.

There are a couple of issues of concern. The garbage collection time is larger in the case of LGC for some programs. The reason is that the cost of consulting the liveness DFA may outweigh the combined benefits of fewer garbage collections and fewer markings per garbage collection. The other issue is illustrated by the program lambda. As can be seen from the table in Figure 10, the number of touched cells[7] in this example is much higher for LGC. This increase is due to excessive sharing among heap nodes in this program. Note that a node re-visited because of sharing is not explored any further during RGC. However, this curtailment cannot happen in LGC because of the possibility that the node, re-visited in a different liveness state, may mark a set of cells different from the earlier visit.

6   Collecting More Garbage Can Never Slow Things Down

Since garbage collection is effectively asynchronous to the allocator thread, one might worry as to how *robust* our measurements are. For example, while LGC would, in general, collect more garbage than RGC in the same heap state, might LGC do a larger number of collections for some programs? We prove below that

---

[7] These are the cells visited during the marking phase, often more than once due to sharing.

this cannot happen. This result applies to classical mark-and-sweep and copying garbage collectors and, we believe, also to generational collectors.

Lemma 1. *For the same mutator, a liveness-based collector can never do more garbage collections than a reachability-based collector.*

Proof. Assume, as before, that time is measured in terms of the number of **cons** cells allocated. Now run two copies of the mutator, one with RGC and one with LGC, in parallel. Memory allocations by **cons** happen simultaneously, but the times of garbage collections diverge.

To prove the lemma, it is enough to show the truth of the following statement: After every LGC invocation, the count of LGC invocations is no greater than RGC invocations. The base case holds since the first invocations of both GCs happen at the same time. Assume the statement to be true after n invocations of LGC. Since LGC copies a subset of reachable cells, its heap would contain no more cells than RGC heap at the end of the nth invocation. Thus either RGC is invoked next before LGC, or LGC and RGC are both invoked next at the same time. In either case, the statement holds after $n + 1$ invocations of LGC.

7   Related Work

Previous attempts to increase the space efficiency of functional programs by additional reclamation of memory fall in two broad categories. In the first, the program itself is instrumented to manage reclamation and reallocation without the aid of the garbage collector. Such attempts include: sharing analysis based reallocation [12], deforestation techniques [13,14,15], methods based on linear logic [16] and region analysis [17]. Closer to our approach, there are methods that enable the garbage collector to collect more garbage [18,6] by explicitly nullifying pointers that are not live. However, the nullification, done at compile time, requires sharing (alias) analysis. Our method, in contrast, does not require sharing because of the availability of the heap itself at run time. To the best of our knowledge, this is the first attempt at liveness-based marking of the heap during garbage collection.

8   Conclusions

We have defined a notion of liveness on structured data; this generalises classical liveness and strong liveness. We started with a general fully context-sensitive analysis which we proved correct with respect to a minefield semantics (this models the effect of garbage collection between every evaluation step).

To avoid scalability issues (and to avoid performing part of the liveness computation at run time) we defined an 0-CFA version of this liveness analysis in which demands for function f at all calling contexts are conflated into a single demand σ_f. This enabled us to treat the liveness equations symbolically obtaining context-free grammars for liveness at each GC point (calls to user functions and to **cons**). These were then converted to DFAs for run-time consultation by the garbage collector. Experiments confirm the precision of the analysis.

To obtain performance figures we compared a reachability-based garbage collector with a liveness-based collector. This showed a decrease in the number of GCs, more garbage collected per invocation. A significant benefit of LGC is that programs can run in smaller memory when compared to RGC. This is potentially useful in situations where memory is limited—as with embedded systems. For a majority of programs, the garbage collection times were reduced.

One issue we highlighted was that while fewer nodes were marked (and hence more garbage collected), sometimes **cons** cells could be visited and traversed multiple times with different sets of liveness paths to explore; this risks infinite looping if extended to languages with cyclic data structures. Avenues of further work include static analysis to avoid revisiting cells known to have been visited. One possibility is to record a representation of the liveness paths already visited from each **cons** cell; the classical mark bit indicates that all paths have been visited from the cell.

Acknowledgements. We thank the anonymous referees for their helpful comments. Thanks are also due to Hemanshu Vadehra for a preliminary implementation of the prototype system. Amey Karkare was supported for this work by the DST/SERC fast track scheme for young scientists.

References

1. Röjemo, N., Runciman, C.: Lag, drag, void and use—heap profiling and space-efficient compilation revisited. In: ICFP (1996)
2. Karkare, A., Sanyal, A., Khedker, U.: Effectiveness of garbage collection in MIT/GNU Scheme (2006), http://arxiv.org/abs/cs/0611093
3. Shaham, R., Kolodner, E.K., Sagiv, M.: Estimating the impact of heap liveness information on space consumption in Java. In: ISMM (2002)
4. Chatterjee, R., Ryder, B.G., Landi, W.A.: Relevant context inference. In: POPL (1999)
5. Cherem, S., Rugina, R.: A practical escape and effect analysis for building lightweight method summaries. In: Krishnamurthi, S., Odersky, M. (eds.) CC 2007. LNCS, vol. 4420, pp. 172–186. Springer, Heidelberg (2007)
6. Lee, O., Yang, H., Yi, K.: Static insertion of safe and effective memory reuse commands into ML-like programs. Science of Computer Programming (2005)
7. Khedker, U.P., Sanyal, A., Karkare, A.: Heap reference analysis using access graphs. TOPLAS (2007)
8. Karkare, A., Khedker, U., Sanyal, A.: Liveness of heap data for functional programs. In: Heap Analysis and Verification Workshop, HAV (2007), http://research.microsoft.com/~jjb/papers/HAV_proceedings.pdf
9. Chakravarty, M.M.T., Keller, G., Zadarnowski, P.: A functional perspective on SSA optimisation algorithms. In: COCV (2003)
10. Mohri, M., Nederhof, M.J.: Regular approximation of context-free grammars through transformation. In: Junqua, J.C., van Noord, G. (eds.) Robustness in Language and Speech Technology, pp. 251–261. Kluwer Academic Publishers (2000)

11. Hopcroft, J.E., Ullman, J.D.: Introduction to Automata Theory, Languages, and Computation. Addison-Wesley Longman Publishing Co., Inc., Boston (1990)
12. Jones, S.B., Metayer, D.L.: Compile-time garbage collection by sharing analysis. In: FPCA (1989)
13. Wadler, P.: Deforestation: Transforming programs to eliminate trees. In: Ganzinger, H. (ed.) ESOP 1988. LNCS, vol. 300, pp. 344–358. Springer, Heidelberg (1988)
14. Gill, A., Launchbury, J., Jones, S.L.P.: A short cut to deforestation. In: FPCA (1993)
15. Chitil, O.: Type inference builds a short cut to deforestation. In: ICFP (1999)
16. Hofmann, M.: A type system for bounded space and functional in-place update. In: ESOP (2000)
17. Tofte, M., Birkedal, L.: A region inference algorithm. TOPLAS (1998)
18. Inoue, K., Seki, H., Yagi, H.: Analysis of functional programs to detect run-time garbage cells. TOPLAS (1988)

deGoal a Tool to Embed Dynamic Code Generators into Applications

Henri-Pierre Charles, Damien Couroussé, Victor Lomüller, Fernando A. Endo, and Rémy Gauguey

CEA, LIST, Département Architecture Conception Logiciels Embarqués,
F-38054 Grenoble, France
firstname.lastname@cea.fr

Abstract. The processing applications that are now being used in mobile and embedded platforms require at the same time a fair amount of processing power and a high level of flexibility, due to the nature of the data to process. In this context we propose a lightweight code generation technique that is able to perform data dependent optimizations at run-time for processing kernels.

In this paper we present the motivations and how to use deGoal: a tool designed to build fast and portable binary code generators called *compilettes*.

1 Introduction

Today, software development is facing two competing objectives:

- Improve programmers efficiency by using generic and expressive programming languages
- Generate efficient machine code to achieve the best execution speed and energy efficiency

These two objectives are competing because the more expressive and abstract a programming language is, the more difficult it is for a code generation tool-chain to produce efficient machine code.

We believe that code optimization, driven by run-time data characteristics, is a promising solution to tackle this issue. To achieve this, we propose deGoal: a lightweight runtime solution for code generation.

deGoal was designed with the limitations of embedded systems computing power and memory in mind: our bottom-up approach allows code generation of specialized kernels, at runtime, depending on the execution context, the features of the targeted processor, and furthermore on the *data to process*: their characteristics and their values. Runtime code generation is achieved thanks to tiny *ad hoc* code generators, called *compilettes*, which are embedded into the application and produce machine code at runtime. *Compilettes* have only the strict necessary processing intelligence to perform the required code optimizations. As a consequence, code generation is:

A. Cohen (Ed.): CC 2014, LNCS 8409, pp. 107–112, 2014.

1. *very fast*: 10 to 100 times faster than typical JITs or dynamic compilers which allow to use code generation inside the application and during the code execution, not in a virtual machine.
2. *lightweight*: the typical size of *compilettes* is only a few kilobytes which allows its use on constrained memory micro controllers such as the Texas Instrument MSP430 which has only 512 bytes of available memory [1]. Standard code generators, such as LLC of the LLVM infrastructure, have Mbytes of memory footprint, making their use impossible in this context.
3. *produce compact code*: as we are able to generate only the needed specialized code and not all variants at the same time.
4. *portable* across processor family: i.e. a *compilette*is portable on RISC platforms or on GPU platforms.
5. able to perform *cross-jit* applications, i.e. a *compilette* can run on one processor model and generate code for an other processor and download the generated code.

2   Introduction to the deGoal Infrastructure

The **deGoal** infrastructure integrates a language for kernel description and a small run-time environment for code generation. The tools used by the infrastructure are architecture agnostic, they only require a python interpreter and an ANSI C compiler. We briefly introduce the language, how applications are written with **deGoal** and how they're are compiled and executed.

2.1   Kernel Description

We use a dedicated language to describe the kernel generation at runtime. This language is mixed with C code, this latter allowing to control the code generation performed in *compilette*s. This combination of C and **deGoal** code allows to efficiently design a code generator able to:

1. inject immediate values into the code being generated,
2. specialize code according to runtime data, e.g. selecting instructions,
3. perform classical compilation optimizations such as loop unrolling or dead code elimination.

deGoal uses a pseudo-assembly language whose instructions are similar to a neutral RISC-like instruction set. The goal is to achieve:

– A rich instruction set focused on vector and multimedia instructions.
– The capability to use the run-time information in the specialized code.
– Cross-platform code generation: the architecture targeted by the *compilette* may also be different from the architecture on which the code generator runs.
– Fast code generation, thanks to the "multiple time" compilation scheme. The intermediate representation (IR) is processed at static compile time. At run time the application has only to generate binary code mixed with data.

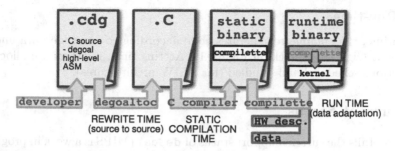

Fig. 1. deGoal work flow: from the writing of applications source code to the execution of a kernel generated at run-time

Table 1. deGoal support status

Architecture	Port status	SIMD support	Instruction bundling
ARM Thumb-2 (+NEON/VFP)	✓	✓	N/A
STxP70 (STHORM)	✓	N/A	✓
PTX (NVIDIA)	✓	✓	N/A
ARM32	✓	✗	N/A
MSP430	✓	N/A	N/A
K1	✓	✓	✓
MIPS	∊	✗	N/A

2.2 Compilation Chain

To achieve fast code generation, the compilation chain is split into several steps that run at different "times" (Figure 1).

Static Compilation. The *compilette* is rewritten into a standard C file by the degoaltoc tool. The C version of the *compilette* is then statically compiled and linked to the targeted architecture deGoal back-end using the C compiler of the target platform.

Runtime. The application first invokes the *compilette* to generate the machine code of the kernel, once the optimizing data from the execution context are available. The kernel can then be executed as a standard procedure.

Given that the back-end is composed of portable C functions, our compilation chain is able to generate cross-platform code.

2.3   Run-time

At runtime, the *compilette* generates code according to run-time data and environment (rightmost block on Figure 1). At this time, registers are allocated, instructions scheduled and bundled (for VLIW architectures).

3   Current Status

Table 1 details the current support status of deGoal (MIPS is a work in progress). The column "SIMD support" shows the ability to take advantage of hardware vectors efficiently. The last column indicates if deGoal is able to generate code for VLIW processors.

The core infrastructure is licensed under a BSD style license but all hardware-specific developments are restricted to their respective owners.

4   Related Works

There is an extensive amount of literature about approaches related to our work with deGoal. Other works are related :

Java JIT mix interpretation and dynamic compilation for hotpots. Such techniques usually require large memory to embed JIT framework, and performance overhead. Some research works have tried to tackle these limitations: memory footprint can be reduced to a few hundreds of KB [6], but the binary code produced often presents a lower performance because of the smaller amount of optimizing intelligence embedded in the JIT compiler [12].

Java JITs are unable to directly take data value as parameters. They use indirect hotspot detection by tracing the application activity at runtime.

In deGoal, the objective is to reduce the cost incurred by runtime code generation. Our approach allows to generate code at least 10 times faster than traditional JITs: JITs hardly go below 1000 cycles per instruction generated while we obtain 25 to 80 cycles per instruction generated on the STxP70 processor.

LLVM [9] (Low Level Virtual Machine) is a compilation framework that can target many architectures, including x86, ARM or PTX. One of its advantages is the unified internal representation (LLVM IR) that encode a virtual low-level instruction with some high-level information embedded on it. Various tools were built on top of it.

In deGoal, we don't use IR at run-time, we keep only calls (with parameters) to binary code generators.

Partial evaluation Our approach is similar to partial evaluation techniques [4,8], which consists in pre-computing during the static compilation passes the maximum of the generated code to reduce the run-time overhead. At run-time, the finalization of the machine code consists in: selecting code templates, filling pre-compiled binary code with data values and jump addresses.

Using deGoal we compile statically an *ad hoc* code generator (the compilette) for each kernel to specialize. The originality of our approach relies in the possibility to perform run-time instruction selection depending on the *data* to process [2].

DyC [7] is a tool that creates code generators from an annotated C code. Like `C, it adds some tokens such as @ to evaluate C expressions and inject the results as an immediate value into the machine code.

deGoal is different from DyC because the parameters given to the binary run-time generators can drive specialized optimization such as loop-unrolling or vectorizers.

5 Application Domain Examples

As examples, here are some references of work in different application domains where *compilettes* have been used:

Specialized memory allocator: memory allocators are specialized depending on the size of the memory to manage. *Lhuilier et al* [10] built an example with a very low memory footprint, able to adapt itself to the size of data set.

Hardware support thanks to the fast generation code scheme we are able to generate specialized code which run faster with a low overhead. We have used this support in

Mono-core specialization in an MPSoC context where each node is able to generate an optimized version of a matrix multiplication function [5].

GPU code specialization on an NVIDIA GPU we have developped a "cross-JIT" approach where a CPU generate a specialized GPU code depending on data sets [3].

Microcontrollers with hardware support for floating point arithmetics, where we are able to generate on the fly $10\times$ faster specialized floating point routines [1].

Video compression need specialized code depending on data sets as shown in [11]. deGoal can be used in this domain.

Thanks to the low memory footprint of both code generator and generated code, deGoal is a perfect match for embedded systems.

This article is only an introductory tutorial; results with discussions about acceleration and produced code size can be found in the following bibliography.

References

1. Aracil, C., Courousse, D.: Software acceleration of floating-point multiplication using runtime code generation. In: Proceedings of the 4th International Conference on Energy Aware Computing, Istanbul, Turkey (December 2013)
2. Charles, H.P.: Basic infrastructure for dynamic code generation. In: Proceedings of the Workshop "Dynamic Compilation Everywhere", in Conjunction with the 7th HiPEAC Conference, Paris, France (January 2012)

3. Charles, H.P., Lomüller, V.: Data Size and Data Type Dynamic GPU Code Generation. In: GPU Design Pattern. Saxe-Coburg publications (2012)
4. Consel, C., Noël, F.: A general approach for run-time specialization and its application to C. In: Proceedings of the 23th Annual Symposium on Principles of Programming Languages, pp. 145–156 (1996)
5. Couroussé, D., Lomüller, V., Charles, H.P.: Introduction to Dynamic Code Generation – An Experiment with Matrix Multiplication for the STHORM Platform. In: Smart Multicore Embedded Systems, ch. 6, pp. 103–124. Springer (2013)
6. Gal, A., Probst, C.W., Franz, M.: HotpathVM: An effective JIT compiler for resource-constrained devices. In: VEE 2006, pp. 144–153. ACM, New York (2006)
7. Grant, B., Mock, M., Philipose, M., Chambers, C., Eggers, S.J.: DyC: An expressive annotation-directed dynamic compiler for C. Theor. Comput. Sci. 248(1-2), 147–199 (2000)
8. Jones, N.D.: An introduction to partial evaluation. ACM Comput. Surv. 28, 480–503 (1996), http://doi.acm.org/10.1145/243439.243447
9. Lattner, C.: LLVM: An Infrastructure for Multi-Stage Optimization. Master's thesis, Computer Science Dept., University of Illinois at Urbana-Champaign, Urbana, IL (2002)
10. Lhuillier, Y., Couroussé, D.: Embedded system memory allocator optimization using dynamic code generation. In: Proceedings of the Workshop "Dynamic Compilation Everywhere", in Conjunction with the 7th HiPEAC Conference, Paris, France (January 2012)
11. Sajjad, K., Tran, S.M., Barthou, D., Charles, H.P., Preda, M.: A global approach for mpeg-4 avc encoder optimization. In: 14th Workshop on Compilers for Parallel Computing (2009)
12. Shaylor, N.: A just-in-time compiler for memory-constrained low-power devices. In: Java VM 2002, pp. 119–126. USENIX Association, Berkeley (2002)

Improving the Performance of X10 Programs by Clock Removal

Paul Feautrier[1], Éric Violard[2], and Alain Ketterlin[2]

[1] INRIA, UCBL, CNRS & École Normale Supérieure de Lyon, LIP, Compsys
[2] INRIA & Université de Strasbourg

Abstract. X10 is a promising recent parallel language designed specifically to address the challenges of productively programming a wide variety of target platforms. The sequential core of X10 is an object-oriented language in the Java family. This core is augmented by a few parallel constructs that create *activities* as a generalization of the well known fork/join model. Clocks are a generalization of the familiar barriers. Synchronization on a clock is specified by the `Clock.advanceAll()` method call. Activities that execute *advances* stall until all existent activities have done the same, and then are released at the same (logical) time.

This naturally raises the following question: are clocks strictly necessary for X10 programs? Surprisingly enough, the answer is no, at least for sufficiently regular programs. One assigns a date to each operation, denoting the number of advances that the activity has executed before the operation. Operations with the same date constitute a *front*, fronts are executed sequentially in order of increasing dates, while operations in a front are executed in parallel if possible. Depending on the nature of the program, this may entail some overhead, which can be reduced to zero for polyhedral programs. We show by experiments that, at least for the current X10 runtime, this transformation usually improves the performance of our benchmarks. Besides its theoretical interest, this transformation may be of interest for simplifying a compiler or runtime library.

1 Introduction

Due to physical limitations, today computers all have explicit parallelism. This is true over the whole power spectrum, from embedded systems to high performance number crunchers, in which millions of cores must contribute to a common task. Efficient programming of such architectures is one of the most important challenge of the next decade. Among the many solutions which have been proposed – parallel programming libraries, domain specific languages, automatic parallelization – one of the most interesting is the use of parallel programming languages: languages in which parallel constructs are first class citizens, on a par with standard control constructs like the sequence or the loop. This approach has two advantages. Firstly, it hides the intricate details of parallel programming at the hardware or operating system level. Second, and most importantly,

A. Cohen (Ed.): CC 2014, LNCS 8409, pp. 113–132, 2014.

the programmer can express the problem inherent parallelism. Such parallelism might be difficult to infer from a sequential implementation.

The recent years have seen the creation of many such languages, among which Titanium [1], Chapel [2], Co-Array Fortran [3], UPC [4], and Habanero Java [5]. This paper deals with X10 [6], which is being developed at IBM Research. However, we believe that our techniques – if not our results – can be adapted without difficulties to other languages. Basically, parallelism is expressed by syntactic constructions, `async/finish` in X10 or `cobegin/coend` in Chapel. For some algorithms, it is necessary to restrict temporarily the degree of parallelism, using synchronization objects, called clocks in X10 or phasers in Habanero Java. These primitives are somewhat redundant with the `finish` construct, and may be used interchangeably in some circumstances. The aim of this paper is to explore these redundancies for X10, and to evaluate their impact on program performance.

Our key contributions are:

- we give a general scheme for clock elimination, which applies only to static control programs,
- we show that this scheme is correct and does not lose parallelism,
- for polyhedral programs, the control overhead of the target program can be reduced or even eliminated by loop transformations,
- experiments show that for the latest version of the X10 compiler and runtime, the proposed transformation improves the running time for fine grain parallel programs.

The rest of the paper is structured as follows. We will first give as much information on X10 as is necessary to understand our approach. The interested reader is referred to [6] for an in-depth coverage. We will then define the polyhedral subset of X10. While our approach is not limited to this subset, it gives the best results in the case of polyhedral programs.

1.1 The X10 Language

The Base Language. X10 is an object oriented language of the Java family. It has classes and methods, assignments and method invocation, and the usual control constructs: conditionals and loops. Dealing with method invocation necessitates interprocedural analysis, and is beyond the scope of this paper. The exact shape of assignments is irrelevant in this work.

X10 has two kind of loops: the ordinary Java loop:

```
for(<initialization>; <tests>; <increment>) S
```

and an enumerator loop:

```
for(x in <range>) S
```

where the type of the counter x is inferred from the type of the range.

Concurrency. Concurrency is expressed in X10 by two constructs, async S and finish S, where S is an arbitrary statement or statement block. Such constructs can be arbitrarily nested, except that the whole program is always embedded in an implicit or explicit finish, which creates the main activity. The effect of async S is to create a new *activity* or lightweight thread, which executes S in parallel with the rest of the program. The effect of finish S is to launch the execution of S, then to wait until all activities which were created inside S have terminated.

X10 also allows the distribution of work on a set of logical places (typically, various nodes of a compute cluster), in a way that is transparent to the organization of activities. This aspect is orthogonal to the work presented in this paper, and will not be further discussed.

Synchronization. In some cases, it may be necessary to synchronize several parallel activities. This can be achieved using *clocks*. Implicit clocks are created by clocked finish constructs. Activities are *registered* to the clock associated to the innermost enclosing clocked finish if created by a clocked async construct. An activity deregisters itself from its associated clock when it terminates. Synchronization occurs when an activity executes the Clock.advanceAll() primitive. This activity is held until all registered activities have executed a matching Clock.advanceAll(), at which time all registered activities are released. In the following text, and in the interest of brevity, Clock.advanceAll() will be abbreviated into advance. X10 also has explicit clocks, which are first class objects and are always accessed through references. Their analysis poses difficult points-to problems which are beyond the scope of this paper.

Clocks can be seen as generalization of the classical barriers. The main differences are that activities may be distributed among several clocks which work independently, and that this distribution is dynamic as it can change when an activity is created or terminated. Refer to Figure 1 for a sample X10 program.

Intuitively, it should be clear that an unclocked finish or a set of advances can be used interchangeably. In both cases, several activities are stalled until all of them have reached a synchronization point. If a clock is used, then all clocked activities are released for further processing, while in the case of a finish, they are destroyed. The aim of this paper is to explore this analogy, both from the point of view of expressiveness and from the point of view of performance.

1.2   The Polyhedral Subset of X10

In general, analysis of arbitrary programs in a high level language like X10 is difficult, due to the presence of dynamic constructs like while loops, tests, and method invocation. Hence, many authors [7] have defined the so-called polyhedral model, in which many analyses can be done at compile time. The polyhedral subset of X10 has been defined in [8]. The present section is a summary of this work. An X10 program is in the polyhedral model if its data structures are arrays and its control structures are loops. An enumerator loop is polyhedral if the range is an integer interval. The bounds of the range and the array subscripts must be affine functions of surrounding loops counters and integer parameters.

If these conditions are met, one can define statement instances, iteration domains, and an order of execution or happens-before relation. Statement instances are named by position vectors, which are deduced from abstract syntax trees (AST).

Consider the following example and its AST:

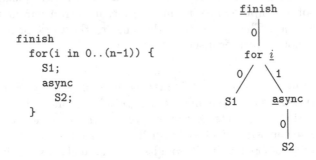

```
finish
  for(i in 0..(n-1)) {
    S1;
    async
      S2;
  }
```

Fig. 1. A Sample Program

The position vector for an elementary statement S is obtained by following the unique path in the AST from the root to S. In the example, the position vector of S_1 is $[f, 0, i, 0]$ and that of S_2 is $[f, 0, i, 1, a, 0]$, where f stands for finish and a stands for async. Let x and y be two position vectors, and let us write $x \prec y$ for "instance x happens before instance y". To decide whether $x \prec y$, first expand $x \ll y$, where $\ll$ is the ordinary lexicographic order. Then, remove a term if, after elimination of a common prefix, the first letter one encounter on the left is an a. This rule reflects the fact that the only temporal effect of async S is to postpone the execution of S. The reader may care to check that in the above example, instances of S_2 are unordered, while $S_1(i)$ happens before $S_2(i')$ if $i < i'$.

Another construction is necessary for programs that use clocks. The simplest case is that of one-clock programs (or of innermost clocked finishes). One must distinguish the unclocked happens-before relation, for which advances are treated as ordinary statements, and the clocked happens-before, noted $\twoheadleftarrow$. Let $\mathcal{A}$ be the set of advances inside one clocked finish. The advance counter at operation u is defined as:

$$\phi(u) = \text{Card}\{u' \in \mathcal{A} \mid u' \prec u\}.$$

When the effect of clocks is taken into account, one can prove that if $\phi(u) < \phi(v)$, then u happens before v. As a consequence, the clocked happens-before relation is:

$$u \twoheadleftarrow v \equiv \phi(u) < \phi(v) \lor u \prec v.$$

Since for polyhedral programs $\mathcal{A}$ is a union of disjoint polyhedra, and $u' \prec u$ is a disjunction of affine inequalities, the set $\{u' \in \mathcal{A} \,|\, u' \prec u\}$ is the set of integer points which belong to a union of polyhedra. The cardinal of this set can be computed in closed form using the theory of Ehrhart polynomials, for which there exists efficient libraries [9].

2 A Generic Transformation Strategy

Our goal is to remove clocks from X10 programs. To understand the idea of this transformation, consider Figure 2: the center graph depicts the execution of an imaginary X10 program, where activities are represented by vertical boxes that contain regular instruction executions and clock synchronization operations. These activities "align" on their calls to `Clock.advanceAll()`. The code on the left side of the figure is one possible source of this program. The idea of the transformation is to extract "slices" (or phases) across activities, represented by horizontal dashed boxes on the graph. A possible corresponding program appears on the right of the figure: the usage of clocks has been replaced by the barrier ending `finish` blocks. We will prove in the next section that both programs execute the same operations in the same order, except for clocks and the number (and duration) of activities.

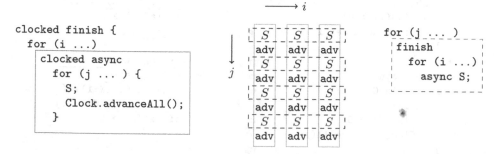

Fig. 2. Parallelism and synchronization in X10, with and without clocks

This transformation, can be implemented by a straightforward technique. Starting with a given `clocked finish` block, the result of the transformation can be sketched as follows:

```
for (d ...) // where d is a monotonically increasing phase number
    finish S_d // the original finish block restricted to phase d
```

Writing the transformed program this way assumes that it is possible 1) to determine the number of phases of the program, either statically or dynamically, 2) to execute the given block for a given phase only (the *restriction* of the block to that phase), and 3) to repeatedly execute the original block. The rest of this section explores these three issues.

2.1   Motivating Example

Our goal in this section is three-fold. First, it is important to understand what class of programs the transformation can be applied to. Second, the example will help pinpointing potential optimizations. And third, we want to empirically validate our intuition that managing clocks is more expensive than creating activities.

Our working example appears on the left of Figure 3. The finish block creates only two activities in addition to the main activity. Each of these execute a loop that does some work (in abstract instructions S0 and S1), and then conditionally synchronizes with the other. A set of input parameters, contained in arrays a0 and a1, drives the control of the program and the synchronization scheme. These parameters make it impossible to statically derive how many phases the program has, and how many executions of S0 and S1 are performed in each phase.

```
clocked finish {
  clocked async {
    for (i in 0..(N-1)) {
      S0(i);
      if (a0(i) > 0)
        Clock.advanceAll();
    }
  }
  clocked async {
    for (i in 0..(N-1)) {
      S1(i);
      if (a1(i) > 0)
        Clock.advanceAll();
    }
  }
}
```

```
1   cont = true;
2   for (d=0 ; cont ; d++) {
3     cont = false;
4     finish {$\phi$ := 0;
5       async { $\phi_0$ := $\phi$;
6         for (i in 0..(N-1)) {
7           if (d == $\phi_0$) S0(i);
8           if (a0(i) > 0)
9             ++ $\phi_0$;
10        }
11        if (d<$\phi_0$) cont = true; }
12      async { $\phi_1$ := $\phi$;
13        for (i in 0..(N-1)) {
14          if (d == $\phi_1$) S1(i);
15          if (a1(i) > 0)
16            ++ $\phi_1$;
17        }
18        if (d<$\phi_1$) cont = true; }
19      if (d<$\phi$) cont = true; }
20  }
```

Fig. 3. An example program, before and after transformation

The resulting program appears on the right of Figure 3. The transformation can be broken into four successive steps:

1. The finish block is wrapped inside a loop over d, whose iterations represent the various phases of the execution (line 2 on Fig. 3). The exit condition is represented with a boolean, named cont, whose role is detailed in the fourth phase.

2. Every activity gets its own local "counter" (named ϕ, ϕ_0 and ϕ_1 in the example),[1] initialized at the start of the activity by capturing the value of the parent activity's counter if any (lines 4, 5, and 12). Local counters are maintained by replacing calls to `Clock.advanceAll()` by an incrementation (lines 9 and 16).

3. All instructions that have an effect visible outside the `finish` block are guarded (lines 7 and 14), and the guard condition checks whether the value of the local counter matches the currently executed phase (given by d).

4. Finally, when any activity reaches its end, the value of the local counter has reached its maximum value for that activity. This maximum value is the index of the last phase for which this activity has work to do. A simple test decides whether the loop on d should continue iterating (lines 11, 18, and 19).[2]

To evaluate the performance impact of the transformation, we still need to give some definition to `S0(i)` and `S1(i)`. In the experiment below, we use some "dummy" code of the form:

```
for (t in 1..T)
    a(i) += garbage(k%4)
```

that is to say, two accesses to arrays plus two arithmetic operations (subject to optimization). The `T` parameter is used to control the amount of work performed by one call to either `S0` and `S1`: on a recent processor, we have observed that such a loop takes roughly `T` nanoseconds. To run either the original or the modified program, the arrays `a0` and `a1` are filled with randomly generated values with equiprobable signs.

Figure 4 shows the execution times in milliseconds of both versions with $N = 100$ as a function of the parameter `T`. The original version uses clocks to synchronize both activities, whereas the modified version simply repeats the whole `finish` block as many times as necessary (therefore creating many more activities). These curves are surprisingly close to each other. For moderately heavy instruction grain (here between 10 and 100 μs per call to `S0` or `S1`), it seems that the cost of handling clocks is approximately as high as executing around 50 instances of the block (including the creation of activities). This accomplishes our third goal, and validates our intuition that clocks are expensive.

2.2   Applicability and Correctness

There are two main aspects in the generic transformation:

1. guarding the instructions, so as to have them execute during the right phase;
2. maintaining phase numbers ("dates") during each iteration of the loop on d.

---

[1] The local counter of the activity executing the body of `finish`, named ϕ, is useless here and was left for completeness only.

[2] Activities could be aborted once their local counter is above the value of d: this aspect is more or less orthogonal to our goal, and is ignored here.

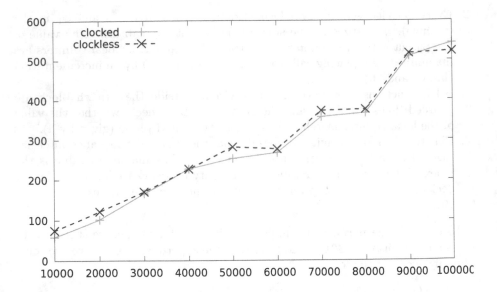

Fig. 4. Clocked and clockless execution times (in milliseconds)

Let us for a moment assume that the second aspect is enforced. In that case, it is easy to see that both versions of the program are equivalent. For, if two instructions of the original block are executed during different phases, then they will be executed inside different **finish** blocks in the transformed program. And if they are executed during the same phase, they will still be executed in the right order, since the transformed block is a copy of the original block, and thus faithfully reproduces program order. Therefore, correctness of the transformation is guaranteed if phase numbers can be correctly maintained.

Maintaining correct dates at all times, *i.e.*, during every iteration of the d-loop, however, is not possible for all programs. Here is a simple modification of our previous example, where the body of the i-loop inside the first **async** becomes:

```
if (a0(i) > 0) {
  a0(i) = -1;
  Clock.advanceAll();
}
```

Here, code executed at date d updates a value that will be used at a later date (an iteration d' with $d' > d$). This means that later iterations of the d-loop will not be able to maintain phase numbers correctly, leading to an incorrect result.

The general criterion to distinguish programs that can be transformed correctly is the following: every iteration of the d-loop must perform exactly the same sequence of advance counter incrementations. To formally capture this notion, let us define *control variables*: a variable that is used in a conditional branch (including loop back-edges), or to update another control variable (with arrays considered as single variables).[3] Then, a program will be correctly transformed, if the history of each control variable is the same in each iteration of the d loop, *i.e.* if control variables which are live-in at the begining of the d loop are not modified within the loop. For sequential structured programs, this can be checked by many classical algorithms, including reaching definition analysis and transformation to SSA. These algorithms can be extended to parallel programs: see for instance [10], where a Concurrent Static Single Assignment form is defined for programs with parallel construct similar to those of X10, including post / wait synchronization. The results of this analysis are approximate. For polyhedral X10 programs, it is possible to do better, as shown in [8].

2.3 Optimization Opportunities

The generic transformation described above uses a very costly strategy: re-executing the original code again and again, inhibiting the execution of almost all instructions at each iteration. Even though this cost seems to be amortized even for moderately heavy computations, the whole structure of the transformed program is unsatisfactory. This section tries to highlight characteristics of the transformed program that may lead to further simplification. The various steps of the intuitive transformation provide important clues on classes of programs where this applies.

The first aspect is about the local counters that have to be maintained to model the "date" inside an activity. In some cases, the date may be available at compile time as a closed form function of loop counters. Or it can be precomputed to avoid repeated incrementations of the local counter. In our example, precomputation would fill two arrays d0 and d1, indexed on i and containing the date at iteration i. The code of the first activity becomes:

```
for (i in 0..(N-1))
    if (d == d0(i)) S0(i);
```

In other cases, like the ones described in the next section, dates are functions of the enclosing loop counters, and do not need dedicated storage.

The second aspect is very much related to the first, and relates to the upper bound of the enclosing loop. When dates can be calculated statically, it is immediate to compute or memorize their maximal value (which is the upper bound on d) . This also removes the need of a boolean variable and tests at the end of activities.

The third aspect relates to the interplay between statement guards and loop bounds. In our example, we have reached a situation where a loop iterates from 0 to $N - 1$, but where only a sub-range of this iteration space leads to actual execution. It is therefore possible to adjust the range of the loop to cover only the relevant sub-range. In our example, the first activity becomes:

---

[3] In practice, the collection of control-variables can be restricted to programming constructs containing at least one call to Clock.advanceAll().

```
while (d0(i0) == d) {
    S0(i0);
    ++ i0;
}
```

where i0 is a global counter, suitably initialized and preserved across activities.

We have given an informal account on how a program with clocks removed can be further simplified and optimized. The next section describes a class of programs where these optimizations can be systematically applied, and details their implementation.

2.4   General Polyhedral Programs

Polyhedral programs with clocks have the property that a date can be computed directly for any instruction, by counting the number of advances performed before an instance of the given instruction. This removes the need to maintain explicit counters, and provides symbolic expressions involving loop counters and symbolic parameters. One can always evaluate the number of integer points inside a (parametrized) polyhedron, and therefore assign a monotonically increasing rank to any instance of an instruction. Under reasonable assumptions, i.e., that loops have unit steps, such ranks are integer-valued polynomials with rational coefficients [11].

An example program appears on Figure 5, with date expressions placed in comments. Note that the counting happens in two phases: first, the starting date of an activity is computed, and second the date of instructions are computed relative to the activity's starting date.

```
                                    for (d in 0..(N-2+M*(M-1)/2))
clocked finish                        finish
  for (i in 0..(N-1)) {                 for (i in 0..(N-1)) {
    clocked async {  // i                 async {
      for (j in 0..(M-1)) {                 for (j in 0..(M-1)) {
        S0(i,j);     // i+j*(j-1)/2           if (d == i+j*(j-1)/2)
        for (k in 0..(j-1)) {                   S0(i,j);
          S1(i,j,k); // i+j*(j-1)/2+k         for (k in 0..(j-1)) {
          Clock.advanceAll();                  if (d == i+j*(j-1)/2+k)
    } } }                                        S1(i,j,k);
    Clock.advanceAll();              } } }
  }                                   }
```

Fig. 5. A polyhedral program with polynomial dates (in comments) on the left, and the result of the transformation, on the right

The transformation process starts by computing the maximal date at which an instruction of the original finish block executes. This can be done by maximizing for each instruction individually, and then taking the maximum of the results. This maximum, $N-2+M(M-1)/2$ in our example, is the upper bound of the loop wrapped around the original block. Then, calls to `Clock.advanceAll()` are removed, and guards are placed around statements. The result appears on the right part of Figure 5.

After having inserted guards around statements, the last step is to examine whether the guards have an impact on the bounds of the loops that enclose the statement. Our example illustrates this situation: after transformation, the innermost loop becomes:

```
for (k in 0..(j-1))
    if (d == i+j*(j-1)/2+k)
        S1(i,j,k);
```

A trivial rewriting of the guard shows that even though the loop iterates over a range of values for k, the whole loop will actually execute S1(i,j,k) at most once. This construct can therefore be replaced by:

```
k = d - i - j*(j-1)/2;
if (0<=k && k<=j-1)
    S1(i,j,k);
```

which tests whether the single value selected by the guard is inside the range of the loop.

Note that we started with a depth three loop nest. Then a new loop level was added around this nest. And finally the deepest level is removed. This is likely to reduce the overhead introduced by the transformation. This optimization may be extended to loops containing several statements (at the same or different dates). However, it applies only when date expressions are linear in the nearest enclosing loop counter, which we think is a very common case. Actually, for this not to be the case, an innermost statement-bearing loop should also contain another loop 1) containing only advances, and 2) with a bound being a function of its parent loop counter. Here is the simplest example of such a construction:

```
for (y in ...) {
    S(...);
    for (z in 0..y)
        Clock.advanceAll();
}
```

We think this pathological case and its variations are sufficiently infrequent not to cause real trouble in practice.

Note that after a loop is removed, the statement is still guarded, but with a condition involving inequalities. Therefore, there is no possibility of re-applying the same "iteration space collapsing", but nothing says that the new guard may not imply bound adjustments on the enclosing loops. The next section shows an example of such chained loop adjustments.

2.5   Polyhedral Programs with Affine Dates

We have seen that when polynomial dates are available, the resulting program can be optimized by combining guards and loop bounds. However, dealing with polynomials of high degree is difficult and may restricts how far optimizations can go. It is therefore interesting to consider the particular case of affine dates. In that case, all obstacles to optimization are lifted, and one can hope to be able to optimize the transformed program up to the point where it has the same complexity as the original program.[4]

Whenever the original program induces dates that are all affine forms in the enclosing loop counters (and parameters), we are guaranteed that the deepest loop level can be removed. In fact, this last level of loop contains only guarded statements, and the guards are of the form $d = \alpha_0 i_0 + \ldots + \alpha_n i_n$, where $i_0, \ldots, i_n$ are the counters of the enclosing loops. Such a guard always determines at most one value of the counter of the nearest loop. This property appears in the program in Figure 6. The left part shows the original clocked finish block (dates appear in comments), whereas the right part shows the mechanically transformed program. Since dates are affine, one can immediately apply the "iteration space collapsing" optimization mentioned in the previous section. The first loop on j then becomes:

```
if (i<=d && d<=N-1)
    S0(i,d);
```

and the second loop on j can be transformed as well (note that we do not keep a variable to store the value of j, but rather substitute it immediately).

The major advantage of having affine dates is the fact that the resulting program can be further optimized. We are going to illustrate these additional optimizations on the example program in Figure 6, and then we will show how the program transformations involved are strongly related to the problem of code generation from a polyhedral model of a program. We will then show, in the next section, how existing tools can be adapted to directly produce the optimized version.

Regarding the example of Figure 6, the first step is to replace constructs of the form async if (...) S(...) with if (...) async S(...), because there is no need to create an activity that does nothing. All these initial modifications lead to the following program:

```
for (d in 0..(2*N-2))
  finish
    for (i in 0..(N-1)) {
      if (i<=d && d<=N-1)
        async S0(i,d);
```

---

[4] Note that the complexity in terms of the number of executions of individual instructions is always the same on both versions. Here we refer to the complexity of the associated control, i.e., the number of times guards and loop exit conditions are evaluated.

```
                                    for (d in 0..(2*N-2))
   clocked finish {                   finish {
     for (i in 0..(N-1)) {              for (i in 0..(N-1)) {
       clocked async // i                 async
         for (j in i..(N-1)) {              for (j in i..(N-1)) {
           S0(i,j); // i+j-i = j             if (d == j)
           Clock.advanceAll();                 S0(i,j);
         }                                  }
       Clock.advanceAll();
       clocked async // i+1               async
         for (j in 0..(i-1)) {              for (j in 0..(i-1)) {
           S1(i,j); // i+1+j                 if (d == i+j+1)
           Clock.advanceAll();                 S1(i,j);
         }                                  }
     }                                  }
   }                                  }
```

Fig. 6. A polyhedral program with affine dates on the left, and the corresponding program after clock removal and before optimization on the right

```
   if (i+1<=d && d<=2*i)
     async S1(i,d-i-1);
 }
```

At this point, all remaining optimizations are made possible by the comparison of the various inequalities that apply to the individual instructions. Since our goal is to reduce the time taken by evaluating the guards, we are going to rearrange this code to eliminate useless guards and uselessly large bounds.

The first batch of useless evaluations of guards is caused by the d<=N-1 condition, because at this point d is supposed to iterate from zero to 2*N-2. This means that half of the values of d will simply fail to satisfy the condition. Eliminating these useless tests requires that the range of d is split into two sub-ranges, the first of which makes the condition trivially true, and the second which makes it false. The result appears in Figure 7(a). Range-splitting globally enlarges the code, but removes any occurrence of S0 in the loop iterating over the second sub-range. Note also that condition i+1<=d around S1 has become trivially true in the second loop, and is therefore also omitted.

The second set of unnecessary tests is caused by the remaining conditions, which in all cases are stricter than the surrounding loop bounds. The range of the first loop on i can be split into three sub-ranges, namely 0..(d-1), d, and (d+1)..(N-1): the first leads to the bulk of the work, the second selects only S0, and the third leads to nothing. The result of bound adjustment appears in Figure 7(b). What was just done on upper bounds can now be done on lower bounds as well: the condition d<=2*i appears twice inside loops whose lower bound on i is zero, for any value of d. Therefore, the lower bound can be adjusted as well. The details are left to the reader.

```
for (d in 0..(N-1))              for (d in 0..(N-1))
  finish                           finish {
    for (i in 0..(N-1)) {            for (i in 0..(d-1)) {
      if (i<=d)                        async S0(i,d);
        async S0(i,d);                 if (d<=2*i)
      if (i+1<=d && d<=2*i)              async S1(i,d-i-1);
        async S1(i,d-i-1);           }
    }                                async S0(d,d);
  for (d in N..(2*N-2))            }
    finish                         for (d in N..(2*N-2))
      for (i in 0..(N-1)) {          finish
        if (d<=2*i)                    for (i in 0..(N-1)) {
          async S1(i,d-i-1);             if (d<=2*i)
      }                                    async S1(i,d-i-1);
                                       }
   (a) After range splitting on d    (b) After bound adjustments
```

Fig. 7. The program transformed from Fig. 6, after various further optimizations

3   Polyhedral Implementation and Optimized Control

The approach we have taken in the previous section consists in a succession of elementary transformations: wrapping a loop around the original code, placing guards around elementary statements, and adjusting iteration domains according to the guards. In contrast, in the polyhedral model, all these transformations can be represented in a uniform framework, and polyhedral operations can be used to manipulate the program. A polyhedral model of an instruction (a polyhedron, for short) is made up of two distinct parts: first, an ordered list of dimensions, and second a set of constraints (inequalities) on the values of the various dimensions. There are three types of dimensions: 1) syntactic dimensions, which are usually constants, 2) loop iterators, and 3) parallel constructs indicators, which are the abstract symbols f(inish) and a(sync). Figure 8 displays the polyhedra corresponding to the instructions appearing in the original program of Figure 6. The left part of the figure shows an abstract syntax tree, which is convenient to read the various dimensions. The right part shows the polyhedra, using the notation of the iscc *polyhedral calculator*, part of the barvinok library [9]. Note that polyhedra can be parametrized (by N in our case), and that constant dimensions can be written literally, *i.e.*, {[f,0,...]: ...} is equivalent to {[f,p_0,...]: p_0=0 and ...}.

All manipulations necessary for the elimination of clocks can now be formulated as operations on polyhedra:

1. Introducing dates is performed by adding a dimension, at the very end of the list of dimensions since the date may depend on any of the enclosing loop counters. For instance, the definition of S0 becomes:

   S0 := [N]->{[f,0,i,0,a,0,j,0,d]: 0<=i<N and i<=j<N and d=j};

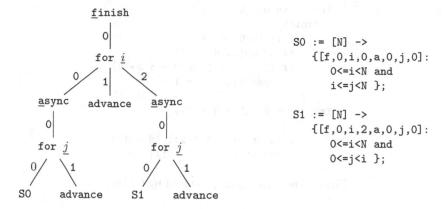

```
finish
    0|
  for i
 0 / 1| \ 2
async  advance  async
  0|              0|
for j            for j
0/ \1           0/ \1
S0   advance   S1   advance
```

```
S0 := [N] ->
  {[f,0,i,0,a,0,j,0]:
     0<=i<N and
     i<=j<N };

S1 := [N] ->
  {[f,0,i,2,a,0,j,0]:
     0<=i<N and
     0<=j<i };
```

Fig. 8. An AST for the program on Figure 6, and the corresponding polyhedra

2. Representing the whole program simply consists in computing the union of the individual instruction polyhedra: [5]

   `P := S0+S1;`

3. Iterating on dates first is performed by changing the order of the dimensions. This is written as:

   `U := {[f,p0,i,p1,a,p2,j,p3,d]->[d,f,p0,i,p1,a,p2,j,p3]}(P);`

   This does not do anything, but is an important indication to the next step.

4. Producing the final code is performed by generating a program scanning the resulting polyhedron U. We use the CLooG algorithm [12], which produces a new loop nest with a loop scanning dates (d) first, and whose body contains various constructions (finish, async, loops, and instructions) in the order prescribed by the various other dimensions.

The final code (after trivial cosmetic post-processing) appears on Figure 9: CLooG has adjusted all loop bounds (even though it could have gone further). The same result could be obtained by applying, e.g., some variation of Fourier-Motzkin elimination for bound adjustment [13]. However, reconstructing the structure would still need additional work. CLooG does both iteration domain computation *and* code generation.

4   Experimental Results

To evaluate the effect of eliminating clocks on execution time, we have used eight different polyhedral programs with affine dates. All these programs are parametrized by a number N that determines the number of activities and the number of iterations of loops in various ways. Their execution is depicted on Figure 10 for $N = 6$: vertical lines represent activities, horizontal dashed lines

---

[5] For this union operation the dimension of the various lists must coincide; this is trivially achieved by padding with zeros. No modification is necessary in our example.

```
for (d in 0..(N - 1))
  finish
    for (i in 0..d) {
      async S0(i, d);
      if (d >= i + 1 && 2 * i >= d)
        async S1(i, d - i - 1);
    }
for (d in N..(2 * N - 2))
  finish
    for (i in (d - d / 2)..(N - 1))
      async S1(i, d - i - 1);
```

Fig. 9. The final result, produced by CLooG

represent phases of execution, and dots represent individual instruction executions (distinct dot shapes represent distinct static instructions). For instance, the penultimate iteration domain on Figure 10 corresponds to the program shown on the left of Figure 6.

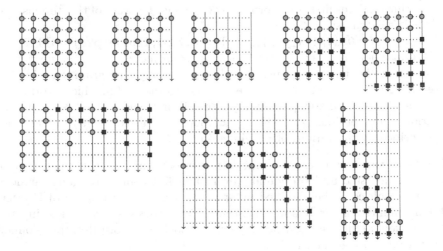

Fig. 10. Example iteration spaces, here for $N = 6$. All examples spawn $O(N)$ activities, last for $O(N)$ clock steps, and execute $O(N^2)$ instructions.

To compare the clocked and clockless versions of each program, we have measured their execution times (averaged over 20 executions). We have used a not-quite-recent X86-64 compatible AMD machine with 24 cores (two sockets of 12 cores). X10 programs were compiled with the official release of X10, version 2.3.1, available from http://x10-lang.org/. All programs have been run with $N = 100$. Because the elimination of clocks affects only the control of the program, and not its actual work, we have varied the time taken by a single instruction execution (a call of the form $S_k(i,j)$ in all cases) the same way we did in Section 2.1: a single parameter T controls how much time a single execution of any $S_k(i,j)$ takes. The goal of the experiment is therefore to measure the difference in execution times as a function of T.

The results are shown on Figure 11. Every graph shows the execution time of both versions. In all cases, the clockless version runs faster than the version with clocks. Rows of three graphs show the times of a given program for various values of T (the workload): every graph displays ten evenly spaced values of T, with one order of magnitude variation from one graph to the next.

Since X10 is not the only language allowing finish/async programming, we have also conducted preliminary experiments with Habanero-Java [5] (version 1.3.1), with results similar to those presented here.

There are several lessons to learn from Figure 11. First, eliminating clocks always has a positive impact on execution time. This validates our intuition that clocks are expensive to manage. At least their use is more expensive than launching more activities (by a factor $O(N)$ in our case). We acknowledge that this is fairly dependent on implementation issues, but we also think that it will be easier to optimize activity creation rather than clock synchronization. Future implementations of X10 (and related languages, like Habanero and Chapel [2]) may change this situation.

Examination of the leftmost column of Figure 11 shows the relatively irregular behavior of programs using clocks with fine-grain instructions: it looks as if the frequent advances make the actual time difficult to predict. Clockless programs display a smoother, quasi-linear curve. Again, this heavily depends on the implementation of the activity scheduler, but it seems clear that clockless programs are "easier" to schedule over an arbitrary number of threads.

The third lesson learned is that, as expected, the difference between versions vanishes when the workload is reasonably large, because the time spent in control becomes negligible compared to the time spent on computation. Less obvious is that this happens for values of T around one million (on our machine, about 1 millisecond). Considering the kind of programs we have used (loops over arrays, where instructions access one or more arrays), there is little chance that this workload is reached. This means that for fine-grain programs, the transformation is probably advantageous, providing significant speedup in most cases.

5 Related Work

There exists a large body of literature on barriers and clocks, their analysis, optimization and verification. Nearest to the subject of this paper is work on optimal barrier placement [14,15,16] and verification [17]. While apparently related to the present work, Chau-Weng Tseng paper [18] deals in fact with a completely different problem, namely how to distribute work among threads in order to minimize synchronization. Several authors have argued that barriers or clocks can be implemented more efficiently than task or activity creation, and have advocated algorithms for minimizing the number of tasks. To the best of

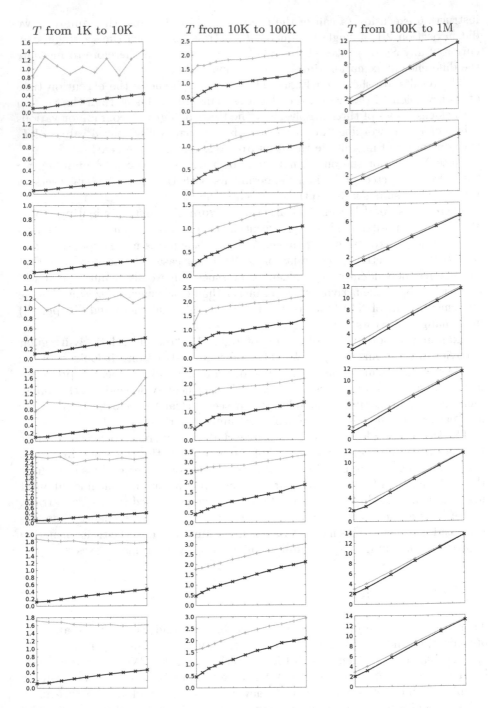

Fig. 11. Execution times in seconds for clocked (—|—) and clockless (—✳—) versions, for various scales of workload

our knowledge, the word *SPMDization* was coined by Padua and Paek in [19]. A recent discussion of the same idea is by Zaho et. al. [20] in which an algorithm, which amount to moving parallel loops outside sequential loops with barrier insertion is proposed. Our contention here is that moving in the opposite direction may be beneficial in some cases. Choosing between the two solutions depends on many factors: the target system, the compiler and runtime and the source program. For instance, if the target is hardware, where it is almost impossible to dynamically create activities and synchronization is cheap, using clocks might be the best solution. Our work shows that the situation is exactly the reverse for software.

6 Conclusion

When generating a parallel program, either manually or automatically, one has to choose between two extreme program shapes: one a sequence of parallel constructs, the other a parallel composition of sequential threads. Obviously, these two extreme cases can be combined to produce many intermediate solutions.

In the first approach, it is usually possible to restrict synchronization to one barrier after each parallel block. This corresponds to the exclusive use of `async` / `finish` in X10, and is especially suitable for vector or data-parallelism. In the second approach, it is usually not possible, except in the case of embarrassingly parallel programs, to construct independent threads. Residual dependences must be satisfied using clocks or phasers [5]. This work shows that deciding which approach gives the best performance is not obvious, and must be approached experimentally. Our main contribution is a systematic method for converting a large class of clocked programs into unclocked ones. Our algorithms can easily be automated, thus simplifying the comparison process. Let us emphasize that our transformation is not limited to polyhedral programs or fragments. The only real constraint is that no control variable which is live-in at the beginning of the considered fragment is modified. This condition is trivially satisfied for polyhedral programs, in which case further optimizations are enabled.

This paper has introduced a program transformation that acts on an explicitly parallel program, an unusual characteristic in the polyhedral framework. Such an ability opens up a large space of new potential optimizations, extending the scope of automatic parallelization. Taking the cost of synchronization primitives into account must also be extended and further generalized, to cover cases where implementations may have different semantics and/or relative overheads. Also, the cost of synchronization is only one part of the picture, and more work is needed to combine synchronization costs with more "traditional" transformation objectives in the polyhedral framework, like, e.g., temporal and spatial locality. Finally, we plan to investigate the use of parallel-to-parallel program transformations in dynamic optimization frameworks, where switching between various versions of the same program can alleviate the variation of synchronization costs linked to changing runtime conditions.

References

1. Yelick, K., Semenzato, L., Pike, G., Miyamoto, C., Liblit, B., Krishnamurthy, A., Hilfinger, P., Graham, S., Gay, D., Colella, P., et al.: Titanium: A high-performance Java dialect. Concurrency Practice and Experience 10(11-13), 825–836 (1998)
2. Chamberlain, B., Callahan, D., Zima, H.: Parallel programmability and the Chapel language. International Journal of High Performance Computing Applications 21(3), 291–312 (2007)
3. Numrich, R.W., Reid, J.: Co-array Fortran for parallel programming. SIGPLAN Fortran Forum 17(2), 1–31 (1998)
4. UPC Consortium and others: UPC language specifications. Lawrence Berkeley National Lab. Tech. Report LBNL–59208 (2005)
5. Cavé, V., Zhao, J., Shirako, J., Sarkar, V.: Habanero-java: The new adventures of old X10. In: PPPJ 2011, pp. 51–61. ACM (2011)
6. Saraswat, V., Bloom, B., Peshansky, I., Tardieu, O., Grove, D.: X10 language specification version 2.2 (March 2012), http://x10.sourceforge.net/documentation/languagespec/x10-latest.pdf
7. Feautrier, P., Lengauer, C.: The polyhedral model. In: Padua, D. (ed.) Encyclopedia of Parallel Programming. Springer (2011)
8. Yuki, T., Feautrier, P., Rajopadhye, S., Saraswat, V.: Array dataflow analysis for polyhedral X10 programs. In: PPoPP (2013)
9. Verdoolaege, S., Seghir, R., Beyls, K., Loechner, V., Bruynooghe, M.: Counting integer points in parametric polytopes using Barvinok's rational functions. In: Algorithmica (2007)
10. Lee, J., Padua, D.A., Midkiff, S.P.: Basic compiler algorithms for parallel programs. In: PPoPP 1999, pp. 1–12. ACM (1999)
11. Clauss, P.: Counting solutions to linear and nonlinear constraints through Ehrhart polynomials: Applications to analyze and transform scientific programs. In: ICS 1996, pp. 278–285. ACM (1996)
12. Bastoul, C.: Code generation in the polyhedral model is easier than you think. In: PACT 2013, Juan-les-Pins, pp. 7–16 (2004)
13. Ancourt, C., Irigoin, F.: Scanning polyhedra with DO loops. In: Proc. Third SIGPLAN Symp. on Principles and Practice of Parallel Programming, pp. 39–50. ACM Press (April 1991)
14. Aiken, A., Gay, D.: Barrier inference. In: POPL 1998, pp. 342–354 (1998)
15. Kamil, A., Yelick, K.: Concurrency analysis for parallel programs with textually aligned barriers. In: Ayguadé, E., Baumgartner, G., Ramanujam, J., Sadayappan, P. (eds.) LCPC 2005. LNCS, vol. 4339, pp. 185–199. Springer, Heidelberg (2006)
16. Darte, A., Schreiber, R.: A linear-time algorithm for optimal barrier placement. In: PPoPP 2005, pp. 26–35. ACM (2005)
17. Vasudevan, N., Tardieu, O., Dolby, J., Edwards, S.A.: Compile-time analysis and specialization of clocks in concurrent programs. In: de Moor, O., Schwartzbach, M.I. (eds.) CC 2009. LNCS, vol. 5501, pp. 48–62. Springer, Heidelberg (2009)
18. Tseng, C.W.: Compiler optimizations for eliminating barrier synchronization. In: PPoPP 1995, pp. 144–155. ACM (1995)
19. Padua, D.A., Paek, Y.: Compiling for scalable multiprocessors with Polaris. Parallel Processing Letters 07(04), 425–436 (1997)
20. Zhao, J., Shirako, J., Nandivada, V.K., Sarkar, V.: Reducing task creation and termination overhead in explicitly parallel programs. In: PACT 2010, pp. 169–180. ACM (2010)

Taming Control Divergence in GPUs through Control Flow Linearization

Jayvant Anantpur and Govindarajan R.

Supercomputer Education and Research Centre
Indian Institute of Science
jayvant@hpc.serc.iisc.ernet.in, govind@serc.iisc.ernet.in

Abstract. Branch divergence is a very commonly occurring performance problem in GPGPU in which the execution of diverging branches is serialized to execute only one control flow path at a time. Existing hardware mechanism to reconverge threads using a stack causes duplicate execution of code for unstructured control flow graphs. Also the stack mechanism cannot effectively utilize the available parallelism among diverging branches. Further, the amount of nested divergence allowed is also limited by depth of the branch divergence stack.

In this paper we propose a simple and elegant transformation to handle all of the above mentioned problems. The transformation converts an unstructured CFG to a structured CFG without duplicating user code. It incurs only a linear increase in the number of basic blocks and also the number of instructions. Our solution linearizes the CFG using a predicate variable. This mechanism reconverges the divergent threads as early as possible. It also reduces the depth of the reconvergence stack. The available parallelism in nested branches can be effectively extracted by scheduling the basic blocks to reduce the effect of stalls due to memory accesses. It can also increase execution efficiency of nested loops with different trip counts for different threads.

We implemented the proposed transformation at PTX level using the Ocelot compiler infrastructure. We evaluated the technique using various benchmarks to show that it can be effective in handling the performance problem due to divergence in unstructured CFGs.

Keywords: GPU, Control Divergence, Control Flow Graph.

1 Introduction

There has been a tremendous increase in the use of GPUs in general purpose programming, especially to accelerate data parallel code. The emergence of programming models such as CUDA [17], OpenCL [13] etc., has fuelled the use of GPUs.

Programming models such as CUDA, OpenCL, etc., use the Single Instruction Multiple Threads (SIMT) computation model [17]. In this model a large number of threads run in parallel on Single Instruction Multiple Data (SIMD) cores using hardware multithreading to hide the stalls due to long latency instructions. A group of threads, called a warp, is scheduled to execute on the SIMD processors. Each thread in a warp executes the same instruction. The execution of a branch instruction can cause the control flow to diverge. The existing hardware solution to handle branch divergence serializes

A. Cohen (Ed.): CC 2014, LNCS 8409, pp. 133–153, 2014.

execution of the two paths till a reconvergence point [10]. Branch divergence is one of the major sources of performance bottlenecks in GPUs [7] [12] [16] [22]. The diverging threads are reconverged at the immediate post-dominator (IPDOM) of the branch instruction.

IPDOM guarantees earliest reconvergence for structured CFGs but not for unstructured CFGs. Unstructured CFGs (for definition see section 3.2) can result due to the use of programming language constructs such as goto, break statements, short circuiting operations, etc., and also due to compiler optimizations such as function inlining [22]. The work by Wu et al. [22] characterizes the use of unstructured control flow in GPU applications. As per their findings, unstructured CFGs are common in GPU applications and benchmarks (in 40% of the Parboil, Rodinia and Optix benchmarks).

In the case of unstructured CFGs, some basic blocks between the divergent branch and its IPDOM may get executed multiple times due to different paths to reach those blocks from the divergent branch. Diamos et al. [7] proposed a combined hardware and software solution for this problem and found a reasonable reduction in dynamic instruction counts for several real applications. Their proposed solution identifies the thread frontier of each block - set of basic blocks where all other diverged threads may be executing - and then checks for stalled threads waiting in the thread frontier.

Serial execution of different paths of a branch cannot effectively utilize the parallelism among the paths especially in the case of nested branches and nested loops. In the case of nested branches, the different execution paths cannot be interleaved to extract parallelism among them. Rhu et al. [16] proposed a modification to the existing hardware stack to enable interleaved execution of divergent control flow paths. They showed performance improvement by utilizing the available parallelism among the diverging control flow paths. In the case of nested loops, when the inner loops have different trip counts for different threads of the same warp, threads with smaller trip counts have to wait for the threads with larger trip counts. Han et al. [12] proposed a compiler transformation to reduce the effect of divergence due to varying trip-counts. It merges a divergent loop with one or more outer surrounding loops into one loop.

Another limitation of the hardware reconvergence stack is that its depth increases as the nesting level of branches increases.

In this paper we describe a simple compile time transformation to convert unstructured CFGs to structured CFGs. The transformation uses a predicate variable to guard the execution of basic blocks in a CFG. The guard variable acts like a software Program Counter to decide which basic block to execute next. The transformation implements the control flow as a simple "if-then" structure, linearizing the CFG. The proposed transformation is powerful to convert any unstructured CFG to a structured one. It does not duplicate the user code unlike in the earlier approach of Zhang et al. [23]. Carter et al. [5] proved that any node-splitting technique used to convert an irreducible graph to a reducible graph can increase the code size exponentially. Our algorithm, though does not fall under node-splitting category, will only cause a linear increase in the code size.

To summarize, our contributions are:

– We propose a very simple and elegant transformation to convert an unstructured CFG to a structured CFG, with just a linear increase in the number of basic blocks and instructions.

– We also demonstrate that the proposed transformation is powerful and versatile. It can be used to handle various performance problems due to branch divergence. In particular it (a) ensures reconvergence at IPDOM and hence no duplicate execution of code, (b) enables interleaved execution of blocks from different parts of a divergent branch and (c) enables merging different invocations of inner loops.
– We show the feasibility of implementing the transformation at PTX level and some initial experimental results.

To the best of our knowledge, our work is the first to use the transformation described to convert an unstructured CFG to a structured CFG and further use this idea to reduce negative effects of branch divergence on GPU performance.

2 Motivation

In this section we discuss in detail the problems due to control divergence in both unstructured and structured Control Flow Graphs (CFG), arising because of the existing hardware reconvergence stack and IPDOM mechanism.

2.1 Control Divergence

In GPUs, a group of consecutive threads, called warps, execute together the same instruction in a lock step manner.

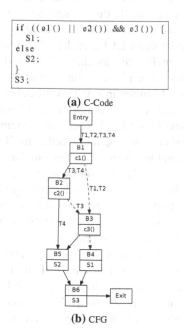

(a) C-Code

(b) CFG

Fig. 1. Short Circuit example

While executing a branch instruction, if the branch condition evaluates to true for some threads and false for the other threads of a warp, then the two parts of the branch statement are executed one after the other, masking out threads based on their branch condition evaluation. This results in smaller groups of threads executing the *then* and *else* parts. These groups are then merged back when control reaches the IPDOM of the branch node. In the case of a structured CFG, IPDOM of the branch node is the earliest reconvergence point, but for an unstructured CFG, there may be other nodes of the graph where some of the diverging groups can potentially reconverge before all the threads reconverge at the IPDOM. So, if all the subgroups are allowed to run without reconverging till the IPDOM, some of the nodes in the CFG may be executed multiple times. This leads to duplicate execution of instructions. We explain this using the example in Figure 1(a). The unstructured CFG is shown in Figure 1(b).

For this example, let us assume a warp with 4 threads T1-T4. Also assume that threads T1-T2 evaluate c1() to true and T3-T4 evaluate it to false. This causes the threads to diverge at the end of block B1. The diverging threads are reconverged at the IPDOM block B6 corresponding to statement S3. Threads T1-T2 take B1→B3 path whereas threads T3-T4 take B1→B2 path. If we assume that thread T3 evaluates c2() to true and T4 evaluates it to false, block B3 will be executed twice, once for threads T1-T2 and then for thread T3. We observe that the problem of branch divergence and repeated execution of basic blocks exacerbates as we go down the unstructured control flow graph. For example, B5 is executed thrice, once for each thread T2, T3 and T4.

2.2 Branch Interleaving

The serial execution of the *then* and *else* parts of a branch also forgoes the potential parallelism that can be achieved by interleaved execution of the two parts.

```
B1  if (c1 == 1) {
B2      S1;
        if (c2 == 1)
B3          S2;
        else
B4          S3;
    } else {
B5      S4;
        if (c3 == 1)
B6          S5;
        else
B7          S6;
    }
```

(a) C-Code Example for Branch Interleaving

```
for (i = 0; i < 2; i++) {
    S1;
    for (j = 0; j < cond; j++)
        S2;
    S3;
}
```

(b) C-Code Example for Loop Merging

Thread	i=1	i=2
T1	cond=10	cond=15
T2	cond=15	cond=10

(c) Trip Counts for Loop Merging Example

Fig. 2. Branch Interleaving and Loop Merging Examples

Consider a branch with multiple basic blocks in each part of the branch as shown in Figure 2(a). The beginning of each block is shown on the left side. In this example, if we assume that the *then* parts execute before *else*, the basic blocks will execute in the order B1, B2, B3, B4, B5, B6, B7. If the execution in the *then* part stalls due to unavailability of operands, e.g. consider a load in B2 that results in an L1/L2 cache miss, with its use in B3, the available ILP in B4 or other basic blocks cannot be utilized to mask latencies in B3. This is because the execution of B4 cannot start until B3 finishes. Thus SIMD cores may remain unused until the operands needed for B3 are ready. One of the main reasons for stalls is the high latency for memory accesses. In the absence of enough threads to hide the high latency for memory accesses, the ability to execute code from other paths of divergent branches can improve the utilization of the hardware and also improve the performance. If the blocks can be ordered differently, e.g. B1, B2, B5, B3, B6, B4, B7, then the stall on use in B3 can potentially be avoided. Since execution stalls when a needed operand is not available, the blocks can be ordered so as to increase the distance between definition and use of an operand. So, if the definition is a memory load in B2 and the use is in B3, then execution of B5 between B2 and B3 can avoid the stall in B3.

2.3 Loop Merging

Consider a kernel with a nested loop in which the inner loop has different trip counts for different threads. Threads of a warp diverging on the inner loop reconverge at the end of that loop. So, threads with smaller trip counts of the inner loop have to wait for all other threads of the warp to finish the inner loop execution, before proceeding further.

Consider the example in Figure 2(b). Figure 2(c) shows a scenario where the two threads have different trip counts for the inner loop. With the existing reconvergence mechanism, both iterations of the outer loop will execute 15 iterations of the inner loop. In the first iteration of the outer loop, thread T1 finishes the inner loop execution after 10 iterations but has to wait for thread T2 to finish its remaining 5 iterations. Instead, if thread T1 is allowed to execute statement S3 and start next iteration of the outer loop, it can join thread T2 in the execution of the inner loop. With this capability of executing different invocations of a loop for different threads of a warp, the hardware can be used more efficiently.

2.4 Hardware Stack Depth

The reconvergence mechanism using hardware stack, handles branch divergence by pushing two entries on to the hardware stack, one each for the two paths of the branch. The entry consists of PC of the path, an active mask representing the set of threads in the warp that follow this path and the reconvergence PC.

```
B1      if (c1) { // branch 1
B2        if (c2) { // branch 2
B4          if (c3) // branch 3
B6            S1;
            else
B7            S2;
B8          S3;
        else
B5          S4;
B9        S5;
        else
B3        S6;
B10     S7;
```

(a) C-Code

PC	Active Mask	RPC
B6	1000	B8
B7	0100	B8
B8	1100	B9
B5	0010	B9
B9	1110	B10
B3	0001	B10
B10	1111	-

(b) Reconvergence Stack during execution of S1

Fig. 3. Stack Depth Example

Each entry is popped when the control flow corresponding to it reaches the reconvergence PC (IPDOM) of the divergent branch node. In this way the stack depth increases for nested divergent branches and hence cost of the hardware needed to support nested branches also increases.

In the example shown in Figure 3(a), let us assume 4 threads and for each branch one thread takes the *else* path and the remaining threads take the *then* path. Also assume that the *else* path is pushed onto the stack first and then the *then* path. Initially there is only one entry on the stack corresponding to all the threads executing block B1. The execution of branch 1 adds two entries to the stack corresponding to blocks B2 and B3. Then the execution of branches 2 and 3 will add two entries each to the stack. So when S1 is executing, there are 7 entries on the stack as shown in Figure 3(b).

All the above mentioned problems with the existing hardware stack based reconvergence mechanism can be solved with our technique of linearizing a control flow graph.

3   Linearization Transformation

In the previous section we saw that the reconvergence mechanism using IPDOM suffers from duplicate execution for an unstructured CFG. Our proposed transformation converts an unstructured CFG to a structured CFG and hence eliminates the problem of duplicate execution.

In this section we will discuss the linearization transformation in detail, show that it transforms an unstructured CFG to a structured CFG, prove correctness of the transformation and then analyze the increase in code size.

3.1   Linearization

Linearization algorithm is based on the idea of predicated/guarded execution of the basic blocks of a CFG.

(a) Transformed Code

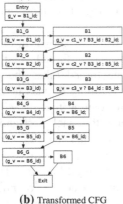

(b) Transformed CFG

Fig. 4. Transformed Short Circuit Example

For each basic block of the input CFG, the transformation creates a guard basic block to guard its execution; the guard condition is set by its predecessors. We will explain this with the short circuit example from Figure 1. The transformed code is shown in Figure 4(a) and the corresponding CFG is shown in Figure 4(b).

Execution of the entry block assigns B1_id to the guard variable as block B1 is the only successor of the entry block. As the condition in the first branch statement evaluates to true, code for block B1 is executed and the guard variable is set to index of the successor of B1 based on the branch condition, i.e., value of c1_v, where c1_v contains the result of function call c1(). (Note that in the original code, based on the value of c1_v, control transfers either to block B2 or B3). This way at the end of execution of block B1, the guard variable contains index of the next block to be executed, i.e. B2_id or B3_id. Assuming that block B1 sets the guard variable to the index of block B3, execution of block B2 is skipped and block B3 is executed (i.e. the guard condition for block B3 evaluates to true and code for block B3 is executed). This way the execution continues till block B6. As can be seen from Figures 4(a) and (b), linearization algorithm transforms the input CFG into a sequence of predicated blocks.

3.2   Unstructured CFG to Structured CFG

In this subsection, we explain formally how linearization converts an unstructured CFG to a structured CFG.

Definition 1. *An edge from block B_i to B_j is said to be unstructured if any of the following three conditions is satisfied:*

- *Block B_i has multiple successors, block B_j has multiple predecessors, and neither of B_i or B_j dominates nor postdominates the other,*
- *Block B_j is in a loop, block B_i is not in the same loop and B_j does not dominate all other blocks of the loop,*
- *Block B_i is in a loop, block B_j is not in the same loop and B_i does not postdominate all other blocks of the loop*

For example, in Figure 1(b), edges B2→B3, B2→B5 and B3→B5 are unstructured edges as they satisfy the first condition. Edges B1→B5 and B2→B3 in Figure 6(b) are marked as unstructured edges as they jump into the loop formed by blocks B3, B4 and B5. In Figure 5(b), edge B3→B6 and B2→B5 are unstructured edges as they jump out of the loop formed by blocks B2, B3 and B4.

Zhang et al. [23] showed that repeated applications of their three transformations convert all possible unstructured programs into structured programs. The three transformations proposed by them are (a) Forward Copy - for unstructured edges in an acyclic CFG, (b) Backward Copy - for incoming edge of a loop and (c) Cut - for outgoing edge of a loop. Based on the prior works by Zhang et al. [23], Wu et al. [22], and our extensive study of unstructured CFGs from various benchmark suites, we claim that the 3 conditions specified in the definition of an unstructured edge cover all possible cases of unstructuredness.

We call a CFG containing an *unstructured edge*, an *unstructured CFG (UCFG)*. For the discussion in this subsection we define *unstructured region* to be the region encompassing all blocks of the input CFG except for the Entry and Exit blocks. Also we use the term *unstructured block* to refer to any block from an unstructured region. In the next section we will present an algorithm to find the minimal *unstructured region* of an *unstructured edge*.

Now we will describe the algorithm to transform an UCFG into a structured CFG.

Definition 2. *The common immediate dominator, CIDOM, D of a set of blocks B in a CFG is a block such that D dominates all the blocks in B and there does not exist any other block $\hat{D}$ such that $\hat{D}$ dominates all the blocks in B and D dominates $\hat{D}$.*

Definition 3. *The common immediate postdominator, CIPDOM, P of a set of blocks B in a CFG is a block such that P postdominates all the blocks in B and there does not exist any other block $\hat{P}$ such that $\hat{P}$ postdominates all the blocks in B and P postdominates $\hat{P}$.*

So, a block that dominates all the blocks in *B*, will dominate the *CIDOM*. Similarly, a block that postdominates all the blocks in *B*, will postdominate the *CIPDOM*.

Algorithm 1. Linearization

```
1.  procedure LinearizeUnstructuredRegion(Ureg)
2.    idom ← immedDom(Ureg)
3.    ipdom ← immedPostDom(Ureg)
4.    prevGuard ← 0, prevBlock ← 0
5.    for all blk ∈ Ureg, inRevPostOrder do
6.      guard = createGuard(blk)
7.      addGuardVarAssign(blk)
8.      addBrEdge(guard, blk)
9.      if isFirstBlock(blk) then
10.         addEdge(idom, guard)
11.     end if
12.     if prevGuard ≠ 0 then
13.         addEdge(prevGuard, guard)
14.     end if
15.     if prevBlock ≠ 0 then
16.         addEdge(prevBlock, guard)
17.     end if
18.     if isLastBlock(blk) then
19.         addEdge(guard, ipdom)
20.         addEdge(blk, ipdom)
21.     end if
22.     prevGuard ← guard
23.     prevBlock ← blk
24.     if isSrcOfRetreatingEdge(blk) then
25.         beGuard ← createBEGuard(blk)
26.         addEdge(guard, beGuard)
27.         addEdge(blk, beGuard)
28.         beDst ← getBackEdgeDst(blk)
29.         beDstGuard ← getGuard(beDst)
30.         addBrEdge(beGuard, beDstGuard)
31.         prevGuard ← beGuard
32.         prevBlock ← 0
33.     end if
34.   end for
35. end procedure
```

Our algorithm for transforming unstructured graphs first computes the *CIDOM* and *CIPDOM* of the input CFG. The next step is to generate a reverse post-order (also known as depth first order [1]) for all the blocks in the unstructured region, starting from the *CIDOM* up to the *CIPDOM*. The reverse post-order ensures that before a block is traversed all its predecessors are traversed. This helps to minimize the number of guard checks during execution of the transformed CFG. This is similar to the case of using a reverse post-order traversal in an iterative algorithm for a forward data-flow problem. For example in Figure 4(b), if block B5 was before block B3, then the linearized CFG would have needed a back edge to execute block B5 after block B3. In case of a back edge in a CFG, the reverse post-order contains the destination of the back edge before the source and hence the linearized CFG contains a back edge for it.

Algorithm 1 shows the steps to linearize an unstructured region. The blocks in the input unstructured region are traversed in the reverse post-order and for each block, a guard block is created (line 6). An assignment is added to each unstructured block, to set the guard variable to the block id of one of its successor blocks in the original CFG (line 7). The guard block is populated with an instruction to branch to the unstructured block - block from the original CFG in an unstructured region - when the guard variable value matches the block's index (line 8). The guard block corresponding to the first unstructured block is added as a successor of the *CIDOM* of the unstructured region (lines 9-11). The other successor of the guard block is the guard block for the next unstructured block in the reverse post-order (lines 12-14). This is the successor on the fall through edge of the guard block. Lines 15-17 add a guard block as successor of the previous unstructured block in the reverse post-order. The successor of the last guard block is the *CIPDOM* of the unstructured region (lines 18-20).

Applying this algorithm on the unstructured CFG in Figure 1(b), we get the transformed CFG in Figure 4(b). B1_G to B6_G are the guard blocks (line 6). In blocks B1-B5, an assignment is added to set the guard variable to the id of the appropriate successor block (line 7). Each of B1_G to B6_G contains the guard variable check (line 8). Block B1_G is made the successor of the entry block (lines 9-11). As per lines 12-14, blocks B2_G to B6_G are made successors of blocks B1_G to B5_G respectively.

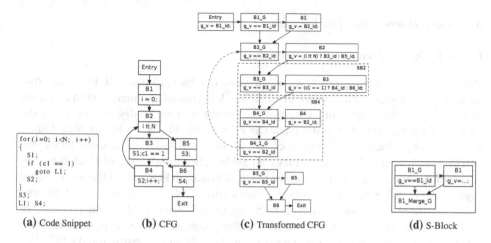

(a) Code Snippet   **(b)** CFG   **(c)** Transformed CFG   **(d)** S-Block

Fig. 5. Jump out of a loop

Blocks B2_G to B6_G are also added as successors of blocks B1 to B5 respectively (lines 15-17). Finally lines 18-20 add Exit as the successor of blocks B6 and B6_G.

For a block which is the source of a retreating edge (i.e. an edge in which the destination appears before source in the reverse post-order), another guard block is created (lines 24-33). For the retreating edge B4→B2 in Figure 5(b), block B4_1_G is created and a back edge is added to block B2_G as shown in Figure 5(c). None of the blocks in the loop of this back edge, other than the two blocks of the back edge, can be the destination of any other back edge, as that will make the CFG unstructured (jump into a loop). In other words, in the reverse post-order of an unstructured CFG, none of the blocks that lie between the destination and source of a retreating edge, can become the destination of any other back edge unless its source also lies between them. This condition ensures that any two loops in the transformed CFG are either nested or disjoint. If there exists an edge in the input CFG to any of such blocks then destination of the corresponding back edge in the transformed CFG will be moved up, to the closest back edge destination. So, if there was an edge from B5 to B3 in Figure 5(b), then in the linearized CFG the back edge destination would be moved to B2_G.

The transformation converts a CFG into a sequence of if-then statements such that each branch guard block is the IPDOM of its predecessor branch guard block.

3.3 Converting Irreducible Graph to Reducible Graph

The linearization transformation can be applied to any unstructured CFGs including irreducible graphs. Figures 6(c) and (d) show an irreducible graph and its transformed version. In this case the transformed CFG has been obtained by traversing the blocks in the order B1, B2, B3. Even if they were traversed in the order B1, B3, B2, the resultant transformed CFG would still be a reducible graph. Since B1 has two successors viz., B2 and B3, the reverse post-order traversal can select any one of them and so both the orders mentioned above are possible in the reverse post-order.

3.4 Correctness of the transformation

Claim 1: The transformed CFG is structured.

Proof Sketch: To aid in the proof, we will assume that for each block B_i in the unstructured region, in addition to a guard block, a block is created as a merge point as shown in Figure 5(d). The merge block acts as the source of a back edge in case B_i is the source of a retreating edge in the input CFG e.g block B4_1_G in Figure 5(c). Otherwise the merge block is an empty block and is combined with the successor block. We call this combination of the three blocks, an *S-block*, in which the guard block is the entry block and the merge block is the exit block. So for each block B_i in the unstructured region an S-block SB_i is created in the transformed CFG. The transformed CFG can be thought of as a linearized graph of the S-blocks such that (a) if B_i is the predecessor of B_j in the reverse post-order, then SB_i is the predecessor of SB_j in the linearized CFG, and (b) if there is a retreating edge from B_j to B_i in the unstructured CFG, then a back edge from SB_j to SB_i is added in the linearized CFG. As explained before this creates either disjoint or nested loops. The CFG of the blocks in an S-block does not contain an unstructured edge. This is because (a) for any edge in the CFG either the source dominates the destination or the destination postdominates the source, and (b) the CFG has no loops. So, the CFG of the blocks in an S-block is structured. The CFG formed using the S-blocks (i.e. CFG whose nodes are S-blocks) is also a structured CFG because (a) if there are no loops in the unstructured CFG, then each S-block has only one predecessor and one successor, and (b) if there are loops in the unstructured CFG, then they are either nested or disjoint, and each loop is a natural loop [1]. These two conditions ensure that the CFG formed using the S-blocks is also structured. Since the CFG formed using the S-blocks is structured and also the CFG of the blocks in any S-block is structured, the linearized CFG is structured.   ∎

S-blocks which do not have back edges have empty merge blocks. Each empty merge block has only one successor. Hence it can be eliminated by connecting its predecessors to its successor. It can be seen that the resultant CFG is also structured using the same reasoning as given above. Figure 5(c) shows the S-blocks corresponding to blocks B3 and B4 labelled as SB3 and SB4 respectively. SB3 does not show the empty merge block.

Claim 2: Linearization transformation preserves semantics of the input CFG.

Proof Sketch: We make the following 4 observations regarding the transformation: (1) it does not delete any basic block from the original CFG, (2) it adds guard blocks and they do not modify any user defined variables, (3) it replaces conditional and unconditional branch statements in unstructured blocks by assignments to the guard variable and (4) it adds an assignment to the guard variable in unstructured blocks that do not have branch statements. These observations imply that if the order of execution of blocks in the original CFG is the same as in the transformed CFG then the transformation preserves the semantics of the input CFG.

First we will prove that for every execution order of blocks in the original CFG the execution order of those blocks in the transformed CFG is the same. When the control reaches a basic block, say B_i, in the original CFG there are 3 possibilities:

- B_i has no successors. In this case in the original CFG, the execution stops. In the transformed CFG, at the end of the execution of B_i, the guard variable is set to an unused value and hence no other blocks can execute and the execution stops.
- B_i has one successor. In this case in the original CFG, the control will transfer to the successor block. In the transformed CFG, the guard variable will be assigned the index of the successor block and hence only that block can execute next.
- B_i has two successors. In the original CFG, the branch condition at the end of B_i decides the next block to be executed. The transformed CFG sets the guard variable to the index of the next block to be executed.

This shows that if the original CFG executes block B_j after block B_i, the transformed CFG will also execute block B_j after B_i. The transformed CFG may execute one or more guard blocks between B_i and B_j, but since the guard blocks do not modify any of the original program state, their execution will not have any effect on the final output of the program. This proves that the order of execution of blocks in the original CFG remains the same after the transformations.

Next we will prove that for every execution order of the original CFG blocks in the transformed CFG, there is an equivalent order of those blocks in the original CFG. The transformed CFG has two types of blocks viz., guard blocks (GB) and original CFG blocks (OB). So we need to prove that for every execution order of the OBs in the transformed CFG, the original CFG has an equivalent execution order of them.

Consider two OBs, B_i and B_j. If the transformed CFG executes B_j after B_i with no other OB executing between them, then it means B_i sets the guard variable to the index of B_j. This is possible only if B_j is a successor of B_i in the original CFG and the branch condition in B_i evaluates to a value such that the branch to B_j is taken, so the original CFG also executes B_j after B_i.

This proves that the transformation preserves the semantics of user code.   ∎

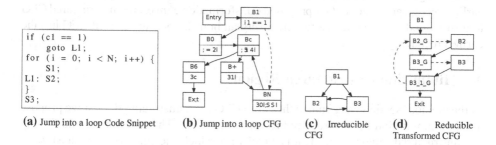

```
if (c1 == 1)
    goto L1;
for (i = 0; i < N; i++) {
    S1;
L1: S2;
}
S3;
```

(a) Jump into a loop Code Snippet   **(b)** Jump into a loop CFG   **(c)** Irreducible CFG   **(d)** Reducible Transformed CFG

Fig. 6. Jump into a loop and Irreducible Graph Example

3.5 Analysis of Increase in Code Size

Claim 3: Increase in code size due to the transformation is linear in the number of blocks and instructions.

Proof Sketch: One guard block is created for (a) each basic block in the unstructured region and (b) each retreating edge in the unstructured region. Hence the total number of new blocks added is the sum of number of blocks and number of retreating edges in an unstructured region. The number of retreating edges in a CFG cannot be more than the number of blocks in the CFG. Hence the total number of new blocks added is at most two times the total number of blocks in the original CFG.

Each guard block adds one instruction to compare the guard variable with a block index. For each block in the unstructured region with (a) a fall through edge to its successor, one instruction is added to set the guard variable, and (b) a branch edge to its successor, the branch instruction is replaced with an assignment to the guard variable. This shows that the total number of new instructions added is at most twice the number of blocks in an unstructured region.   ∎

In contrast to this, the transformations presented by Zhang et al. [23] can have exponential increase in the code size in their Forward Copy transformation. Even the Backward Copy transformation makes a copy of the loop to peel its first iteration. Carter et al. [5] proved that exponential blowup in the size of the CFG is unavoidable when a node-splitting technique is used to convert an irreducible flow graph to a reducible one. They have also stated that their results do not apply to techniques which use predicate variables to guard statements. Since our technique uses predicate variables to guard blocks, the results proved by Carter et al. do not apply to our technique.

3.6 Earliest Reconvergence

In this section we will show that the transformed CFG has the earliest reconvergence point for any divergent branch. The IPDOM of a guard block is the successor on its fall through edge. In Figure 5(c), threads diverging at block B2_G will reconverge at block B3_G and threads diverging at block B4_1_G will reconverge at block B5_G. So each fall through edge successor of a guard block acts as a reconvergence point and since threads can only diverge at a guard block they are immediately reconverged on the fall through edge successor. In a structured CFG, the IPDOM of a divergent branch is its earliest recovergence point. Our proposed transformation converts an unstructured CFG to a structured CFG and hence for any divergent branch, the transformed CFG has the earliest reconvergence point.

4   Minimizing Unstructured Region

In the previous section we assumed the entire CFG to be unstructured. First we propose an algorithm to find the unstructured region in the CFG. The intuition behind finding the unstructured region is to identify blocks for which the linearization transformation is applied. Further, the size of a transformed CFG linearly increases with size of the unstructured region and the unstructured CFG may contain subregions which are structured. To reduce unnecessary code bloat of structured subregions, we propose an algorithm to identify structured regions within the unstructured region.

To be able to apply the transformation only on an unstructured region, it should have a single entry point and a single exit point.

Definition 4. *The* unstructured region *of an unstructured edge is defined as a set of blocks, UR, such that*

- *it is bounded by blocks D and P, where D is the* CIDOM *and P is the* CIPDOM *of all the blocks in the set (D and P are not in the set),*
- *it contains blocks of the unstructured edge,*
- *for any edge $B_k \rightarrow B_l$, where $B_l \in UR$, either $B_k \in UR$ or $B_k = D$,*
- *for any edge $B_k \rightarrow B_l$, where $B_k \in UR$, either $B_l \in UR$ or $B_l = P$.*

Algorithm 2. Unstructured Region

---

1. **procedure** FindUnstructuredRegion()
2. $UE = set\_of\_all\_unstruct\_edges$
3. **for all** $edge \in UE$ **do**
4. $UN1 \leftarrow \phi$
5. $UN1.insert(edge.src, edge.dst)$
6. $Done \leftarrow false$
7.   **while** $Done = false$ **do**
8. $cidom = findIdom(UN1)$
9. $cipdom = findIpdom(UN1)$
10. $N1 \leftarrow BlksDomBy(cidom)$
11. $N2 \leftarrow BlksThatCanReach(cipdom)$
12. $N3 \leftarrow BlksPostDomBy(cipdom)$
13. $N4 \leftarrow BlksReachableFrom(cidom)$
14. $UN2 \leftarrow (N1 \cap N2) \cup (N3 \cap N4)$
15.   **if** $UN2 = UN1$ **then**
16. $Done \leftarrow true$
17.   **end if**
18. $UN1 \leftarrow UN2$
19.   **end while**
20. **end for**
21. **end procedure**

The algorithm to find the minimal unstructured regions is shown in Algorithm 2. It iterates over all unstructured edges in a CFG and finds the unstructured region for each edge. The first step is to mark the source and destination of an unstructured edge as unstructured blocks *UN1* (line 5). Then it finds their *CIDOM* and *CIPDOM* (line 8). Using *CIDOM* and *CIPDOM* as the entry and exit points of the unstructured region, the algorithm adds blocks to the region as per the two criteria: (a) blocks dominated by *CIDOM* and that can reach the *CIPDOM*, and (b) blocks postdominated by *CIPDOM* and that can be reached from *CIDOM*(lines 9-13). Since these steps can add more blocks to the set of unstructured blocks, i.e. *UN1*, they are repeated until no new blocks are added to the set of unstructured blocks.

Algorithm 2 identifies all blocks in an unstructured region. Any non-overlapping structured region is not included in the unstructured region. The unstructured regions of two unstructured edges cannot partly overlap, i.e. they are either disjoint or one will contain the other (including the case where they are the same).

4.1 Structured Region

The unstructured regions found by Algorithm 2 may contain structured sub-regions, i.e. regions with single entry and single exit, and no unstructured edge in them.

Definition 5. *A structured region is defined as a set of blocks, SR, such that*

- *it is bounded by blocks D and P where D is the* CIDOM *of all the blocks in SR except for D, and P is the* CIPDOM *of all the blocks in SR except for P and*
- *it contains both D and P but does not contain any unstructured edge.*

Since a structured region has only one entry block and one exit block, if control does not reach the entry block, it cannot reach any of the blocks between the entry and exit, including the exit. Also, the hardware stack based reconvergence mechanism guarantees earliest reconvergence for a structured region. Hence, the cost of linearization is reduced by guarding only the entry block of a structured region and not linearizing the structured region. This helps maintain the original structure of the CFG for the region and hence reduce the side effects of linearization on the other compilation passes. The algorithm to find structured regions is presented in Algorithm 3.

4.2 Optimizations

To further reduce the cost of guard checks, the linearization algorithm optimizes the transformed CFG to remove unnecessary guard checks, nest guard checks, etc. To be able to decide which checks can be eliminated or nested under some other checks, the transformed CFG is analyzed to find the possible values the guard variable can take at each guard block.

Algorithm 3. Structured Region

---

1. **procedure** FindStructuredRegion()
2. **for all** $blk \in set\_of\_all\_unstruct\_blks$ **do**
3. $structRegion \leftarrow false$
4.   **if** $isImmedDom(blk)$ **then**
5. $ipdom \leftarrow immedPostDom(blk)$
6.   **if** $blk = immedDom(ipdom)$ **then**
7. $idom \leftarrow blk$
8. $N1 \leftarrow visit(idom, ipdom)$
9. $N1 \leftarrow N1 \cup visit(ipdom, idom)$
10. $structRegion \leftarrow true$
11.   **for all** $n1 \in N1$ **do**
12.   **if** $hasUnstructEdge(blk)$ **then**
13. $structRegion \leftarrow false$
14.   **else if** $(ipdom \neq pdom(n1))$ **then**
15. $structRegion \leftarrow false$
16.   **else if** $(idom \neq dom(n1))$ **then**
17. $structRegion \leftarrow false$
18.   **end if**
19.   **end for**
20.   **if** $structRegion = true$ **then**
21. $SN \leftarrow N1$
22.   **end if**
23.   **end if**
24.   **end if**
25. **end for**
26. **end procedure**

The first step is to find the guard values that can reach a guard block from its predecessor unstructured blocks. The next step is to propagate the guard values on the two successor edges of a guard block. As mentioned before, there are two types of guard blocks, viz., a guard block created for an unstructured block (GB) and a guard block created for a re-treating edge (RGB). The branch edge of a GB is to an unstructured block and is taken only when its guard check is true, which means for only one of the input guard values the branch edge is taken and all other values flow through the fall through edge. In case of a RGB, both the branch and fall-through edges are to guard blocks. The branch edge can be taken for more than one guard value (e.g., in case of loop merging in Figure 8(b), the branch edge of B6_1_G is taken if the guard value is either B2_id or B4_id),

Hence all those values will flow on the branch edge and the remaining values will flow on the fall through edge.

The transformed CFG is iteratively analyzed to propagate the guard values on the input and output edges of each guard block, till no new values are seen at the input of any guard block. The iterative algorithm is guaranteed to terminate as i) the cardinality of the set of guard values at the input of a guard block in each iteration is non-decreasing, ii) once a guard value is added to the input set of a guard block, it is never removed, and iii) the cardinality of the set of all possible guard values is equal to the number of unstructured blocks, At the end of this analysis, values of the guard variable flowing on edges into and out of each guard block are known.

Now we briefly describe some optimizations to reduce the guard checks:

- (O1) If only one incoming edge of a guard block has the matching guard value (i.e. the value being checked by the guard block) then the destinations of all other incoming edges are changed to the next guard block to avoid execution of the guard check on paths containing those edges. Similarly, if only one incoming edge of a guard block does not have the matching guard value, then the destination of that edge is changed to the next guard block.

- (O2) If block B_i dominates block B_j in the original CFG, then the guard block for B_j can be nested within the guard block for B_i so that the guard check for B_j is executed only if the guard check for B_i is true.
- (O3) If a guard block has only one predecessor and if that predecessor is a block from an unstructured region, then the guard block is merged with its predecessor.

5 Applications of Linearization

In this section we will discuss some applications of the linearization transformation.

5.1 Branch Interleaving

As discussed in the motivation section, existing hardware reconvergence stack mechanism using IPDOM forgoes the potential parallelism achievable by interleaved execution of other basic blocks. We propose to use the linearization transformation to exploit parallelism among the two paths of a divergent branch.

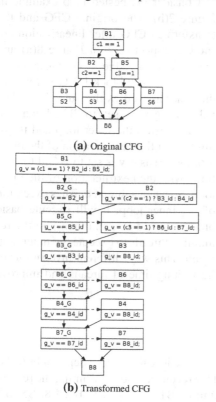

(a) Original CFG

(b) Transformed CFG

Fig. 7. Branch Interleaving Example

Consider the example in Figure 2(a). The original CFG and the transformed CFG are shown in Figures 7(a) and 7(b) respectively. The transformed CFG has basic blocks from the two arms of the branch statement interleaved. A thread executing the branch statement will execute blocks from either of the two arms. Assuming stall-on-use model, i.e. a core stalls when the value needed is not available in the register, we can identify blocks with potential stalls. For example, if block B2 loads a variable which is used in blocks B3 and B4, then a core can stall while executing an instruction that uses the variable, if the load instruction results in a cache miss. As shown in Figure 7(b), block B5 is inserted between blocks B2 and B3. So, if some threads of a warp take B1→B2 path and others take B1→B5 path, then executing instructions from block B5 after block B2 can help hide the long latency of a load in block B2. In contrast, existing hardware support for branch execution always traverses the blocks in the depth-first order until the IPDOM and hence incur the stalls.

Linearization can also be used to reduce stalls in a block which loads a variable as well as uses it. For example, if block B6 loads a variable and uses it, then it can be split into two sub blocks, B6_1 and B6_2, such that the load instruction is in B6_1 and use of the variable is in B6_2. The execution of these two blocks then can be separated by inserting one or more blocks from the other arm of the branch instruction in B5.

5.2   Loop Merging

In nested loops, if the threads of a warp have different trip counts for the inner loop then threads with smaller trip counts will have to wait for the thread with the largest trip count.

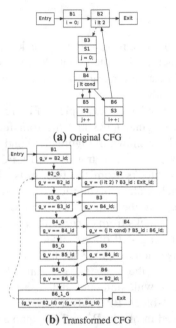

(a) Original CFG

(b) Transformed CFG

Fig. 8. Loop Merging Example

We can use the linearization transformation to let the threads with smaller trip counts proceed further and join the remaining threads in the execution of the inner loop but for a different invocation of the inner loop.

Consider the nested loop example in Figure 2(b). The original CFG and the transformed CFG after linearization are shown, respectively, in Figure 8(a) and (b). The back edge from basic block B6_1_G to basic block B2_G is for both the inner as well as the outer loop. The value of g_v is set to B2_id when a thread finishes the inner loop and is going to start the next iteration of the outer loop, whereas g_v is set to B4_id to continue with the next iteration of the inner loop. So when a thread finishes execution of the inner loop, it will execute basic blocks B2 and B3, and then join the remaining threads to execute the inner loop again. This way, different invocations of the inner loop can be overlapped to reduce the waiting time of threads and improve performance.

5.3   Hardware Stack Depth Reduction

The proposed linearization technique can be used to reduce the nesting depth of branches and hence the depth of the hardware stack used for reconvergence. Assuming the reverse post order traversal of the CFG in Figure 3(a) to be B1, B2, B4, B6, B7, B8, B5, B9, B3 and B10, it can be seen that threads diverging at block B2_G will reconverge at block B4_G and hence the depth of the reconvergence stack at B4_G will be the same as the depth at B2_G. Proceeding further, we see that the stack depth does not increase. Hence, to restrict depth of the reconvergence stack to a certain limit, branches beyond that nesting depth limit can be linearized.

Table 1. Linearization Transformation Statistics, PTX-Number of PTX Instructions, BB-Number of Basic Blocks, Reg-Number of registers used by the compiled code, SASS-Number of instructions in the assembly code, Bf-before transformation, Af-after transformation, AfOpt-after optimizing the transformed code, Incr-Increase(=AfOpt/Bf)

BM	PTX				BB				Reg			SASS		
	Bf	Af	AfOpt	Incr	Bf	Af	AfOpt	Incr	Bf	AfOpt	Incr	Bf	AfOpt	Incr
hotspot [3],[4]	269	289	275	1.02	19	30	20	1.05	30	30	1.00	383	390	1.02
hearwall [3],[4]	1422	1442	1432	1.01	192	206	196	1.02	32	32	1.00	2667	2681	1.01
mcx [9]	1358	1447	1408	1.04	138	185	148	1.07	57	63	1.10	1139	1252	1.10
mum [2]	232	259	256	1.10	37	51	47	1.27	22	32	1.45	202	226	1.12
nqueen [2]	164	175	169	1.03	30	37	31	1.03	16	18	1.12	145	148	1.02
particlefilter [3],[4]	52	63	54	1.04	10	17	10	1.0	13	13	1.00	52	51	0.98
ray [2]	780	869	805	1.03	84	148	90	1.07	43	50	1.16	933	966	1.03

6 Experimental Evaluation

We evaluated our proposed algorithm by implementing it in the Ocelot [8] compiler framework. The transformation is done at the PTX (version 2.3) IR level. The CFG constructed by Ocelot front end is transformed into a linearized CFG and then the modified PTX code is JIT compiled. We used CUDA toolkit version 4.2 [18] and Tesla C2070 GPU (Fermi) [19]. The CUDA code was compiled with the default optimization level. Each benchmark was run 10 times and the average of the execution time is reported. We used CUDA profiler to measure the runtime and other performance counters.

The proposed transformation avoids duplicate execution of basic blocks and also ensures early reconvergence which are the primary benefits of converting an unstructured CFG to a structured CFG. Further the transformation is expected to reduce the number of global loads and stores. These improvements come, however, at the cost of increased code size. We report these performance metric in our experimental framework.

We compared number of PTX instructions (PTX), number of basic blocks (BB), number of registers used (Reg) and number of assembly instructions (SASS) in the original and transformed code. Table 1 shows the increase in number of PTX instructions per kernel. It is less than 5% for 6 out of 7 benchmarks. The maximum increase in code size is 10% in *mum* benchmark. Table 1 also shows the increase in number of basic blocks per kernel. It is less than 10% for 5 out of the 7 benchmarks and a maximum of 27% in *mum*. The improvements with the optimizations are shown in column AfOpt. Even though the upper bound for increase in code size is linear in terms of the number of basic blocks, the observed increase is less than 7% on an average.

Out of the 7 benchmarks, 4 show an increase of 10% or more in the number of registers. This is one of the major side effects of doing the transformations at the PTX level. In the next subsection we discuss how this transformation can be implemented at a lower level of IR. The increase in the number of assembly instructions is up to 12%.

Table 2 shows the runtime performance numbers measured using CUDA profiler counters. Except for the execution time, other metrics reported are aggregate numbers for all threads on all SMs. For benchmarks *mcx* and *mum* the number of global loads decrease by 4.4% and 48.5% respectively. Also the number of global stores decrease for benchmarks *mcx* (13.3%), *mum* (68.7%) and *heartwall* (2.5%). Benchmark *mum* also shows an improvement of 17.5% in the number of dynamic instructions executed.

Table 2. Runtime profile per kernel, ExecTime - execution time in micro seconds, InstExec - number of assembly instructions executed, GlobalLd - number of global load instructions executed, GlobalSt - number of global store instructions executed, Before - before transformation, AfterOpt - after optimizing the transformed code

BM	ExecTime(us)		InstExec		GlobalLd		GlobalSt	
	Before	AfterOpt	Before	AfterOpt	Before	AfterOpt	Before	AfterOpt
hotspot	342	360	4.32×10^6	4.57×10^6	2.92×10^4	2.92×10^4	1.1×10^4	1.1×10^4
heartwall	4.22×10^4	4.23×10^4	4.68×10^8	4.71×10^8	3.21×10^7	3.21×10^7	7.82×10^6	7.62×10^6
mcx	3.15×10^6	3.97×10^6	2.64×10^{10}	3.05×10^{10}	2.48×10^8	2.37×10^8	8.06×10^7	6.99×10^7
mum	2242	2224	7.80×10^6	6.43×10^6	1.69×10^5	8.76×10^4	5.99×10^4	1.87×10^4
nqueen	112	110	5.94×10^4	5.96×10^4	3	3	256	256
particlefilter	187	205	1.02×10^5	1.49×10^5	1.85×10^4	1.85×10^4	64	64
ray	163	173	1.82×10^6	1.89×10^6	2048	2048	4096	4096

Table 3. Increase in Number of PTX instructions, Orig - Before transformation, Ocelot - After transformations proposed by Wu et al. [22], Linear - After our transformations

BM	Orig	Ocelot	Linear
hotspot	237	242	240
heartwall	1422	1452	1432
particlefilter	54	78	62

Table 4. Reduction in number of instructions executed, Orig - Before transformation, After - After transformations without any optimizations, O1 to O4 are the optimization levels

BM	Orig	After	O1	O2	O3	O4
hotspot	4.32×10^6	4.90×10^6	4.98×10^6	4.88×10^6	4.76×10^6	4.57×10^6
heartwall	4.68×10^8	4.69×10^8	4.69×10^8	4.69×10^8	4.68×10^8	4.71×10^8
mcx	2.64×10^{10}	3.7×10^{10}	3.36×10^{10}	3.26×10^{10}	3.18×10^{10}	3.05×10^{10}
mum	7.80×10^6	6.90×10^6	6.66×10^6	6.66×10^6	6.60×10^6	6.43×10^6
nqueen	5.94×10^4	6.01×10^4	6.05×10^4	6.05×10^4	6.03×10^4	5.96×10^4
particlefilter	1.02×10^5	1.77×10^5	2.14×10^5	1.86×10^5	1.68×10^5	1.49×10^5
ray	1.82×10^6	2.50×10^6	2.16×10^6	2.13×10^6	2.09×10^6	1.89×10^6

We analyzed the slowdown in *mcx* and found it to be due to the increase in number of registers from 57 to 63. Since the register allocator cannot use more than 63 registers on the GPU used in our experiments, code is introduced to spill registers to global memory. This increases the number of cache misses and the load on the memory system. Benchmark *mum* also has an increase in the number of registers from 22 to 32 and hence the occupancy drops from 0.833 to 0.667 reducing the performance improvement in spite of a significant reduction in the numbers of global loads and stores.

Table 3 shows the comparison with the algorithm by Wu et al. [22]. We could get only 3 benchmarks working with their implementation in the Ocelot framework. Since our transformation does not duplicate user code, the increase in code size is less than due to their transformation. For benchmarks *hotspot* and *particlefilter* we had to use CUDA toolkit version 4.0.

Table 4 shows the effect of our proposed optimizations. Optimization level O4 has, in addition to the three optimizations described in section 4.2, some miscellaneous optimizations. As shown in the table, each of these optimizations helps in reducing the number of instructions executed. Higher optimization levels include the optimizations done by the lower optimization levels, e.g. O3 has, in addition to the optimizations done by O1 and O2, the optimization to merge guard blocks with their predecessors.

We used PTX as the IR because of the availability of its documentation and the Ocelot [8] compilation framework. But ideally this transformation should be done as late in the compilation process as possible to avoid its side effects on flow analyses, optimizations, register allocation, etc. Implementing the transformation at a lower level IR can reduce the major side effect of increase in register pressure and hence reduction in the occupancy, e.g. benchmarks *mum* and *mcx* are severely affected because of the increase in number of registers. Unfortunately, there is not enough information in public domain, about assembly level instructions of NVIDIA GPUs and hence we could not implement the linearization algorithm at that level.

The proposed transformation can be implemented at the assembly level with one additional integer register needed to hold the guard variable and one additional predicate register needed to hold result of the guard check (in case of loop merging, an additional predicate register per loop to be merged is needed). To make sure that the transformation will have enough registers left, the register allocator can be restricted to use that many fewer registers. We also believe that the costs and benefits of linearization can be estimated more accurately at an assembly level IR than at PTX IR.

7   Related Work

Wu et al. [22] implemented a transformation pass at the PTX level, to convert unstructured control flow to structured control flow. The transformations are equivalent to the ones used in Zhang's [23] work. These transformations duplicate user code, whereas, our proposed transformations do not. Thread Frontier [7] uses a combined hardware and software solution to handle unstructured control flow. It identifies the thread frontier of each basic block and using extra hardware prioritizes basic blocks and checks for stalled threads waiting in the thread frontiers. Our proposed solution does not need any hardware support and it uses predicated execution to linearize CFGs.

Han et al. [12] have proposed a compiler transformation to merge a divergent loop with one or more outer surrounding loops into a single loop. Even though they also transform the CFG to achieve loop merging, our algorithm uses the idea of linearization to reconverge threads. Stratton et al. [20], Wang et al. [21] and Coutinho et al. [6] discuss various compile time analyses to identify non-divergent branches which can be used to skip linearization of non-divergent branches.

Rhu et al. [16] suggested a dual-path stack to keep the two divergent paths of a branch in parallel. This enables interleaved execution of threads from both the paths. Dynamic warp formation [10] regroups threads dynamically into new warps based on their next program counter values. Dynamic Warp subdivision [15] exploits intra-warp latency hiding, by dynamically subdividing warps and allowing them to run ahead. Thread block compaction [11] uses a common block-wide stack for divergence handling. New warps are formed from threads of a block at divergent branches. They also suggest using likely convergence points to converge threads earlier than IPDOM.

The work on obfuscating C++ programs via control flow flattening [14] converts the high level constructs into if-then-goto constructs and changes the target addresses of goto statements so that they will be determined dynamically.

8 Conclusion

In this paper, we presented a simple and elegant transformation to handle the performance problems arising due to branch divergence in GPUs. We showed that the transformation converts an unstructured CFG to a structured CFG with linear increase in the number of instructions. We also discussed three applications of the transformations viz., branch interleaving, loop merging and reduction in reconvergence stack depth. We described the implementation of this technique at the PTX IR level with only up to 10% increase in code size. As future work, we will use a lower level IR and also develop heuristics for its various applications.

Acknowledgements. We thank the anonymous reviewers for their suggestions and comments. We also thank Vaivaswatha N. and other members of the Lab for HPC for discussions and feedback on improving the paper. The first author acknowledges the funding received under Google India Ph.D. Fellowship.

References

1. Aho, A.V., Lam, M.S., Sethi, R., Ullman, J.D.: Compilers Principles, Techniques and Tools, 2nd edn. Pearson
2. Bakhoda, A., Yuan, G., Fung, W., Wong, H., Aamodt, T.: Analyzing CUDA workloads using a detailed GPU simulator. In: ISPASS (2009)
3. Che, S., Boyer, M., Meng, J., Tarjan, D., Sheaffer, J.W., Lee, S.H., Skadron, K.: Rodinia: A Benchmark Suite for Heterogeneous Computing. In: IISWC (2009)
4. Che, S., Sheaffer, J.W., Boyer, M., Szafaryn, L.G., Wang, L., Skadron, K.: A Characterization of the Rodinia Benchmark Suite With Comparison to Contemporary CMP Workloads. In: IISWC (2010)
5. Carter, L., Ferrante, J., Thomborson, C.: Folklore Confirmed: Reducible Flow Graphs are Exponentially Larger. In: POPL (2003)
6. Coutinho, B., Sampaio, D., Pereira, F.M.Q., Meira Jr., W.: Divergence Analysis and Optimizations. In: PACT (2011)
7. Diamos, G., Ashbaugh, B., Maiyuran, S., Kerr, A., Wu, J., Yalamanchili, S.: SIMD Re-Convergence At Thread Frontiers. In: MICRO (2011)
8. Diamos, G., Kerr, A., Yalamanchili, S., Clark, N.: Ocelot: A dynamic compiler for bulk-synchronous applications in heterogeneous systems. In: PACT (2010)
9. Fang, Q., Boss, D.A.: Monte Carlo Simulation of Photon Migration in 3D Turbid Media Accelerated by Graphics Processing Units. Optics Express 17(22), 20178–20190 (2009)
10. Fung, W.W.L., Sham, I., Yuan, G., Aamodt, T.M.: Dynamic warp formation and scheduling for efficient gpu control flow. In: MICRO (2007)
11. Fung, W.W.L., Aamodt, T.M.: Thread block compaction for efficient simt control flow. In: HPCA (2011)
12. Han, T.D., Abdelrahman, T.S.: Reducing Divergence in GPGPU Programs with Loop Merging. In: GPGPU (2013)
13. OpenCL, http://www.khronos.org/opencl
14. László, T., Kiss, Á.: Obfuscating C++ programs via control flow flattening. Annales Universitatis Scientarum Budapestinensis de Rolando Ëotvös Nominatae, Sectio Computatorica 30, 3–19 (2009)

15. Meng, J., Tarjan, D., Skadron, K.: Dynamic Warp Subdivision for Integrated Branch and Memory Divergence Tolerance. In: ISCA (2010)
16. Rhu, M., Erez, M.: The Dual-Path Execution Model for Efficient GPU Control Flow. In: HPCA (2013)
17. Nvidia. CUDA C Programming Guide (October 2010)
18. Nvidia, https://developer.nvidia.com/cuda-toolkit-42-archive
19. Nvidia, http://www.nvidia.com/content/PDF/fermi_white_papers/ NVIDIA_Fermi_Compute_Architecture_Whitepaper.pdf
20. Stratton, J.A., Grover, V., Marathe, J., Aarts, B., Murphy, M., Hu, Z., Hwu, W.W.: Efficient Compilation of Fine-Grained SPMD-threaded Programs for Multicore CPUs. In: CGO (2010)
21. Wang, S., Hung, M., Hwang, Y., Ju, R.D., Lee, J.: Pointer Based Divergence Analysis in the SSA Form. In: CPC (2013)
22. Wu, H., Diamos, G., Li, S., Yalamanchili, S.: Characterization and Transformation of Unstructured Control Flow in GPU Applications. In: The First International Workshop on Characterizing Applications for Heterogeneous Exascale Systems, CACHES (June 2011)
23. Zhang, F., D'Hollander, E.H.: Using hammock graphs to structure programs. IEEE Trans. Softw. Eng., 231–245 (2004)

Exploitation of GPUs for the Parallelisation of Probably Parallel Legacy Code

Zheng Wang[1], Daniel Powell[2], Björn Franke[2], and Michael O'Boyle[2]

[1] School of Computing and Communications, Lancaster University, United Kingdom
z.wang@lancaster.ac.uk
[2] School of Informatics, University of Edinburgh, United Kingdom
d.c.powell@sms.ed.ac.uk, {bfranke,mob}@inf.ed.ac.uk

Abstract General purpose GPUs provide massive compute power, but are notoriously difficult to program. In this paper we present a complete compilation strategy to exploit GPUs for the parallelisation of sequential legacy code. Using hybrid data dependence analysis combining static and dynamic information, our compiler automatically detects suitable parallelism and generates parallel OPENCL code from sequential programs. We exploit the fact that dependence profiling provides us with parallel loop candidates that are highly likely to be genuinely parallel, but cannot be statically proven so. For the efficient GPU parallelisation of those probably parallel loop candidates, we propose a novel software speculation scheme, which ensures correctness for the unlikely, yet possible case of dynamically detected dependence violations. Our scheme operates *in place* and supports speculative read and write operations. We demonstrate the effectiveness of our approach in detecting and exploiting parallelism using sequential codes from the NAS benchmark suite. We achieve an average speedup of 3.2x, and up to 99x, over the sequential baseline. On average, this is 1.42 times faster than state-of-the-art speculation schemes and corresponds to 99% of the performance level of a manual GPU implementation developed by independent expert programmers.

Keywords: GPU, OpenCL, Parallelization, Thread Level Speculation.

1 Introduction

GPUs have become ubiquitous in a wide range of computing devices and consumer electronics appliances. They provide a powerful resource for parallel processing and can deliver great performance improvements for suitably mapped algorithms. Realising this potential, however, is challenging due to the complexity of their programming.

Auto-parallelisation technology can greatly reduce the barrier for GPU programming by automatically generating parallel code from sequential programs. However, one of the main problems is the static undecidability of the underlying data dependence problem [9]. Static analysis attempts to determine if two memory references are dependent, in which case their sequential order needs to

A. Cohen (Ed.): CC 2014, LNCS 8409, pp. 154–173, 2014.

be retrained for correctness, limiting the amount of parallelism, which can be exploited. Static analysis is necessarily conservative and despite large research efforts, frequently fails to deliver, e.g. for complex, pointer-based C code [25].

Off-line profile-guided parallelisation is a recent development, which seeks to complement static analysis with profiling information [8,7,24,30]. Using such a scheme, a program is profiled with different input data sets and dependencies are determined using dynamic memory traces. Although correctness cannot be guaranteed, given enough input data sets, the probability of correctly identifying a genuinely parallel loop increases. In this paper, we seek to exploit such probably parallel loops. In addition, we want to avoid generating potentially unsafe code or asking the user for final approval. This means, we have to rely on speculative parallelisation [19].

Current speculation schemes are designed to deal with the occasional dependence violation and, consequently, provide efficient rollback capabilities. In our case, we can rely on profiling information and we only attempt to speculatively parallelise loops, where there is almost no chance of misspeculation. We require speculation support purely as a safety net, which might not be used at all. Hence, we can afford a more expensive rollback mechanism in favour of faster checks.

In this paper we combine profile-guided parallelisation, OPENCL code generation and software thread level speculation (SW-TLS) to exploit highly-likely parallelism on the GPU. Our compiler uses static and profile-based dynamic dependence analysis to detect parallelism and to automatically generate parallel OPENCL code with in place dependence checking. We exploit that parallel loop candidates are "almost always" genuinely parallel, but escape static analysis.

To provide safety we concurrently execute a sequential version of the program alongside our speculatively parallelised one. In the unlikely case of a dependence violation we abort parallel execution and rely on the results of the sequential program. This simple mechanism enables us to design a simple, yet efficient dependence checking mechanism for GPUs while at the same time, providing correctness for speculative parallel executions.

We have implemented our scheme using the LLVM compiler framework and have evaluated its effectiveness in detecting and exploiting parallelism in benchmarks, which are known to be manually parallelisable, but present a challenge to automatic parallelisation approaches. On an NVIDIA GPU platform, our approach achieves an average speedup of 3.2x (up to 99x), which is 1.42 times faster than its nearest competitor and delivers 99% of the performance level of a manual GPU implementation.

2 Motivation

Consider the code fragment in figure 1 (a). This loop is extracted from the sequential version of the BT benchmark from the NAS benchmark suite. While conservative, static analysis fails to parallelise this loop due to the inter-procedural call to function binvcrhs at line 14 where an output dependence (i.e. write after write) to array lhs has to be assumed (inlining of binvcrhs would not eliminate the possible aliasing problem). Without further information, this loop would

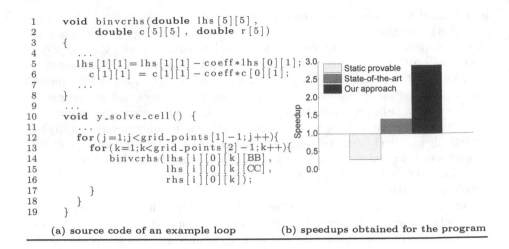

```
1      void binvcrhs(double lhs[5][5],
2          double c[5][5], double r[5])
3      {
4          ...
5      lhs[1][1]=lhs[1][1]-coeff*lhs[0][1];
6      c[1][1] = c[1][1]-coeff*c[0][1];
7          ...
8      }
9          ...
10     void y_solve_cell() {
11         ...
12     for(j=1;j<grid_points[1]-1;j++){
13       for(k=1;k<grid_points[2]-1;k++){
14         binvcrhs(lhs[i][0][k][BB],
15                  lhs[i][0][k][CC],
16                  rhs[i][0][k]);
17       }
18     }
19     }
```

(a) source code of an example loop   **(b) speedups obtained for the program**

Fig. 1. An example that static analysis fails to discover parallelism. No speedups were observed by only exploring statically provable parallelism. Profiling-based analysis, on the other hand, can provide us with additional information: no dependencies have been encountered in any trial run. By exploiting this information, we can use the GPU to execute both statically and probably parallel loops (with speculation support) and to achieve speedups rather than a slowdown. Our approach gives a speedup of 2.9x which is 2 times faster than a speedup of 1.45x given by the state-of-the-art GPU speculation scheme.

have to be executed in sequential on the CPU (as it is too expensive to do so on the GPU). Although we can still execute statically provable, parallel parts of the loops on the GPU, we will have to introduce additional synchronisation and communication between the sequential CPU and parallel GPU computation. The additional overhead, however, could be expensive and can outweigh the benefit of parallel GPU execution. In fact, as can be seen from figure 1 (b), doing so leads to a slowdown of 3.6x over the sequential code on a NVIDIA GTX 580 platform described in section 6.

Profile-based dependence analysis, on the other hand, provides use with the additional information that *no actual data dependence* inhibits parallelization for given sample inputs. While we still cannot prove absence of data dependences for *every possible input*, we can classify this loop as a highly-likely parallel candidate. We can then speculatively execute this loop in parallel on the GPU with dependence violation checking together with a rollback scheme to ensure correctness if a true dependence violation is discovered at runtime. This is safe and potentially fast. As shown in figure 1 (b), a state-of-the-art GPU speculation scheme, Paragon [21], gives a speedup of 1.45x for this particular benchmark. Though the result of using Paragon is encouraging, it can be further improved. Paragon requires a large buffer to record the speculative accessing addresses, which will be used in a separate dependence checking procedure to check the

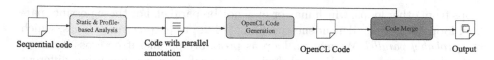

Fig. 2. Our compiler framework first uses static and profiled-based analysis to identify parallel candidates. Those parallel candidates are then translated into OpenCL kernels. Dependence checking code is added to perform dependence checking for those candidates that cannot be statically proven to be parallelizable but no dependence violation was discovered during profiling. Finally, the generated parallel OpenCL program is merged with the original sequential program as output.

potential violations of speculative accesses. This, however, can result in expensive indirect memory accessing overhead on the GPU. We would like to avoid this overhead.

As described later in this paper, our novel *in-place* dependence checking approach does not require a buffer to store the speculative accesses. It results in a speedup of 2.9x, two times faster than Paragon. With a novel dependence checking scheme, we then build a compiler framework to automatically generate parallel OpenCL code from sequential code using dependence profiling information and without user interaction, allowing us to exploit GPU parallelism for highly-likely parallel legacy code.

This example demonstrates that static analysis is overly conservative. Profiling based analysis, by contrast, opens up opportunities to exploit GPU parallelism for highly-likely parallel code. In the following three sections, we will first provide an overview of our compiler framework and then describe our parallelism detection and speculation schemes in details.

3   Overview

Our compiler uses both static and profile-driven dynamic analyses to automatically discover parallelism from sequential code and to generate parallel OPENCL code. For this, we also perform loop and array layout optimisations. At runtime, a safety net is provided for probably parallel loops that require dependence violation checking. Our prototype compiler is implemented using LLVM.

3.1   Compile Time

Figure 2 depicts our compilation framework. Our compiler uses three steps to generate parallel GPU code: parallelism detection, OPENCL code generation and code merging.

Parallelism Detection. We currently target loop-level parallelism. In particular, we use static analysis to separate definitely sequential and definitely parallel loops from other loops, which may or may not be parallel. For these possibly parallel loops we rely on dependence profiling [24,26] to extract those loops, which are *probably parallel*. We mark a loop as probably parallel if no cross-iteration dependences have been observed during any profiled execution using different data inputs. These loops are candidates for speculative parallel execution. The output of this stage is a program with OPENMP-like annotations to parallel and probably parallel loops, which include privatisable variables.

OpenCL Code Generation. The annotated program is passed to an OPENCL code generator [5], which automatically converts data-parallel loops and parallel reduction loops into OPENCL kernels. Each data-parallel loop is translated to a separate kernel using the OPENCL APIs, where each iterator of the loop is replaced by a global work-item ID. Checking code is added to speculative references, which may lead to a dependence violation in probably parallel loops. The details of our speculative checking scheme are described in section 5. Furthermore, as the currently OpencCL implementation does not support I/O operations, our approach does not speculatively parallelize any loops with I/O operations.

Code Merging. The last compilation stage merges the generated parallel OPENCL code with the original, sequential program into a single program. As such, the output program consists of both the original, safe implementation in addition to the generated OPENCL parallel code. Additional code will be automatically generated to spawn two processes to run both versions and validate results at runtime with the support a lightweight library.

3.2   Runtime

The combined use of static analysis and dependence profiling provides us with sufficient confidence that no data dependences exist in probably parallel loops, although this cannot be proven. The low expected probability of encountering any future dependences motivates us to speculatively execute such loops in parallel, without provisions for rollback to an earlier, safe state. Instead, we speed up what we expect to be the common case, i.e. parallel execution without dependence violation. In particular, we do not maintain rollback state or memory write buffers. Obviously, such as scheme will make the occurrence of a data dependence expensive to resolve, however, we do not expect this to happen frequently.

Runtime Dependence Checking. Inspired by a CPU-based SW-TLS scheme [16], we propose a *in place* dependence checking scheme for GPUs. Checking only needs to be applied to speculative memory references in probably parallel loops. Statically provable parallel loops do not require any runtime checking at all. For every access to a speculative variable (i.e. a variable of which a read and write access may cause an dependence violation with speculative parallel execution), our compiler automatically converts the memory reference to a speculative read/write operation. Dependences are checked *in place* and on the fly, and any

```
1    void binvcrhs_spec(__global double (*lhs)[5],
2                       __global int (*rd_log_lhs)[5],
3                       __global int (*wr_log_lhs)[5],
4                       ...,
5                       __global int* spec_flag,
6                       __global int iter_id)
7    {
8        ...
9        _rval_0 = specLD_double(&lhs[1][1],
10                           &wr_log_lhs[1][1],&rd_log_lhs[1][1],
11                           iter_id,spec_flag);
12
13       _rval_1 = specLD_double(&lhs[0][1], ...);
14
15       //speculatively store the result to lhs[1][1]
16       specST_double((_rval_0-coeff*_rval_1), &lhs[1][1],
17                           &wr_log_lhs[1][1], &rd_log_lhs[1][1],
18                           iter_id,spec_flag);
19       ...
20   }
21
22   __kernel void y_solve_cell_L0 (...)
23   {
24       ...
25       iter_id = get_global_id(1) * get_global_size(0)
26                 + get_global_id(0) + init_iter_num;
27       ...
28       binvcrhs_spec(lhs, rd_log_lhs, wr_log_lhs,
29                     lhs, rd_log_lhs, wr_log_lhs,
30                     rhs, rd_log_lhs, wr_log_lhs,
31                     spc_flag, iter_id);
32   }
```

Fig. 3. A simplified OpenCL-based code for the statically undecidable parallel loop shown in figure 1. A speculative version of the original function **binvcrhs** is generated in which every access to the speculative variable **lhs** is replaced with a speculative load/store operation.

violation will be reported to the control thread on the CPU. An example of the generated code can be found in figure 3, where reads and writes to the speculative variable **lhs** are replaced with a speculative load and store operations, respectively.

Recovery from Dependence Violations. We use competitive scheduling to deal with unexpected, but possible dependence violations. For this, we launch *both* the parallel and the original, sequential program simultaneously. Each version runs as a separated process which has its own memory space. We immediately terminate the parallel version on detection of a dependence violation. Otherwise, if no dependence violations have been observed, the version first to finish kills the slower competitor. The speculative execution will only commit if no violation is detected through all speculative execution. Maximum execution time is capped to time of sequential execution.

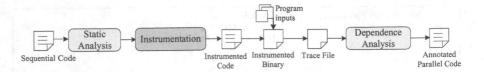

Fig. 4. The process of profile-based dependence analysis. Our compiler only uses profile-guided analysis for code regions where static analysis has bailed out.

4   Compile Time: Parallelism Detection and Code Generation

4.1   Parallelism Detection

To determine whether or not speculate we use the following hybrid approach: (i) use static analysis wherever possible and results are conclusive, (ii) use profile-guided analysis only for dependence checking where static analysis has bailed out, and (iii) identify parallel loop candidates using combined static and dynamic dependence information.

Figure 4 illustrates our hybrid static and dynamic parallelism detection approach. We use a customised memory dependence analysis path from LLVM v3.4 for static analysis. We then perform profile-guided analysis with similar capabilities as [24], but we only instrument memory operations, which previous static analysis could not resolve with certainty. The instrumented sequential application is recompiled and executed with several different inputs in sequential to generate traces of memory operations. Different program inputs are provided by the user. Each loop will be profiled once during trace collection. Loop traces are further analysed to determine if data dependences occurred during execution. Any loop that does not contain cross-iteration data dependences is then marked as *probably parallel*. Additionally, traces can be used to support static reduction recognition.

Speculative Variables. Tracking of speculative memory accesses is expensive, hence it is desirable that we only track those accesses that can potentially cause a dependence violation. Here we rely on static analysis to generate a list of variables that require speculative tracking, i.e. those which are subject to *may*-dependences. In particular, we do *not* track the accesses to read-only and thread-private variables. For the remaining speculative accesses we insert suitable wrappers, which invoke the appropriate checking functions.

4.2   Code Generation

Definitely parallel and probably parallel loops are treated similarly except probably parallel loops have references to arrays replaced with speculative loads and stores. Parallel loops are translated in a straightforward manner into kernels. A standard two-stage algorithm [3] is used to translate a parallel reduction loop. Each parallel loop is translated to a separate kernel using the OPENCL APIs where each iterator is replaced by a global work-item ID.

```
1   double specLD_double(__global double *a, __global int *wr_log,
2            __global int *rd_log, int iter_id, __global int *flag)
3   {
4       double value;
5       atom_max(rd_log, iter_id);
6       value = a[0];
7       if (*wr_log > iter_id) /*Condition 1*/
8           *flag = FAIL;
9       return value;
10  }
11
12  double specST_double(__global double *a, __global int *wr_log,
13          __global int *rd_log, int iter_id, __global int *flag, double value)
14  {
15      atom_max(wr_log, iter_id);
16      if (*wr_log > iter_id) { /*Condition 2*/
17          *flag = FAIL;
18      }
19      a[0] = value;
20      if (*rd_log > iter_id) { /*Condition 3*/
21          *flag = FAIL;
22      }
23      return value;
24  }
```

Fig. 5. The OpenCL implementation of our speculative load and store. Dependence checking is combined with speculative loads and stores.

5   Runtime: Safe Speculative Execution

5.1   Runtime Dependence Checking

Dependence checking is combined with speculative loads and stores. Hence, we only need to check dependence violations for addresses that are actually accessed at runtime. Figure 5 shows the OPENCL implementation of speculative load and store operations. Dependence checking is performed *in place*. For each speculatively accesses address, we create a suitable entry in either a read or write log, i.e. the rd_log and wr_log variables in figure 5. The read and write logs are created on the GPU global memory, which are used to store the ID of the highest iteration that has read/written to the corresponding memory address a (lines 5 and 15). As OPENCL does not support barriers for GPU threads across work groups, we use the atom_max operation provided by OPENCL to make sure only the *highest* iteration ID is stored in the log. The value in the log entry will be monotonically increasing[1] over time. Using the logs, we can simply determine whether a speculative load/store is successful.

5.2   Violation Detection

Speculative Load. A speculative load is successful if there have been no speculative store to the same memory location by a GPU thread that executes a

---

[1] For a program with multiple GPU kernels, the iteration ID passed to the speculative load and store functions starts from the maximum iteration number of the previous probably parallel loop. Therefore, the number is monotonically increasing for multiple speculative kernels.

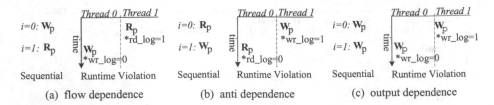

Fig. 6. Three cross-iteration dependence and the possible runtime violations due to GPU thread scheduling. All the three violations can be successful detected by our dependence checking scheme with the read (rd_log) and write (wr_log) buffers as shown in figure 5.

later loop iteration. This condition is checked in line 7. If the memory location is written in a later iteration, i.e. (*wr_log>iter_id), a violation will be reported (line 8).

Speculative Store. Conversely, a speculative store is successful as long as there has been no speculative accesses (either loads or stores) to the same address by later iterations. This condition is checked in lines 16 and 18. If a later iteration attempts to write to the same location, i.e., (*wr_log>iter_id), or read from it, i.e., (*rd_log>iter_id), a violation is detected.

We continue the discussion of our violation detection mechanism for all possible types of runtime dependence violations. It is worth noting that our scheme is *exact* and does not report any false positives. In addition, if cross-iteration dependent accesses are executed in the correct sequential order by virtue of the GPU thread scheduler, it will correctly handle this situation and not flag any violation.

Our OPENCL code generator maps each loop iteration to an OPENCL work item to be executed by one GPU thread. Hence, no dependence violations are possible within one iteration. Though, cross-iteration dependence violations are possible due to the arbitrary order of thread scheduling on the GPU. In this case, Figure 6 enumerates all three possible cross-iteration violations. Here we show the sequential dependence of two consecutive iterations that must be respected and the potential violation due to GPU thread scheduling.

Flow Dependence. Figure 6(a) illustrates a violation of a flow dependence (i.e. read after write), where the use of p in iteration 1 happens before p is updated by thread 0, which executes iteration 0. This violation will be detected in function specST. It is *rd_log=1 and iter_id=0 and also Condition 3 (line 18) of figure 5 holds, such that a violation will be reported.

Anti Dependence. In figure 6(b), the use of p happens after it has been updated by the a later iteration. This causes an anti-dependence (i.e. write after read) violation, which will be captured by function specLD. In this case, it is *wr_log=1 and iter_id=0 and Condition 1 (line 7) of figure 5 holds, such that a violation will be reported.

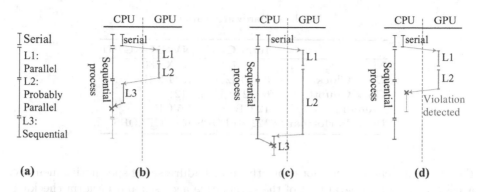

Fig. 7. Three different parallel execution scenarios for the sequential program shown in (a) : speculative execution runs faster with no conflict (b) , sequential execution runs faster (c), violation are found for speculative execution (d)

Output Dependence. Figure 6(c) is an output dependence (i.e. write after write) violation. After thread 1 has updated p, this memory location is overwritten by thread 0, which executes a previous iteration. In this case, it is *wr_log=1 and iter_id=0 and Condition 2 (line 16) in figure 5 holds, such that a violation will be reported.

5.3   Recovery from Dependence Violations

Speculative parallel executions can fail despite prior dependence profiling. We use a *competitive scheduling* scheme where we simultaneously execute a sequential version of the program alongside the parallelised program on a spare core of the host CPU. If a dependence violation is reported, we simply abort speculative parallel execution and use the result produced by the safe, sequential run as the output of the program. Competitive scheduling caps the maximum execution time to that of the sequential program.

Figure 7 depicts our competitive scheduling scheme. This example contains three loops: a statically proven parallel loop $L1$, a probably parallel loop $L2$, and a statically proven sequential loop $L3$. In our scheme, loops $L1$ and $L2$ will be executed on the GPU and the sequential loop $L3$ will be executed on the host CPU. There are three possible scenarios. If the speculative version finishes first and does not observe any dependence violations, it terminates the sequential version (figure 7(b)). If the sequential version finishes first, it will abort the parallel speculative version (figure 7(c)). Finally, if the speculative version detects a dependence violation, it aborts and the sequential version will eventually finish (figure 7(d)) successfully.

5.4   Comparison to other Approaches

Our speculative checking scheme has several advantages when compared to other state-of-the-art GPU thread level speculative schemes, e.g. Paragon [21]. Unlike

Table 1. Hardware platform

	Intel CPU	NVIDIA GPU
Model	Core i7	GTX 580
Core Clock	3.6 GHz	1544 MHz
Core Count	6 (12 w/HT)	512
Memory	12 GB	1.5 GB
Peak Performance	122 GFLOPS	1581 GFLOPS

Paragon, our scheme does not explicitly record addresses of speculative memory accesses. It is an integral part of the speculative accesses and perform checking on the fly. As such, our scheme does not have the indirect memory access overhead resulting from the address bookkeeping buffer, a problem which hampers Paragon's performance. Our scheme is particularly well suited for sparse data applications (e.g. using sparse matrices) where only a small number of the total index space is accessed by the program. Unlike Paragon, load and store logs (i.e rd_log and wr_log) can be re-used between multiple speculative kernels without the need for clearing them in-between. Finally, Paragon uses a naive violation detection scheme where an output dependence violation will be reported if there is more than one write to the same memory address. This naive scheme may cause false positives (i.e. a successful speculative execution is reported as violation) when an address has been updated multiple times within the same loop iteration or a write dependence is honoured. By contrast, our precise violation detection scheme is *exact* and does not suffer from this problem.

6   Experimental Setup

Platform. We evaluate our approach on a CPU-GPU mixed system with an Intel Core i7 CPU and an NVIDIA GTX 580 GPU. The system runs with a openSUSE 12.3 with Linux kernel 3.7.10. Table 1 gives detailed information of our platform.

Benchmarks. We have used the *sequential* NAS benchmark v.2.3 suite for which manually parallelised CPU and GPU implementations are available. To parallelise the code, we use a profiling-based auto-parallelisation tool to analyze data dependences and generate parallel OpenCL code. The tool parallelises loops with speculative checking, which are found to be parallelisable during profiling but cannot proven statically. For all loops that can be statically proven to be safe to parallelise, the tool parallelises them straightforward. The compiler parallelises up to three-level of a nested loops to create as many GPU threads as possible. Whenever possible, we try to avoid the CPU-GPU communications and synchronisation by running a parallel loop on the GPU. We avoid to parallelize a loop that accounts for less than 1% of the whole-program execution time unless there is a consecutive parallel or probably parallel loop candidate after it (so that we can remove a CPU-GPU synchronisation point).

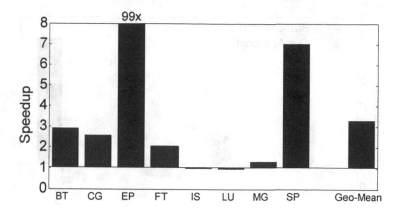

Fig. 8. Speedups over the sequential execution of our approach. We achieve on average a speedup of 3.2x and has never significantly slowed down the program over the sequential execution.

Compiler and Evaluation Runs. All programs have been compiled using GCC 4.4.7 with the -O3 option. Each experiment was repeated 5 times and the average execution time was recorded. All the benchmarks were profiled using the smallest input (class S) and evaluated with a larger input class (class A).

Comparison. Our approach is evaluated against *Paragon* [21], the closest competitor. In Paragon, probably parallel loops are discovered at program runtime by profiling those statically undecidable loops. However, we found doing so is very expensive. To provide a fair comparison, we make offload the profiling stage offline and provide Paragon with the same probably parallel code so it is speculate on exactly the same loops as our approach. We therefore only evaluate the efficiency of speculation rather than accuracy of parallelism discovery and profiling overhead. The Paragon scheme relies on OpenCL code generation. Again, we use the same OpenCL code generator to provide a fair evaluation. In addition to Paragon, we also compare our approach to two manually parallelised implementations of the NAS benchmark suite: an OPENMP version and an OPENCL implementation (SNU NPB [22]). Both versions were implemented by independent programmers. The two manual implementations provide a good estimation of the upper bound performance with the help of user assistance.

7   Experimental Results

In this section we first evaluate our approach against the sequential baseline. We then compare our approach to a scheme that only parallelises statically decidable loops on GPUs. This is followed by comparisons to a state-of-the-art GPU speculation scheme and manually parallelised implementations. Finally, we take a closer look at the limitations of static analysis and our speculation overhead, and discuss of dependence violations.

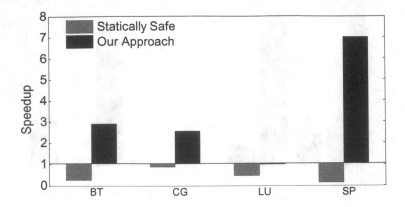

Fig. 9. Comparisons of Paragon and our in-place GPU speculation scheme. Our scheme achieves higher speedups on more benchmarks when compared to Paragon.

7.1   Overall Results

Figure 8 shows the speedups achieved by our scheme. The performance numbers presented are speedups over the sequential execution on the CPU. On average our scheme achieves a speedup of 3.2x. Furthermore, by co-running the original sequential program alongside the parallelised GPU program, our scheme has never significantly slowed down the program.

As can be seen from figure 8, great performance improvement can be observed by exploiting GPU parallelism for probably parallel loops. This is exemplified by the embarrassing parallel benchmark EP where a speedup of 99x was observed. Parallel GPU execution can benefit for other benchmarks too. For benchmarks BT, CG and SP, we achieved a speedup of at least 2.6x and up to 7x. For benchmarks FT and MG, we only achieved modest speedups due to the available parallelism and cost of speculation. For benchmarks LU and IS, no speedups were observed on our platform. For LU, a new algorithm is required to get improved performance on the GPU [22,5]. For IS, the parallel loop only accounts for 27% of the sequential execution and it is not worth to parallelise it on the GPU. Nonetheless, our competitive scheduling scheme caps the execution time to the time of the sequential run if the parallel GPU execution is not profitable.

7.2   Comparison with the Statically Safe Approach

We compare our approach to a conservative approach that only parallelises those statically proved parallel loops on the GPU and runs the rest part in sequential on the CPU. Obviously, no speculation is needed for such a scheme but data transfers and synchronisation are required to synchronise between the CPU and the GPU threads.

Figure 9 compare our approach with such a statically safe scheme. Here, some of the benchmarks are omitted because static analysis fails to discover parallelism

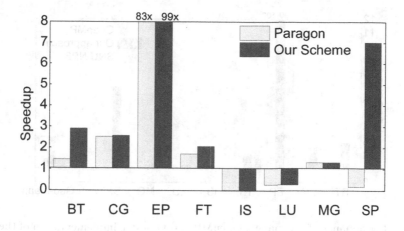

Fig. 10. Comparison of Paragon and our in-place GPU speculation scheme. Our approach achieves higher speedups on more benchmarks when compared to Paragon.

of them. As can be seen from this figure, no speedups were observed for the conservative, safe scheme. This is due to the communication and synchronisation overhead associated with the switch between the CPU and GPU executions, where shared variables have to be synchronized among the two devices. This comes at the cost of expensive communications and synchronisation which outweigh the benefit of GPU parallel executions. Our approach, by contrast, avoids this overhead by running two consecutive static and probably parallel loops on the GPU so that we can keep the data on the GPU and avoid the otherwise required CPU-GPU data transfers. Unlike the disappointing results of the static scheme, our profiled-based, GPU speculation scheme is able to achieve speedups for all the four programs except LU where a change of algorithms is require to achieve speedups on the GPU [22].

Overall, the static parallelisation technology is too conservative to exploit GPU parallelism despite the abundant available parallelism for the majority benchmarks. By contrast, our approach outperforms the static parallelisation approach by a factor of 7.

7.3   Comparison with Paragon

Figure 10 compares our GPU speculation scheme with Paragon. We factor out the performance achieved by co-running of the sequential code and focus solely on the quality of the GPU speculation scheme. Note that we applied the same OPENCL code optimization to both approaches; therefore, the performance variations are mainly down to the difference of the speculation schemes.

This figure clearly demonstrates the advantages of our approach. As can be seen from this diagram, the overhead of Paragon can be significant for some benchmarks. For example, Paragon is not able to achieve speedups for SP while our approach gives a speedup of over 7x. For this benchmark, the indirect

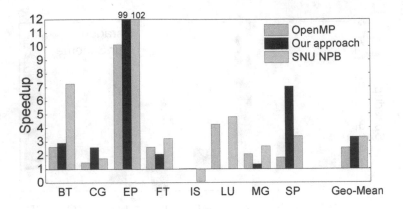

Fig. 11. Performance of the manual OpenMP and OpenCL implementation of the Nas benchmark suite and our automatically generated parallelised code

memory accessing and initialization overhead of Paragon clearly outweighs the benefit of Gpu parallel execution. Besides SP, our scheme also outperforms Paragon on benchmarks BT and FT, with a speedup up to 2 times higher. For benchmarks CG, EP and MG, speculative checking only needs to be performed on a few speculative variables and both approaches deliver similar performance. Finally, for benchmarks IS and LU, none of the two schemes achieve performance improvement due to the restriction of the program and the Gpu architecture as explained in section 7.1. Overall, our scheme outperforms Paragon by achieving higher speedups whenever it is profitable to exploit Gpu parallelism.

7.4 Comparison to Manually Parallelized Code

We also compare our approach to two manually parallelised implementations developed by independent programmers: (1) the OpenMP version of the Nas benchmark suite [1] for the Cpu and (2) SNU NPB [22], an OpenCL implementation of the Nas benchmark suite for the Gpu. The SNU NPB provides a good estimation of the up-bound performance that our Gpu speculation scheme can achieve. The results are shown in figure 11.

As can be seen from this diagram, exploiting Gpu parallelism for highly-likely parallel code can be beneficial. Example benchmarks include BT, CG, EP and SP where Gpu execution significantly outperforms the OpenMP Cpu execution by a factor up to 10. It is not supervised that a manually parallelised Gpu implementation without speculation overhead outperforms our automatic scheme, but our approach is able to achieve a level of performance close to the manual implementation. For benchmarks CG and SP, our approach even outperforms the manual Gpu implementation with advanced Gpu memory optimizations such as dynamic index reordering applied by our OpenCL code translator [5]. For benchmarks FT and MG, our approach is not as good as the OpenMP implementation. This is restricted by the programs themselves as the Cpu-Gpu communications

Table 2. Numbers of statically decidable and undecidable parallel loops of the manual OpenMP implementation

Benchmark	Manual	Statically Decidable	Statically Undecidable
BT	54	23	31
CG	19	17	2
EP	1	0	1
FT	6	0	6
IS	1	0	1
LU	29	12	17
MG	12	5	7
SP	70	41	29

is relatively high compared to computation. This can be seen from the fact that the manually parallelised GPU code only outperforms the OpenMP CPU code by a small margin. For benchmark LU, the algorithm in the sequential code has to be changed to a hyperplane one to achieve speedups on the GPU [22]. This is of course out of the scope of our automatic approach. Finally, for IS, none of the three parallel versions can gain speedups because the execution time of this program is dominated by serial code.

Overall our automatic approach performs well. The average 3.2x speedup achieved by our approach is very close to the 3.3x speedup of the manually parallelised OPENCL implementation. Moreover, our approach also outperforms the OPENMP implementation on the majority of the benchmarks by exploiting GPU parallelism.

7.5 Analysis

Limitation of Static Analysis. Table 2 shows the number of parallelised loops of the OpenMP implementation and among those how many are statically decidable and undecidable. For benchmark CG, a considerable number of the parallelised loops are statically decidable. However, for most of the programs, merely relying on static analysis is not enough to exploit program parallelism, which actually misses a significant amount of parallel opportunities. For example, for benchmarks EP, FT and IS, static analysis fails to detect any of the manually parallelised loops. Static analysis fails to explore parallelism for these three benchmarks including EP where a speedup of 90x is available. Dependence profiling information, on the other hand, can provide us with additional information, enabling us to discover those parallel opportunities. By contrast to static analysis, our hybrid static and dynamic parallelism detection scheme identifies all the parallel loops specified in OpenMP implementation. This table shows that profile-based analysis is a powerful technique that allows us to discover parallelism for highly-likely parallel legacy code.

Speculation Costs. Figure 12 shows the overhead of the speculation for each benchmark. In this diagram, the program runtime is broken down into two parts: speculation overhead and non-speculative GPU parallel execution. The

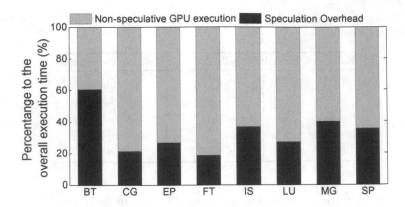

Fig. 12. Speculation overhead compared to the unsafe parallel execution without speculation on the GPU

two breakdowns are shown as the percentage to the overall program runtime. As can be seen from this diagram, the speculation overhead varies from one program to the other. Depending on the number of probably parallel loops and the frequency of speculative accesses, the overhead varies from 60% to 15% relative to the whole-program execution time. For some benchmarks, such as CG, FT and SP, the speculation overhead is relatively low, around 20%. This is because speculation only needs to be applied on a few arrays. For benchmark LU, the program execution time is dominated by the synchronisation and communication overhead due to the restriction of the program algorithm and thus the speculation overhead is not significant. For benchmarks IS, MG and BT, the overhead is more than 30% of the whole-program execution time, because of the high frequent speculative access to variables. Particularly, benchmark BT has the highest speculation overhead which accounts for 60% of the total program execution time. For this benchmark, 31 out of the 54 parallel loops cannot be statically determined and speculation has to be performed on those statically undecidable loops. Despite the speculation overhead, our approach is still able to achieve a speedup of 2.9x rather than a 3.6x slowdown of a static approach (see section 2). On average, the speculation overhead is 28% across all benchmarks.

Dependence Violation. Possibly a little surprising, in none of the above experiments dynamic dependence violations have been detected. This indicates that our profile-guided parallelisation approach correctly identifies probably parallel loops. Whilst it is easy to construct a counter example, it suggests that many loops are genuinely parallel even though static analysis is unable to prove this. In fact, we have compared the loops identified by our analysis with those parallelised in the manually derived OPENMP reference implementation of the benchmarks and confirm equivalence (subject to insertion of speculation code).

8 Related Work

Whilst specific pieces of related work have already been discussed earlier on we will provide a brief overview of TLS and profile-guided parallelisation approaches as far as relevant for this paper in the following paragraphs.

*Thread-Level Speculation (*TLS*)* Padua and Rauchwerger [20] are early pioneers of software based TLS. Their framework speculatively executes a loop as a *doall* and applies a fully parallel data dependence test to determine if it had any cross-iteration dependencies; if the test fails, then the loop is re-executed serially. There are other automatic parallelisation techniques that exploit parallelism in a speculatively execution manner [28,29], some of which require hardware support [2]. Matthew *et al.* [4] have manually parallelised the SPECINT-2000 benchmarks with TLS. Their approach relies upon the programmer to discover parallelism as well as runtime support for parallel execution. SW-TLS has been the topic of many research papers, e.g. [14,15,17,12]. All of these papers focus on individual speculation schemes, but share the assumption that dependence violations have a significant probability > 0. In fact, it is generally assumed that speculative parallel code is either generated by a traditional compiler using static analysis [31] or directly by the programmer [18]. This is different to our work, where profiling information is available and probably parallel loops have been identified for speculative execution.

Profile-Guided Parallelisation Static analyses are *fundamentally* limited by the undecidability of the underlying data flow problem [9]. This is not only of theoretical interest, but has practical implications: parallelizing compilers using static analysis are severely limited in detecting parallelism and fail to provide speedups across standard industry benchmarks representative of whole classes of real-world applications [24]. Profile-guided data flow analyses, on the other hand, have been proven to detect significantly more parallelism than their static counterparts [7,11,13], but are lacking safety, i.e. critical data dependencies can be missed. As profile-guided parallelisation has gained popularity in the academic community, several papers have investigated methods for making profile collection more efficient [8,27]. Some interactive parallelisation tools incorporate dynamic information [23], but typically this is restricted to mapping support and not used for dependence testing.

Automatic Generation of GPU Programs Some of the recent work target CUDA [10] or OPENCL [5] code generation from an already parallelized program, such as OPENMP programs. Unlike these approaches where the program parallelism needs to be identify and verify by the programmer, our compiler automatically detects parallelism from sequential code without user assistance.

Speculative Parallel Executions for GPUs The Paragon compiler [21] is the nearest work. Unlike our approach where profiling is performed off-line, Paragon uses profiling information at program runtime to determine parallelism of the statically undecidable loops by recording all the memory access. This approach, however, can incur significant overhead at program runtime. Furthermore, Paragons dependence checking scheme requires a buffer to record the memory access of speculative variables. This could lead to indirect memory accessing overhead for a separated checking process and the buffer will need to be initialized before being used. By contrast to Paragons, our in place dependence checking scheme does not have this overhead. Finally, Hayashi et al. [6] propose a scheme to automatically generated OpenCL code for Java parallel constructors and preserve precise exception semantics.

9   Conclusion

In this paper we have presented a holistic approach to exploit parallelism for highly-likely parallel legacy code on commodity GPUs. Building on prior work on profile-guided parallelization, we proposed a novel GPU-based speculation scheme to provide correctness guarantees for probably parallel loops. Our scheme discards expensive check-pointing for rollback that is not suitable for GPUs, but instead provides faster checking of dependences for speculative parallel execution regions, which are identified as probably parallel by our profile-guided analysis. Our novel approach allows dependence checking to be done in place with speculative accessing operations. We thus only need to perform checking on the addresses where speculative accesses actually take place. Our approach has been evaluated on benchmarks that are rich in parallelism, but hard to parallelize using traditional static analyses. By exploiting GPU parallel execution, we avoid the expensive overhead that otherwise would be required for serial CPU executions. We have demonstrated the effectiveness of our in-place GPU speculation scheme by comparing it to a state-of-the-art GPU-based speculation scheme. Experimental results show that our technique outperforms the state-of-the-art by a factor of 1.45. This translates to 99% of the performance of a manual OPENCL implementation without speculation overhead where the probably parallel loops have been manually verified. Our future work will explore the combination of CPU and GPU speculation schemes for auto-parallelisation on heterogeneous systems.

References

1. NAS parallel benchmarks 2.3, OpenMP C version,
   http://phase.hpcc.jp/Omni/benchmarks/NPB/index.html
2. Ahn, W., Duan, Y., Torrellas, J.: Dealiaser: Alias speculation using atomic region support. In: ASPLOS 2013 (2013)
3. AMD. AMD/ATI Stream SDK, http://www.amd.com/stream/
4. Bridges, M., Vachharajani, N., Zhang, Y., Jablin, T., August, D.: Revisiting the sequential programming model for the multicore era. IEEE Micro 28(1) (2008)
5. Grewe, D., Wang, Z., O'Boyle, M.: Portable mapping of data parallel programs to opencl for heterogeneous systems. In: CGO 2013 (2013)
6. Hayashi, A., Grossman, M., Zhao, J., Shirako, J., Sarkar, V.: Speculative execution of parallel programs with precise exception semantics on gpus. In: LCPC 2013 (2013)
7. Ketterlin, A., Clauss, P.: Profiling data-dependence to assist parallelization: Framework, scope, and optimization. In: MICRO 2012 (2012)
8. Kim, M., Kim, H., Luk, C.-K.: Sd3: A scalable approach to dynamic data-dependence profiling. In: MICRO 43

9. Landi, W.: Undecidability of static analysis. ACM Lett. Program. Lang. Syst. 1(4) (December 1992)
10. Lee, S., Eigenmann, R.: Openmpc: Extended openmp programming and tuning for gpus. In: SC 2010 (2010)
11. Mak, J., Faxén, K.-F., Janson, S., Mycroft, A.: Estimating and exploiting potential parallelism by source-level dependence profiling. In: EuroPar 2010 (2010)
12. Mehrara, M., Hao, J., Hsu, P.-C., Mahlke, S.: Parallelizing sequential applications on commodity hardware using a low-cost software transactional memory. In: PLDI 2009 (2009)
13. Mishra, V., Aggarwal, S.K.: Partool: A feedback-directed parallelizer. In: Temam, O., Yew, P.-C., Zang, B. (eds.) APPT 2011. LNCS, vol. 6965, pp. 157–171. Springer, Heidelberg (2011)
14. Oancea, C.E., Mycroft, A.: A lightweight model for software thread-level speculation (TLS). In: PACT 2007 (2007)
15. Oancea, C.E., Mycroft, A.: Set-congruence dynamic analysis for thread-level speculation (TLS). In: Amaral, J.N. (ed.) LCPC 2008. LNCS, vol. 5335, pp. 156–171. Springer, Heidelberg (2008)
16. Oancea, C.E., Mycroft, A., Harris, T.: A lightweight in-place implementation for software thread-level speculation. In: SPAA 2009 (2009)
17. Oancea, C.E., Mycroft, A., Harris, T.: A lightweight in-place implementation for software thread-level speculation. In: SPAA 2009 (2009)
18. Prabhu, M.K., Olukotun, K.: Using thread-level speculation to simplify manual parallelization. In: PPoPP 2003 (2003)
19. Rauchwerger, L.: Speculative parallelization of loops. Springer, Heidelberg (2011)
20. Rauchwerger, L., Padua, D.A.: The LRPD test: Speculative run-time parallelization of loops with privatization and reduction parallelization. IEEE Trans. Parallel Distrib. Syst. 10(2) (1999)
21. Samadi, M., Hormati, A., Lee, J., Mahlke, S.: Paragon: Collaborative speculative loop execution on gpu and cpu. In: GPGPU 2012 (2012)
22. Seo, S., Jo, G., Lee, J.: Performance characterization of the nas parallel benchmarks in opencl. In: IISWC 2011 (2011)
23. Thies, W., Chandrasekhar, V., Amarasinghe, S.P.: A practical approach to exploiting coarse-grained pipeline parallelism in C programs. In: MICRO 2007 (2007)
24. Tournavitis, G., Wang, Z., Franke, B., O'Boyle, M.F.: Towards a holistic approach to auto-parallelization: Integrating profile-driven parallelism detection and machine-learning based mapping. In: PLDI 2009 (2009)
25. Vandierendonck, H., Rul, S., De Bosschere, K.: The paralax infrastructure: Automatic parallelization with a helping hand. In: PACT 2010 (2010)
26. Vanka, R., Tuck, J.: Efficient and accurate data dependence profiling using software signatures. In: CGO 2012 (2012)
27. Vanka, R., Tuck, J.: Efficient and accurate data dependence profiling using software signatures. In: CGO 2012 (2012)
28. Wallace, S., Calder, B., Tullsen, D.M.: Threaded multiple path execution. In: ISCA 1998 (1998)
29. Wu, P., Kejariwal, A., Caşcaval, C.: Compiler-driven dependence profiling to guide program parallelization. In: Amaral, J.N. (ed.) LCPC 2008. LNCS, vol. 5335, pp. 232–248. Springer, Heidelberg (2008)
30. Yu, H., Li, Z.: Fast loop-level data dependence profiling. In: ICS 2012 (2012)
31. Zhai, A., Wang, S., Yew, P.-C., He, G.: Compiler optimizations for parallelizing general-purpose applications under thread-level speculation. In: PPoPP 2008 (2008)

A Flexible and Efficient ML Lexer Tool Based on Extended Regular Expression Submatching

Martin Sulzmann* and Pippijn van Steenhoven**

Hochschule Karlsruhe - Technik und Wirtschaft

Abstract. Lexical analysis has many applications beyond the first phase of compilation in programming language processing. We argue that extended regular expressions combined with the ability to extract submatch information significantly increase the expressiveness of lexer specifications. We show that such an expressive lexical analysis can be done efficiently using some novel automata-based methods. The approach has been implemented in an ML lexer tool which is compatible with `ocamllex`. Experimental results confirm that our approach is competitive with respect to existing ML lexer tools.

1 Introduction

The task of lexical analysis consists of identifying patterns of character sequences also known as lexeme [1]. Patterns are typically described by regular expressions. Thus, scanning can be performed efficiently by applying automata-based methods.

In this paper, we introduce an *efficient* lexical analysis approach based on *extended* regular expressions with support for intersection and negation in combined with *submatching*. As we will explain in more detail later, extended regular expressions and submatching provide the means to support clean and concise lexer specifications. While earlier works [10,9] supports either one of the two, we are the first to support both extensions. Powerful regular expression libraries such as [11] provide also a rich feature set but can possibly exhibit a running time which can be exponential in the size of the input. Our lexical analysis approach has a guaranteed linear run-time.

Specifically, our contributions are:

- We introduce a novel and expressive scanner approach based on extended regular expressions combined with submatching (Section 2).
- The expressiveness of our approach poses new challenges when it comes to efficient scanning (Section 3). We present an efficient automata-based method to track submatches connected to extended regular expressions. Our method combines and extends prior work on partial derivative automata-based submatching [14] and partial derivatives of an extended regular expression [4] (Section 4).

---

* `martin.sulzmann@hs-karlsruhe.de`
** `pip88nl@gmail.com`

A. Cohen (Ed.): CC 2014, LNCS 8409, pp. 174–191, 2014.

- We have implemented the approach in an ML lexer tool `dreml` which is compatible with `ocamllex` (Section 5).
- We present empirical measurements which show that our approach is competitive with respect to existing ML lexer tools (Section 6).

Related work is discussed in Section 3 and Section 6. Section 7 concludes. Our tool including benchmark examples is available via

`https://github.com/pippijn/dreml/`

2   Expressiveness

We start off with a cursory overview of the novel features of our lexer tool. We make use of standard math notation for regular expression patterns r:

$$r ::= \epsilon \mid \phi \mid l \in \Sigma \mid r + r \mid rr \mid r^* \mid \neg r \mid r \cap r \mid x : r$$

Letters l are taken from a finite alphabet Σ. Symbol ϵ denotes the empty word and ϕ denotes the empty language. The next forms describe alternation, concatenation and Kleene star. In examples, we write r^+ as a short-hand for rr^*. In patterns, we will write Σ as a short-hand for $l_1 + ... + l_n$ where $l_i \in \Sigma$. Choice and concatenation are assumed to be right-associative. The novelty lies in negation ($\neg$), intersection ($\cap$) and the submatch annotation $x : r$. We assume that pattern variables x are linear, i.e. occurrences are distinct.

As observed in [10], negation is useful for C comments of the form /* ... */. A pattern to match C comments may be written as

$$\text{/*}(x : \neg(\Sigma^* \text{*/} \Sigma^*))\text{*/}$$

Describing the same language without negation would require a longer, more complex and cumbersome expression:

$$\text{/*}((\Sigma \setminus \{\text{*}\})^*(\varepsilon + \text{*}^*(\Sigma \setminus \{\text{/}, \text{*}\})))^* \text{*/}$$

Submatch annotations are highly useful to directly extract subparts during lexical analysis to avoid clumsy post-processing steps. See the above example where we directly extract the comment text. Another typical use case for submatching are C preprocessor directives, particularly the `#include` directive. A lexical analysis is only interested in the name of the included file, which can be extracted using a pattern such as `#include` $W^* \text{"}(x : (\Sigma \setminus \{\text{"}\})^*)\text{"}$.

Matching a valid include-directive with this pattern will record the file name in the pattern variable x. For example, consider input `#include "stdio.h"`, the resulting matching environment will consist of the set $\Gamma = \{(x : \texttt{stdio.h})\}$. The file name can then be extracted and used in a semantic action or post-processing step.

The combination of submatching and extended regular expressions is highly useful as shown by our final example. Via submatching we can specify a base pattern for C integer literals, not including hexadecimal literals:

$$r_{int} = (num : (0 \ldots 9)^+)(suf : (l + L + u + U)^*)$$

after which *num* contains the number and *suf* the type suffix. Via intersection we can restrict the pattern for octal integer literals by requiring it to begin with a zero followed by anything not containing digits 8 or 9:

$$r_{oct} = r_{int} \cap (0, (\Sigma \setminus \{8, 9\})^*)$$

In general, intersection is particularly useful in the presence of composed regular grammars. A library of standard regular expressions may define a set of valid C identifiers, which may then be restricted in specialized lexers used to verify a coding style or perform syntax highlighting based on coding conventions.

3   Efficient Submatching

Our lexer tool takes as input a sequence of patterns $(r_1, ..., r_n)$. Each r_i represents the pattern for a particular class of lexeme. The common lexical analysis approach is to seek for the longest matching pattern by testing each pattern r_i in parallel. Thus, the scanning problem can be reduced to a single pattern r. The particular challenge we face is that each r is composed of submatch annotations and extended operations such as negation and intersection. During scanning we need to efficiently keep track of submatchings.

Earlier works [6,7] advocate the use of Thompson NFAs [15] for tracking of submatches efficiently. Roughly, the NFA non-deterministically searches for possible (sub)matchings without having to back-track. Thus, a linear running time can be guaranteed.

To deal with extended regular expressions, the Thompson transformation approach from regular expressions to NFA requires some significant changes. To deal with negation, we must first turn the underlying NFA into a DFA and then build the negation of the DFA. The DFA construction is costly and may incur some exponential explosion on the size of the automata. Similar issues arise in case of intersection where we must build the product automata. Interestingly, real world regular expression tools such as re2 [5] which rely on the Thompson NFA construction do *not* support negation and intersection (but for only very limited cases).

The work in [10] describes how to support extended regular expressions by adapting Brzozowski's derivative operation [3]. A DFA for recognizing expressions is obtained by interpreting regular expression as states. Transitions among states are obtained via the derivative operation which symbolically transforms regular expressions by taking away the leading letters. The results in [10] show that the resulting DFAs are generally optimal in size. However, like the Thompson NFA method, the Brzozowski method possibly suffers from an exponential explosion in the size of the automata. Furthermore, the work in [10] does not consider submatching which we consider a highly useful feature.

In conclusion, it is entirely possible to extend earlier works [6,7,10] with missing features such as submatching and extended regular expressions. However, we decide to take a different route which allows us to stick to NFAs.

To support submatching and extended regular expressions, our idea is to rely on the concept of Antimirov's partial derivatives [2]. Specifically, we build upon our own prior work [14] where we show to construct an NFA submatch automata for standard regular expressions via partial derivatives.

Like Brzozowski's derivative operation, the partial derivative operation performs a symbolic transformation on regular expressions to take away the leading letters. The difference is that Brzozowski's derivatives yield a DFA whereas Antimirov's partial derivatives yield an NFA. Roughly, the partial derivative operation takes an expression r and a letter l and yields a set of alternatives $\{r_1, ..., r_n\}$ where each r_i is a partial derivative. We find that $L(r) = L(l(r_1 + ... + r_n))$.

For example, for expression a^*a the set of partial derivatives with respect to a is $\{\epsilon, a^*a\}$. Each expression is a possible successor state. Antimirov shows that the number of partial derivatives is finite and linear in the size of the initial regular expressions. Thus, we obtain a fairly compact NFA.

Important for our work is that recently the partial derivative operation has been generalized to include additional operations such as negation and intersection [4]. As we will show in the upcoming section, we can thus extend the NFA submatch construction in [14] to the case of extended regular expressions. Experiments in the later Section 6 confirm that our approach works well in practice.

4   Extended Partial Derivative Submatch Automata

We present the details of the NFA construction for tracking submatches for an expression which may contain negation and intersection. For the construction of the automata, we use Antimirov's partial derivatives method [2] extended to the case of intersection and negation [4].

Before we dive into the technical details, we illustrate the key ideas of the construction via some example which for simplicity makes use of submatching only. For pattern $(x : a) + (y : ab)$ our construction yields the following transitions. Error states and the respective transitions are omitted for brevity.

$$(x : a) + (y : ab) \xrightarrow{(a,(x \to a))} (x : \epsilon)$$
$$(x : a) + (y : ab) \xrightarrow{(a,(y \to a))} (y : b)$$
$$(y : b) \xrightarrow{(b,(y \to b))} (y : \epsilon)$$

In the Antimirov method, NFA states can symbolically be represented by regular expressions r. There are no ϵ-transitions because the Antimirov method builds new states by taking away the leading letter. For state $(x : a) + (y : ab)$ the set of partial derivatives w.r.t. letter a is $\{(x : \epsilon), (y : b)\}$. Following [7], transitions are tagged by matchings such as $(x \to a)$ for which we use function notation.

For example, consider the transition arrow $\xrightarrow{(a,(x \to a))}$ where in case we find the input letter a we obtain the matching $(x \to a)$. Matchings are accumulated to compute the bindings for submatch annotations. For example, running the above NFA on input word ab yields the final binding $y \rightarrow ab$.

In detail, here is a sample run of the NFA on input ab where we only follow a specific path.

$$
(x : a) + (y : ab)
$$
$$
\xrightarrow{(a,(y \rightarrow a))} (y : b)
$$
$$
\xrightarrow{(b,(y \rightarrow b) \circ (y \rightarrow a))} (y : \epsilon)
$$

Accumulation of tags is via function composition. We follow the standard definition of function composition with the exception that we concatenate the codomains of submappings with the same domain, i.e.

$$
(y \rightarrow w_2) \circ (y \rightarrow w_1) = (y \rightarrow w_1 w_2)
$$

Thus, we arrive at the final binding $y \rightarrow ab$.

The main challenge is to extend the partial derivative operation to the case of negation and intersection while retaining all the good properties (i.e. finite number of partial derivatives). Thankfully for us, this problem has been solved in [4]. The idea is to represent the *extended* partial derivative result as a disjunctive normal form. That is, as a set of alternatives where each alternative is a conjunction of expressions which is again represented as a set. For example, the normal form representation of $((a + b)^* \cap b^*) + c$ is $\{\{(a + b)^*, b^*\}, \{c\}\}$. In our setting, we additionally need to keep track of submatchings connected to each alternative. Hence, we need to refine the normal form in [4] to include submatching.

4.1   Extended Partial Derivatives with Submatchings

Extended regular expressions:

$$
r ::= \epsilon \mid \phi \mid l \in \Sigma \mid r + r \mid rr \mid r^* \mid \neg r \mid r \cap r \mid x : r
$$

Normal form representation:

$$
\begin{array}{ll}
\bar{r}^n ::= \{r_1, ..., r_n\} & \text{Conjunctive clause} \\
f, g ::= (x_1 \rightarrow w_1, ..., x_n \rightarrow w_n) & \text{Matchings} \\
\mathcal{R} ::= (\bar{r}^n, f) & \text{Conjunctive clause with matchings} \\
\mathbb{R} ::= \{\mathcal{R}_1, ..., \mathcal{R}_n\} & \text{Alternatives of conjunctions}
\end{array}
$$

Conjunctive clause to expression: Alternatives of conjunction to expression:
$$
\{r\} \downarrow = r \qquad\qquad\qquad \{\} \Downarrow = \phi
$$
$$
(\{r\} \cup \bar{r}) \downarrow = r \cap \bar{r} \downarrow \qquad (\{(\bar{r}^n, f)\} \cup \mathbb{R}) \Downarrow = \bar{r}^n \downarrow + (\mathbb{R} \Downarrow)
$$

Fig. 1. Extended Partial Derivatives Normal Form

Distributivity of concatenation, intersection and negation:

$$\mathbb{R} \odot_g r' = \{(\{rr' \mid r \in \bar{r}^n\}, f \circ g) \mid (\bar{r}^n, f) \in \mathbb{R}\}$$

$$\mathbb{R}_1 \odot \mathbb{R}_2 = \{(\overline{r_1}^n \cup \overline{r_2}^m, f_1 \circ f_2) \mid (\overline{r_1}^n, f_1) \in \mathbb{R}_1, (\overline{r_2}^m, f_2) \in \mathbb{R}_2\}$$

$$\ominus \mathbb{R} = \begin{cases} \{(\{\neg\phi\}, id)\} & \text{if } \mathbb{R} = \{\} \\ \odot_{(\bar{r}^n, f) \in \mathbb{R}} \bigcup_{r \in \bar{r}^n} (\{\neg r\}, id) & \text{otherwise} \end{cases}$$

Collection of ϵ bindings:

$$x : r\downarrow_\epsilon = (x \to \epsilon) \circ r\downarrow_\epsilon \qquad \epsilon\downarrow_\epsilon = id \qquad r_1 r_2\downarrow_\epsilon = (r_1\downarrow_\epsilon) \circ (r_2\downarrow_\epsilon)$$

$$\neg r\downarrow_\epsilon = id \qquad r_1 \cap r_2\downarrow_\epsilon = r_1\downarrow_\epsilon \circ r_2\downarrow_\epsilon$$

$$r^*\downarrow_\epsilon = \begin{cases} r\downarrow_\epsilon & \text{if } \epsilon \in L(r) \\ id & \text{otherwise} \end{cases} \qquad r_1 + r_2\downarrow_\epsilon = \begin{cases} r_1\downarrow_\epsilon & \text{if } \epsilon \in L(r_1) \\ r_2\downarrow_\epsilon & \text{if } \epsilon \in L(r_2) \end{cases}$$

Extended partial derivatives with submatching:

(1) $\dfrac{\partial}{\partial_a}(\phi) = \dfrac{\partial}{\partial_a}(\epsilon) = \dfrac{\partial}{\partial_a}(b) = \{\}$ **(2)** $\dfrac{\partial}{\partial_a}(a) = \{(\{\epsilon\}, id)\}$

(3) $\dfrac{\partial}{\partial_a}(x : r) = \{(\{(x : \bar{r}^n\downarrow)\}, (x \to a) \circ f) \mid (\bar{r}^n, f) \in \dfrac{\partial}{\partial_a}(r)\}$

(4) $\dfrac{\partial}{\partial_a}(r_1 + r_2) = \dfrac{\partial}{\partial_a}(r_1) \cup \dfrac{\partial}{\partial_a}(r_2)$

(5) $\dfrac{\partial}{\partial_a}(r^*) = \dfrac{\partial}{\partial_a}(r) \odot_{last_{fv(r)}} r^*$

(6) $\dfrac{\partial}{\partial_a}(r_1 r_2) = \begin{cases} \dfrac{\partial}{\partial_a}(r_1) \odot_{id} r_2 & \text{if } \varepsilon \notin L(r_1) \\ \dfrac{\partial}{\partial_a}(r_1) \odot_{id} r_2 \cup \dfrac{\partial}{\partial_a}(r_2) \odot_{r_1\downarrow_\epsilon} \epsilon & \text{otherwise} \end{cases}$

(7) $\dfrac{\partial}{\partial_a}(r_1 \cap r_2) = \dfrac{\partial}{\partial_a}(r_1) \odot \dfrac{\partial}{\partial_a}(r_2)$

(8) $\dfrac{\partial}{\partial_a}(\neg r) = \ominus \dfrac{\partial}{\partial_a}(r)$

Fig. 2. Extended Partial Derivatives with Submatching

Figure 1 describes the necessary adjustments. $\mathbb{R}$ describes the possible outcomes of the (shortly defined) extended partial derivative operation $\frac{\partial}{\partial_a} r$. Each component in $\mathbb{R}$ consists of a pair $(\bar{r}^n, f)$ where $\bar{r}^n$ is a set of conjunctions $\{r_1, ..., r_n\}$ and f the associated matching function (i.e. mapping of pattern variables to matched words). The translation of $\mathbb{R}$ to the underlying regular expression is straightforward. See operations $\cdot \downarrow$ and $\cdot \Downarrow$. By construction $\bar{r}^n$ is always non-empty whereas $\mathbb{R}$ can possibly be equal to the empty set. For example, consider $r = \{(\{(a+b)^*, b^*\}, f), (\{c\}, g)\}$ for which we find $r \Downarrow= ((a+b)^* \cap b^*) + c$.

Our refinement of the extended partial derivative operation $\frac{\partial}{\partial_a} r$ with sub-matching is given in Figure 2. We largely follow the definition given in [4] with of course some necessary adjustments due to submatching. For the definition of $\frac{\partial}{\partial_a} r$ we require auxiliary operations $\odot_g$, $\odot$ and $\ominus$. These operations apply standard distributivity laws on expressions in normal form and additionally perform operations on matching functions.

For operation $\odot_g$, g is generally the identity function. There are two special non-identity use cases. For Kleene star, g can be customized such that we keep the matchings for all iterations or (as it is standard) only the last match. For concatenation where the first component matches ϵ, we must collect all "ϵ" bindings in combination with the operator $\downarrow_\epsilon$. Both special cases will be shortly explained in more detail. Operation $\odot$ combines conjunctive clauses which requires us to build the composition of the associated matching functions.

Operation $\ominus$ effectively cancels any submatchings which arise below negation by simply recording the identity matching function id. The reason is that we can not give any well-defined meaning to these submatchings. For example, consider $x : \neg(y : a^*)$. Suppose the pattern matches some word. Then, pattern variable x will bind any word not containing any letter a. Clearly, the binding of y is nonsensical here because (due to the outer negation) there cannot be any match for a^*.

Next, we take a look at the various cases of the extended partial derivative operation $\frac{\partial}{\partial_a} r$. Base cases (1), (2) are straightforward and so is case (4) which deals with choice.

Case (3) deals with submatch annotations $x : r$. The result is a set of alternatives where each conjunctive clause component $\bar{r}^n$ resulting from $\frac{\partial}{\partial_a} r$ is turned into an expression by applying $\cdot\downarrow$ to satisfy the syntactic forms of extended regular expressions. For each submatching f connected to a conjunctive clause, we compose the 'top-level' match $x \to a$ with f to build the overall submatching for each alternative in $\frac{\partial}{\partial_a}(x : r)$.

Case (5) deals with the Kleene star. We unfold the Kleene star once and then concatenate the result with r^*. In case of submatchings within r, the common approach is to keep only the "last" match. This is achieved via $last_{fv(r)}$ whose special purpose is to cancel all "outer" mappings connected to any variable in $fv(r)$ where $fv(r)$ refers to all pattern variables in r. [1] For example,

$$(y \to w_2) \circ last_{\{y\}} \circ (y \to w_1) = (y \to w_1)$$

For concatenation $r_1 r_2$, case (6), there are two subcases depending if r_1 is nullable, i.e. $\epsilon \in L(r_1)$. The nullable test for extended regular expression is straightforward and omitted for simplicity. In case r_1 is not nullable, we only apply the partial derivative operation on r_1 and concatenate the result with r_2. The $\odot$ operation carries the identity function because the matchings for r_2 yet have to be computed.

---

[1] Is is also possible to tailor our approach to record the matchings for each iteration. We ignore this variation here for brevity.

If r_1 is nullable, we can simply drop r_1 and apply the partial derivative operation on r_2. What about the bindings in r_1? We clearly can not ignore them. For example, consider

$$\underbrace{((x : (y : a)^*) + (z : b^*))}_{r_1} r_2$$

Expression r_1 matches ϵ. This implies that the bindings of nullable subexpressions within r_1 are equal to ϵ. Both alternatives are here nullable. The left alternative $(x : (y : a)^*)$ yields $(x \to \epsilon, y \to \epsilon)$ and the right alternative yields $z \to \epsilon$. However, we will only report $(x \to \epsilon, y \to \epsilon)$ because we follow here a greedy left-most matching strategy which strictly favors *left-most* matches.

Collection of "ϵ bindings" is achieved via $r_1\!\downarrow_\epsilon$. By assumption r_1 is nullable. Hence, we recurse over the structure of r_1 and consider all submatch annotations which match ϵ. We attach the resulting bindings $r_1\!\downarrow_\epsilon$ to the bindings in $\frac{\partial}{\partial_a}(r_2)$ by slightly abusing the $\odot$ operator. The concatenated expression ϵ yields elements $r\epsilon$ in conjunctive clauses. We silently assume that $r\epsilon$ will be immediately simplified to r.

Cases **(7)** and **(8)** deal with intersection and negation and make use of the respective distributivity operators. Recall that we do not track any submatchings within negation.

4.2   Submatch NFA Construction

The construction of the actual submatch automata proceeds as follows. We repeatedly apply the $\frac{\partial}{\partial}\cdot$ operation to compute the set of all states, starting with the pattern r. This set is finite as verified in [4]. Hence, we can apply the following fixpoint construction:

$$fix(\{r_1, ..., r_n\}) := \text{let } x = \{r_1, ..., r_n\} \cup \bigcup_{a \in \Sigma, r_i \in \{r_1,...,r_n\}}$$
$$\text{in if } x = \{r_1, ..., r_n\}$$
$$\text{then } \{r_1, ..., r_n\}$$
$$\text{else } fix(x)$$

The set $fix(\{r\})$ denotes the set of states of the automata resulting from r where r is the initial state and any state $r' \in fix(r)$ where $\epsilon \in L(r')$ is a final state.

We assume that transitions are recorded in some set T where T is defined as follows:

$$T = \{r_1 \xrightarrow{(a,f)} r_2 \mid \begin{array}{l} \text{for each } r_1, r_2 \in fix(\{r\}) \wedge a \in \Sigma \text{ where} \\ \text{for some } (\bar{r}^n, f') \in \frac{\partial}{\partial_a} r_1 \text{ we have that } f' = f \text{ and } r_2 = \bar{r}^n\!\downarrow\} \end{array}$$

We describe the execution of the submatch automata of r on some input word. Transitions operate on a configuration $\{r_{1_{f_1}}, ..., r_{n_{f_n}}\}$ which is a set of active states r_i attached with the so far accumulated matching function f_i. The initial configuration is $\{r_{id}\}$. For input symbol a, the derivation step from one configuration to the next is as follow:

$$\{r_{1_{f_1}}, ..., r_{n_{f_n}}\} \xrightarrow{a} \{r'_{g \circ f_i} \mid r_{i_{f_i}} \in \{r_{1_{f_1}}, ..., r_{n_{f_n}}\} \wedge r_{i_{f_i}} \xrightarrow{(a,g)} r' \in T\}$$

That is, we build the set of follow states which are reachable via a transition and extend the current matching function. [2]

We may encounter duplicate states because submatching may be ambiguous. For example, consider the pattern $(x : a^*) + (y : a^*)$ where for input a we either obtain the matching $(x \to a)$ or $(y \to b)$. Following [14], we remove duplicates by giving preference to states which are to the left in the order as generated by the partial derivative operation. We assume that two expressions r_1 and r_2 are duplicates if they are syntactically equal assuming that all submatch annotations $(x : r)$ are replaced by r.

Thus, we follow the greedy left-most submatching strategy for the submatchings connected to a pattern describing a lexeme. Recall that our lexer tool guarantees to compute the longest matching among all lexeme patterns by running each pattern in parallel.

4.3   Example

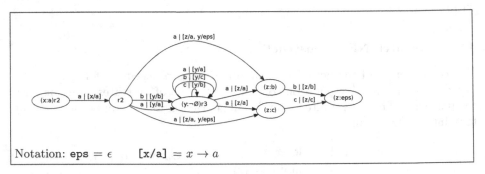

Notation: **eps** $= \epsilon$ **[x/a]** $= x \to a$

Fig. 3. $r = (x : a)r_2$ where $r_2 = (y : \neg c, r_3)$ and $r_3 = (z : ab + ac)$

We consider some example to explain the construction in more detail. We assume the alphabet $\Sigma = \{a, b, c\}$ and the pattern expression $r = (x : a)r_2$ where $r_2 = (y : \neg c)r_3$ and $r_3 = (z : ab + ac)$, thus $r = (x : a)(y : \neg c)(z : ab + ac)$. The resulting NFA is given in Figure 3 where we exclude error states for brevity. Below, we consider a few steps of the extended partial derivative construction.

We start off with the initial pattern r. The computation of the extended partial derivative of r for letter a is as follows.

---

[2] In our informal execution notation at the beginning of this section, the extended matching is put over the derivation arrow whereas in our formalization the extended matching is now attached to the resulting state.

$$\frac{\partial}{\partial_a}(r) = \frac{\partial}{\partial_a}((x:a)r_2)$$
$$= \frac{\partial}{\partial_a}(x:a) \odot_{id} r_2$$
$$= \{(\{x:\bar{r}^n\downarrow\}, (x \rightarrow a) \circ f) \,|\, (\bar{r}^n, f) \in \frac{\partial}{\partial_a}(a)\} \odot_{id} r_2$$

Intermediate step:
$$\frac{\partial}{\partial_a}(a) = \{(\{\varepsilon\}, id)\}$$
$$= \{(\{x:\varepsilon\}, (x \rightarrow a))\} \odot_{id} r_2$$
$$= \{(\{(x:\varepsilon)r_2\}, (x \rightarrow a))\}$$
$$= \{(\{r_2\}, (x \rightarrow a))\}$$

In the last step, we apply the simplification $\epsilon r = r$. For brevity, such simplifications are omitted in the formal description in Figure 2.

Computation of $\frac{\partial}{\partial_b}(r)$ and $\frac{\partial}{\partial_c}(r)$ yield $\{(\{\phi r_2\}, (x \rightarrow b))\}$ and $\{(\{\phi r_2\}, (x \rightarrow c))\}$ which are equivalent to the error state.

We continue with the set of derived terms from the previous iteration, in this case just r_2 which is equal to $(y : \neg c)(z : ab + ac)$. We start off with building the extended partial derivative for the letter a. For the first component of the concatenated pattern $(y : \neg c)(z : ab + ac)$ we find $\epsilon \in L(\neg c)$. Hence, in the first step we apply the 'otherwise' case for concatenation. See case **(6)** in Figure 2.

$$\frac{\partial}{\partial_a}((y : \neg c)(z : ab + ac))$$
$$= \frac{\partial}{\partial_a}(y : \neg c) \odot_{id}(z : ab + ac) \cup \frac{\partial}{\partial_a}(z : ab + ac) \odot_{y:\neg c\downarrow_\epsilon} \epsilon$$

Intermediate step:
$$\frac{\partial}{\partial_a}(\neg c) = \{(\{\neg\phi\}, id)\}$$
$$= \{(\{(y : \neg\phi)(z : ab + ac)\}, (y \rightarrow a))\} \cup \frac{\partial}{\partial_a}(z : ab + ac) \odot_{y:\neg c\downarrow_\epsilon} \epsilon$$

Intermediate steps:

(1) $y : \neg c\downarrow_\epsilon = (y \rightarrow \epsilon)$

(2) $\frac{\partial}{\partial_a}(z : ab + ac) = \{(\{z : b\}, (z \rightarrow a)), (\{z : c\}, (z \rightarrow a))\}$
where we simplify ϵb to b and ϵc to c

(3) Application of $\odot_{y:\neg c\downarrow_\epsilon} \epsilon$
invokes another simplification step, $b\epsilon$ to b and $c\epsilon$ to c

$$= \{(\{(y : \neg\phi)(z : ab + ac)\}, (y \rightarrow a)), (\{z : b\},$$
$$(z \rightarrow a, y \rightarrow \epsilon)), (\{z : c\}, (z \rightarrow a, y \rightarrow \epsilon))\}$$

The remaining states and transitions are computed similarly.
Here is a sample execution for input aab.

$$\{((x : a)r_2)_{id}\}$$
$$\xrightarrow{a} \{(r_2)_{(x \rightarrow a)}\}$$
$$\xrightarrow{a} \{((y : \neg\phi)r_3)_{(x \rightarrow a, y \rightarrow a)}, (z : b)_{(x \rightarrow a, y \rightarrow \epsilon, z \rightarrow a)}, (z : c)_{(x \rightarrow a, y \rightarrow \epsilon, z \rightarrow a)}\}$$
$$\xrightarrow{b} \{((y : \neg\phi)r_3)_{(x \rightarrow a, y \rightarrow ab)}, (z : \epsilon)_{(x \rightarrow a, y \rightarrow \epsilon, z \rightarrow ab)}\}$$

State $(z : \epsilon)$ is the only final state. Hence, the resulting matching is $(x \rightarrow a, y \rightarrow \epsilon, z \rightarrow ab)$.

5   The dreml Tool

Our tool aims to be a fully compatible drop-in replacement for `ocamllex` [9] with extended regular expression support and minor additional usability features. We give some examples in `dreml` syntax and discuss the current state of our implementation.

5.1   Lexer Example

We consider some of the earlier examples from Section 2 which deal with C-style comments and integer literals. Recall that both examples make use of submatching in combination with negation and intersection. Here are the examples in dreml syntax.

```
(* Shortcut definitions for regular expressions. *)
let digit = ['0'-'9']
let lowercase = ['a'-'z']
let suffix = ['l' 'L' 'u' 'U']
let int = (digit+ as num)(suffix+ as suf)

(* Lexer specifications. *)
rule c_token = parse
| "/*" (~(_* "*/" _*) as s) "*/"   { Comment s }
| int & (['^'0'] _*)               { IntLiteral (Decimal, num, suf) }
| int & ('0' (['^'8' '9']*))       { IntLiteral (Octal, num, suf) }
...
| _                                { failwith "invalid character" }
```

The `dreml` tool follows the `ocamllex` syntax which already has support for submatching. In addition, `dreml` adds support for negation and intersection.

- ~ for negation of regular expressions,
- & for their intersection,
- `re as name` to introduce a pattern variable binding **name** referring to the text matched by **re**,
- (...) for grouping of expressions, not introducing a pattern variable,
- 'a' to match a single character, and
- "abc" as shorthand for the concatenation of characters in the string.
- ['0'-'9'] for character classes
- ['^'8' '9'] for negated character classes.

The earlier C comment text extraction is an almost literal translation to `dreml`. The earlier octal number specification

$$r_{int} = (num : (0 \ldots 9)^+)(suf : (l + L + u + U)^*)$$

is written in dreml syntax as follows

```
let int = (digit+ as num)(suffix+ as suf)
```

The shortcut definition `int` introduces pattern bindings `num` and `suf`. We can refer to these bindings inside the semantic actions of patterns. For example, consider

```
| int & ('0' ([^'8' '9']*))        { IntLiteral (Octal, num, suf) }
```

where on the right-hand side we refer to bindings `num` and `suf` which arise from `int`. Note that the negated character class `[^'8' '9']` corresponds to $(\Sigma \setminus \{8, 9\})^*$.

The above refines our earlier specification by including decimal numbers. Decimal numbers are required to start with a non-zero digit, since the base pattern requires at least a leading digit.

```
| int & ([^'0'] _*)                { IntLiteral (Decimal, num, suf) }
```

Readers familiar with Perl style regular expressions will notice that the `ocamllex` syntax slightly differs from Perl. The purpose of the `ocamllex` syntax is to match the OCaml syntax more closely, thus making it easier for syntax highlighting source code editors to properly display the code. Most notably the two key differences to the Perl style syntax are:

- Characters and strings must be explicitly quoted with `''` and `""`, respectively.
- The ML-style `_` operator replaces `.` as wildcard character representing Σ.

5.2   Lexer Engine

$$\text{Concatenation}$$
$$\phi r = r\phi = \phi \qquad \varepsilon r = r\varepsilon = r$$

$$\text{Choice}$$
$$r + r = r \qquad \neg\phi + r = r + \neg\phi = \neg\phi$$

$$\text{Kleene star}$$
$$r^{*^*} = r^* \qquad \varepsilon^* = \varepsilon \quad \phi^* = \varepsilon$$

$$\text{Intersection}$$
$$r \cap r = r \qquad \phi \cap r = r \cap \phi = \phi$$

$$\text{Negation}$$
$$\neg(\neg r) = r$$

Fig. 4. Simplification rules for regular expression patterns

Simplifications. To reduce the number of states during the NFA submatch automata construction, we apply simplifications on regular expression patterns. See Figure 4. For example, via the rules for concatenation we can replace state

ϕr_2 from the earlier Section 4.3 by the canonical error state ϕ. In $r + r = r$ we assume that the "right" r will be removed to maintain the greedy left-most nature of our NFA submatch engine.

Simplification rules are applied from left to right and are guaranteed to terminate as we strictly produce a smaller expression. It is straightforward to verify that simplification rules are equivalence preserving.

Character classes. Currently, character classes are desugared into plain regular expressions. We plan to provide 'native' support for character classes and adopt ideas in [10] to support Unicode.

Execution. The current `dreml` prototype follows an interpreter style table-driven approach. We are in the process of supporting full code generation. Our plan is to support two back-ends: a table-based one using a modified version of our prototype implementation, and a code-based back-end using mutually recursive functions. An implementation of such code generation already exists in the Thompson DFA based `re2ml` [12] tool. This older tool supports neither extended regular expressions nor pattern submatching. Our development of `dreml` will supersede this tool.

Tokenization. At the time of submission, we only provide limited tokenization support because we do not fully support the `Lexing` interface in `ocamllex`. This interface abstracts processing of arbitrary streams as well as plain strings. Position information is extracted by notifying the library when matching a full lexeme. The underlying library takes care of all details concerning buffering. Hence, the implementation effort to achieve full support for tokenization is rather straightforward.

Redundancy Check. Using our extended regular expression automata construction, we can decide whether the language of an expression r_1 is a subset of the language of another expression r_2. If it is, and r_1 occurs after r_2, a greedy left-most match will never reach it. We can notify the user of this problem. `re2ml` implements this check in an ad-hoc way, due to the lack of extended regular expressions. In `dreml`, we can accurately solve the equation

$$
\begin{aligned}
& L(r_1) \subseteq L(r_2) \\
\Leftrightarrow\ & L(r_1) \setminus L(r_2) = \emptyset \\
\Leftrightarrow\ & L(r_1) \cap \neg L(r_2) = \emptyset \\
\Leftrightarrow\ & L(r_1 \cap \neg r_2) = \emptyset
\end{aligned}
$$

by constructing the automata for $r_1 \cap \neg r_2$. If the resulting automata accepts no language, i.e. it is empty or contains no final state, the equation is true and we can issue a warning.

6   Empirical Results

We benchmark the performance of dreml. Benchmarks are executed under
Ubuntu Linux 3.8.0 with 3.4GHz Intel Quad Core and 8GB RAM. Our benchmarks focus on the size of the resulting automata and the time spent on the
automata construction. We also consider timing results for (sub)matching but
for all cases we ignore the cost of tokenization. The contenders are ocamllex and
ml-ulex which are lexing tools part of OCaml [8] and respectively SML/NJ [13].
For experiments, we use OCaml 4.00.1 and SML/NJ 110.74. ocamllex supports
submatching and ml-ulex supports extended regular expressions based on the
ideas described in [10]. Neither tool supports both features like our dreml tool.

The comparison to ocamllex is interesting, as we aim to produce a drop-
in replacement for this tool. However, dreml is strictly implemented in OCaml
and currently only supports a table-driven approach whereas the ocamllex DFA
matching engine is implemented in C. Our measurements show that we already
obtain good performance results.

A comparison with ml-ulex is more representative, since both SML/NJ and
ocamlopt[3] produce relatively straightforward native code.

In our first benchmark, we consider a C lexical grammar specification. The
ml-ulex and dreml variant make use of extended regular expressions whereas
the ocamllex variant uses a more clumsy workaround with standard regular
expressions. Both ocamllex and dreml use submatching which is not supported
by ml-ulex.

Tool	States
ml-ulex	171
ml-ulex (minimized)	167
ocamllex	127
dreml	60

Fig. 5. Number of automata states

Figure 5 shows the number of automata states. Note that since ocamllex has
a very low automata size limit, the grammar we use does not include keywords
and simply collapses all of them into the identifier rule with a subsequent
table lookup. As can been seen, our non-deterministic automata is the smallest
(as expected). The reason why the DFA produced by ocamllex is smaller than
the minimized ml-ulex DFA is unclear to us.

Figure 6 shows the timing result matching against a larger C file. Timings
for ocamllex and dreml include variations where we do not perform any submatching. That is, effectively ignore the context of C comments and the path
of include directives. As can been seen, for both cases performance results are

---
[3] The "optimizing" OCaml native compiler merely performs some inlining, which was
turned off for the tests.

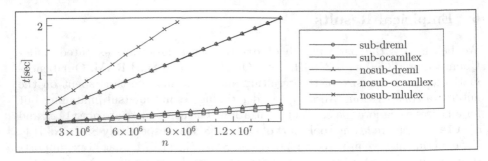

Fig. 6. Time taken lexing a Mozilla source file of n bytes

comparable. This indicates that submatching generally does not incur any severe run-time penalty.

The timings for `ml-ulex` (which does not support submatching) appear to be the worst. We would have expected its timings to be similar to, or even slightly better, due to the DFA-based approach, than the ones for the NFA-based `dreml`. We suspect the 'bad' timing behavior of `ml-ulex` might be due to the fact that the input file is read in chunks of 4KB. Hence, we observe overhead due to IO.

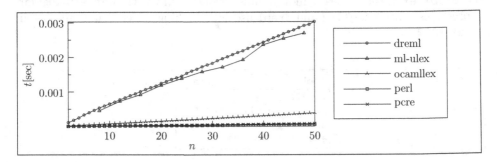

Fig. 7. Running a^* on n bytes

Figure 7 shows the timing results for matching a simple pattern against some large file. `dreml` and `ml-ulex` are comparable whereas `ocamllex` is much faster due to its C-based table engine. For comparison, we also include results for Perl and PCRE.

The next two benchmarks measure the time spent on constructing the automata. Figure 8 considers the pattern a^n which is a short-hand for a concatenated n times. Clearly, the pattern is deterministic. Hence, `dreml` will also produce a DFA. As expected, the `dreml` NFA method causes some unnecessary overhead. Interestingly, `ocamllex` performs the worst.

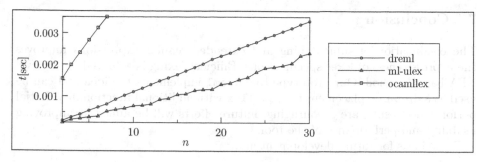

Fig. 8. Constructing automata for a^n

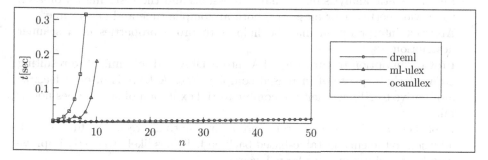

Fig. 9. Constructing automata for $(a + b)^* b(a + b)^n$

Figure 9 shows a worst-case scenario for DFA approaches. Performance results of `ml-ulex` and `dreml` are similar for the extended regular expression $(\neg(\neg a \cap \neg b))^*$. Obviously, we assume here that the above is not simplified to $(a + b)^*$.

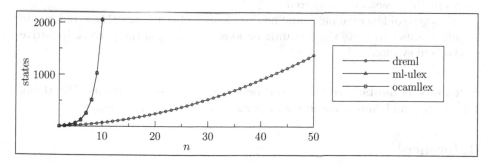

Fig. 10. Automata size for $(a + b)^* b(a + b)^n$

The exponential behavior of `ocamllex` and `ml-ulex` is due to the exponential size of the DFA automata. See Figure 10. In contrast, the NFA approach in `dreml` shows polynomial growth.

7   Conclusion

The combination of submatching and extended regular expressions improves the expressiveness of lexer specifications. Efficient lexing is achieved via a novel NFA-based method. Our prototype tool `dreml` implements the idea and can be used as a drop-in replacement for `ocamllex` with additional functionality. Initial performance results are encouraging. Future efforts will be aimed at improving usability and performance of the tool.

Some ideas for future development are:

- Add Unicode support, building on the ideas implemented in `ml-ulex` and presented in [10]. This would improve compile time performance even for non-Unicode patterns.
- Perform static analysis on regular expressions and the resulting automaton to provide better error messages, both at compile time and at runtime. Abstract interpretation may be helpful to prove properties of a scanner description.
- Provide an option to turn the NFA into a DFA and minimize the resulting DFA, at the expense of increased compile time. A DFA is often a feasible alternative to NFAs, when the combinatorial explosion of states does not or minimally occur.
- Implement an ML code generator producing mutually recursive functions in addition to the current table-based back-end. This is likely to vastly improve matching performance for large lexemes.
- Investigating the possibilities within a generic submatching based lexer engine.
  It would be interesting to include the semantic action functions in the AST data structure representing patterns. These functions would replace the variable names and using GADTs[4], we might be able to construct a statically typed heterogeneous matching environment. Initial attempts at this failed, so further research is required.
  This type of lexer engine would not be compatible with `ocamllex`, but would allow a user to write the semantic actions directly into the pattern in native OCaml syntax.

Acknowledgments. We thank the reviewers for their comments. We thank John Reppy and Aaron Turon for their `ml-ulex` benchmark examples.

References

1. Aho, A.V., Lam, M.S., Sethi, R., Ullman, J.D.: Compilers: Principles, Techniques, and Tools, 2nd edn. Addison-Wesley Longman Publishing Co., Inc., Boston (2006)
2. Antimirov, V.M.: Partial derivatives of regular expressions and finite automaton constructions. Theoretical Computer Science 155(2), 291–319 (1996)

---

[4] Generalised Algebraic Data Types.

3. Brzozowski, J.A.: Derivatives of regular expressions. J. ACM 11(4), 481–494 (1964)
4. Caron, P., Champarnaud, J.-M., Mignot, L.: Partial derivatives of an extended regular expression. In: Dediu, A.-H., Inenaga, S., Martín-Vide, C. (eds.) LATA 2011. LNCS, vol. 6638, pp. 179–191. Springer, Heidelberg (2011)
5. Russ Cox. re2 – an efficient, principled regular expression library, http://code.google.com/p/re2/
6. Cox, R.: Regular expression matching can be simple and fast (but is slow in java, perl, php, python, ruby,...) (2007), http://swtch.com/~rsc/regexp/regexp1.html
7. Laurikari, V.: NFAs with tagged transitions, their conversion to deterministic automata and application to regular expressions. In: SPIRE, pp. 181–187 (2000)
8. OCaml, http://caml.inria.fr/pub/docs/manual-ocaml
9. ocamllex, http://caml.inria.fr/pub/docs/manual-ocaml-4.00/manual026.html
10. Owens, S., Reppy, J., Turon, A.: Regular-expression derivatives reexamined. Journal of Functional Programming 19(2), 173–190 (2009)
11. PCRE - Perl Compatible Regular Expressions, http://www.pcre.org/
12. re2ml: Code-based replacement for ocamllex without submatching support, https://github.com/pippijn/re2ml
13. Standard ML of New Jersey, http://www.smlnj.org/
14. Sulzmann, M., Lu, K.Z.M.: Regular expression sub-matching using partial derivatives. In: Proc. of PPDP 2012, pp. 79–90. ACM (2012)
15. Thompson, K.: Programming techniques: Regular expression search algorithm. Commun. ACM 11(6), 419–422 (1968)

The PAPAGENO Parallel-Parser Generator

Alessandro Barenghi[1], Stefano Crespi Reghizzi[1,2], Dino Mandrioli[1],
Federica Panella[1], and Matteo Pradella[1,2]

[1] Dipartimento di Elettronica, Informazione e Bioingegneria - Politecnico di Milano
[2] National Research Council - Institute of Electronics, Computer and Telecommunication
Engineering (CNR-IEIIT)
{alessandro.barenghi,stefano.crespireghizzi,
dino.mandrioli,federica.panella,matteo.pradella}@polimi.it

Abstract. The increasing use of multicore processors has deeply transformed
computing paradigms and applications. The wide availability of multicore systems had an impact also in the field of compiler technology, although the research on deterministic parsing did not prove to be effective in exploiting the
architectural advantages, the main impediment being the inherent sequential nature of traditional LL and LR algorithms. We present PAPAGENO, an automated
parser generator relying on operator precedence grammars. We complemented
the PAPAGENO-generated parallel parsers with parallel lexing techniques, obtaining near-linear speedups on multicore machines, and the same speed as Bison
parsers on sequential execution.

Keywords: Parser generation, Parallel Parsing, Operator Precedence Grammars.

1 Introduction

Parsing, or syntactic analysis, plays a fundamental role in a wide variety of computing
applications, ranging from compilation to browsing of structured and semi-structured
data, natural language processing and genomics. In the last years all these fields have
experienced increasingly demanding requirements in terms of time and energy consumption or size of the data sets to be processed, which urged for new effective parsing
solutions. Some attempts have been made to devise new parsing algorithms, or obtain
relevant speedups from the classic deterministic ones, by exploiting the computing capability offered by modern multiprocessor architectures, but they had almost no success
except for a few overly specific cases (as e.g. for ad-hoc parsers for XML and HTML).

The classical parsing algorithms used for deterministic context-free (DCF) languages,
such as LR and LL, can be efficiently implemented (in linear-time) on sequential machines, however they do not achieve speedups on multicore architectures due to their
inherent sequential nature: if an input string is split into several parts, handled by different processors, the parsing actions may require communication among the different
processing nodes, with considerable additional overhead. Although this work is no place
for a comprehensive survey, we point out the works of Mickunas and Schell [1] and the
more recent ones of [2] as an example of such issues.

A. Cohen (Ed.): CC 2014, LNCS 8409, pp. 192–196, 2014.

Recently we focused on a subclass of DCF the *Operator precedence languages* (OPLs), and their grammars (*Operator precedence grammars*, OPGs) which have been defined by Robert Floyd a few decades ago [3], and represent a precursor of LR languages. OPLs have some limits in terms of expressive power and they had been soon overtaken by parsing techniques based on the more expressive LR family: still, OPGs are adequate for many common programming languages [4]. The remarkable – and until now unnoticed – aspect of OPLs, is that differently from the larger class of DCF languages they enjoy a property of *local parsability*, which makes them suitable for efficient parallel parsing. Local parsability means that parsing of any substring of a string according to an OPG depends only on information that can be obtained from a local analysis of the portion of the substring under processing and is, thus, not influenced by parsing of other substrings [5,6].

In this work we present a generator of deterministic parallel parsers (PAPAGENO) for syntactic grammars specified as OPGs, which exploits their local parsability property. To our knowledge, PAPAGENO is the first general-purpose practical generator of efficient deterministic parallel parsers. It features significant speedups in parsing of both general programming languages and standard data representation languages. In this work we improve the tool features presented in [5,6] through the effective coupling of the parallel parsing with a parallel lexical analysis. Moreover, we show that it is possible, exploiting a moderately tailored parallel lexical analysis, to describe the Lua programming language with OPGs.

2   Parallel Parser Generation with PAPAGENO

We first recall the essentials of OPGs and of the corresponding bottom-up parsers (more details in [4,5,7]).

A grammar rule is in *operator form* if its right hand sides (r.h.s.) have no adjacent nonterminals; an *operator grammar* (OG) contains only such rules. Without loss of generality, we can also assume that the rules of the grammar have no repeated r.h.s. and renaming rules are absent.

OPGs exploit three binary partial relations on the set of terminal symbols, named *precedence relations*, which can be automatically derived from the rule set of the grammar: between any two terminals the *equal in precedence* ($\doteq$), *yields precedence* ($\lessdot$), *takes precedence* ($\gtrdot$) relations may hold. An OPG is defined as an OG where between any pair of terminal symbols there is at most one precedence relation. Precedence relations are inspired by the notion of precedence between the operators of arithmetic expressions: in the same way as e.g. the precedence of product over sum controls the parsing and evaluation of an arithmetic expression, similarly the relations between the terminal symbols guide deterministically the parsing of a string.

Precedence relations, in particular, determine the local parsability property of OPGs: in any partially reduced string, any segment delimited by a pair $\lessdot$ and $\gtrdot$, where $\doteq$ holds between consecutive terminal characters within it (possibly separated by a nonterminal), corresponds to the r.h.s. of a grammar rule. The parsing of the sentence can start from an arbitrary position in the string: when the parsing algorithm identifies a segment with the aforementioned pattern through examining the precedence relations,

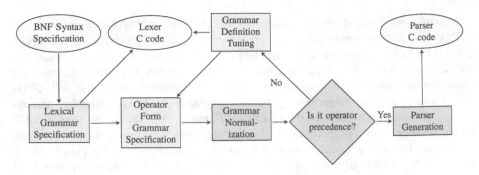

Fig. 1. Typical development flow of a parser, employing PAPAGENO. The human operator stages are marked in green, while the PAPAGENO automated staged are marked in blue.

it reduces it to the corresponding l.h.s. (which is unique if the grammar has no repeated r.h.s.) and the reduction by means of the chosen rule will never be affected or invalidated by the processing of other portions of the whole string.

A very efficient parallel parsing algorithm can be devised from this parsing strategy: the input string is split in different parts, each one parsed in parallel by independent processors. The choice of the positions where the string is split is fully arbitrary, differently from other proposed parallel parsing algorithms, f.i. [8], which require each substring to start at the beginning of suitable (language-dependent) syntactic units (e.g. loops, blocks, etc.). The partial parsing trees generated by the different processors can then be pairwise combined with constant-time transformations and reduced into the final tree, possibly with a further or – seldom – multiple parallel passes, depending on the structure of the syntax trees.

3   Tool Structure, Performances and Applications

PAPAGENO offers a practical tool to automatically generate parallel parsers starting from the description of a grammar in a GNU Bison-like syntax. It has been conceived to be a drop-in replacement to Bison-generated parsers, allowing to exploit the benefits of automatically generated parallel parsers with a minimum codebase re-engineering effort. The generated parser can thus be combined with a scanner generated by GNU Flex in the same way a Bison generated parser does, and does not rely on any external libraries, except the common C library.

The parallel workers are implemented exploiting POSIX threads, and have been successfully benchmarked with Linux and MacOS X implementations. To prevent thread interlocking due to the memory allocation performed via the `libc` allocation functions, the generated parser adopts a pooled allocation strategy to handle both the parsing stack involved in the process and the construction of the AST. As it is frequent to check whether the current symbol under analysis is a terminal or a nonterminal, its belonging to one of the two sets is bit-packed within the same integer value representing the symbol, thus yielding a fast checking strategy by means of bit-masks. To ease portability, the position of the packed bit is designer-tunable, while the tool provides a suitable default value for x86(64) and ARM architectures.

In order to optimize r.h.s. matching at reduction time, the r.h.s. of the grammar rules are stored in a prefix trie, so that the recognition of the correct reduction is performed in linear time with respect to the longest r.h.s. of the grammar and is fully independent from the grammar size. To prevent a performance loss from the scarce spatial locality of a trie, the data structure is effectively linearized into a constant vector at parser generation time, thus yielding efficient memory accesses upon look-up.

We have been able to successfully generate a full JSON parallel parser, together with a straightforward lexer, proving the practicality of parallel parsing through OPGs of data description languages. Contrary to common belief, we note that the parallelization of the lexing phase becomes relevant when dealing with operator precedence parsing, as the running times of the parser and the lexer are comparable for lightweight syntax languages such as JSON. For instance, parsing a 10 MB JSON file with 8 workers, we obtain a $3.18\times$ speedup ($3.6\times$ against Bison) employing a parallel lexer coupled to the PAPAGENO generated parser, while the speedups drop to $2.08\times$ ($2.29\times$ against Bison) when employing a sequential lexer.

We have also been able to tackle the parsing of the Lua programming language, assuming some sensible, and much widespread, programming practices are employed when writing Lua sources. Parsing Lua through OPGs has been possible thanks to a proper lexing stage which allows a more natural expression of the grammar in operator precedence form through token renaming, in a fashion similar to the one proposed by Floyd for an ALGOL-like language in [9], and by De Bosschere for Prolog in [10]. We note that this enriched lexer can still be parallelized effectively: we achieved near linear improvements in our current tests.

The overall parser design workflow with PAPAGENO is summarized in Figure 1. The figure shows the novel and enriched role of lexical analysis w.r.t. to classical compilers: the lexical analysis in fact, besides being carried over in parallel, has also the goal of producing an intermediate code better suited for an operator precedence parsing.

4   State of the Project

The current state of PAPAGENO provides a working tool to generate parallel parsers starting from the grammar description. The violations to the constraint on the absence of repeated right hand side rules in the grammar is pointed out to the parser designer and an automated r.h.s. elimination algorithm is run assist developers. Currently, we provide the JSON sequential lexer and parallel parser with the codebase as a working example to ease the understanding of the toolchain. Interested users should thus be able to express their preferred language in an OPG compliant syntax with a limited effort. The number of parallel parsing threads can be chosen at parsing run-time, simply providing it as an input parameter to the parsing function, allowing efficient adaptation to the target platform capabilities. Moreover, we perform fully parallel lexing of JSON and Lua, obtaining further speedups. The generated parsers were tested on x86_64, ARM 926, and ARM Cortex-A architectures retaining the same performance across all the platforms. We are planning to enlarge the set of languages supported by OPGs and the corresponding lexical specifications. Further improvements involve a more methodical approach to the parallelization of the lexing stage, and the integration with incremental parsing methods such as [11], which are particularly well suited to our operator precedence parallel parsing algorithm, is also considered. In addition, we are considering the possibility of tackling other data description languages: among them restricted XML documents may offer a viable topic for further research. In particular, we note that current parallel XML parsers, such as [2] employ a language specific approach to tackle the problem, often resorting to linear-time sequential preprocessing passes. The codebase of PAPAGENO is available at: https://github.com/PAPAGENO-devels/papageno

References

1. Mickunas, M.D., Schell, R.M.: Parallel compilation in a multiprocessor environment. In: Proceedings of the 1978 Annual Conference, pp. 241–246. ACM, New York (1978)
2. You, C.H., Wang, S.D.: A data parallel approach to XML parsing and query. In: HPCC, pp. 520–527. IEEE (2011)
3. Floyd, R.W.: Syntactic Analysis and Operator Precedence. J. ACM 10(3), 316–333 (1963)
4. Grune, D., Jacobs, C.J.: Parsing techniques: A practical guide. Springer, New York (2008)
5. Barenghi, A., Crespi Reghizzi, S., Mandrioli, D., Pradella, M.: Parallel parsing of operator precedence grammars. Inf. Process. Lett. 113(7), 245–249 (2013)
6. Barenghi, A., Viviani, E., Crespi Reghizzi, S., Mandrioli, D., Pradella, M.: PAPAGENO: A parallel parser generator for operator precedence grammars. In: Czarnecki, K., Hedin, G. (eds.) SLE 2012. LNCS, vol. 7745, pp. 264–274. Springer, Heidelberg (2013)
7. Crespi Reghizzi, S., Mandrioli, D.: Operator Precedence and the Visibly Pushdown Property. Journal of Computer and System Science 78(6), 1837–1867 (2012)
8. Sarkar, D., Deo, N.: Estimating the speedup in parallel parsing. IEEE Trans. on Softw. Eng. 16(7), 677 (1990)
9. Floyd, R.W.: Syntactic analysis and operator precedence. J. ACM 10(3), 316–333 (1963)
10. De Bosschere, K.: An Operator Precedence Parser for Standard Prolog Text. Softw., Pract. Exper. 26(7), 763–779 (1996)
11. Ghezzi, C., Mandrioli, D.: Incremental parsing. ACM Trans. Program. Lang. Syst. 1(1), 58–70 (1979)

String Analysis for Dynamic Field Access

Magnus Madsen and Esben Andreasen

Aarhus University
{magnusm,esbena}@cs.au.dk
http://cs.au.dk/~{magnusm,esbena}

Abstract. In JavaScript, and scripting languages in general, dynamic field access is a commonly used feature. Unfortunately, current static analysis tools either completely ignore dynamic field access or use overly conservative approximations that lead to poor precision and scalability.

We present new string domains to reason about dynamic field access in a static analysis tool. A key feature of the domains is that the equal, concatenate and join operations take $\mathcal{O}(1)$ time.

Experimental evaluation on four common JavaScript libraries, including jQuery and Prototype, shows that traditional string domains are insufficient. For instance, the commonly used constant string domain can only ensure that at most 21% dynamic field accesses are without false positives. In contrast, our string domain $\mathcal{H}$ ensures no false positives for up to 90% of all dynamic field accesses.

We demonstrate that a dataflow analysis equipped with the $\mathcal{H}$ domain gains significant precision resulting in an analysis speedup of more than 1.5x for 7 out of 10 benchmark programs.

1 Introduction

JavaScript is a notoriously difficult language for static analysis due to its many dynamic features, including a flexible object-model, prototype-based inheritance, dynamic property accesses[1], non-standard scope rules, coercions, and the eval-construct [3, 5, 6, 9, 10, 13].

This paper focuses on the problem of dynamic property accesses in points-to or dataflow analysis of JavaScript, that is, reads or writes to objects where the property names are computed on-the-fly. This involves statements such as v = o[p] or o[p] = v where the value of p is not statically known. A simple sound approach is to treat the first statement as a read of *any* property of o and the second statement as a write to *all* properties of o. However, such an approach loses the benefits of field-sensitivity. And, as the following sections illustrate, it is too imprecise in practice. In JavaScript, string manipulations and dynamic property accesses are common, and to paraphrase an old mantra: *"One man's string is another man's heap location"*.

---

[1] In JavaScript a field is called a property and reading/writing a field is called a property access. We will use this terminology for the remainder of the paper.

A. Cohen (Ed.): CC 2014, LNCS 8409, pp. 197–217, 2014.

Dynamic Reads. The JavaScript code below shows three different ways of accessing a property of an object o.

```
1  x = o.p;                  // a static read of 'p'
2  x = o["p" + "q"];         // a dynamic read of 'pq'
3  x = o[c ? "p" : "q"];     // a dynamic read of 'p' or 'q'
```

Line 1 is straightforward to analyze. Line 2 can be handled using syntactic constant folding. However, if the concatenation involves variables or heap locations the syntactic approach is no longer viable, instead some kind of string analysis is required. Line 3 is even more nefarious for a static analysis. If the statement is analyzed using the constant string lattice – without context sensitivity or path sensitivity – the result will be $\top$ (corresponding to any property) and thus it is unknown which property is read from o. A sound analysis will then conservatively include *all* properties accessible on the o object in the result. However this includes all properties available in the prototype hierarchy of o! If o is a regular object and its prototype is Object[[proto]] then around 10 properties are involved, including functions such as toString and __defineSetter__. If the internal prototype object is Array[[proto]] then the problem is exacerbated by an *additional* 20 properties, including mutators such as pop, push, and reverse, leading to even more spurious flow.

Dynamic Writes. The JavaScript code below shows three different ways to store a value into an object property.

```
1  o.p = function() {}
2  o.["p" + "q"] = function() {}
3  o.[c ? "p" : "q"] = function() {}
```

The first two statements can be handled like in the previous section. However, the third statement requires extra care. If it is not known to which property a value is written, then the analysis must conservatively write it to *all* properties of that object using a weak update, i.e. by joining the new value into the existing values. Thus, after the last statement, any property of object o can point to the function defined on line 3.

Dynamic Reads and Writes. Even more precision is lost when dynamic reads and writes are combined as shown below:

```
o[p][q] = function() {};
```

If neither p nor q are known by the analysis, e.g. if the constant string lattice is $\top$ for both, then p could potentially be the string "__proto__" and as a result o[p] could be the internal prototype object of o. If o is a regular object then this would be the Object[[proto]] object. Thus, the write will cause the function to be written to *all* properties of the Object[[proto]] object which is shared by *all* JavaScript objects. In Java, for instance, this would correspond to overriding all fields and methods of the java.lang.Object with a spurious function. To handle such scenarios, a better string abstraction is required, in particular, the abstraction of p and q should be able to rule out property names such as __proto__. Furthermore, should a loss of precision occur for p, then the abstraction of q should still limit the damage done to Object[[proto]] by writing to just a few of its properties.

Event Handlers. An additional challenge occurs for JavaScript web applications. In JavaScript, an event handler may be registered on a HTML object by writing to several special properties, e.g. onclick, ondblclick, onload and onsubmit. For instance, writing a function value to the onclick property registers that function as a callback which is executed whenever the user clicks the mouse on its corresponding HTML object.

A sound analysis must take such registrations into account. If a dynamic property write occurs, where a HTML object is the base object, and the analysis cannot rule out that the write occurs to one of these special properties, then it must conservatively assume that an event handler registration occurs. This can lead to spurious event handler registration and spurious dataflow.

Usage in Practice. According to a study of JavaScript behavior by Richards et al. [14]: 8.3% of all property reads are dynamic and 10.3% of all property writes are dynamic (c.f. Section 5.2 in [14] and the associated web page[2]). Furthermore, as Table 5 shows, many popular JavaScript libraries contain several hundred dynamic property reads and writes.

Contributions. In summary our paper makes the following contributions:

- We describe twelve different string abstractions – five previously known and seven new. We focus on abstractions which require $\mathcal{O}(1)$ space and support the equal, concatenate and join operations in $\mathcal{O}(1)$ time. We place a strong emphasis on the precision and performance of the equal operation.
- We experimentally evaluate each string abstraction on four common JavaScript libraries: jQuery, Prototype, MooTools and jQuery UI. We base our evaluation on concrete executions of each library thus providing an analysis independent upper bound on the precision of each string abstraction.
- We propose a precise and efficient string abstraction $\mathcal{H}$ for reasoning about dynamic property accesses. Experiments show that $\mathcal{H}$ has no spurious flow for up to 90% of all dynamic property accesses compared to at most 21% for the constant string abstraction.
- We equip a dataflow analysis with the proposed $\mathcal{H}$ string abstraction and show that it leads to a significant improvement in precision and performance. In particular, the analysis achieves a speedup of at least 1.5x for 7 out of 10 benchmark programs.

---

[2] http://dumbo.cs.purdue.edu/js/analysis-charts/events.html

2   Related Work

We begin with a discussion of prior work related to string analysis and JavaScript.

String Analysis. Costantini et al. presents an abstract interpretation-based framework for string analysis and instantiates the framework for four different abstract domains [4]: a) The *character inclusion* domain, which tracks what characters *may* or *must* occur within the string, b) the *prefix/suffix* domain, which tracks the k first and last characters of the string, c) the *bricks* domain, where a brick $b = [\mathcal{P}(s)]_{min}^{max}$ represents all strings that can be generated by concatenating elements of $\mathcal{P}(s)$ between min and max times, and d) the *string graph* domain for which we refer the reader to [4] for details. Costantini et al.'s work does not discuss string equality which is a key issue for our work. Another difference is that Costantini et al. focus on the theoretical aspects of the strings domains, whereas we provide an experimental evaluation of the precision and performance of the domains.

Christensen et al. presents the Java String Analyzer [2] (JSA), a static analysis tool which approximates string expressions in a Java program by a regular language. The technique is based on translation from the control-flow graph into the def-use graph, which is then translated to a context-free grammar and finally widened into a regular language. JSA has found a wide variety of applications; including verification of generated SQL statements and validation of dynamically constructed HTML. In comparison to our work Christensen et al. focus on string analysis in general, whereas we focus on string analysis for reasoning about dynamic property accesses. Furthermore, we place a strong emphasis constant time and space bounds for our abstract domains compared to the potentially exponential time bound for the whole JSA analysis.

Zheng et al. present Z3-str a general purpose string solver based on the Microsoft Z3 SMT solver [16]. The solver models strings as a primitive type together with booleans and integers. Its supported operations include concatenation, equality, sub-string and replace. Kiezun et al. present HAMPI a string solver based on constraints on regular languages and fixed-size context-free languages [11]. In relation to our work, general purpose string solvers such as Z3-str and HAMPI, are heavy-weight. We aim to construct a light-weight string domain, which can be used in any points-to or dataflow analysis, to address the problem of dynamic property accesses.

JavaScript Analysis. Guarnieri et al. present GATEKEEPER, a tool for static enforcement of security policies for JavaScript programs [6]. The authors present an Andersen-style [1] inclusion-based, context-insensitive, points-to analysis for JavaScript. GATEKEEPER classifies whether JavaScript "widgets" are safe with respect to a security policy by inspecting information from the computed points-to sets and call graph. GATEKEEPER cannot soundly reason about dynamic property accesses and thus must resort to runtime enforcement of the security policy for every dynamic read or write (c.f. Section 3.2.2, [6]).

Guarnieri et al. present ACTARUS, a static taint analysis for JavaScript [7]. ACTARUS tracks information flow to ensure that data from an untrusted source cannot reach a high-integrity sink. The analysis, like the GATEKEEPER project, is based on inclusion-based points-to analysis. ACTARUS handles dynamic property accesses (called reflective property accesses in their paper) by keeping known string constants separated and creating new abstract objects when strings objects are concatenated (Section 3.3 in [7]). Yet, abstraction must be introduced at some point, and it is not clear from the paper, how this is implemented in ACTARUS.

Jensen et al. present the Type Analysis for JavaScript (TAJS) tool based on inter-procedural dataflow analysis [10]. The analysis aims for soundness and goes to great lengths to faithfully model the semantics of JavaScript. The string abstraction is based on the constant string lattice extended to track whether the string may or must be a number-string. In more recent work, Jensen et al. extends TAJS with the *Unevalizer*, a technique for analyzing certain invocations of `eval` [8]. For this purpose, the string lattice is extended to track strings which are valid JavaScript identifiers or contain characters which are valid inside identifiers. Jensen et al. originally identified the problem of dynamic property writes to HTML objects [9].

Sridharan et al. present *correlation tracking*, a technique for identifying and tracking dynamic property reads and writes which are related [15]. The purpose of their technique is to ensure that e.g. for-each-in loops which copy properties from one object o_{src} to another o_{dst} maintain the relation s.t. $o_{dst}[p] = o_{src}[p]$. Thus, preserving field sensitive precision. We believe that correlation tracking is a step in the right direction for scaling points-to and dataflow analyses for large JavaScript libraries. However, not all dynamic property accesses are correlated and this paper presents an orthogonal way to improve precision.

In summary, except for Sridharan et al., most work use very simple techniques for dealing with dynamic property accesses.

3   String Domains

In this section we present some existing and several new abstract string domains. We have marked the domains which we believe are new to the literature with the $\star$ symbol.

Assumptions. We assume, for the rest of the paper, an underlying points-to or dataflow analysis with a standard field-sensitive heap abstraction. It is our goal to design string lattices which can be used together with the analysis without increasing its running time.

String Operations. JavaScript has around 15 built-in string operations. We consider the abstract equality ($\hat{=}$), abstract concatenation ($+$) and lattice join ($\sqcup$) operations central for reasoning precisely and efficiently about dynamic property accesses. The $\hat{=}$ operation is applied at every dynamic property access to decide which property names may be referenced. Thus, it must be both *precise* – to rule out many property names – and *efficient* since it will be evaluated often. Similarly, the + and ⊔ operations should be efficient, while maintaining as much knowledge about the underlying strings as possible. Additional string operations are discussed in Section 3.16. All domains described in the following have finite height, thus widening is not required to ensure termination.

3.1   Constant String

The *constant string* lattice C tracks a single concrete string. The lattice is elements are $\bot, \top$ and $s \in Str$ where $\bot$ and $\top$ are the bottom and top elements, respectively. The $\bot$ element represents no concrete strings, whereas $\top$ represents all possible concrete strings. The lattice supports the equal, concatenate and join operations in $\mathcal{O}(n)$ time in the length of the string. In practice most strings are short so we do not consider the linear complexity to be a problem. The constant string lattice is the standard solution used by much prior work (as discussed in Section 2) and is used as the baseline abstraction in Section 4.2.

3.2   String Set

The *string set* lattice SS is the powerset lattice ordered by subset-inclusion of a bounded number of concrete strings. The lattice elements are $\top$ and $\{s | s \in \mathcal{P}(Str) \wedge |s| \leq k\}$ where s is a set of up to k strings and $\top$ represents all possible concrete strings. The lattice supports the equal, concatenate and join operations in $\mathcal{O}(k^2 \times n)$ time, where k is the bound and n is length of the longest string.

3.3   Length Interval

The *length interval* lattice $\mathcal{I}$ is the interval lattice on the string length. It tracks the minimum and maximum length of the concrete strings it represents. The length interval lattice can distinguish property names which are usually short, from data strings such as HTML code, image data or other serialized data. The interval representation is standard, with a bounded width k, and supports the equal, concatenate and join operations in $\mathcal{O}(1)$ time. Finally, we note that the length interval lattice can be useful for coercions from strings to booleans as it tells us whether the string may be the empty string, and thus can coerce to `false`.

3.4   Length Hash ⋆

The length interval lattice $\mathcal{I}$ loses much precision whenever strings of disparate length are joined. We propose to overcome this by introducing the length hash lattice $\mathcal{LH}$. The length hash lattice tracks *a set of string length hashes* instead of tracking the minimum and maximum string length. We take a universe of fixed size $U = \{0 \ldots b\}$ and a hash function $h : S \to U$ s.t. each string length

```
def concat(A: Long, B: Long): Long = {
  var R: Long = Long.reverse(B);
  var C: Long = 0L;
  for (i <- 0 until b) {
    r = Long.rotateLeft(r, 1);
    if ((A & R) != 0L) {
      C |= (1 << i);
    }
  }
  return C;
}
```

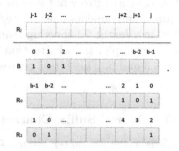

Fig. 1. Implementation of fast hash concatenation in Scala. In Java/Scala bit positions are indexed in the opposite direction of what we have described on thus `rotateLeft` is used instead of a right rotate.

Fig. 2. The top part of the figure shows the bitvector R_j, obtained by reversing and right-rotating B j times. The bottom part is an example where R_0 and R_2 are obtained from the bitvector B.

hashes to a particular bucket in the universe. The lattice is the powerset lattice of U ordered by subset-inclusion (i.e. $\bot$ is the empty set and represents no concrete strings). If we fix b at the word size of the target architecture we can efficiently implement $\mathcal{LH}$ as a bitset. The equal and join operations can then be implemented as bitwise operations in $\mathcal{O}(1)$ time.

Concatenation is more tricky. If we require the hash function h to be distributive, s.t. $(h(s_1 + s_2) = h(s_1) + h(s_2) \mod b)$, then concatenation can be implemented precisely. Concatenation of the abstract strings $\hat{s}_1$ and $\hat{s}_2$ is computed by summing all lengths in $\hat{s}_1$ with all lengths in $\hat{s}_2$ and taking the modulus. A naive implementation calculates these sums inside two nested loops. The complexity of this implementation is $\mathcal{O}(b^2)$ where b is the size of the universe. This is $\mathcal{O}(1)$ since b is a fixed constant, but in practice $b = 64$ and thus the naive implementation may require up to 4096 iterations.

A better solution achieves $\mathcal{O}(b)$ time by only iterating through the lengths of $\hat{s}_1$ and summing with the lengths of $\hat{s}_2$ *simultaneously* by using a few clever bit operations. Let A and B be the bitvectors representing $\hat{s}_1$ and $\hat{s}_2$ respectively. We observe that the k'th position in the resulting bitvector C depends on all $A[i]$ and $B[j]$ where $i + j \equiv k \mod b$.

We define R_j to be the bitvector obtained from B by first reversing it and then right rotating the result j positions. Thus, e.g. R_0 is the reverse of B and R_2 is the reverse of B right rotated two positions, as shown in Figure 2.

We can now compute $C[k]$ by evaluating $A \wedge R_{k+1} \neq 0$, since $R_{k+1}[i] = B[(b-1-i) + (k+1) \mod b] = B[k-i \mod b] = B[j]$ and thus:

$$C[k] = (A \wedge R_{k+1} \neq 0) = \bigvee_{i=0}^{b-1} A[i] \wedge B[j]$$

which is equivalent to what is computed by the naive implementation. The code in Figure 1 implements this strategy. In a synthetic benchmark the above code resulted in a factor 70 speedup compared to the naive implementation.

As an example, the abstraction of {abc, abcdef} is a bitset containing the elements 3 and 6. This bitset represents all strings of length $\{l | l = 3 + b * i \vee l = 6 + b * i, \forall i \geq 0\}$.

3.5   Prefix and Suffix Characters

The *prefix-suffix character* lattice PS tracks the first and last character symbol of the string. It is formed as the cartesian product of two constant character lattices; one for the prefix and one for the suffix. The lattice supports the equal, concatenation and join operations in $\mathcal{O}(1)$ time.

In jQuery HTML tags can be passed into to the $-function to construct new HTML elements. Inside the $-function[3], the following test is used to inspect whether an argument is an HTML tag:

```
var length = selector.length;
if (selector.charAt(0) === "<" &&
    selector.charAt(length - 1) === ">" &&
    length >= 3) {
```

The prefix-suffix character lattice can analyze code like the above by providing information about whether the first and last character *may* or *must not* be the < and > characters, respectively.

3.6   Character Inclusion

The *character inclusion* lattice CI tracks what character symbols *may* and *must* occur within a string. It is formed as the cartesian product of the four sub-lattices: c_{may}, c_{must}, e_{may} and e_{must}. The c_{may} and c_{must} lattices are powerset lattices of character symbols ordered by subset- and superset inclusion, respectively. The e_{may} and e_{must} boolean lattices tracks whether the concrete set of strings may or must include the empty string or a character symbol which is not representable by c_{may} or c_{must}. As an example, the empty string, and the strings foo and moo are represented as:

$$CI = (c_{\text{may}} = \{\text{f}, \text{m}, \text{o}\}, c_{\text{must}} = \{\text{o}\}, \top_{e_{\text{may}}}, \bot_{e_{\text{must}}})$$

The equal operation of CI_1 and CI_2 is implemented as:

1. If CI_1 or CI_2 is $\bot_{CI}$ then the result is $\bot_{\text{bool}}$, i.e. if one (or both) of the lattices represents the empty set of concrete strings then the results represents the empty set of concrete booleans (denoted by $\bot_{\text{bool}}$).
2. If $c_{\text{must}}^1 \cap c_{\text{may}}^2 = \emptyset$ or $c_{\text{must}}^2 \cap c_{\text{may}}^1 = \emptyset$ the result is **False**, i.e. if a character *must* be in CI_1 but at the same time is *definitely not* present in CI_2 the strings cannot be the same (and vice versa).

---

[3] jQuery v. 1.8.3, line 114.

3. If $c^1_{may} \cap c^2_{may} = \emptyset$ and $e^1_{may} = e^2_{may} = \bot$ then the result is **False**, since no characters overlap between $\mathcal{CI}_1$ and $\mathcal{CI}_2$, and none of them are the empty string.
4. If $\mathcal{CI}_1$ must contain the empty string or an unrepresented character and $\mathcal{CI}_2$ definitely does not (or vice versa) the result is **False**, since either contains characters which the other does not.
5. Otherwise the result is $\top_{bool}$, i.e. the concrete set of **true** and **false**.

We implement the character inclusion lattice using two bitsets. The first bitset tracks may-information and the second tracks must-information. In each bitset we use a bit to track whether the string may/must be the empty string or contain an unrepresentable character. The remaining bits are reserved for character symbols. If we use a word size of 64 this leaves space for 63 character symbols.

We represent character symbols in the ASCII range from 32 to 95, which includes the characters 0-9, A-Z, the special characters ! "#$%&'()*+,-./:;<=>?@ and space. Lowercase letters can be accommodated by converting them to uppercase, i.e. the character inclusion lattice is case-insensitive. In summary, the bitset-based character inclusion lattice supports the equal, concatenate and join operations in $\mathcal{O}(1)$ time.

3.7 Index Predicate ⋆

The *index predicate* lattice ($\mathcal{IP}$) tracks whether a boolean valued predicate $\rho(c)$ may or must hold for the character symbol c at index i of the string, where the index is bounded by a constant b. That is, the lattice only tracks the predicate for the first b characters. Most property names are short, and thus having incomplete information for long strings is unlikely to be a problem in practice. We can instantiate the lattice with predicates like the following:

- *Lowercase / Uppercase* – whether the character at index i may or must be a lowercase or uppercase letter. This is useful for property names that use camel casing, e.g. `hasOwnProperty`.
- *Underscore* – whether the character at index i may or must be an underscore. Like above, this is useful for "hidden" property names with underscores, e.g. `__defineGetter__`.
- *Digit* – whether the character at index i may or must be a digit. If all character symbols must be digits then the entire string represents a number.
- *Non-identifier Character* – whether the character at index i may or must be a non-identifier character. (A generalization of the `idPart` in *Unevalizer* [8])
- *Whitespace* – whether the character at index i may or must be white space (i.e. space, tabs or newline) which is useful for e.g. `split`.

The index predicate lattice is the cartesian product of two powerset lattices of indices i_{may} and i_{must} and the length interval lattice. The length interval lattice is used to handle concatenation precisely.

We implement the i_{may} and i_{must} lattices as bitsets for the first 64 string indices. The length interval lattice uses the standard representation. The join operation is straightforward to implement in $\mathcal{O}(1)$ time. The equal operation can be implemented similarly to the equal operation for the character inclusion lattice. The concatenate operation, however, requires more legwork. If the strings $s_1 = (i^1_{\text{may}}, i^1_{\text{must}})$ and $s_2 = (i^2_{\text{may}}, i^2_{\text{must}})$ are concatenated and the length of s_1 is not an interval, but a concrete number, then concatenation is simply a matter of merging the i^1_{may} and i^2_{may} bitsets using the concrete length of s_1 as an offset. On the other hand, if the length of the string s_1 is an interval then the i^1_{may} and i^2_{may} bitsets must be merged by all offsets in that interval. Similarly for the must bitsets, as shown in Figure 3.

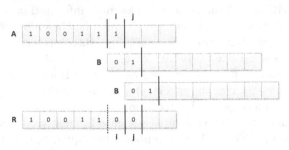

Fig. 3. Concatenation of two index predicate lattices A and B for the i^1_{must} and i^2_{must} sets, respectively. Here the length of A is between $[5, 6]$. The example shows how the indices i and j are computed by bitwise-and.

3.8   Sliding Index Predicate ⋆

The *sliding index predicate* lattice $\mathcal{SIP}$ tracks a boolean valued predicate for pairs of consecutive characters. That is, the predicate is of the form $\rho : \text{Char} \times \text{Char} \rightarrow \text{Bool}$, where the two characters are adjacent inside the string. We can instantiate the lattice with predicates like the following:

- Gemination - whether two consecutive characters are the same. E.g. in the property names __defineGetter_ and __defineSetter_ there are three geminations, one for the preceding underscores, one for the double t's and one for the succeeding underscores.
- Inversions - whether two consecutive characters are inverted with respect to their lexicographical ordering. E.g. in the property name valueOf the characters v and a are inverted. If no characters may be inverted then the characters in the string must be sorted.

The sliding index predicate lattice is similar to the index predicate lattice. However, in addition to may- and must- bitsets and the length interval lattice, it must be equipped with the prefix-suffix lattice. This lattice is required for the concatenation operation: When s_1 and s_2 are concatenated the prefix-suffix is used to evaluate the predicate for the last character of s_1 and the first character of s_2 thus ensuring that knowledge of the predicate is preserved for all consecutive pairs of characters in the resulting string.

3.9   Prefix Suffix Inclusion ⋆

The *prefix-suffix inclusion* lattice $\mathcal{PSI}$ is inspired by the prefix-suffix and character inclusion lattices. It tracks the *set of characters* that the first and last character in the string *may* or *must* be. As for the character inclusion lattice, it tracks whether the string is the empty string or if the prefix/suffix may be a non-representable character symbol. Its representation is based on no less than *four* bitsets: May- and must- bitsets for both the prefix and suffix character. Equal, concatenation and join is implemented as bitwise operations in $\mathcal{O}(1)$ time.

The prefix-suffix inclusion lattice can rule out equality of the concrete string prototype and the abstract string $\hat{s}$, if the first character of $\hat{s}$ is *definitely not* p or the last character of $\hat{s}$ is *definitely not* e.

3.10   String Hash ⋆

The *string hash* lattice $\mathcal{SH}$ lattice is inspired by the length hash lattice, but instead of hashing the string length, it hashes the string itself: It uses a hash function $h : S \to U$ which takes the sum of all character codes in the string and hashes it into a bucket (as described in Section 3.4). The strength of the string hash lattice is that it can keep separate strings for which the other lattices might lose all information. Consider the example:

$$\texttt{"foo"} \mathbin{\hat{=}} (\texttt{"The"} \sqcup \texttt{"quick"} \sqcup \texttt{"brown"} \sqcup \texttt{"fox"})$$

Here, for instance, the length interval, the length hash and the character inclusion lattices lose information and cannot rule out that the strings may be equal. In contrast, the four strings hash to 33, 29, 40 and 13, respectively, and "foo" hash to 4, and thus the abstraction is able to rule out equality between the left and right side. We implement the string hash lattice as a single bitset which supports equal, concatenate and join in $\mathcal{O}(1)$ time. Concatenation is implemented in the same way as the length hash lattice and requires the hash function to be distributive (see Section 3.4).

3.11   Number Strings ⋆

In JavaScript it is common for numbers to be coerced to strings. We introduce the number string lattice $\mathcal{N}$ to track JavaScript numbers encoded as strings. It is the powerset lattice of the elements ∞, $-\infty$, NaN, $\mathbb{N}$ and Other ordered by subset-inclusion:

$$\mathcal{N} = (\mathcal{P}\{\infty, -\infty, \text{NaN}, \mathbb{N}, \text{Other}\}, \subseteq)$$

Here ∞ represents the number "positive infinity" which coerced to a string yields "Infinity", similarly $-\infty$ coerces to "-Infinity", NaN represents "not-a-number" which coerces to "NaN" and $\mathbb{N}$ which represents any natural number which coerces to itself as a string. The number string lattice is implemented as a bitset and supports equal, concatenate and join operations in $\mathcal{O}(1)$ time. With respect to concatenate, we take a pragmatic approach and let it return ⊤, i.e. all lattice elements.

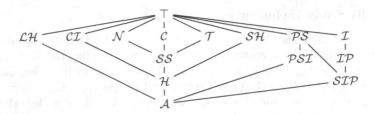

Fig. 4. A diagram showing how the precision of the lattices relate to each other. As an example, the precision of the prefix-suffix lattice $\mathcal{PS}$ lattice is fully subsumed by the prefix-suffix inclusion lattice $\mathcal{PSI}$.

3.12 Type Strings ★

In JavaScript the `typeof` operator inspects the runtime type of a value and returns one of the string constants: `boolean`, `function`, `object`, `string` and `undefined`. The `typeof` operator is widely used in jQuery, for instance[4]:

```
stop: function(type, clearQueue, gotoEnd) { // ...
    if (typeof type !== "string") { // ...
```

Here the behaviour of the `stop` function depends on the type of its first argument. We introduce the type string lattice $\mathcal{T}$ to explicitly track the five strings returned by `typeof`:

$$\mathcal{T} = (\mathcal{P}(\{\texttt{Bool}, \texttt{Func}, \texttt{Obj}, \texttt{Str}, \texttt{Undef}, \texttt{Other}\}), \subseteq)$$

The `Other` element, as for the number string lattice, represents all strings other than the type strings. We implement the lattice as a single bitset which supports the equal and join operations in $\mathcal{O}(1)$ time.

3.13 The Hybrid Lattice ★

We introduce the hybrid string lattice $\mathcal{H}$ as the cartesian product of the string set $\mathcal{SS}$ (Section 3.2), character inclusion $\mathcal{CI}$ (Section 3.6) and string hash $\mathcal{SH}$ (Section 3.10) lattices. The intuitive idea behind the lattice is to track a few concrete strings with full precision and then "fallback" to the character inclusion and string hash lattices when there are too many strings to track. As will be shown in Section 4, the hybrid lattice achieves almost the same precision as the combination of all presented lattices.

3.14 Lattice Relations

Figure 4 shows how the precision of the lattices relate to each other. As discussed in the previous section, the figure shows that the hybrid string lattice $\mathcal{H}$ is at least as precise as the string set $\mathcal{SS}$, character inclusion $\mathcal{CI}$ and string hash lattices $\mathcal{SH}$. We call the cartesian product of all lattices $\mathcal{A}$.

---

[4] jQuery v1.8.3, line 9,046.

Table 1. Overview of lattice characteristics

	C	SS	I	LH	PS	CI	IP	PSI	SH	N	T	H
New			✓		✓	✓	✓	✓	✓			✓
Structural	✓	✓		✓		✓	✓		✓	✓		✓
Subset		✓		✓		✓	✓	✓	✓	✓	✓		✓
Parametric						✓	✓	✓	✓			✓
Space	$|s|$	$k \times |s|$	2	1	2	2	4	5	1	1	1	$k \times |s| + 3$

3.15 Overview

We briefly summarize some characteristics of the presented lattices:

New We believe that the lattice is new to the literature.
Structural The lattice tracks the structure of the string. As an example, the prefix-suffix lattice PS tracks the first and last character of the string.
Subset The lattice subset or superset-based.
Parametric The lattice has different instantiations. For instance, the index predicate lattice IP can be instantiated with different predicates.
Space The space (memory) required to represent a single lattice element. In machine words, except for C and SS which must store the entire string(s).

Table 1 shows an overview of these characteristics.

3.16 Additional String Operations

We now describe some additional string operations which the lattices support.

charAt and charCodeAt. The $charAt(i)$ and $charCodeAt(i)$ string functions return the character or character code at position i inside the string.

- PS– if the index is zero then the prefix-suffix lattice knows the precise result.
- IP– the index predicate lattice can provide an upper bound on what character symbols may occur at index i. E.g. if the predicate is `isUpperCase` and it holds for index i, then the character must be in the set $[A - Z]$.
- CI– the character inclusion lattice can provide an upper bound on what character symbols may occur at index i.

indexOf, lastIndexOf and Search. The $indexOf(s)$ and $lastIndexOf(s)$ functions return the index of respectively the first and last occurrence of s in the string. If s is not contained in the string, the value -1 is returned.

- CI– if the query string is a single character the character inclusion lattice can decide whether that character may or must occur within the string. It cannot give the precise index, but it can decide whether the -1 value should be part of the return value.

– $\mathcal{IP}$– if the query string is a single character and some property of that character is tracked by the index predicate lattice, then a set of indices can be returned. E.g. if the query string is an uppercase A and the index predicate lattice tracks uppercase letters, then the lattice can provide all indices where uppercase letters may occur.

– $\mathcal{I}$– the length interval lattice can provide a bound on the returned index.

Substring. The *substring(b, e)* function returns the substring beginning at position b and ending immediately before position e.

– $\mathcal{I}$ & $\mathcal{LH}$– the length interval and length hash lattices simply restrict their intervals to the range $[b, e]$.

– $\mathcal{PS}$– if the extracted string is a prefix, i.e. if $b = 0$, then the prefix-suffix lattice can retain its first component.

– $\mathcal{CI}$– the character inclusion lattice can retain its *may-set* of character symbols, but its *must-set* must be replaced by $\top$.

– $\mathcal{IP}$ & $\mathcal{SIP}$– the index predicate and sliding index predicate lattices can retain all their information for the substring.

4   Evaluation

We have described the theoretical properties of the lattices and now turn to their practical application by considering the research questions:

– **Q1**: How precise are the lattices, independent of any particular analysis, for reasoning about strings used in dynamic property accesses?

– **Q2**: To what degree does a more precise string lattice, for dynamic property accesses, improve the overall precision and performance of a static analysis?

4.1   Dynamic Analysis

We investigate Q1 by performing a dynamic analysis of strings and dynamic property accesses in four large JavaScript libraries. Inspired by Liang et al. [12] the dynamic analysis is used to provide a (static-) analysis independent upper bound on the precision of each lattice. That is, the best precision each lattice can possibly provide for a set of concrete execution traces.

We instantiate the string set lattice with $k = 3$ (see Section 3.2), the length interval lattice with width $k = 20$ (see Section 3.3), the index predicate lattice with the uppercase predicate (see Section 3.7) and the remaining lattices are instantiated as described in their respective sections.

Benchmarks. We collect concrete execution traces for the four large JavaScript libraries shown in Table 5. The traces expose a total of 80,000 dynamic property accesses of which 60,000 are reads. We obtained the traces by loading twelve

Library	Lines	Reads		Writes	
		Locations	Properties	Locations	Properties
jQuery-1.9.1	9,597	400	7.0	124	5.8
jQuery-1.8.1	9,301	377	12.0	102	8.3
jQuery-1.7.1	9,266	401	6.8	101	6.6
Prototype-1.7.0	7,036	226	9.8	43	14.7
MooTools-1.4.5	5,976	281	13.7	110	14.2
jQueryUI-1.8.24	11,377	265	8.1	75	7.4

Fig. 5. The JavaScript libraries used for the dynamic analysis evaluation. Here the *locations* column indicates the number of syntactic occurrences of dynamic property accesses. The *properties* column indicates the average number of property names read-/written by a dynamic property access expression.

popular websites according to the Alexa rankings[5]. The complete list of websites is available in Appendix A. Since jQuery is prevalent, we include three different versions. The websites are automatically modified to use instrumented versions of the libraries which record information about every dynamic property access.

We explain Table 5 by example. The table shows that the jQuery-1.9.1 source code has 400 dynamic property read expressions and 124 write expressions. For the read expressions, an average of 7.0 properties are read by each expression, and an average of 5.8 properties are written by each expression.

Concrete Traces. We instrument the source code to register the following for every dynamic property access o[p]:

$$\mathcal{T} = (\mathcal{R}, \mathcal{L}, \mathcal{E}, \mathcal{P}_o, \mathcal{P}_p) \text{, where}$$

– $\mathcal{R}$ is a unique identifier for the concrete *run*.
– $\mathcal{L}$ is the physical *location* of the dynamic property access in the source code.
– $\mathcal{E}$ is the *expression tree* corresponding to how the property name, which is being used for the dynamic property access, was created. An expression tree is a tree where the leaves are string constants and the internal nodes are string operations, which are equipped with their source code location.
– $\mathcal{P}_o$ is the set of properties available on the object o itself.
– $\mathcal{P}_p$ is the set of properties available on the prototype objects of o.

Here $\mathcal{R}$ and $\mathcal{L}$ is meta data about the concrete trace and $\mathcal{E}, \mathcal{P}_o, \mathcal{P}_p$ is information about the dynamic property access. As an example, the execution of the code snippet on the left produces the trace on the right.

Here `Toplevel` is the name of the toplevel "function", $\mathcal{E}$ is the expression tree for the string concatenation of `"p"` and `"q"`, $\mathcal{P}_o$ contains a and b (i.e all properties of o) and $\mathcal{P}_p$ contains all properties of the `Object[[prototype]]` object.

---

[5] http://www.alexa.com/topsites

```
x = new Object();
x.a = 42;
x.b = 21;
z = x["p" + "q"];
```

$$\mathcal{T} = (0, \texttt{input.js:4}, \texttt{Toplevel}, \mathcal{E}, \mathcal{P}_o, \mathcal{P}_p)$$

$$\mathcal{E} = \texttt{Concat}(\texttt{input.js:4}, \texttt{"p"}, \texttt{"q"})$$

$$\mathcal{P}_o = \{\texttt{a}, \texttt{b}\}$$

$$\mathcal{P}_p = \{..., \texttt{toString}, \texttt{valueOf}, ...\}$$

Abstract Traces. We simulate the effects of abstraction by merging several concrete traces into a smaller set of abstract traces. We merge concrete traces which share the same location $\mathcal{L}$ to obtain a single abstract trace for that location. In particular, given two concrete traces $\mathcal{T}^1 = (\mathcal{R}^1, \mathcal{L}^1, \mathcal{E}^1, \mathcal{P}_o^1, \mathcal{P}_p^1)$ and $\mathcal{T}^2 = (\mathcal{R}^2, \mathcal{L}^2, \mathcal{E}^2, \mathcal{P}_o^2, \mathcal{P}_p^2)$ we define the abstract trace $\hat{\mathcal{T}} = (\mathcal{L}, \hat{\mathcal{E}}, \hat{\mathcal{P}}_o, \hat{\mathcal{P}}_p)$ where

$$\mathcal{L} = \mathcal{L}^1 = \mathcal{L}^2 \qquad \hat{\mathcal{E}} = \{\mathcal{T}_\mathcal{E}^1, \mathcal{T}_\mathcal{E}^2\} \qquad \hat{\mathcal{P}}_o = \mathcal{T}_{\mathcal{P}_o}^1 \cup \mathcal{T}_{\mathcal{P}_o}^2 \qquad \hat{\mathcal{P}}_p = \mathcal{T}_{\mathcal{P}_p}^1 \cup \mathcal{T}_{\mathcal{P}_p}^2$$

The generalization to multiple traces is straightforward.

We now consider two scenarios. First, we evaluate the precision of the lattices on the abstract traces where the expression tree $\mathcal{E}$ is fully evaluated before any abstraction. That is, if an abstract trace has the two expressions trees $\mathcal{E}_1 = "a"$ and $\mathcal{E}_2 = "b" + "c" + "d"$ then we consider the abstraction $\alpha("a") \sqcup \alpha("bcd")$, i.e. concatenation occurs *before* abstraction. Second, we evaluate the precision when concatenation occurs *after* abstraction. For instance, we would evaluate $\alpha("a") \sqcup (\alpha("b") + \alpha("c") + \alpha("d"))$. Here α is the abstraction function which lifts a concrete string into the abstract domain.

Precision without Concatenation. Figure 6 shows the percentage of dynamic property access locations with *zero* false positives for each lattice. That is, a value of 100% implies that the lattice is complete for all dynamic property accesses. A value of 50% implies that half of all locations of dynamic property accesses have at least one false positive. The figure shows two bars for each lattice; the light bar represents locations with false positives involving properties in the base object, and the dark bar represents false positives involving properties in the prototype objects.

We observe that the constant string lattice ensures that at most 50% of all dynamic property accesses involving base object properties have zero false positives. If we consider prototype properties, the number drops to 31%. This means that for more than half of all dynamic property accesses the constant string lattice will cause spurious flow. For the string set lattice the percentages are not surprisingly higher at 72% and 58%, respectively. The character inclusion lattice achieves the highest precision with 79% and 78% of all dynamic property accesses having zero false positives. Remarkably, the prefix-suffix inclusion lattice achieves nearly the same precision, even though it only tracks information about the first and last characters in the string. The hybrid lattice achieves 89% and 86% which is only slightly lower than the all lattice (the product of all lattices). The number string and type string lattices achieve less than 25% of property accesses with zero false positives and are omitted from the graphs.

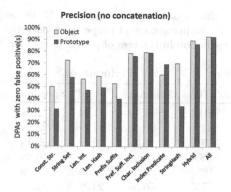

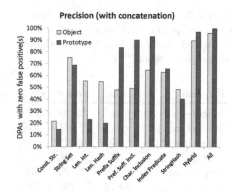

Fig. 6. Precision *without* concatenation, measured as the number of dynamic property accesses with zero false positives

Fig. 7. Precision *with* concatenation, measured as the number of dynamic property accesses with zero false positives

We attribute the difference in precision for object and prototype properties to the fact that most objects have fewer properties than their corresponding prototype object(s).

Precision with Concatenation. Figure 7 shows the percentage of dynamic property accesses with *zero* false positives for each lattice restricted to traces which involve at least one concatenation. This restriction reduces the number of concrete traces from 80,000 to around 8,000. Note that this implies that Figures 6 and 7 are not directly comparable.

We observe, when concatenation is involved, the constant string lattice is only able to achieve a zero false positive rate of 21% and 14% for object and prototype properties. Again, the character inclusion lattice achieves the best precision with 64% and 93% property accesses with zero false positives. The hybrid lattice achieves 90% and 97% which is only slightly less than all the lattices combined. The number string and type string lattices achieve less than 10% with zero false positives and are omitted from the graphs.

We leave the evaluation of the sliding index predicate as future work for two reasons: First, initial experiments on the index predicate lattice showed that it has very poor performance for concatenation. Second, it was not clear to us what kind of predicate would be a good discriminator for property names.

We answer Q1 by concluding that the precision of the constant string lattice is worse than most other of the presented lattices. Furthermore, the hybrid string lattice $\mathcal{H}$ achieves almost the same precision as all the lattices combined.

4.2 Static Analysis

We investigate Q2 by comparing the precision and performance of a static analysis equipped with the constant string lattice $\mathcal{C}$ and the proposed hybrid string lattice $\mathcal{H}$.

Table 2. Static Analysis results. Lines is the number of lines of source code. Nodes is the number of control-flow graph nodes. PAs↓ is the percentage of property reads with improved precision. PointsTo↓ is the average reduction in the size of points-to sets for *all* property reads.

			Precision		Performance		
Program	Lines	Nodes	PAs↓	PointsTo↓	Constant	Hybrid	Speedup
3d-cube.js	343	2,794	14%	10%	1.7s	1.0s	1.6x
3d-raytrace.js	443	2,874	57%	41%	38.5s	4.7s	8.2x
access-nbody.js	170	828	9%	7%	0.3s	0.2s	2.1x
astar.js	355	1,406	68%	58%	5.9s	0.3s	16.8x
crypto-md5.js	295	1,422	93%	93%	0.3s	0.2s	1.8x
garbochess.js	2,812	15,795	78%	77%	56.3s	24.3s	2.3x
javap.js	1,400	5,104	28%	27%	7.5s	7.3s	1.0x
richards.js	541	1,602	3%	2%	3.7s	3.3s	1.1x
simplex.js	450	2,056	73%	72%	0.6s	0.3s	2.0x
splay.js	398	1,016	2%	2%	0.4s	0.4s	1.0x

Dataflow Analysis. We have implemented an inter-procedural, flow-sensitive and context-insensitive dataflow analysis for JavaScript in the style of Jensen et al. [10]. The analysis can be instantiated with different string lattices without any changes to the rest of the abstraction.

Benchmarks. We evaluate the analysis on the programs shown in Table 2. The `3d-cube.js`, `3d-raytrace.js`, `access-nbody.js` and `crypto-md5` programs originate from the Mozilla SunSpider benchmark suite, `richards.js` and `splay.js` originate from the Google Octane benchmark suite and `astar.js`, `garbochess.js`, `javap.js` and `simplex.js` were collected from GitHub and various sources on the Internet. The table lists the benchmark name, number of lines of code and the number of control-flow graph nodes in the first three columns. We use these benchmarks, instead of the libraries from the previous section, since we know of no analysis which is yet able to analyze such large and complex libraries.

Precision. We compare the precision of the string lattices in two ways. First, we compute for how many property read locations that the points-to sets are smaller. Second, we compute on average how much smaller the points-to sets are. We look at all property reads and not just dynamic property reads. The reason is that spurious flow in one dynamic property access may cause imprecision in a non-dynamic read. Thus, by looking at all reads we get a clearer picture of overall analysis precision.

The PAs↓ column in Table 2 shows the percentage of property reads where the use of the hybrid string lattice results in a smaller points-to set than the constant string lattice, that is, the percentage of reads where the hybrid string lattice yields at least one less pointer than the constant string lattice. The results show that for 5 of the 10 programs at least 50% of all property reads have improved precision, and that all programs show some improvement. The PointsTo↓ column shows how much smaller on average the points-to sets are for all property reads. The results show that the hybrid lattice ensures significantly smaller sets and that for 5 of the 10 programs the reduction is more than 40%. Thus the hybrid lattice improves precision for many property accesses and is effective at reducing spurious flow compared to the constant string lattice.

Performance. The last three columns of Table 2 compare the analysis time with the two different lattices. The results show that for 7 of the 10 programs the analysis is more than 1.5x faster, and for 5 of the programs the analysis is more than 2.0x faster. We attribute this to the fact that the analysis is more precise with the hybrid lattice and propagates less spurious flow. In the case of `javap.js`, `richards.js` and `splay.js` there is no significant speedup. In case of `richards.js` and `splay.js` this can be explained by the fact that these two benchmarks gain little in terms of improved precision. The `javap.js` program appears to be an outlier which gains significantly improved precision, but no corresponding boost in performance. Naturally, the degree of speedup will vary from analysis to analysis. In particular, if the analysis is efficient at representing and propagating large point-to sets the performance improvement will likely be less pronounced.

We answer Q2 by concluding that the hybrid string lattice $\mathcal{H}$ is preferable to the commonly used constant string lattice $\mathcal{C}$. We have shown that the hybrid string lattice leads to significantly improved precision and performance.

5   Conclusion

We have described twelve different string abstractions – five previously known and seven new – for reasoning about dynamic property accesses in static analysis of JavaScript. Experimental evaluation on four common and large JavaScript libraries, including jQuery, suggests that dynamic property accesses are prevalent and that the standard approach of tracking strings with the constant string lattice is insufficient. We have presented the hybrid lattice $\mathcal{H}$ which supports the equal, concatenate and join operations in $\mathcal{O}(1)$ time. Experimental results on 10 JavaScript programs show that the hybrid string lattice leads to significantly improved precision and performance when used in a dataflow analysis.

References

1. Andersen, L.O.: Program Analysis and Specialization for the C Programming Language. PhD thesis, DIKU, University of Copenhagen (1994)
2. Christensen, A.S., Møller, A., Schwartzbach, M.I.: Precise Analysis of String Expressions. In: Cousot, R. (ed.) SAS 2003. LNCS, vol. 2694, pp. 1–18. Springer, Heidelberg (2003)
3. Chugh, R., Meister, J.A., Jhala, R., Lerner, S.: Staged Information Flow for JavaScript. In: PLDI, pp. 50–62 (2009)

4. Costantini, G., Ferrara, P., Cortesi, A.: Static Analysis of String Values. In: Qin, S., Qiu, Z. (eds.) ICFEM 2011. LNCS, vol. 6991, pp. 505–521. Springer, Heidelberg (2011)
5. Crockford, D.: JavaScript: The Good Parts. O'Reilly Media, Inc. (2008)
6. Guarnieri, S., Livshits, V.B.: GATEKEEPER: Mostly Static Enforcement of Security and Reliability Policies for JavaScript Code. In: USENIX Security Symposium, pp. 151–168 (2009)
7. Guarnieri, S., Pistoia, M., Tripp, O., Dolby, J., Teilhet, S., Berg, R.: Saving the World Wide Web from Vulnerable JavaScript. In: ISSTA, pp. 177–187 (2011)
8. Jensen, S.H., Jonsson, P.A., Møller, A.: Remedying the Eval that Men Do. In: ISSTA, pp. 34–44 (2012)
9. Jensen, S.H., Madsen, M., Møller, A.: Modeling the HTML DOM and Browser API in Static Analysis of JavaScript Web Applications. In: Proc. 8th Joint Meeting of the European Software Engineering Conference and the ACM SIGSOFT Symposium on the Foundations of Software Engineering, ESEC/FSE (September 2011)
10. Jensen, S.H., Møller, A., Thiemann, P.: Type Analysis for JavaScript. In: Palsberg, J., Su, Z. (eds.) SAS 2009. LNCS, vol. 5673, pp. 238–255. Springer, Heidelberg (2009)
11. Kiezun, A., Ganesh, V., Guo, P.J., Hooimeijer, P., Ernst, M.D.: HAMPI: A Solver for String Constraints. In: ISSTA, pp. 105–116 (2009)
12. Liang, P., Tripp, O., Naik, M., Sagiv, M.: A Dynamic Evaluation of the Precision of Static Heap Abstractions. In: OOPSLA, pp. 411–427 (2010)
13. Maffeis, S., Mitchell, J.C., Taly, A.: An Operational Semantics for JavaScript. In: Ramalingam, G. (ed.) APLAS 2008. LNCS, vol. 5356, pp. 307–325. Springer, Heidelberg (2008)
14. Richards, G., Lebresne, S., Burg, B., Vitek, J.: An Analysis of the Dynamic Behavior of JavaScript Programs. In: PLDI, pp. 1–12 (2010)
15. Sridharan, M., Dolby, J., Chandra, S., Schäfer, M., Tip, F.: Correlation tracking for points-to analysis of javaScript. In: Noble, J. (ed.) ECOOP 2012. LNCS, vol. 7313, pp. 435–458. Springer, Heidelberg (2012)
16. Zheng, Y., Zhang, X., Ganesh, V.: Z3-str: A Z3-based String Solver for Web Application Analysis. In: ESEC/SIGSOFT FSE, pp. 114–124 (2013)

A Appendix

The concrete traces were scraped from the following websites:

URL	Library	Version
http://jquery.com/	jQuery	1.9.1
http://www.chacha.com/	jQuery	1.9.1
http://themeforest.net/	jQuery	1.8.1
http://www.guardian.co.uk/	jQuery	1.8.1
http://adf.ly/	jQuery	1.7.1
http://stackoverflow.com/	jQuery	1.7.1
http://www.fixya.com/	jQuery UI	1.8.24
http://www.goal.com/en-us/	jQuery UI	1.8.24
http://www.6.cn/	MooTools	1.4.5
http://www.aeriagames.com/	MooTools	1.4.5
http://hubpages.com/	Prototype	1.7.0
http://www.last.fm/	Prototype	1.7.0

Addressing JavaScript JIT Engines Performance Quirks: A Crowdsourced Adaptive Compiler

Rafael Auler[1], Edson Borin[1], Peli de Halleux[2],
Michał Moskal[2], and Nikolai Tillmann[2]

[1] University of Campinas, Brazil
{auler,edson}@ic.unicamp.br
[2] Microsoft Research, Redmond, WA, USA
{jhalleux,micmo,nikolait}@microsoft.com

Abstract. JavaScript has long outpaced its original target applications, being used not only for coding complex web clients, but also web servers, game development and even desktop applications. The most appealing advantage of moving applications to JavaScript is its capability to run the same code in a large number of different devices. It is not surprising that many compilers target JavaScript as an intermediate language. However, writing optimizations and analyses passes for a compiler that emits JavaScript is challenging: a long time spent in optimizing the code in a certain way can be excellent for some browsers, but a futile effort for others. For example, we show that applying JavaScript code optimizations in a tablet with Windows 8 and Internet Explorer 11 increased performance by, on average, 5 times, while running in a desktop with Windows 7 and Firefox decreased performance by 20%. Such a scenario demands a radical new solution for the traditional compiler optimization flow. This paper proposes collecting web clients performance data to build a crowdsourced compiler flag suggestion system in the cloud that helps the compiler perform the appropriate optimizations for each client platform. Since this information comes from crowdsourcing rather than manual investigations, fruitless or harmful optimizations are automatically discarded. Our approach is based on live measurements done while clients use the application on real platforms, proposing a new paradigm on how optimizations are tested.

Keywords: Adaptive compilation, JavaScript engines, just-in-time compilation.

1 Introduction

JavaScript started as a simple non-professional scripting language in 1995 to support small-scale client-side logic in the earliest versions of the Netscape Navigator web browser. By now the language has become so pervasive that it invaded even non-web domains previously reserved for classic programming languages. With the availability of high performing virtual machines like Node.js [28] and efficient Just-in-Time (JIT) compilation technology, not only are complex web

A. Cohen (Ed.): CC 2014, LNCS 8409, pp. 218–237, 2014.

applications moving its logic to client-side JavaScript, but server applications are also being coded in JavaScript as much of the server-side programming logic fits nicely with JavaScript closures. Overall, JavaScript's popularity made the language common for coding web clients, web servers, game development and even desktop applications [1].

The most appealing advantage of moving applications to JavaScript is its capability to run the same code in a large number of different devices. This was a major factor for the design of TouchDevelop [29], a modern, device independent browser-based programming language and development environment. TouchDevelop offers a platform for users to create scripts in its own custom language, designed for simplicity of programming on touch devices. As far as we are aware, TouchDevelop is currently the most advanced environment for programming on the phone. While the original purpose was to create simple scripts selecting coding structures with your finger, it turned out to be so easy to program that it began being adopted as a teaching environment in schools, by hobbyist programmers, and even by professional developers using their phone to program while on the go.

TouchDevelop scripts inherit the characteristics of their platform and run on the browser as JavaScript code, so there is a compiler that translates the TouchDevelop language to JavaScript. JavaScript is a hot target for compilers, as seen by the increasing number of projects that compile code to it, such as the Google Web Toolkit [2] by Google, TypeScript [7] by Microsoft, Dart [5] by Google or the Emscripten [30] used in the LLVM [10] community.

However, the ability to run on many different environments also brings new challenges when it comes to ensure good performance of the scripts. Since clients have different browsers to choose from and each browser implements its own JavaScript engine (e.g. SpiderMonkey [3], V8 [9], JavaScriptCore (aka. Nitro) [8] or Chakra [6]), optimizing the JavaScript code becomes a guessing game because each engine has its own optimizations and limitations.

Moreover, writing optimizations and analyses passes for a compiler that emits JavaScript is further complicated because of the time spent in optimizing code, which affects user experience when the compilation is not offline, as in TouchDevelop. The compiler can spend a significant amount of time to apply an optimization that is worthless for a particular JIT engine or even make the script slower. There is a number of possible causes: the underlying JIT engine may already apply this kind of optimization; changing the code in a particular way may preclude further JIT optimizations by the browser; or perhaps this particular issue was never the true performance bottleneck of this system. Overall, it is expensive to handle all particularities of each platform.

To overcome these problems, we developed a crowdsourced approach to drive our JavaScript compiler optimizations. We use a benchmark set of TouchDevelop scripts to exercise common performance bottlenecks and compile these scripts with different optimizations in different clients, storing the results of each client in the cloud. This enables us to characterize how each system responds to our optimizations and this information gets uploaded to the cloud. When another user that uses the same platform compiles the TouchDevelop script to JavaScript, the system queries the cloud to know the best set of flags, or optimizations to apply, that best suits her system.

In this paper we describe this system in detail and report on our experience with our crowdsourced flag inference to circumvent JIT engines limitations. We also present a set of optimizations that addresses common language implementation issues when compiling to JavaScript that is able to speed applications up by 30x.

The main contributions of this work are as follows:

− We identify how JavaScript performance can vary from browser to browser and present three optimizations that handle the limitations of each JavaScript engine regarding common language implementation issues;

− We describe an approach to performance data crowdsourcing of web client software;

− We present a compiler flag suggestion system for a compiler that targets the JavaScript language;

− We implement and test these concepts in a real web-based programming environment used by tens of thousands of users, TouchDevelop, and present data from more than a thousand users that collaborated with the project.

This paper is organized as follows. Section 2 presents our benchmark selection, Section 3 discusses how performance data is reported to the cloud, Section 4 presents the overall structure of the TouchDevelop compiler, Section 5 presents the experimental results, Section 6 discusses related work and Section 7 presents the conclusions.

2   Selection of Benchmarks

The selection of benchmarks shapes the development of compiler optimizations and the performance bottlenecks identification. At the same time that it is at the crux of the performance study of any computer system [27], it is also impossible to build a set of programs that exercises the execution paths of all possible programs that can be written in a general purpose programming language.

To commit to a specific set of benchmarks is an important step, and therefore we chose the benchmarks from the Computer Languages Benchmarks Game (CLBG) [4] because of the benefit of comparing the TouchDevelop language performance with several other languages that had the same programs implemented using them. Table 1 presents the 8 chosen benchmark programs from the Computer Language Benchmarks Game.

Our benchmark selection includes all of the CLBG programs, except for those that use thread support, since TouchDevelop does not support multi-threading nor does the underlying language that TouchDevelop compiles to, JavaScript.

The CLBG website also publishes results and implementations of the same programs in optimized JavaScript. This enables us to compare the performance of the code generated by the TouchDevelop compiler against a manually written version of the same program in JavaScript.

Table 1. Description of the selected benchmark programs taken from the CLBG website [4]

Program	Description
n-body	Perform an N-body simulation of the Jovian planets
fannkuch-redux	Repeatedly access a tiny integer-sequence
fasta	Generate and write random DNA sequences
spectral-norm	Calculate an eigenvalue using the power method
reverse-complement	Read DNA sequences and write their reverse-complement
mandelbrot	Generate a Mandelbrot set and write a portable bitmap
k-nucleotide	Repeatedly update hashtables and k-nucleotide strings
binary-trees	Allocate and deallocate many binary trees

3   Live Crowdsourced Performance Measurement

A primary issue in the live performance measurement of web client software, which is the measurement of the users experience while they are using the platform, is how to cope with the diversity of platforms where the measurements are taking place. Specifically, how to compare and keep track of the performance of the web client software if the computers that run it are constantly changing?

For example, a naïve comparison can mistakenly report code performance improvements between two measurements simply because the latest measurement took place in a client device that is more powerful than the device where previous measurements were taken. To tackle this issue, we first start by aggregating data by each different platform string taken from the *User Agent* string in HTTP requests. We tallied over 30 different client platforms that were using the TouchDevelop web client. This allows us to examine separately the behavior on each different kind of platform.

Table 2 shows the number of synchronization requests to update the web client with respect to the cloud data, a measurement of the activity by platform. Along with the data required to identify the platform, we also send to the server the wall time that this device took to run our benchmarks in JavaScript. For example, the first line shows the platform with the highest activity measured, a version of the Windows Phone 8 with the Internet Explorer 10 browser with 11,756 requests, whose average time to complete the execution of the JavaScript benchmark is 688.86 ms and the standard deviation is 266.84 ms. This data was extracted from a batch of 50,000 requests.

Categorizing the performance data with respect to the platform string is useful, but not enough. Table 2 shows that in a given platform, there is a very high standard deviation between all the measurements of the run time to complete the same task. While identifying devices by the *User Agent* string gives some characteristics of the client system, we are not able to fully identify underlying hardware configuration, which plays a crucial role in the final system speed and cause significant differences in the reported run time to complete the same task.

Table 2. Frequency of use of the 5 most popular TouchDevelop web clients by platform string, in number of synchronization requests (total of 50,000 requests by 32 different platforms during August 2013)

Platform	Requests	Average Time to Complete Benchmark (ms)
Windows Phone 8.0.10211.0 with IE10	11,756	688.86 ± 266.84 ms
Windows 7 Desktop with Chrome	6,046	149.52 ± 172.47 ms
Windows 8 Desktop with Chrome	5,731	144.93 ± 140.82 ms
Windows Phone 8.0.10328.0 with IE10	3,998	623.18 ± 219.17 ms
Windows 8 Desktop with IE10	3,336	572.26 ± 1638.84 ms

To allow us to study the performance improvement of web clients regardless of the client speed, we adopted the run time of the JavaScript version of the programs featured in our subset of the Computer Language Benchmarks Game run on a particular small input, as a reference time for this platform, the *unit time*. It is an indication of the processing power of the platform, measured by the time it took to complete (the lower, the better).

Time measurements reported to the cloud comes with the unit time as well, along with the raw time required to complete a task. The raw time is divided by the reference time, and finally this ratio is reported as an approximated task performance score.

Figure 1 shows a diagram explaining how different devices report performance results to the cloud. The raw run time required to run a certain task, for example, a script execution, is divided by the unit time, a reference of its computational power.

Clients collecting
performance

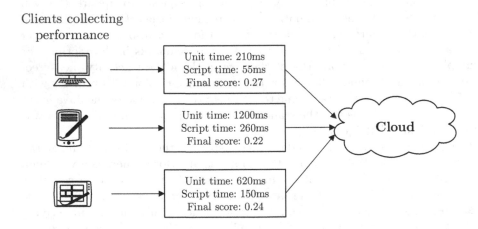

Fig. 1. A diagram showing how performance of different client devices is reported back to the cloud

For example, a desktop with Mozilla Firefox 23 typically executes the *unit benchmark* in 210 ms, while a slower smartphone with Internet Explorer 10 in 1200 ms and an intermediary tablet device with Chrome in 600 ms. Suppose we want to test the execution speed of a script S. The script execution time is very different across these devices, but the run time of S divided by the unit time will be closer even among different devices, since the slowdown caused by the different device speed is factored out.

A special case is that of measuring our optimizations effects on the benchmark programs, as reported in this paper. The benchmark measurements are normalized against the JavaScript version of each corresponding individual benchmark in JavaScript running the exact same input, rather than the time taken to run the *unit benchmark*.

3.1 Distribution of Client Performance Scores

Figure 2 shows a histogram of the time a device needs to complete the execution of our reference benchmark in JavaScript, giving an overview of the range of TouchDevelop clients performance. The client *unit time* piggybacks on every synchronization request to the cloud, allowing us to examine how fast our client platforms are. The histogram shows three distinct classes:

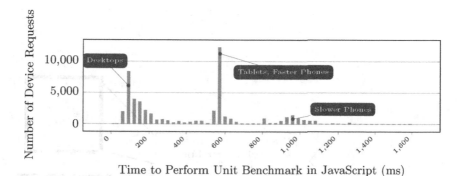

Fig. 2. Unit time histogram (50,000 client requests)

1. **Desktops**: With an average of 70ms to complete the JavaScript benchmark, these represent the fastest edge in the devices spectrum.
2. **Tablets and Faster Phones**: They have an average of 570ms to complete the benchmark and represent the latest generation smartphones and tablets.
3. **Low-end Phones**: They have a wider variation and greater diversity in models, but typically completes the benchmark in approximately 1 second, 10 times slower than desktops. Their worse performance is due to a combination of simpler hardware and JIT engines.

4   TouchDevelop Compiler Overview

The TouchDevelop compiler is the component that translates scripts written in the TouchDevelop language to pure JavaScript running on the following browsers: Internet Explorer 10+, Chrome 22+ for PCs, Macs and Linux, Firefox 16+ for PCs, Macs and Linux, Safari 6+ for Macs, Mobile Safari on iOS 6+ for iPad, iPhone and iPod Touch and Chrome 18+ for Android. Figure 3 shows a diagram with an overview of how scripts are executed.

The complete software stack involves two layers of translators, the first translating TouchDevelop scripts to JavaScript, and the second translating JavaScript to machine code. We use a black-box approach to the second layer and we do not focus on investigating its internals, but we wish to infer its capabilities by analyzing performance results. This section discusses only the first layer.

The script on the left-hand side of Figure 3 is the input script written by the user. Since the script code can call asynchronous functions (e.g. consume a web service), the *Execution Manager*, the component responsible for ensuring correct script execution, must remember the context of the call in order to resume script execution when the request response arrives. However, there is no support for direct jump to a specific point of the code in JavaScript. To overcome this issue, the Execution Manager splits the script code into several separate native JavaScript functions and executes them in a continuation-passing style [11].

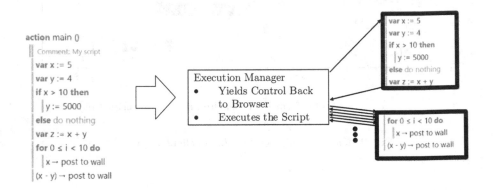

Fig. 3. Overview of TouchDevelop scripts execution

In the script, every point that is a target of a jump starts a new JavaScript function. Besides asynchronous calls, this is also true for loop structures because the Execution Manager must also ensure that the browser user interface (UI) update stack runs periodically, which does not happen if a loop structure runs for too much time without returning to the Execution Manager. In this case, the

UI may look frozen or, in an even worse scenario, the browser may terminate the script (after possibly asking the user), which is undesirable, particularly for games. The Execution Manager avoids this situation by deciding the next program segment to run; if a time budget is exceeded, it yields control back to the browser by means of a call to a `setTimeout` function to resume script execution later.

Owing to the lack of a jump construct in JavaScript, the continuation-passing style execution is a common language implementation technique and we targeted two optimizations at improving this kind of execution. The next subsections present all three code transformations we employed to optimize the execution of the scripts compiled to JavaScript code.

4.1 Safety Checks Elimination

Prior to every use of a value in the TouchDevelop language or in any other language where sanity checks must be performed, the value must be checked for **undefined** references (see Figure 4). In the case of TouchDevelop, where first-time programmers are the language target audience, the detection of uses of the **undefined** value makes it easier to understand and spot bugs. The removal of these safety checks can propagate the error inside a runtime function and cause crashes outside the scope of the TouchDevelop script, that is, errors in the JavaScript run time library that intimidates novice programmers unaware of the underlying infrastructure.

```
function ok1(a0) {
    if (a0 == undefined)
        TDev.Util.userError("using invalid value");
}
```

Fig. 4. Code excerpt for the safety check

Figure 4 shows a separate function to check for undefined references. We put the code in a separate function to help us distinguish this code in our profiler; inlining the calls to this function has no difference in performance.

Figure 5 shows the results of profiling, on an Internet Explorer 10 desktop platform, of the execution of the Mandelbrot program from the CLBG implemented as a TouchDevelop script. Mandelbrot spends most of its time in a loop body calculating values of the pixels of a fractal image. Function `arun6` is this loop body and, therefore, corresponds to time spent executing the actual algorithm.

All other functions are execution overhead. The `ExecutionManager` entry is the time spent inside the Execution Manager while it is giving back control to the browser or to the next script fragment scheduled. The `ok1` and `ok2` functions are safety checks for 1 and 2 arguments operations respectively. Therefore, 72%

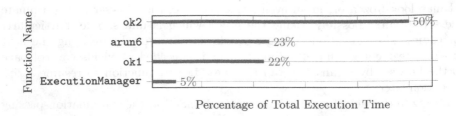

Percentage of Total Execution Time

Fig. 5. Profiling of the Mandelbrot benchmark script in Internet Explorer 10 for a desktop machine

of the script execution time is spent checking whether values are undefined for the Mandelbrot when running on Internet Explorer.

This motivated the construction of analyses passes to remove unnecessary, redundant checks for which we can either prove that the tested value is never undefined or that has already been checked in the past and was not changed since then.

4.2   Stack Frame Bypass

Recall that if the script calls an asynchronous function, the Execution Manager needs to remember the point where the script stopped in order to resume the execution when the response comes, and how this can be addressed by the continuation-passing style of execution. It also needs to remember all of the caller action local variables. This context-saving performed by the Execution Manager requires the maintenance of a data structure to hold the call stack with stored local variables for the current action.

To allow this, each time the script needs to call an *action*, the TouchDevelop analogue for a function, the Execution Manager first needs to build an object to hold all locals of this action and then call the first function fragment to start its execution. Furthermore, the explicit stack frame causes an additional overhead: each local read and write translates to JavaScript object accesses instead of a JavaScript local variable access.

However, if the action does not call other actions and does not have loop structures, there is no point in building expensive, explicit stack frames because there is no need to resume execution of the action: it executes once and exits back to the caller. It is possible to build a call graph and remove the stack frame from leaf functions with these properties. When this is done, the script can bypass the Execution Manager and call the leaf function directly, as it would call a JavaScript helper function, since the execution manager does not need to instantiate a special stack anymore.

Figure 6 shows the call graph construction where we can see that Action F is a simple leaf function that can be emitted as a native JavaScript function. An important observation is that if an action only calls other actions that don't need context and it does not have loop structures or calls to asynchronous functions,

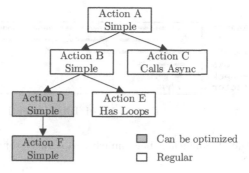

Fig. 6. A call graph identifying optimization opportunities for actions whose stack frame can be removed

it also does not need a context itself. To implement this, we employ a bottom-up analysis of the call graph, which enables us to remove the stack frame at multiple levels, not only leaf functions.

4.3 Block Chaining

The Execution Manager is an expensive mechanism in script execution because after a script fragment finishes, it hands over control back to the Execution Manager along with an indication of the next fragment to execute, which means the regular program flow always involves visiting the Execution Manager several times. This is especially true for loop constructs because they involve going back to some previous point in the script and this is accomplished by isolating the loop body into a separate JavaScript function that will be called every iteration.

At the end of each loop iteration, it must return back to the Execution Manager that in turn calls the fragment again to execute the next iteration. It is not possible to bypass the Execution Manager by emitting a native `for` or `while` construct in JavaScript because if the loop body makes an asynchronous call, it is no longer possible to resume execution to the next program point. Furthermore, giving control to the script for too much time, for instance, over many iterations of a loop, can delay the browser UI update thread and make the app looks unresponsive.

For a loop-intensive benchmark like the Pfannkuchen program, which repeatedly calculates permutations using a complex loop structure, this mechanism generates a considerable overhead. Figure 7 shows the profiling of this program running on Chrome 29 for desktops, and we see that the Execution Manager actually spends more time than the application itself.

Figure 8 presents a technique to avoid excessive returns to the Execution Manager by chaining fragments execution: instead of returning the next fragment to execute, a fragment can call the next fragment itself, bypassing the Execution Manager. To avoid that a really long loop takes control of the thread making

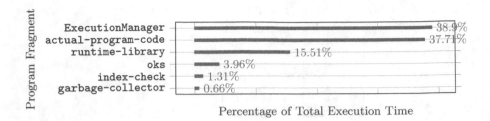

Percentage of Total Execution Time

Fig. 7. Profiling of the Pfannkuchen benchmark script in Chrome 29 for a desktop machine

the app unresponsive, we add a *trip count* to mark how many iterations skipped the Execution Manager and once a threshold is met, it finally returns to the Execution Manager. Notice that this parameter affects the call nesting level and should be tuned by platform, since some systems, most notoriously the Mobile Safari browser, implement a very shallow call stack.

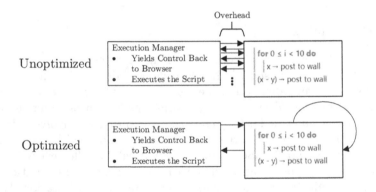

Fig. 8. Chaining blocks of execution to bypass the Execution Manager

Even taking care of the trip count, this technique can reduce responsiveness of the application unnecessarily. It is important to have the crowdsourced performance measurements to know where it is profitable to apply this optimization. The next section dives into the crowdsourced performance results and discuss the effectiveness of all these optimizations.

5   Results

We show the crowdsourced compiler flag recommendation system in practice with an experiment to test the performance of the three optimizations implemented for JavaScript code emission. Users of TouchDevelop were prompted to

Platform	Safety Checks Elimination	Stack Frame Bypass	Block Chaining	Suggested Flags
Tablet with Windows 8 and IE 10	5.8	5.8	5.6	sfb
Desktop with Windows 8 and Chrome	1.1	1.2	1.1	-
Desktop with Windows 8 and IE 10	2.6	2.6	2.6	sfb
Desktop with Windows 7 and Chrome	1.1	1.4	1.1	f
Tablet with Windows 8 and IE 11	4.5	5.0	6.0	sfb
Cellphone with IE 10	1.5	1.5	1.7	sfb
Desktop with Windows 7 and Firefox	0.9	0.8	1.6	b
Desktop with Windows 7 and IE 10	1.3	1.3	1.3	-

Fig. 9. Color-coded recommendation table that suggests which flags to apply on each client browser platform

help with benchmark measurements and, once accepted, a single benchmark with random flags ran on their platform and the results were uploaded back to the cloud. We collected more than 1,000 measurements, allowing us to draw clear conclusions for 8 different platforms. The results appear in Figure 9.

The second line shows that the Windows 8 with Chrome platform has, on average, 10% performance improvements after *Safety Checks Elimination*, 20% after *Stack Frame Bypass*, 10% with *Block Chaining* and therefore no special flags are recommended for this platform. In order to show that an optimization is really important, the crowdsourced data must show that the average improvements for a given platform surpass 30%. We see this scenario for a Tablet with Windows 8 and IE 11: programs run 4.5 times faster after removing safety checks, 5 times faster after bypassing the stack frame whenever possible and 6 times faster with block chaining. However, we see a 20% performance decrease for Windows 7 with Firefox, showing that changing the code can actually be worse for some platforms and, therefore, the importance of crowdsourcing the performance of optimizations, checking whether we have real improvements.

In order to understand why the crowdsourced data lead to these conclusions, the next subsections describes in detail experiments on a single desktop platform, showing what happens with each browser after each of our optimizations are turned on. Finally, we show how the improvements on a Microsoft Surface RT Tablet platform look like.

5.1 No Optimizations

Figure 10 presents the performance figures for our benchmark implemented in TouchDevelop compared against optimized hand-crafted JavaScript code, for different JIT engines. For example, the program *Binary Trees* in TouchDevelop runs 46.3 times slower than the same algorithm implemented in JavaScript on Chrome 27. Slowdowns of this magnitude are expected because of the runtime

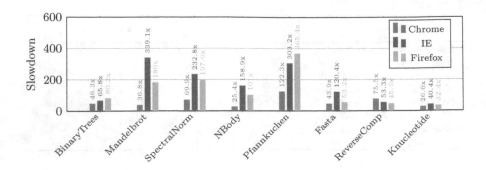

Fig. 10. The slowdown of running each benchmark as a TouchDevelop script, when compared to optimized JavaScript code

mechanism for TouchDevelop scripts, which is continuously interrupting script execution to yield control back to the browser when it is necessary. However, higher slowdowns are a consequence of a performance bottleneck.

The JavaScript optimized performance is only used as a reference and as an upper bound for performance. We focus on the difference of performance between the different JIT engines. Perhaps the most notorious performance result is that of Mandelbrot, a small program that fits almost completely in Figure 11. Its purpose is to calculate a fractal image, and for each pixel of the image it uses a formula to determine whether the pixel is black or white. Its performance running on a desktop with Chrome 27 is 36.8 times slower than the JavaScript version running in the same environment, while on Internet Explorer 10 the slowdown is 339.1 times and on Firefox 21 it is 180 times.

The cause of such large performance differences amongst different JIT engines is a consequence of the different compilation schemes employed by each one, and we need to be aware of these idiosyncrasies and handle them when optimizing for performance. The fact that Internet Explorer 10 runs this script with a slowdown of 339.1 means that either the JavaScript baseline version is too fast or the TouchDevelop version is too slow, when compared to other browsers. In both cases, it is clear that out compiler fails to extract the performance that this browser can deliver for this code fragment as good as we do it for Chrome. Nevertheless, the JavaScript execution time differences of Mandelbrot for both Chrome and Internet Explorer are negligible, showing that the problem is really a bad interaction of our generated JavaScript code and Internet Explorer 10.

The programs *Spectral Norm*, for calculating eigen values, *N Body*, for performing physics simulation and *Pfannkuchen*, for calculating the maximum number of permutations in a math riddle, all suffer similar performance differences between JIT engines.

```
for 0 ≤ i < h do
  var Ci := i * y fac - 1
  for 0 ≤ j < w do
    var Zr := 0
    var Zi := 0
    var Tr := 0
    var Ti := 0
    var Cr := j * x fac - 1.5
    var run loop := true
    for 0 ≤ k < 50 do
      if run loop then
        Zi := 2 * Zr * Zi + Ci
        Zr := Tr - Ti + Cr
        Tr := Zr * Zr
        Ti := Zi * Zi
        If Tr + Ti > 4 then
          run loop := false
        else do nothing
      else do nothing
    if run loop then
      ⊡pic→ set pixel(i, j, colors→ white)
    else
      ⊡pic→ set pixel(i, j, colors→ black)
```

Fig. 11. Main loop of the Mandelbrot algorithm implemented in TouchDevelop, accessible via *https://www.touchdevelop.com/iyyydbkw*

5.2   Safety Checks Elimination

Figure 12 presents the results of the safety checks elimination, an optimization we wrote for the TouchDevelop compiler, and its effects on different JIT engines.

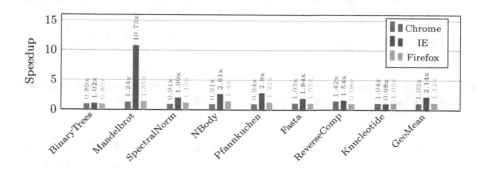

Fig. 12. Elimination of safety checks: Speedups over baseline with no optimizations

The graph now shows the speedup of the optimized script code versus the unoptimized version. We see that one of the pathological cases, Mandelbrot, got its performance substantially improved (10.73 times faster) in Internet Explorer 10, bringing its slowdown, when compared to the native JavaScript version, to 31.6 times for Internet Explorer. Chrome 27 executes the same program with

29.7 times of slowdown, while without optimizations it executed with 36.8 times of slowdown.

The elimination of safety checks has almost no effect on Chrome, but it is really important for Internet Explorer, showing that the knowledge of the underlying platform that is running our script is crucial to drive which optimizations our compiler should apply.

5.3   Stack Frame Bypass

Figure 13 presents the effect of bypassing the creation of a separate stack frame for actions in which it is not necessary to have one. The graph shows the cumulative effect of applying both the elimination of safety checks and stack frame bypass. The greatest speedup remains that of Mandelbrot thanks to the elimination of safety checks. The stack frame bypass affects only Spectral Norm, which is a program whose inner loop depends on calling a helper action and therefore exercises this kind of bottleneck. However, the platforms see uneven improvements. Firefox 21 benefits the most out of this optimization, with an speedup of 9.11 times, while Internet Explorer 10 had 2.83 times, the lowest improvement, and Chrome 27 had 3.92 times.

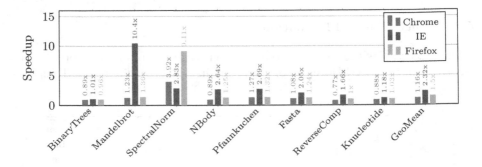

Fig. 13. Adding stack frame bypass: Speedups of safety checks elimination added with stack frame bypass over baseline with no optimizations

For Firefox 21, Spectral Norm started with a slowdown of 197.6 times and, after this optimization, finished with a slowdown of 21.7 times, one of the lowest slowdowns for TouchDevelop scripts execution.

5.4   Block Chaining

Figure 14 shows the final improvements of all optimizations, including *block chaining*, when compared with the baseline without optimizations for a desktop computer. The *block chaining* boosts Mandelbrot speedup in Internet Explorer 10 to be 21.19 times faster, making its original slowdown, when compared to pure JavaScript, to be of 16 times, as opposed to 339.1 times without optimizations.

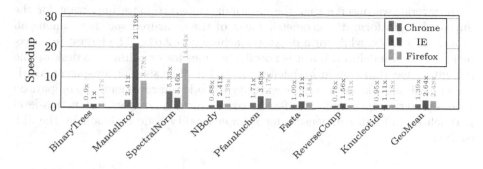

Fig. 14. Adding block chaining: Speedups of all optimizations over baseline with no optimizations

The speedup of Mandelbrot for Firefox 21 boosts from 1.36 times to 8.78 times faster, showing that, for Firefox, the block chaining mechanism is much more important than the elimination of safety checks. The block chaining in Firefox is also responsible for making Spectral Norm 14.64 times faster, doubling the gain obtained by *stack frame bypass*.

5.5 Surface RT with IE 11

So far, we have presented the effects of three code optimizations when generating JavaScript code for desktop browsers. However, the main audience for the TouchDevelop project are mobile users, since it is a touch-friendly integrated development environment. The combination of the software JIT methods with the underlying simpler hardware platform creates yet another effects on the results. The final effect of applying all three optimizations described in this paper when running on a Microsoft Surface RT tablet with Internet Explorer 11 appears in Figure 15.

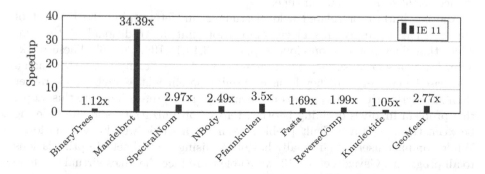

Fig. 15. All optimizations speedups over baseline performance for Surface RT with Internet Explorer 11

In general, we observe that these optimizations are more important for the Surface RT platform: the geometric mean of the measured speedups among all programs is 2.77x, while for a desktop machine it is 2.64x. The largest improvement is still Mandelbrot, but it is now 34.49 times faster, while on a desktop the maximum speedup seen in Mandelbrot is 21.19x. The simpler low-power ARM-based hardware platform is more sensitive to code improvements in comparison with a power-hungry Intel out-of-order core, which can extract instruction-level parallelism and can compensate for a lower quality code emission by the JIT engine.

6   Related work

In this work we study how we can infer optimization flags based on crowdsourced performance data for a compiler that produces JavaScript code. Since JavaScript performance is largely dependent on the JIT compilation techniques employed by the JavaScript interpreter, it is important to know which browser will run this code. However, we assume no knowledge about the underlying JIT compilation mechanism – instead, we expect to draw all necessary conclusions from our collected data. On the other hand, there are several other studies that focus on tuning the underlying JavaScript JIT compilation mechanism to improve performance [12,21,22,23,24] or on selecting the best JavaScript framework to program with [17]. For instance, Lee and Moon [22] study, for mobile web browsers, how the JIT engine can be turned on or off in order to avoid waiting for the compilation of a code that may be not frequently executed enough to pay off the compilation time. Furthermore, mobile web browsers are such an important cellphone use case that they deserve a specific study on how to render pages with the minimum use of battery: Zhu and Vijay [31] analyze how to leverage heterogeneous multiprocessor systems to render mobile web pages fast enough to the user while maximizing power efficiency. Notice that although our data collection mechanism cannot receive power information from our users, for homogeneous systems, our recommendation system also improves power efficiency when it reduces total script execution time.

Another important related field of study is in determining the best set of optimizations to apply on a given compilation unit for traditional, static compilers that does not rely on cloud support [13,14,16,19,20,25,26]. These works differ from ours because they are targeted at traditional compilers rather than a web-based compiler, and they focus on producing efficient assembly code rather than JavaScript that runs on top of a JavaScript interpreter. Since, in this scope, this problem involves deciding between tens of optimizations and the ordering between then, it is a difficult problem even for a single well-known platform. While compiler users traditionally have been using a fixed set of optimizations to all programs, Cavazos et al. [13] were able to reduce the Jikes virtual machine execution time on the SPECjvm98 benchmark by 29% on average by employing machine learning techniques to train the Jikes system to recognize methods and decide which subset of optimizations to apply and its order. Pan et al. [25],

Haneda et al. [19] and Pekhimenko et al. [26] also investigate methods to automatically find a good subset of optimizations to apply to a given program.

Perkhimenko et al. apply a similar technique of Cavazos to a commercial static compiler, reporting a compilation run time speed up by a factor of at least 2. To do this, a feature vector – characteristics that describe a method – is computed from a program at compile time (statically) for the commercial compiler Toronto Portable Optimizer (TPO). They extract instruction types and loop-based parameters to describe methods. Our approach, on the other hand, does not suggest flags per program, but it does per platform because we are primarily concerned with dealing with a large number of client platforms, which must be addressed before each program is fine-grainedly tuned. In our technique, we determine the overall optimization efficiency based on the performance reports of a benchmark set. If the benchmarks show improvements in total run time for a given platform, the selected flags are suggested to be used for all programs of this platform. Notice that the benchmark was selected to exercise the language performance bottlenecks.

Perhaps the work with a greater similarity to ours is the GCC MILEPOST project [16], an adaptive compiler framework that was created for research purposes. To our knowledge, the MILEPOST project is the first attempt to use tuning technology using a crowdsourced database to create real-world self-tuning machine learning enabled static compilers. However, their work is targeted at lower level compilation rather than JavaScript code emission, and their challenges are quite different since they do not have to run code on top of an existing JIT infrastructure. Our work, on the other hand, is targeted at learning how to generate efficient code for different browsers and JIT engines using crowdsourced data for a modern, device independent browser-based programming language and development environment. MILEPOST relies on machine learning techniques to train the traditional open-source compiler GCC [15] in how to best optimize programs. Fursin et al. [16] were able to learn a model that improved the performance of the MiBench [18] benchmark by 11%.

7 Conclusion

We present a system that collects web clients performance data to build a crowd-sourced compiler flag suggestion system in the cloud, helping the compiler perform the appropriate optimizations for a given platform. We also show a set of optimizations that address common language implementation issues when targeting JavaScript. Extracting performance and generating quality code for JavaScript is quite challenging, since each JavaScript engine behaves in a different way.

We implement and test these concepts in a real web-based programming environment used by tens of thousands of users, TouchDevelop, allowing us to better explore the crowdsourcing and cloud dimensions of this project. We enhance the TouchDevelop compiler, which translates TouchDevelop scripts to JavaScript, with three new optimizations.

We then present data from more than a thousand users that collaborated with the project, showing a scenario where optimizations, on average, extract 5x speedups in a tablet with Windows 8 and Internet Explorer 11 but reduces performance by 20% in a desktop with Windows 7 and Firefox. This is a consequence of running code on top of complex Just-in-Time compilation engines, which already apply its own optimizations and can make undisclosed code transformations. The crowdsourcing approach allows us to detect such scenarios and disable unfruitful optimizations in a per-platform basis by simply asking the cloud the best set of flags for a given client.

In this work we assume no knowledge about the underlying JavaScript engine. We rely on the crowdsourced performance data in order to overcome the difficulties of increasing the performance of JavaScript and come up with an adaptive compiler that applies a custom set of optimizations for each web client. This automatic compiler flag suggestion system is able to cope with a wide variety of more than 30 different client platforms without any manual effort.

As future work, we intend to leverage an existing system of crowdsourced profiling of the scripts to also record the effects of a particular optimization on the average performance of real-world programs in the field.

References

1. Develop High Performance Windows 8 Application with HTML 5 and JavaScript, http://blogs.msdn.com/b/dorischen/archive/2013/04/26/develop-high-performance-windows-8-application-with-html5-and-javascript-best-practices-amp-tips.aspx
2. Google Web Toolkit Page, http://www.gwtproject.org/
3. Mozilla SpiderMonkey JavaScript Engine, https://developer.mozilla.org/en-US/docs/Mozilla/Projects/SpiderMonkey
4. The Computer Language Benchmarks Game, http://benchmarksgame.alioth.debian.org/
5. The Dart Language Web Page, https://www.dartlang.org/
6. The New JavaScript Engine in Internet Explorer 9, http://blogs.msdn.com/b/ie/archive/2010/03/18/the-new-javascript-engine-in-internet-explorer-9.aspx
7. The TypeScript Language Web Page, http://www.typescriptlang.org/
8. The WebKit Open Source Project, http://webkit.org/
9. V8 JavaScript Engine, http://code.google.com/p/v8
10. Adve, V., Lattner, C., Brukman, M., Shukla, A., Gaeke, B.: LLVA: A low-level virtual instruction set architecture. In: MICRO 36 (2003)
11. Appel, A.W.: Compiling with continuations. Cambridge University Press, New York (1992)
12. Bebenita, M., Brandner, F., Fahndrich, M., Logozzo, F., Schulte, W., Tillmann, N., Venter, H.: SPUR: A trace-based JIT compiler for CIL. In: OOPSLA 2010. ACM (2010)
13. Cavazos, J., O'Boyle, M.F.P.: Method-specific dynamic compilation using logistic regression. In: OOPSLA 2006. ACM (2006)
14. Cooper, K.D., Grosul, A., Harvey, T.J., Reeves, S., Subramanian, D., Torczon, L., Waterman, T.: Acme: Adaptive compilation made efficient. In: LCTES 2005 (2005)

15. Free Software Foundation, Inc. Using the GNU compiler collection, For GCC version 4.9.0. (March 2013)
16. Fursin, G., Miranda, C., Temam, O., Namolaru, M., Yom-Tov, E., Zaks, A., Mendelson, B., Bonilla, E., Thomson, J., Leather, H., et al.: MILEPOST GCC: Machine learning based research compiler. In: GCC Summit (2008)
17. Gizas, A., Christodoulou, S.P., Papatheodorou, T.S.: Comparative evaluation of javascript frameworks. In: 21st International Conference Companion on World Wide Web (2012)
18. Guthaus, M.R., Ringenberg, J.S., Ernst, D., Austin, T.M., Mudge, T., Brown, R.B.: MiBench: A free, commercially representative embedded benchmark suite. In: IISWC 2001. IEEE (2001)
19. Haneda, M., Knijnenburg, P.M., Wijshoff, H.A.: Automatic selection of compiler options using non-parametric inferential statistics. In: PaCT 2005. IEEE (2005)
20. Hoste, K., Georges, A., Eeckhout, L.: Automated just-in-time compiler tuning. In: CGO 2010. ACM (2010)
21. Jeon, S., Choi, J.: Reuse of JIT compiled code in JavaScript engine. In: 27th Annual ACM Symposium on Applied Computing (2012)
22. Lee, S.-W., Moon, S.-M.: Selective just-in-time compilation for client-side mobile javascript engine. In: CASES 2011. ACM (2011)
23. Lee, S.-W., Moon, S.-M., Kim, W.-J., Jin Oh, S., Oh, H.-S.: Code size and performance optimization for mobile JavaScript just-in-time compiler. In: 2010 Workshop on Interaction between Compilers and Computer Architecture (2010)
24. Martinsen, J.K., Grahn, H., Isberg, A.: Using speculation to enhance javascript performance in web applications. IEEE Internet Computing 17(2), 10–19, 3 (2013)
25. Pan, Z., Eigenmann, R.: Fast and effective orchestration of compiler optimizations for automatic performance tuning. In: CGO 2006. ACM (2006)
26. Pekhimenko, G., Brown, A.D.: Efficient program compilation through machine learning techniques. Software Automatic Tuning: From Concepts to State-of-the-Art Results, 335 (2010)
27. Richards, G., Gal, A., Eich, B., Vitek, J.: Automated construction of javascript benchmarks. In: OOPSLA 2011. ACM (2011)
28. Tilkov, S., Vinoski, S.: Node.js: Using JavaScript to Build High-Performance Network Programs. IEEE Internet Computing 14(6), 80–83 (2010)
29. Tillmann, N., Moskal, M., de Halleux, J., Fahndrich, M.: TouchDevelop: Programming cloud-connected mobile devices via touchscreen. In: ONWARD 2011. ACM (2011)
30. Zakai, A.: Emscripten: An LLVM-to-JavaScript compiler. In: SPLASH 2011. ACM (2011)
31. Zhu, Y., Reddi, V.J.: High-performance and energy-efficient mobile web browsing on big/little systems. In: HPCA 2013. IEEE (2013)

A First Step towards a
Compiler for Business Processes

Thomas M. Prinz, Norbert Spieß, and Wolfram Amme

Friedrich Schiller University Jena
07743 Jena, Germany
{Thomas.Prinz,Norbert.Spiess,Wolfram.Amme}@uni-jena.de

Abstract. The verification of business processes is crucial since an erroneous execution causes high costs and damages the reputation of the providing company. The first step towards correct business processes is the verification of structural correctness, i.e., the absence of deadlocks and lack of synchronization.

In this demonstration paper, we present a system which was integrated into the Activiti BPMN 2.0 designer for Eclipse, allowing an immediate user support during the development of business processes. Therefore, an entire business process is transformed into semantically equivalent workflow graphs on which a new structural correctness verification is performed directly. This is done for each modification and the determined failures are visualized directly in the business process. The system can be seen as first step towards a compiler for business processes.

1 Introduction

Business processes are well-established in business management, in the context of service-oriented architectures, and cloud computing. Since business processes are described by graphical specification languages like BPMN 2.0 [1], there is a need for transformations into more technical representations to allow and outperform analyses and verifications, i.e., a compiler. The verification of business processes becomes crucial as business processes are frequently used and could have runtimes over months, whereby an erroneous execution causes high costs and could lasting damage the reputation of the providing company. Therefore, support for the development of correct business processes is essential for all business process development tools.

Structural correctness, which focuses only on the structure of business processes without consideration of data aspects, builds the first step towards correct business processes. Business processes can have two kinds of structural errors: *deadlocks* and *lack of synchronization* [2]. Deadlocks are situations in which the execution within business processes blocks partly or completely, and lack of synchronization are situations in which parts of business processes are executed twice unintentionally because of unsuccessfully joined parallel control flows. The

A. Cohen (Ed.): CC 2014, LNCS 8409, pp. 238–243, 2014.

absence of deadlocks and lack of synchronization in business processes is called *soundness* in the literature [3,4]. However, we prefer to call it structural correctness like Sadiq and Orlowska [2], since soundness describes the overall correctness.

In our previous work [5,6], we have introduced new compiler-based techniques to find structural errors within workflow graphs. Workflow graphs are a more formal representation of business processes containing exactly one *start* and one *end* node, *activities*, *forks*, *joins*, *splits*, and *merges*. Since the algorithm works only on simple workflow graphs, i.e., on workflow graphs in which each edge contains an activity, and business processes can have more than one start and end node, the transformation of the business process model into the workflow graph representation is not a trivial one-to-one transformation.

In this demonstration paper, we present our analysis tool *mojo* which was integrated into the Activiti BPMN 2.0 designer (http://activiti.org), a tool for creating BPMN 2.0 business processes. The resulting system allows immediate and serious support during the development of business processes by visualizing structural errors directly in the graphical model and providing a failure analysis mode, which highlights a selected error. The rest of the paper is structured as follows: Section 2 introduces structural correctness to the reader, Section 3 gives an overview of the implemented system and transformations, whereas Section 4 evaluates their robustness. Eventually, the paper is concluded in Section 5.

2   Informal Description

A formal representation of business processes are workflow graphs. A *workflow graph* is a directed graph $WFG = (N, E)$ such that N consists of activities, forks, joins, splits, merges, and one start as well as one end node. Each activity, split, fork, and the end node have exactly one incoming edge; whereas each activity, merge, join, and the start node have exactly one outgoing edge. Merges and joins have at least two incoming edges, and splits and forks have at least two outgoing edges. Concluding, each node lies on a path from the start to the end node. A workflow graph is called *simple* if for each edge $e = (n_1, n_2) \in E$ the source n_1 or the target n_2 is an activity.

Figure 1 shows a workflow graph with annotated node types. After the instantiation of a workflow graph, a control flow starts at the start node and follows the flow given by the graph. Each node, except a join, i.e., activities, splits, merges, forks, and the end node, can be executed if a control flow reaches one of its incoming edges. However, joins can only fire if all incoming edges are reached by a

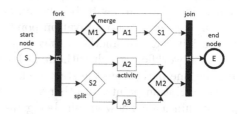

Fig. 1. A workflow graph

control flow. Since data aspects are out of the scope of structural correctness, a

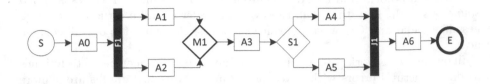

Fig. 2. A workflow graph containing two structural errors

split decides *nondeterministically* which of its outgoing edges will be followed by the control flow. A fork produces a control flow for each of its outgoing edges, i.e., parallelism.

Without loss of generality, each workflow graph is *simple* for the remainder of this paper, since there is a fast transformation from common to simple workflow graphs, e.g., by placing a new activitiy on each edge. It simplifies analyses and algorithms.

Structural correctness describes the absence of deadlocks and lack of synchronization. A *deadlock* appears for a join, if the join was not executed as often as each of its direct predecessor nodes and cannot be executed in future. An executable fork causes a *lack of synchronization* if it may result in simultaneous executions of the same node.

Structural correctness is a standard problem of business processes and has been solved efficiently and with detailed failure information in our previous work [5,6]. The basic idea is to start the analysis for structural correctness at different points (nodes) of a workflow graph, which we call *entrypoints*. It is comparable to a compiler trying to find the next safe program point in order to find further errors after a previous failure. Take the workflow graph of Fig. 2 as example. It contains a deadlock in join $J1$ as well as a lack of synchronization caused by fork $F1$. Starting an analysis in the start node would detect only the lack of synchronization, whereas restarting the analysis at split $S1$ identifies also the deadlock.

We have found out, that *activation points* are good entrypoints for the detection of deadlocks. An activation point *pnt* belongs always to another node n whereas the execution of *pnt* guarantees the future execution of n. Each activation point of a join has to be also an activation point of all of its predecessor nodes, and each closest activation point of a join, i.e., there is at least one path to the join without another activation point, has to be a fork. As a result, a join in a workflow graph without lack of synchronization has a deadlock if on at least one path, from the start node to itself or from itself to itself, lies none of its activation points. In other words, before any control flow ever reaches a join within a workflow graph, being free of lack of synchronization, one of its activation point must be executed.

The identification of lack of synchronization starts in forks, since only forks build more than one control flow causing simultaneous executions of the same node. Generally, two control flows have to be joined before the end node. These joining nodes are called *intersection points*. It is valid, that there are two disjoint paths from the fork to each of its intersection points. If a lack of synchronization occurs at runtime, there is an intersection point of a fork which is not a join, or there is a path from a fork to itself and a path from this fork to the end node, such that both paths are disjoint.

The conditions of deadlocks as well as of lack of synchronization describe supersets of them, since parts of it never occur at runtime, because forgoing deadlocks prevent their execution. Such failures within these supersets are called *potential*. We have proven, that the absence of deadlocks and lack of synchronization corresponds to the absence of potential deadlocks and potential lack of synchronization.

The detection of potential deadlocks can be efficiently implemented via data-flow analyses, being realized in the presented system, whereas the detection of potential lack of synchronization can be done with the help of dominators, post-dominators, loop detection, and decomposition. In summary, compiler-based techniques can be successfully applied to the analysis of workflow graphs.

3   System Overview

The Activiti BPMN 2.0 Designer is an Eclipse plugin which allows for the development of business processes with a subset of BPMN 2.0 model elements. Developed business processes are held as graphical models which can be accessed over an extension point for adding business process verifications. We have created own extensions of this extension point which will be executed for every modification of the business process. These extensions are called *mojo* - our open source business process analysis tool (http://www.bpmn-compiler.org, https://sourceforge.net/projects/bpmojo). Figure 3 visualizes our system. The transformation and structural correctness verification can be used as an extension of Activiti. The following steps are performed by our tool.

At first, the entire business process is transformed into at least one semantically equivalent workflow graph. Therefore, all end events of a BPMN business process are mapped to a single one using the algorithm of Kiepuszewski et al. [7], which was extended for working on workflow graphs instead of Petri nets. The start events of a BPMN business process are merged into a single one using

Fig. 3. The verification system

the rules of the BPMN 2.0 specification [1], e.g., tasks without an incoming edge are combined by a fork and start events are combined by a split.

If the business process is not connected, it is translated into different workflow graphs, whereas each workflow graph will be verified for structural correctness in isolation. Gateways with multiple incoming and multiple outgoing edges are disassembled into two gateways, so that the first gateway has all incoming edges and the second all outgoing edges. XOR gateways are transformed to splits and merges, and AND gateways to forks and joins in conclusion. Finally, each task becomes an activity.

In general, the resulting workflow graphs are not simple regarding to its definition in Section 2. Thus, each edge having no activity as source or sink is replaced by two edges, the first connecting the source with a new activity, whereas the second connects the new activity with the sink. The dependencies between the workflow graph and the graphical model of the business process are built up in each step of the transformation algorithm.

In the second step, our algorithm for structural correctness verification [5,6] is performed directly on each workflow graph. The algorithm finds all potential deadlocks and lack of synchronization, and localizes them precisely. The results of the structural correctness verification are visualized in the graphical model of Activiti: (1) directly in the business process with marks on failure producing nodes, (2) as an error list in the error view of Eclipse, and (3) as a detailed failure highlighting for the failure analysis mode. The failure analysis mode is one of the features of our system (see Fig. 4). It allows for the selection of an error within the error view of Eclipse, which then will be highlighted in the business process in isolation. Therefore, the developer of the business process can find the reasons of these errors.

4   Evaluation

The system was evaluated, using benchmarks of real world business processes, with regard to robustness and performance. On the one hand, the transformation process was tested with the BPMN 2.0 benchmark of IBM http://www.zurich.ibm.com/csc/bit/downloads.html, and, on the other hand, the structural correctness verification was validated and evaluated with the business process benchmark of http://www.service-technology.org/soundness. Both algorithms run stable and take less than one millisecond in the average case (see our previous work [5] for more details). Therefore, the analysis can be done for every modification of the business process, instead only by saving or on demand.

5   Conclusion

In this demonstration paper, we presented a system which allows direct user support during the development of business processes. It is based on the Activiti BPMN 2.0 Designer and our analysis tool *mojo*, transforming an entire

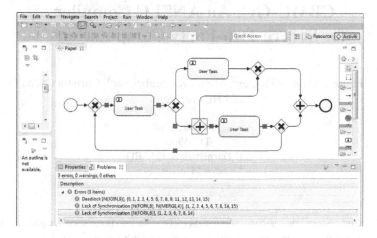

Fig. 4. Visualizing an error in failure analysis mode

business process into semantically equivalent workflow graphs, on which a structural correctness verification is performed. The determined structural errors are directly visualized in the business process, which supports an immediate correction. Furthermore, the system is fast enough to perform the verification for each modification of the business process.

In the future, the system will be extended by analyses considering data aspects, extensive failure explanations, and an automatically correction of structural errors. Furthermore, a coding into a mobile format with a virtual machine is in the scope of our work.

References

1. OMG: Business process model and notation. Specification (2.0) (March 2011)
2. Sadiq, W., Orlowska, M.E.: Analyzing process models using graph reduction techniques. Inf. Syst. 25(2), 117–134 (2000)
3. van der Aalst, W.M.P., Hirnschall, A., Verbeek, H.M.W.: An alternative way to analyze workflow graphs. In: Pidduck, A.B., Mylopoulos, J., Woo, C.C., Ozsu, M.T. (eds.) CAiSE 2002. LNCS, vol. 2348, pp. 535–552. Springer, Heidelberg (2002)
4. Fahland, D., Favre, C., Koehler, J., Lohmann, N., Völzer, H., Wolf, K.: Analysis on demand: Instantaneous soundness checking of industrial business process models. Data Knowl. Eng. 70(5), 448–466 (2011)
5. Prinz, T.M., Amme, W.: Practical compiler-based user support during the development of business processes. In: Service-Oriented Computing - ICSOC 2013 Workshops. Springer, December 2013 (to be published)
6. Prinz, T.M., Amme, W.: Practical compiler-based user support during the development of business processes. Technical Report Math/Inf/02/13, Friedrich Schiller University Jena, 07743 Jena, Thuringia, Germany (June 2013)
7. Kiepuszewski, B., Hofstede, A.H.M.T., van der Aalst, W.: Fundamentals of control flow in workflows. Acta Informatica 39, 143–209 (2002)

CBMC-GC: An ANSI C Compiler
for Secure Two-Party Computations*

Martin Franz[1], Andreas Holzer[2], Stefan Katzenbeisser[3], Christian Schallhart[4],
and Helmut Veith[2]

[1] Deutsche Bank
[2] TU Wien
[3] TU Darmstadt & CASED
[4] Oxford University

Abstract. Secure two-party computation (STC) is a computer security paradigm where two parties can jointly evaluate a program with sensitive input data, provided in parts from both parties. By the security guarantees of STC, neither party can learn any information on the other party's input while performing the STC task. For a long time thought to be impractical, until recently, STC has only been implemented with domain-specific languages or hand-crafted Boolean circuits for specific computations. Our open-source compiler CBMC-GC is the first ANSI C compiler for STC. It turns C programs into Boolean circuits that fit the requirements of garbled circuits, a generic STC approach based on circuits. Here, the size of the resulting circuits plays a crucial role since each STC step involves encryption and network transfer and is therefore extremely slow when compared to computations performed on modern hardware architectures. We report on newly implemented circuit optimization techniques that substantially reduce the circuit sizes compared to the original release of CBMC-GC.

Keywords: Secure Computations, Privacy, Compilers, Circuit Optimization.

1 Introduction

Imagine Alice and Bob as two millionaires who want to determine the richer one among them – but *without* revealing how much they own, neither to the other millionaire nor to somebody else. This is the "millionaires' problem", first described by Yao [18], who thereby initiated research on secure two party computation (STC). Subsequently it has been shown that every computable function over two inputs is also computable in the framework of STC: Two players can evaluate the function on their respective private inputs so that the result of the computation is available to both, without needing to share the inputs with each other.

In modern information processing infrastructures, not only data but also code is becoming more mobile, e.g., in cloud services. Thus, with the increasing amount of sensitive information processed, and facing laws and regulations that are not only hard

---

* This work was supported in part by the Austrian National Research Network S11403 and S11405 (RiSE) of the Austrian Science Fund (FWF) and by the Vienna Science and Technology Fund (WWTF) through grant PROSEED, and by CASED.

A. Cohen (Ed.): CC 2014, LNCS 8409, pp. 244–249, 2014.

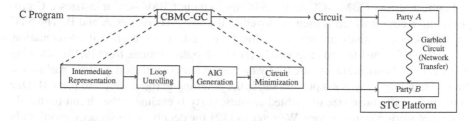

Fig. 1. STC Tool Chain

to understand but even harder to enforce across national boundaries, the demand for technical solutions is growing. These solutions, called Privacy Enhancing Technologies (PETs), assure data secrecy and privacy, even if data is processed on potentially untrusted platforms. The central cryptographic tool enabling such PETs is STC, allowing two distrusting parties to perform arbitrary computations on sensitive data without ever exposing their input in the clear. Hence, no information on the other party's input is revealed, beyond the information derivable from the commonly computed function output.

After 30 years of mainly theoretical studies, increased computational power and advanced cryptographic protocols make it feasible to evaluate reasonably large functions in an STC context [2,5,8,4,17]. The predominant approach to implement STC are Garbled Circuits (GCs), as originally proposed by Yao [19], working in two steps: First, Alice garbles a given circuit and hands this garbled circuit to Bob, together with a set of keys representing Alice's input. Using Oblivious Transfer [16], Bob obtains the set of keys corresponding to his own input, without obtaining any other key, and such that Alice does not know which keys Bob took. With these keys, Bob can evaluate the garbled circuit – unable to learn anything on Alice's input that is not implied by the final output. We refer to [12] for details.

One main obstacle for practical application of STC was the lack of support for general programming languages, as only circuit evaluation [7] or simplified programming languages [13] were supported. Recently at CCS [6], we presented CBMC-GC, the **first STC compiler for full ANSI C.** We argue that practical application of STC should be viewed as a combination of compiler and security research (cf. Figure 1): (i) **STC compilation**, i.e., the STC compiler translates the source code into a circuit that is optimized towards its use in STC and (ii) **STC interpretation**, i.e., the STC framework evaluates generated circuits in a way that ensures the STC guarantees. We believe that this separation of concerns is a crucial step towards broad practical use of STC.

```
1  #include <cbmc-gc.h>

2  void millionaires() {
3      int a, b, result;

4      __CBMC_GC_INPUT_A(1, a);
5      __CBMC_GC_INPUT_B(2, b);

6      result = (a > b)?1:0;

7      __CBMC_GC_OUTPUT(3, result);

8  }
```

Fig. 2. C code for Yao's millionaires' problem

Figure 1 shows CBMC-GC in the STC tool chain. CBMC-GC translates a C program into a circuit which is then deployed to the two STC parties A and B. The STC framework is essentially an interpreter for the circuit. In our current implementation, we use the GC construction proposed in [10] with optimizations from [9,15], allowing XOR-gates to be evaluated at essentially no cost. After compilation, party A garbles the circuit including party A's input and sends the resulting garbled circuit to party B. Due to the potentially huge size of garbled circuits, party B evaluates the circuit on-the-fly instead of storing it in memory. We refer to [12] for details and a security proof, only sketching the STC evaluation.

(1) *Garbling.* Party A assigns to each circuit wire w two random keys K_w^T and K_w^F, each representing one truth value of w (T = true, F = false). For all binary gates $G(u, v) = o$ with input wires u, v and output wire o, party A encrypts each entry $(\mathsf{val}(u), \mathsf{val}(v), \mathsf{val}(o))$ of G's truth table by computing

$$\mathsf{encrypt}_{K_u^{\mathsf{val}(u)}}(\mathsf{encrypt}_{K_v^{\mathsf{val}(v)}}(K_o^{\mathsf{val}(o)})),$$

i.e., $K_o^{\mathsf{val}(o)}$ gets encrypted using the keys $K_u^{\mathsf{val}(u)}$ and $K_v^{\mathsf{val}(v)}$. Therein, $\mathsf{val}(u)$ is the evaluation of u (i.e., the truth value T or F), and hence, if G is, say, an or-gate, party A garbles the entry (F, T, T) by encrypting K_o^T with K_u^F and K_v^T; finally, A permutes the resulting four encrypted keys so that the evaluating party does not see which encrypted key corresponds to which entry of the truth table. If G is an output gate, A encrypts no further key but the plain truth value from G's truth table.

(2) *Evaluation.* The garbled circuit is handed to party B together with the keys corresponding to party A's input. B obtains the keys corresponding to its own inputs with Oblivious Transfer [16], guaranteeing that B only obtains one key per input wire, and guaranteeing that A does not know which keys B has chosen. With these keys, B decrypts inductively the keys for the truth values corresponding to the valuation of the wires in the circuit under the combined inputs of A and B – and importantly, B can only decrypt those. More precisely, for each gate he tries to decrypt all four (permuted) truth table entries; only one decryption will succeed, giving him the necessary key for the subsequent gate.

CBMC-GC solves the millionaires' problem with the source code shown in Figure 2: The procedure `millionaires` is a standard C procedure, where only the input and output variables are specifically marked up, designated as input of party A or B (Lines 4 and 5) or as output (Line 7). But aside this input/output convention, arbitrary C computations are allowed to produce the desired result, in this case a simple comparison (Line 6). This paper presents CBMC-GC v0.9, an improved version of the compiler presented at CCS [6] which combines various techniques known from logic optimization to produce substantially smaller circuits.

2   CMBC-GC in a Nutshell

Our compiler CBMC-GC[1] is based on the software verification tool CBMC [3]. Since CBMC is a bounded model checker for ANSI C, it translates any given C program into

---

[1] http://forsyte.at/software/cbmc-gc/

Table 1. Circuit sizes produced by CBMC-GC v0.8 and v0.9

Benchmark	#gates (v0.8)		#gates (v0.9)	
	total	non-XOR	total	non-XOR
Hamming distance, 320 bit	19031	6038	4010	924
Hamming distance, 800 bit	47816	15143	10119	2344
Hamming distance, 1600 bit	95791	30318	20356	4738
matrix multiplication, 5x5	797751	221625	401250	148650
matrix multiplication, 8x8	3267585	907776	1636096	600768
2000 arithmetic operations	1531601	405640	938671	319584
3000 arithmetic operations	2298441	608668	1417684	479463
median, merge sort, 21 elements	750471	244720	210727	136154
median, merge sort, 31 elements	1840339	602576	550918	348761
median, bubble sort, 21 elements	346380	112800	67050	40320
median, bubble sort, 31 elements	1066470	349600	147600	89280

XOR gates are evaluated at essentially no cost and therefore non-XOR gates are mentioned explicitly. For details on the benchmarks see [6].

a Boolean constraint which represents the program behavior at a bit-precise level up to a bounded number of steps. In a nutshell, we adapted this capability of CBMC to provide the circuits needed for STC. The compilation is divided into four steps, where the first two steps are part of the standard CBMC processing and the second two are specific to STC tasks. For more details on the first two compilation steps, please see [6].

(1) *Intermediate Representation.* The C program gets translated into an intermediate representation—a so-called GOTO program. The only control structures remaining in a GOTO program are guarded GOTOs.

(2) *Loop Unrolling.* Loops and recursive function calls are unrolled up to a specific depth. CBMC-GC tries to compute this depth by a static analysis, but in case of failure, the depth can be specified by the user. After unrolling, we have a loop-free representation of the program.

(3) *AIG Generation.* It remains to translate each program statement into a circuit which encodes the bit-precise semantics of the computation the statement performs. CBMC-GC uses *and-inverter graphs* (AIGs) as an intermediate circuit representation. AIGs are directed acyclic graphs whose nodes represent logical AND gates. The edges of an AIG represent wires between gates. Some of these wires can negate the transmitted signal. Throughout the generation of this intermediate circuit, structural hashing, i.e., the removal of duplicated gates, and constant propagation are performed to keep the resulting circuit small [14]. CBMC-GC incorporates the ABC framework [1] to generate the intermediate representation.

(4) *Circuit Minimization.* XOR gates are preferable due to their small computation costs and therefore the circuit minimization step tries to maximize the number of XOR gates in the resulting circuit while keeping the overall circuit size small. Here, a repeated pattern based subcircuit rewriting is performed in combination with structural hashing, constant propagation, and a simplified version of SAT-sweeping [11].

By compiling the source code with CBMC-GC, we obtain a description of the circuit performing the computation and a mapping between in- and output identifiers and the corresponding circuit pins. Table 1 compares the circuit sizes produced by CBMC-GC v0.8 and CBMC-GC v0.9. The benchmarks were originally used to show the practicality of CBMC-GC v0.8 and are discussed in detail in [6]. We can observe a considerable reduction of circuit sizes when using CBMC-GC v0.9 instead of CBMC-GC v0.8.

References

1. Berkeley Logic Synthesis and Verification Group, ABC: A System for Sequential Synthesis and Verification, Release 30916,
   http://www.eecs.berkeley.edu/~alanmi/abc/
2. Bogetoft, P., Damgård, I.B., Jakobsen, T., Nielsen, K., Pagter, J.I., Toft, T.: A Practical Implementation of Secure Auctions Based on Multiparty Integer Computation. In: Di Crescenzo, G., Rubin, A. (eds.) FC 2006. LNCS, vol. 4107, pp. 142–147. Springer, Heidelberg (2006)
3. Clarke, E., Kroning, D., Lerda, F.: A Tool for Checking ANSI-C Programs. In: Jensen, K., Podelski, A. (eds.) TACAS 2004. LNCS, vol. 2988, pp. 168–176. Springer, Heidelberg (2004)
4. Erkin, Z., Franz, M., Guajardo, J., Katzenbeisser, S., Lagendijk, I., Toft, T.: Privacy-Preserving Face Recognition. In: Goldberg, I., Atallah, M.J. (eds.) PETS 2009. LNCS, vol. 5672, pp. 235–253. Springer, Heidelberg (2009)
5. Goethals, B., Laur, S., Lipmaa, H., Mielikainen, T.: On secure scalar product computation for privacy-preserving data mining. In: ICISC 2004 (2004)
6. Holzer, A., Franz, M., Katzenbeisser, S., Veith, H.: Secure Two-Party Computations in ANSI C. In: CCS 2012 (2012)
7. Huang, Y., Evans, D., Katz, J., Malka, L.: Faster Secure Two-Party Computation Using Garbled Circuits. In: USENIX 2011 (2011)
8. Jagannathan, G., Wright, R.N.: Privacy-preserving distributed k-means clustering over arbitrarily partitioned data. In: KDD 2005 (2005)
9. Kolesnikov, V., Sadeghi, A.-R., Schneider, T.: Improved Garbled Circuit Building Blocks and Applications to Auctions and Computing Minima. In: Garay, J.A., Miyaji, A., Otsuka, A. (eds.) CANS 2009. LNCS, vol. 5888, pp. 1–20. Springer, Heidelberg (2009)
10. Kolesnikov, V., Schneider, T.: Improved Garbled Circuit: Free XOR Gates and Applications. In: Aceto, L., Damgård, I., Goldberg, L.A., Halldórsson, M.M., Ingólfsdóttir, A., Walukiewicz, I. (eds.) ICALP 2008, Part II. LNCS, vol. 5126, pp. 486–498. Springer, Heidelberg (2008)
11. Kuehlmann, A.: Dynamic transition relation simplification for bounded property checking. In: ICCAD 2004 (2004)
12. Lindell, Y., Pinkas, B.: A Proof of Security of Yao's Protocol for Two-Party Computation. Journal of Cryptology 22, 161–188 (2009)
13. Malkhi, D., Nisan, N., Pinkas, B., Sella, Y.: Fairplay — A Secure Two-Party Computation System. In: SSYM 2004 (2004)
14. Mishchenko, A., Chatterjee, S., Brayton, R.: FRAIGs: A Unifying Representation for Logic Synthesis and Verification. Technical report (2005)
15. Pinkas, B., Schneider, T., Smart, N.P., Williams, S.C.: Secure Two-Party Computation Is Practical. In: Matsui, M. (ed.) ASIACRYPT 2009. LNCS, vol. 5912, pp. 250–267. Springer, Heidelberg (2009)

16. Rabin, M.O.: How To Exchange Secrets with Oblivious Transfer. IACR Cryptology ePrint Archive 2005, 187 (2005)
17. Smaragdis, P., Shashanka, M.V.S.: A framework for secure speech recognition. IEEE Transactions on Audio, Speech & Language Processing 15(4), 1404–1413 (2007)
18. Yao, A.C.-C.: Protocols for Secure Computations (Extended Abstract). In: FOCS 1982 (1982)
19. Yao, A.C.-C.: How to Generate and Exchange Secrets. In: FOCS 1986 (1986)

Author Index